FOR VALOUR

P9-CRU-581

FOR VALOUR
CANADIANS AND THE VICTORIA CROSS IN THE GREAT WAR

Series Editor Gerald Gliddon

Contributors
Peter F. Batchelor and Stephen Snelling

Foreword by
Andrew Iarocci, PhD

DUNDURN
TORONTO

GRAND VALLEY PUBLIC LIBRARY

Copyright © Gerald Gliddon, Peter F. Batchelor, and Stephen Snelling, 2015

All rights reserved. No part of this publication may be reproduced, stored in a retrieval system, or transmitted in any form or by any means, electronic, mechanical, photocopying, recording, or otherwise (except for brief passages for purpose of review) without the prior permission of Dundurn Press. Permission to photocopy should be requested from Access Copyright.

Published by arrangement with The History Press using material previously published in the series VCs of the First World War.

Editor: Cheryl Hawley
Design: Jansom
Cover design: Sarah Beaudin
Printer: Webcom

Note: In some cases, the print quality of images in this book has been affected by the age and condition of original material.

Library and Archives Canada Cataloguing in Publication

Gliddon, Gerald 1937-, author
    For valour: Canadians and the Victoria Cross in the Great War / Gerald Gliddon.

Includes bibliographical references and index. Issued in print and electronic formats.
ISBN 978-1-4597-2848-6 (paperback).--ISBN 978-1-4597-2849-3 (pdf).--
ISBN 978-1-4597-2850-9 (epub)

    1. Victoria Cross--Bibliography. 2. Military decorations--Canada. 3. Canada, Candian Armed Forces--Biography. 4. World War, 1914-1918--Canada. 5. Heroes--Canada--Biography. 6. Soldiers--Canada--Biography. I. Title.

CR4885.G65 2015   355.1'3420971   C2015-903962-2

                                                 C2015-903963-0

1   2   3   4   5   19   18   17   16   15

We acknowledge the support of the **Canada Council for the Arts** and the **Ontario Arts Council** for our publishing program. We also acknowledge the financial support of the **Government of Canada** through the **Canada Book Fund** and **Livres Canada Books**, and the **Government of Ontario** through the **Ontario Book Publishing Tax Credit** and the **Ontario Media Development Corporation**.

Care has been taken to trace the ownership of copyright material used in this book. The author and the publisher welcome any information enabling them to rectify any references or credits in subsequent editions.
                                                                    — *J. Kirk Howard, President*

The publisher is not responsible for websites or their content unless they are owned by the publisher.

Printed and bound in Canada.

VISIT US AT

Dundurn.com | @dundurnpress | Facebook.com/dundurnpress | Pinterest.com/dundurnpress

Dundurn
3 Church Street, Suite 500
Toronto, Ontario, Canada
M5E 1M2

CONTENTS

Recipients with Canadian Connections

The Victoria Cross was introduced by Queen Victoria on January 29, 1856, to honour acts of bravery during the Crimean War. The bronze cross bears the inscription "For Valour," and is cast from the metal of captured Russian guns at Sevastopol during the Crimean campaign. It is based on the design of a Maltese Cross and has a one-and-a-half-inch crimson ribbon. The decoration also contains the holder's name and date.

Queen Victoria made the first awards of the VC at a public investiture held in Hyde Park on June 26, 1856, and since then 1,356 have been awarded, the most recent being to Paratrooper Lance Corporal Joshua Leakey, in February 2015.

ABBREVIATIONS

ADS	Advance Dressing Station
BEF	British Expeditionary Force
Bn.	Battalion
BVM	British Victory Medal
BWM	British War Medal
CAMC	Canadian Army Medical Corps
CASC	Canadian Army Service Corps
CEF	Canadian Expeditionary Force
CFA	Canadian Field Artillery
CIB	Canadian Infantry Brigade
CO	Commanding Officer
Col.	Colonel
Cpl.	Corporal
CSM	Company Sergeant Major
CWGC	Commonwealth Graves Commission
DCM	Distinguished Conduct Medal
DFC	Distinguished Flying Cross
DSO	Distinguished Service Order
GC	George Cross
IG	Irish Guards
L/Cpl.	Lance-Corporal
Lt.	Lieutenant
Lt.-Col.	Lieutenant-Colonel
Maj.	Major
Maj.-Gen.	Major-General
MC	Military Cross

MG	Machine-gun
MiD	Mentioned in Despatches
MM	Military Medal
MO	Medical Officer
OTC	Officer Training Corps
Pte.	Private
RAMC	Royal Army Medical Corps
Regt.	Regiment
RE	Royal Engineers
RNWMP	Royal North-West Mounted Police
SAA	Small Arms Ammunition
Sgt.	Sergeant
Sgt.-Maj.	Sergeant-Major
VC	Victoria Cross

FOREWORD

The Victoria Cross, the highest gallantry medal for service to the British Commonwealth, was established by Queen Victoria in 1856, during the Crimean War. The Royal Warrant for the Victoria Cross stated that it may be awarded to persons who served the Crown "in the presence of the enemy, and shall have then performed some signal act of valour or devotion to their country." Soldiers and sailors of all ranks were eligible, as were civilians acting under military command. According to the Royal Warrant no previous distinctions or qualifications, such as long service, wounds, or prior meritorious conduct, were to be taken into account when an application was made. The Victoria Cross is still awarded today for high gallantry in British or Commonwealth service.

The awarding of a Victoria Cross was — and indeed remains — an exceedingly rare distinction: less than 1/55th of 1 percent of the approximately 420,000 men and women who served with the Canadian overseas forces was decorated with the Victoria Cross during the First World War. Recommendations for a Victoria Cross required strong support from commanding officers and, usually, corroborating evidence from at least three eyewitnesses. General eligibility requirements for the decoration evolved during the war. For instance, by late 1916 authorities determined that it would not be awarded to soldiers who had rescued wounded comrades under fire, unless the potential recipient was a designated stretcher-bearer. During the latter part of the war Victoria Crosses typically went to men whose actions were courageous as well as bellicose. Soldiers who overran enemy strongpoints against steep odds, for example, were likely candidates. Lieutenant Samuel Honey's Victoria Cross, earned at Bourlon Wood in September 1918, is a case in point.

First World War British and Dominion soldiers undoubtedly took the award very seriously, although some felt that the medal was awarded inconsistently or perhaps too rarely. Since the eligibility requirements for the Victoria Cross were so rigorous, authorities introduced lesser awards, such as the Military Cross and the Military Medal, to recognize more equitably the innumerable acts of valour exhibited in battle.

The seventy-two recipients of the Victoria Cross whose stories are told in this book each clearly displayed incredible bravery on the battlefield. Interestingly, there is no obvious pattern of common traits in their backgrounds and few clues to suggest that any of them was destined for such a great honour. Captain Francis Scrimger was a thirty-four-year-old physician when he won the VC at the Second Battle of Ypres in April 1915. By contrast, Private Tommy Holmes, a "frail, delicate youth with a contagious smile," was just nineteen years old when he won his VC at Passchendaele in October 1917. Captain Billy Bishop, surely Canada's best-known VC recipient, had failed his first-year exams at the Royal Military College of Canada. It is doubtful that any of Bishop's instructors would have pegged him as a future war hero.

The variety of characters whom we find among Canada's First World War Victoria Cross recipients reminds us of the broad cross section of people who served in Canadian uniform during the war, or were otherwise associated with the Canadian overseas forces. While this book has been prepared to honour their courage in particular, it bears remembering that countless others performed unseen or unrecorded heroic acts that were never formally recognized with an award or honourable mention. Although the First World War is now a century past, and its veterans no longer walk among us, let this book serve as a reminder of the very great stores of courage that helped to bring the Allied forces to final victory.

Andrew Iarocci, PhD
Assistant Professor, Department of History
Western University, London, Ontario

INTRODUCTION

Canada's VCs of the First World War

The country of Canada was part of John Cabot's discovery of North America in 1497, when the French and British laid claim to its lands and potential wealth. The French were the first to establish themselves, which they did on the northeast side of the country. The British established their colony on the Atlantic coast, and in the late eighteenth century moved northward from the United States into Nova Scotia, New Brunswick, and Lower Canada. Soon Britain occupied the majority of the lands to the east and west. In 1867 the two nations joined together in a confederacy, a "Union of Upper British Canada and French Lower Canada," and the country became virtually self-governing. Even so, on paper the country was still subject to the rule of the English Imperial Parliament, which installed a Governor General.

The Boer War in South Africa broke out in October 1899. Three months later the Boers attacked Ladysmith. The war, in which the British Army had received a very bloody nose, ended on May 31, 1902. Canada had taken an active part in the campaign to restore law and order in South Africa, and in doing so had won five Victoria Crosses. The Boers, a skilful enemy, had adapted very well to the terrain and revealed a number of weaknesses in the structure and, more importantly, tactics of the British Army. Over the next twelve years a considerable amount of work was carried out in order to make an efficient, yet small, standing army that would be ready for any major European conflict.

Sam Hughes, the politician and honorary army officer, had been sent to South Africa as a civilian in 1899, when he used influence with British friends to wrangle command of a small force of irregulars. He achieved a slight success in one or two campaigns. He wrote home to newspapers, boasting of his exploits, but he was also very critical of the British Army methods. Consequently he was sent back home, having breached military discipline. After his dismissal by the British Army he was to develop a lifelong distrust of professional soldiers. He also campaigned, but with no success, for the award of a Victoria Cross for himself — actually he reckoned he deserved two!

The British government's declaration of war against Germany was made on August 4, 1914, and on the following day the Duke of Connaught, the Governor General, announced that Canada was also at war with Germany. In reality all member countries of the British Empire, including Canada and the independent colony of Newfoundland, were legally at war as soon as the declaration had been made. However, Canada could and did determine the extent of its military commitment. Colonel the Honourable Sam Hughes, who had been the minister of militia and defence in Robert Borden's Liberal government since October 1911, stated in a press release dated July 30 that preparations were in hand to recruit and equip an initial contingent of 20,000 to 25,000 men. A permanent army of 3,000 men and a militia establishment of over 64,000 or 77,000 was already in existence, but earlier plans made by Hughes' department for the mobilization of this force were not implemented. Instead Hughes anticipated that the enthusiasm of volunteers would quickly provide the numbers required for a Canadian Expeditionary Force (CEF). In the event the majority of these early volunteers joined via existing military depots.

During the weeks that followed the outbreak of war, Canadians from all walks of life and every province enlisted in their thousands. They joined the colours for a variety of reasons, not the least being their links to the Mother Country — more than two thirds of the initial Canadian contingent had been born in the United Kingdom. As immigrants they had brought with them much-needed labour and professional skills, which in turn gave them regular employment and jobs. Growth industries included mining, timber, and the opening up of the northern territories with railway links.

In addition to patriotism there was also pressure from political speeches, newspapers, and religious leaders all of which combined to encourage a rush of volunteers who responded eagerly to Hughes's recruitment campaign. The numbers of a first contingent was set at 25,000 and this figure was exceeded in little over a week. Instigated by Hughes, work began immediately on establishing a vast training camp at Valcartier, sixteen miles from Québec City. With Sam Hughes in command, the first volunteers arrived in August, when the camp was only partially ready for use. During the next few weeks the volunteers assisted in finishing the building of the camp and carried out military training. In response to an enquiry from the British War Office the planned date of embarkation to Britain was given as mid September.

Peter F. Batchelor and Gerald Gliddon
March 2015

1914–1915

On October 3, 1914, the first contingent (almost 31,000) of the Canadian Expeditionary Force (CEF), together with 7,300 horses and equipment, sailed in thirty ships from Gaspé Bay, Quebec, for England. At Cape Race the convoy was joined by the 525-strong Newfoundland Regiment. The original destination for the Canadian troops was Liverpool, but owing to the activity of enemy submarines, the convoy was diverted to Devonport, Plymouth, where the first ships arrived on the morning of October 14. The Canadian troops were met by Lt.-Gen. E.A.H. Alderson, who had taken command in September of what was to become the 1st Canadian Division. Sam Hughes, Canada's minister of militia and defence, who had sailed via New York, was also at the docks ready to greet "his boys."

The Canadian troops entrained for Salisbury Plain, Wiltshire, a vast major British military training area where they were encamped while they carried out their training. Unfortunately conditions were extremely grim for the volunteers, as much of the next few months were blighted by continuously wet weather and muddy conditions. As Colonel A. Fortescue Duguid noted in his excellent *Official History of the Canadian Forces in the Great War 1914–1919;Vol. 1,* "On Salisbury Plain in the 123 days, from mid-October 1914 to mid-February 1915, the rain fell on 89 days...." The rainfall was almost double the average of the previous thirty years.

Medical arrangements were made. No. 1 Stationary Hospital was to remain in London, but No.2 Stationary Hospital was to go to France ahead of the main Canadian Force. This hospital became the first of all Canadian units to disembark in France. The hospital under

Lt.-Col. Shillington was inspected on Salisbury Plain by the king and queen on November 4, and the hospital left for Southampton two days later, sailing to Le Havre on HMT *City of Benares*. For almost two weeks the unit was billeted at Boulogne before entraining for Le Touquet on November 27. Here it opened up the Hôtel du Golf as a hospital equipped with over three hundred beds taking in its first 116 casualties on December 4.

King George V also visited Salisbury Plain on November 4 in order to review the 1st Canadian Division under the command of Lt.-Gen. E.A. Alderson. Exactly three months later, on February 4, 1915, the king inspected the division again, this time on Knighton Down, near Larkshill, prior to it sailing to France where it would become part of the British Expeditionary Force (BEF).

On the outbreak of the war a Capt. Andrew Hamilton Gault had raised the Patricia's Light Infantry, to which he contributed $100,000 to finance and equip a whole regiment. The government temporarily accepted his offer on August 6, 1914, and officially authorized it on August 10, 1914. The regiment was named after the Duke of Connaught's daughter and Light Infantry was chosen by Gault himself. They left Quebec City on September 27 and arrived in England in October. At first they were sent to Bustard Camp on Salisbury Plain, and on November 16 they joined the 80th Brigade of the BEF. Even this early in the war, the regiment was having problems of using the Ross Rifle and were keen to replace it with the British Lee-Enfield 303. On December 20 the regiment left Southampton for France, where they landed the following day. They were the first Canadian unit to be on the battlefield. As with No. 2 Stationary Hospital, the regiment had arrived in France prior to the main Canadian Force and joined the British 27th Division, becoming the first Canadian unit to be in action. They later came back into the fold when they transferred to the 1st Canadian Division on March 3.

The British Expeditionary Force had arrived in France with 84,000 infantry, and by the beginning of 1915 had already sustained casualties in excess of this number, particularly during October and November, when they took part in what became known as First

Ypres, a battle that saw the virtual destruction of the BEF's original regular army units. Over 54,000 casualties were incurred in this series of battles in order to defend the route to the channel ports in the vicinity of the Belgian city of Ypres. In addition to a lack of sufficient manpower the BEF was bedevilled by a shell shortage, which left the British forces at a serious disadvantage to their German adversary.

After their arrival in France the 1st Canadian Division was billeted to the east of Hazebrouck and briefly attached to III Corps, BEF, for initial training and instruction. At the end of February the Canadian Division was ordered into the line in the Fleurbaix area, north of the La Bassée Canal. The Canadians were responsible for nearly 6,500 yards of front and were ready to support the BEF during the Battle of Neuve Chapelle in March 1915.

Although not actively engaged in the attack — the role of the Canadian units here was "to assist by making a demonstration of fire along its entire front with a view to preventing the enemy from sending reinforcements from the neighbourhood of Fromelles to Aubers" — the Canadian Division suffered nearly 300 casualties. Although the village of Neuve Chapelle was captured, the result of this battle was deemed unsatisfactory as there were no other allied gains.

One of the problems encountered in this "demonstration" was the reports of jamming in the Canadian-designed Ross rifle when used in rapid-fire situations. This rifle, basically a hunting rifle, was considered superior to the British Lee-Enfield 303 rifle, in particular by Sam Hughes, a friend of Charles Ross, the rifle's designer. Most Canadian troops were handicapped by the Ross's poor design until 1916, when it was replaced by the British Lee-Enfield 303.

After the battle of Neuve Chapelle the 1st Canadian Division was transferred to the Ypres Salient, where it began taking over front-line positions from French units on April 14. The previous week had been spent training in the areas between Cassel and Poperinghe.

Although it was to be April 23, 1915, before the first Victoria Cross was awarded to a man from a Canadian unit, Irish-born Cpl. Michael O'Leary, 1st Irish Guards, received his VC as early as February 1. His award was won at Cuinchy, south of the La Bassée

Canal, when he attacked two machine-gun posts in succession, killing or capturing their crews. Although he had strong links with Canada, O'Leary was not serving with the CEF at the time he won his decoration. The account of his life, together with those of four other men with strong Canadian connections who won the VC when serving with British Regiments, can be found in the Appendix.

The Canadian Division was put to a very severe test when the Germans introduced a new and very deadly weapon by the release of chlorine gas on the evening of April 22. Together with French colonial and territorial units the Canadians were overwhelmed, leaving the Canadian battalions with their flank unsupported. In a situation with communications and orders at best confused it is to the credit of the units involved, including the "green" Canadians that, although ground was lost to the left of the line by the French, much of the line was held.

Four further VCs were won by Canadians in this April fighting, half of all VCs awarded for this period, the last being to Capt. Francis Scrimger, a medical officer serving with the 14th (Royal Montreal) Battalion. One further VC was awarded to a Canadian in 1915, and that was to Capt. Frederick Campbell at Givenchy on June 15.

The CEF was not actively involved in the later battles of 1915, and was to spend much of the time manning trenches in the Ploegsteert-Wulverghem area.

F. FISHER

St. Julien, Belgium, April 23

On April 22, 1915, the 13th and 15th Bns, 3rd Canadian Infantry Brigade (CIB), were holding the front line trenches north of the River Stroombeek; on 13th Bn's left was the 45th Algerian Div. south of Poelcappelle on the Poelcappelle–St. Julien Road. At 5:00 p.m. the Canadian sentries saw a yellow-green cloud, low to the ground, drifting toward their lines from the German trenches on a front from Steenstraat to Poelcappelle. The cloud turned out to be chlorine gas, released from cylinders on the signal of three red flares dropped from a German aircraft. It took less than eight minutes for the cylinders to be emptied, by which time the gas had reached the French trenches.

Shortly after releasing the gas the Germans launched a fierce artillery bombardment; this was followed at 5:20 p.m. by an assault by the 51st Reserve Div., who clambered over their parapets, many wearing gauze and cotton masks to protect them from the poisonous fumes. Some German soldiers were reluctant to remain close to the gas cloud, and officers were seen using the flats of their swords as "encouragement."

Resistance was very limited among the Algerians, who were understandably terrified by this horrific new weapon that caused many of them to fall to the ground writhing in agony, unable to breathe. The Algerians' retreat left the 13th Bn. with its left flank on the St. Julien–Poelcappelle road unsupported. There was a gap of over 2,000 yards to St. Julien, where its reserve company, two platoons of No. 3 Company and Bn. HQ, were situated. In the middle of this gap, in an orchard some 500 yards north of St. Julien, was a battery of 18-pounders, commanded by Maj. W.B.M. King, 10th (St. Catharines) Battery CFA. King, on his own initiative (the shelling had cut telephone communication and no orders were getting through), opened fire on the German front-line trenches at 5:45 p.m. Although badly affected by the gas, the battery was able to keep firing while large numbers of Algerians streamed through the gun positions. At 7:00 p.m. a large force of Germans was spotted by a French NCO who had stopped at the battery, marching south 200 to 300 yards to the west of the road, their helmets visible over a hedge. Reversing one section of guns, Maj. King opened fire on this target, forcing the German troops to stop and dig in. Maj. King's request to the infantry for help brought a party of sixty men, drawn from 14th and 15th Bns, under Lt. G.W. Stairs, together with a Colt machine gun from the 13th Bn. HQ in St. Julien. No. 24066, L/ Cpl Frederick Fisher, having just recovered from a wound received a few days earlier, was in charge of this machine gun. He made his way to a position in front of the graveyard in St. Julien, and then worked forward to an isolated building that commanded the ground to the north and west where the Germans were entrenching. Once in the building, he brought his gun into action, effectively stopping the German advance and probably saving the guns of the 10th Bty. For this he was awarded the Victoria Cross, as reported in the Supplement to the *London Gazette*, No. 29202, dated June 22, 1915. The date of the action is given in the citation as April 23, but this seems to be incorrect, although Fisher was again in action on this date.

The 10th Bty kept up an intermittent fire until nearly 10:00 p.m. when Maj. King was able to extricate it, and by 11:00 p.m. all his guns had been withdrawn from their very exposed position. Meanwhile, Fisher, having lost four of his original gun-team as casualties, returned to St. Julien and obtained volunteers from the 14th Bn. with whom he again went forward in an attempt to reach his battalion. He reached the front line positions where the 13th Bn. was holding on, with some Canadians now lining the Poelcappelle road at right angles to their original front. Fisher had become separated from his team while setting up his machine gun when he was killed on April 23. Fisher's military record notes that the correct date of death is April 24, 1915, so it would seem likely that Fisher was killed after midnight.

An account of Fisher's heroism, contained in a letter written by Lt. Edward W. Waud Jr., was published in the *Montreal Star* on June 24, 1915:

Fred Fisher and many other poor chaps of our battalion are lying dead near St. Julien. "Bud" made a famous name for himself. He was in charge of a gun team in reserve in the little village of St. Julien. When word of the attack on our line came back he took his team and gun and started for the front trenches. No one knew the way, but came upon some artillery trying to get some big guns out under heavy fire. He set up his machine gun and covered their retirement. Proceeding forward again he cleared a bit of a wood of Germans, becoming separated from most of his team. He then took charge of a French machine gun that had been abandoned, and got it working. He finally found our battalion, and reported to Lieut. J.G. Ross, the MG Officer. He was mounting the gun on the parapet when he was hit in the chest, dying instantly. Lieut. Ross and some of the other officers buried him in the trench.

L/Cpl. Fisher's body was not recovered and his name appears on panel 24 of the Menin Gate Memorial to the Missing at Ypres.

Frederick Fisher was born at Church Street, St. Catharines, Ontario, on August 3, 1894. He had two older brothers, Don and William, and an elder sister, Alice. In 1900 the family moved to Niagara-on-the-

Lake, where his father was manager of the Sovereign Bank. Frederick commenced his schooling at the Niagara Public School until the Fisher family moved again, in 1904, to Dunnville, where they stayed until about 1907 before moving to Montreal. Here Fisher attended Westmount Academy, where a life-sized coloured photograph of him hangs in the rebuilt Westmount High School. In the Westmount Academy Yearbook of 1909 "Bud" Fisher was described as "hard as nails" on the football field.

In 1912 Fisher enrolled at McGill University to study applied science (engineering). He was still a student when war broke out. He was academically capable and a keen sportsman, being a member of the 1914 championship track team as well as the Montreal Amateur Athletics Association.

On August 6, 1914, Fisher enlisted as a private in the 5th Regt. (Royal Highlanders of Canada) and sailed from Valcartier, Quebec, on the *Alaunia*; she was one of the newest ships in the convoy, having been built for Cunard in 1913. Her cargo of 2,062 officers and men disembarked at Plymouth on October 15, 1914; they included the 13th Bn. CEF (forty-five officers and 1,110 other ranks), to which unit Fisher now belonged.

During the battalion's training period on the muddy Salisbury Plain, Fisher was promoted to lance-corporal on December 22, 1914, and on February 11, 1915, he embarked with his battalion on the *Novian* at Avonmouth, arriving at St. Nazaire on February 16. After a long railway journey to Hazebrouck the battalion encamped at Flêtre on February 19, beginning their first tour of duty in March 1915.

Fisher's VC was sent by the War Office on August 5, 1915, to his parents at 576 Lansdown Road, Westmount, Canada, and on April 25, 1916, a ceremony was held in the McGill Union when the picture of L/Cpl. Frederick Fisher VC was unveiled. His parents and sister were present and his mother proudly wore her son's VC. On the same day the McGill Annual was published, and was dedicated to Fisher, the first Canadian to win the Victoria Cross in the First World War and the first of three to be awarded to the 13th Bn. CEF.

A memorial tablet was unveiled at the Royal Highlanders of Canada Armouries, Bleury Street, Montreal, on May 1, 1917, and on

June 12 in the same year a memorial service was held at the Church of St. James the Apostle. In 1970 a plaque was unveiled at Memorial Park, St. Paul Street West, St. Catharines, by the Royal Canadian Legion, and a wreath was laid on behalf of the Fisher family by Kathleen E. Ball of Niagara-on-the-Lake. Fisher's VC remained with the family until the death of his mother in 1946 when his sister, Alice, presented it to the Royal Highland Regiment of Canada.

Fisher's two brothers both served with the Canadian Forces, Don with the 5th Bn.'s automobile section. William was awarded the Military Cross while serving with the Montreal Heavy Artillery. Both brothers died after the war from the effects of their war service. A painting of L/Cpl. Fisher by George J. Coates is held by the Canadian War Museum.

F.W. HALL

Near Ypres, Belgium, April 24

The 8th Bn. (90th Winnipeg Rifles) CEF had moved up to the front line during the evening of April 15, 1915, and took over positions from the French. The battalion found the front to be a series of unconnected lengths of shallow (two-foot deep) trenches with inadequate four-foot breastworks, a few strands of wire, and no traversing. The Canadians spent the next few days improving their trenches and making them more habitable.

Over forty casualties were inflicted on the 8th Bn. by German shelling on April 22, the day of the first gas attack; however, no gas was released on their front and the German infantry did not attack.

The line held by the 2nd Canadian Infantry Brigade (CIB) ran from Berlin Wood across the Gravenstafel–Passchendaele road, and northwest along the valley of the River Stroombeek; it was extended by the 3rd CIB to the newly created salient astride the Keerselaere–Poelcappelle road, some 800 yards from Poelcappelle. The right of the 2nd CIB front was held by the 5th Bn. almost up to the Stroombeek, and continued by the 8th Bn. which joined up with the 15th Bn. of the 3rd CIB.

On the night of April 23, camp kettles full of water were set in the front line and the 8th Bn. made sure that every man had a cotton bandolier to dip in the water to offer them some protection should gas be released on their sector. Three companies were in the front line, with half of C Company in close support and the remaining two platoons, commanded by Capt. Bertram and Lt. O'Grady, further back in dugouts 200 yards south of Bn. HQ at Boetleer Farm. No. 1539 CSM Frederick Hall was in Lt. O'Grady's platoon.

At 3:30 a.m. the following morning a German heavy-artillery barrage was launched all along the line and at 4:00 a.m. sentries saw several Germans, wearing what looked like mine-rescue helmets, climb over their parapets carrying hoses. The British troops watched as what they thought was smoke drifted across no man's land, but it quickly changed to a green colour as it was carried toward the Canadian trenches by the light wind. The artillery bombardment continued for another ten minutes before lifting to shell the support areas, by which time the gas was rolling across the front line trenches. Lt.-Col. Lipsett of the 8th Bn. had telephoned an SOS to his supporting artillery as soon as the gas was reported and immediately a heavy shrapnel fire was opened on the German front where the composite brigade of the 53rd Reserve Division was now advancing behind the gas cloud, causing heavy losses.

The improvised respirators, organized the previous evening, did provide some protection and the advancing German troops were met with a withering fire from those men remaining unaffected by gas. To add to the Canadians' problems, their notoriously unreliable Ross rifles were jamming and men wept in frustration as they used their boots and entrenching tools in order to try and loosen the bolts. The gas cloud passed over the right of the 15th Bn. and the left of the 8th Bn. and it was here, at the junction between the two battalions, that the 4th Reserve Ersatz Infantry Regt. broke through the stricken Canadians. Lt.-Col. Lipsett ordered his reserve half company, C, to try to plug this gap of more than one hundred yards. Very few of the men from C Company reached the gap and those who did witnessed the appalling sight of the gassed survivors of A Company, 15th Bn., vainly trying to escape the choking gas. Not a single officer survived from A Company, which was virtually wiped out; a similar fate befell C Company on their left. Having been ordered by telephone to protect at all costs "Locality C" (the oddly named crest of Gravenstafel Ridge, 800 yards east of Boetleer Farm), Lipsett called up his last remaining reserve, the two remaining platoons of C Company at Boetleer Farm, to plug the gap on his left flank. The time was now about 9:00 a.m.

Under very heavy fire these platoons made their way forward, and when Lt. O'Grady was killed in the advance, CSM Frederick Hall took charge of his platoon. He managed to get his men into position despite severe fire, crossing the 1,500 yards to the front line, then went back part of the way to bring in two wounded men, one after the other. Hearing the cries of a third man, Hall, together with Cpl. Payne and Pte. Rogerson, climbed out of their trench to attempt to rescue the wounded man, who was lying on an exposed raised bank some fifteen yards behind the front line. Both Payne and Rogerson were wounded in the attempt and all three returned to their trench. After a few minutes, Hall again crawled out of the trench, this time alone, and managed to reach the injured man; still lying prone he hoisted the wounded man onto his back, and was about to return to the trench when he raised his head slightly to check his direction. A bullet hit him in the head, causing a fatal wound, and moments later the wounded man was also killed. For this act of courage Frederick Hall was awarded the Victoria Cross.

The *London Gazette* of June 22, 1915, published the citation which read:

No. 1539 Colour-Sergeant Frederick William Hall.

On 24th April 1915, in the neighbourhood of Ypres, when a wounded man who was lying some 15 yards from the trench, called for help, Company Sergeant-Major Hall endeavoured to reach him in the face of a very heavy enfilade fire which was being poured in by the enemy. The first attempt failed and a Non-commissioned Officer and a private soldier who were attempting to give assistance were both wounded. Company Sergeant-Major Hall then made a second most gallant attempt, and was in the act of lifting up the wounded man to bring him in when he fell mortally wounded in the head

The only remaining reserve of the 2nd CIB, C Company of 5th Bn., was rushed to the left to help, and despite considerable losses reached the front line trenches and the position was held. Frederick Hall's VC was presented to his mother, Mrs. Mary Hall, in Winnipeg, having been forwarded to Canada by the War Office on August 5, 1916. CSM Frederick Hall is commemorated on the Menin Gate Memorial to the Missing at Ypres (Panel 24) as his body was never found.

Frederick William Hall, a native of Ireland, was born in Kilkenny on February 21, 1885, the son of Bombadier Frederick Hall, a military bandmaster in the 2/South Lancs Regt., and his wife, Mary. The family moved to England when Frederick junior was very young, and the 1891 census recorded that Frederick and Mary with their five children were living at 81 Ormskirk Street, St. Helens, Lancashire. The young Frederick enlisted in the Cameronians (Royal Scottish Rifles) in February 1901, and was discharged wirth the rank of sergeant in May 1913.

He later emigrated to Canada, and at the outbreak of war Hall was living in Winnipeg, where he was employed as a clerk. He enlisted in the 106th Regt. (Winnipeg Light Infantry), but later transferred to the 8th Bn. (90th Winnipeg Rifles), known as the "Little Black Devils" since 1865. With the rest of the first Canadian contingent, the 8th Bn. assembled at Valcartier Camp, Quebec, where it embarked on the *Franconia*. The convoy of thirty ships, together with escorts, sailed for England on October 3, 1914. The smooth crossing meant there was little demand for the 20,000 boxes of a secret mal-de-mer remedy in the medical stores, and the 2,310 officers and men on board (including 1,153 of the 8th Bn.) disembarked at Plymouth on October 15/16, 1914. The next sixteen weeks were spent at Larkhill South Camp on Salisbury Plain, where above-average rainfall and severe gales produced miserable conditions for the Canadians' stay in England. During this period of training Frederick Hall was first appointed acting sergeant on October 22, and was promoted to colour sergeant on December 1.

On February 10 the 8th Bn. sailed on the *Archimedes* from Avonmouth, disembarking at St. Nazaire on February 13. A tedious railway journey lasting more than forty hours took the Canadians the 500 miles to Strazeele, where their induction into trench life on the Western Front began.

Hall's father died in 1905 and his headstone at St. Helens Cemetery also bears details of his son and his award.

In 1925 Carolyn Cornell of the *Winnipeg Tribune* wrote a series of articles on Canadian Victoria Cross winners and suggested that Pine Street in Winnipeg, where Hall had been living, should be renamed. After some pressure from the Women's Canadian Club of Winnipeg, the city council agreed and Pine Street was renamed Valour Road and commemorated with the erection of a bronze plaque on a lamp post at Portage Avenue. This plaque commemorates three winners of the Victoria Cross in the First World War who were all living in the same block when they joined the CEF: CSM Frederick Hall VC, 8th Bn. (WR), April 24, 1915, Ypres; L/Sgt. Leo Clarke VC, 2nd Bn., September 9, 1916, Pozières; Capt. Robert Shankland VC, DCM, 43rd Bn. (CH of C), October 25, 1917, Passchendaele.

Two of Frederick Hall's brothers also served in the First World War; Ed was a lance corporal in the 2nd Cameronians (Scottish Rifles) and Harry was a sergeant in the 10th Bn., (Canadians) CEF. The Menin Gate Memorial Register shows their mother, Mrs. Mary Hall, living at 43 Union Street, Leytonstone, London, England.

From August 6 to November 14, 2014, the Manitoba Museum in Winnipeg displayed the VC medals awarded to Corporal Leo Clarke, Sergeant-Major Frederick William Hall, and Lieutenant Robert Shankland. The medals were on loan from the Canadian War Museum which had acquired Hall's medals in 2012. Also in November 2014 St. Helens Borough Council announced that roads in the town would be named after VC winners, including Frederick Hall.

E.D. BELLEW

Near Keerselaere, Belgium, April 24

On April 24, 1915, the Canadians of the 8th and 15th Bns (CEF) were holding the trenches on the northeast of the River Stroombeek. To the left of the 15th Bn. the line bent southwest, held by a company of 2nd East Kents, crossed the Poelcappelle road, then curved sharply southward, running west of the villages of Keersclacrc and St. Julien, where the 13th Bn. was positioned on the left of the East Kents; the trenches from Keerselaere to St. Julien were occupied by the 7th Bn. At 4:00 a.m. the release of three red flares from a captive balloon near Westroosebeke signalled another gas attack by the Germans, affecting a front of over 1,000 yards.

The German artillery bombardment, begun an hour before, continued until ten minutes after the release of the gas; when the bombardment ceased German infantry advanced toward the Canadians. The enemy had a numerical superiority of about twenty-four battalions to eight, with the Canadians having the equivalent of only four companies as reserves. By 5:00 a.m. the 7th Bn., 2nd Canadian Infantry Bde. (CIB) saw numbers of the 15th Bn. (3rd CIB) streaming past their rear; infantry of the 4th Reserve Ersatz Infantry

Regt. had broken through the front line where the 3rd CIB was unable to receive artillery support, its supporting batteries being out of range.

The 7th Bn. had arrived at its position just over a day earlier and had dug in with their left flank on St. Julien and the right near Keerselaere. In command was Maj. Victor Odlum who had taken over after Lt.-Col. Hart McHaig had been fatally wounded during the night. Maj. Odlum transferred to 3rd CIB for orders at 5:15 a.m. but, owing to broken-telephone communications, was unable to make contact. At 7:00 a.m. the 4th Marine Brigade launched a renewed attack on the 13th and 7th Bns, the enemy artillery having continued their shelling throughout. The two platoons on the right of the 7th Bn. were supported by two Colt machine guns under Lt. Edward Bellew, the battalion's machine-gun officer, who positioned his gun team on the high ground at Vancouver crossroads. The constant shelling caused many casualties amongst the gunners, so Lt. Bellew manned one gun and Sgt. H.N. Peerless the other, both firing into the Germans who were attacking the company on their right. The shell that killed Sgt. Peerless also wounded Lt. Bellew, but he returned to his gun and continued firing until the machine gun failed. He then snatched up rifles dropped by his killed and wounded men and continued to fire at the enemy before being stunned by another shell, after which he was taken prisoner.

The *Canadian Eye-Witness* reported:

> Lieut E.P.D. Bellew, machine-gun officer of the 7th Battn, hoisted a loaf, stuck on the point of his bayonet, in defiance of the enemy which drew upon him a perfect fury of fire; he fought his gun until it was smashed to atoms, and then continued to use relays of loaded rifles until he was taken prisoner.

It was now about 8:30 a.m. and the 7th Bn. War Diary records, rather tersely, "right flank surrounded and wiped out." There is no doubt that the determined action by Lt. Bellew and Sgt. Peerless was a deciding factor in briefly halting the German advance at this point. The 7th Bn. was still in a desperate situation and, failing to receive either orders or reinforcements from 3rd CIB, by 1:00 p.m.

Maj. Odlum ordered a withdrawal of his surviving men. At 11:15 p.m. Maj. Odlum reported that he had only 350 of all ranks available for duty, with casualties estimated at about 500.

After being captured, Lt. Bellew, together with other prisoners, was taken to Staden where a trial was convened by the Germans. The charge against Bellew was that he had continued to fire after part of his unit had surrendered. A guilty verdict was pronounced and he was sentenced to be shot by firing squad at Staden Church. It was reported that the officer in charge of the firing squad was not convinced of Bellew's guilt and halted the execution at the last minute. A second trial was ordered, which took place at Roulers, at which Lt. Bellew was acquitted. He was taken to a prison camp in Saxony and remained in various camps (six in total) until December 27, 1917, when he was moved to an internment camp in Switzerland owing to poor health, caused by the effects of gas poisoning, shell shock, and the very inadequate diet comprising "pig blood soup, mangold wurzels and bread of 60% sawdust." In Switzerland he was tended by his wife, Charlotte, who had been allowed to join him, and on December 10, 1918, he was repatriated to England.

Details of his bravery were known during his imprisonment but it was decided not to announce the award of his Victoria Cross until after his release. The citation for his VC appeared in the *London Gazette* of May 13, 1919, and he was presented with his medal in Vancouver by Gen. Ross, area-commandant. Lt. Bellew's VC was the first of three to be awarded to the 7th Bn.

Edward Donald Bellew was born on October 28, 1882, at Malabar Hill, Bombay. (Col. Duguid, in his *Official History of the Canadian Forces in the Great War*, states that he was actually "born on the High Seas.") He was the eldest son of Maj. Patrick Bellew, Bengal Army, assay-master of the Bombay Mint, and Letitia Frances Bellew. He was educated in England at Blundell's School, Tiverton, Devon, and at Clifton College, Bristol, before passing out of Royal Military College, Sandhurst, in 1900 where he was prominent in boxing and rugby.

Given the family's military background it was only natural that he should enter the army. His grandfather, Maj. Walter Henry Bellew, assistant quartermaster-general, Indian Army, was one of the last three men with Dr. Brydon, the only survivor of the retreat from Kabul in 1842, while his great-grandfather, Maj.-Gen. Sir Patrick Bellew, was military governor of Quebec in 1798.

Edward Bellew was commissioned into the Royal Irish Regt. as a second lieutenant in May 1901, and after serving in India and Afghanistan retired with the rank of lieutenant in August 1903. On August 24, 1901, in London, England, he married Charlotte Muriel Rees. They had no children.

Emigrating to Canada in 1907, he spent three years ranching and prospecting in Northern British Columbia before joining the Provincial Forestry Service. At Vancouver in 1912 he was appointed assistant to the district engineer of public works employed on harbour engineering. He enlisted in the Canadian Army on August 10, 1914, and was commissioned as a lieutenant in the 11th Irish Fusiliers of Canada.

Following the creation of the Canadian Expeditionary Force at Valcartier, machine-gun officer Bellew and the rest of the men of the 7th Bn. (1st British Columbia), comprising 49 officers and 1,083 other ranks, sailed on October 3, 1914, on the *Virginian*, one of the faster ships in the convoy. Disembarking at Plymouth on October 16, Lt. Bellew suffered the miseries of Salisbury Plain with the rest of the Canadian contingent until February 10, 1915, when the 7th Bn. embarked on the *Cardiganshire* for France, arriving at St. Nazaire on February 15. A railway journey lasting almost two days took the battalion to Belgium where it was deployed in training prior to taking over front-line trenches.

After returning to England from Switzerland, Capt. Bellew (he was promoted on January 2, 1916) returned to Canada in April 1919, and continued his employment with the Canadian Civil Service, who had kept him on the payroll throughout the war, as inspector of dredging in Fraser River. After 1922 it appears that Edward Bellew went into semi-retirement on a ranch at Monte Creek, British Columbia, where he could also indulge in his hobbies of fly-fishing and gardening.

He attended the British Legion dinner in the House of Lords on November 9, 1929, and was also present in 1956 for the VC

Centenary Review at Hyde Park. His last visit to England was in July 1960 for the Second Annual Dinner of the Victoria Cross and George Cross Association at the Café Royal.

Edward Bellew died at the Royal Inland Hospital, Shaughnessy, Kamloops, British Columbia, on February 1, 1961, aged seventy-eight. In June 1958 he had praised this hospital after suffering a light stroke and commented in a letter to Canon Lummis that "the nurses are superlative." He is buried at Hillside Cemetery, Kamloops.

After his death Bellew's VC and other medals passed to his brother-in-law, Mr. S.E. Crossman, of Hendon, London, and when he died the medals were auctioned at Sotheby's of London, on July 5, 1974. They realized a then-record price of £6,000 and were purchased for Stephen B. Roman, a Canadian millionaire who, in turn, presented them to the Royal Canadian Military Institute in Toronto on November 29, 1974. The VC was subsequently stolen and has not been recovered.

In October 2004 The British Columbia Regiment (Duke of Connaught's Own) Association (BCR Association) placed and dedicated a bronze plaque at the Kamloops Cenotaph in Riverside Park commemorating Capt. Bellew, VC. A framed collage of Bellew's photo, citation, 1st BC Regiment cap badge, and replica VC was presented to the mayor of Kamloops for display in the city hall. On September 8, 2008, the BCR Association dedicated a bronze plaque, commemorating Capt. Bellew's action and award, affixed to the brick wall of the café opposite the Vancouver Corner Monument in Belgium.

F.A.C. SCRIMGER

Near Ypres, Belgium, April 25

While Edward Bellew was holding out at Vancouver Crossroads with his machine guns, some 2,500 yards away to the southwest Captain Francis Scrimger, MO of the 14th Bn, and his staff were tirelessly attempting to treat the large numbers of wounded who had been arriving at his Advanced Dressing Station (ADS) since the enemy gas attack on April 22. This was at Shell Trap Farm, which was often the target of enemy artillery. It was during such an attack that Scrimger would win his VC.

On April 22, 1915, the ADS of the 3rd Canadian Field Ambulance was situated with 3rd Canadian Infantry Brigade (CIB) HQ in a large farm to the north of Wieltje. The original, rather grandiose, name of this moated farm had been Château du Nord but it had been aptly christened Shell Trap Farm by the troops (later, on Corps orders, it was renamed Mouse Trap Farm). Capt. Francis Scrimger, MO of the 14th Bn., Royal Montreal Regt., 3rd CIB, was in charge of this ADS, having just arrived from England to replace Capt. Boyd who had been wounded.

At 5:00 p.m. the German gas attack, accompanied by a violent artillery bombardment, was launched along much of the front line. Eye-witnesses reported large numbers of Belgian hares running from the oncoming gas cloud among equally dazed and bewildered French Colonial troops. Some of the gassed soldiers were treated at Scrimger's ADS while it was under shellfire.

Reinforcements were being rapidly sent forward, although German artillery cut many telephone wires and a very confused situation existed with unfounded rumours circulating between the various units, but at 7:00 p.m. the Canadian front line was still basically intact.

Due to confusing reports and the lack of real information, and spurred on by rifle bullets hitting the walls of the château, the Staff Captain, 3rd CIB, Capt. Harold MacDonald, organized all available HQ personnel, including cooks and batmen, for the immediate defence of Shell Trap Farm.

By 9:00 p.m. Brig.-Gen. Turner VC, 3rd CIB, received orders to mount a counterattack on the enemy digging in at Kitchener's Wood. He was advised that a British battalion would be coming to support the Canadians but, despite the efforts of Capt. MacDonald to find the un-named British battalion, it had already been ordered elsewhere. Turner therefore ordered the counterattack to be launched with the only battalions available, the 10th and 16th, mounting their attack at 11:30 p.m.

The 10th Bn. was guided to its assembly position some 500 yards northeast of Shell Trap Farm by the ubiquitous Capt. MacDonald. The 1,500 men advanced in waves, their flanks unsecured and with only three artillery batteries in support. There was one more artillery piece in support: a single gun of the 75th Battery RFA, firing from Shell Trap Farm, but with only sixty rounds available. The attack formation had emanated from 3rd CIB HQ with the orders signed by the brigade major, Lt.-Col. Garnet Hughes, son of the Canadian minister of defence, Sir Sam Hughes. The men had covered about half the 1,000 yards to the wood when the Germans were alerted. Flares illuminated the Canadians, and two-thirds of the officers, all the company commanders, and about a half of the other ranks fell.

Meanwhile, by 1:30 a.m., the 3rd (Toronto) and 2nd (Eastern Ontario) Bns reported to Brig.-Gen. Turner; the 3rd took up positions along the road 300 yards south of Shell Trap Farm while the 2nd Bn. was ordered to support the attack on Kitchener's Wood. News of the

16th Bn's plight was brought to Bde. HQ after 2:00 a.m. by Maj. Godson-Godson, adjutant of the battalion, who gave his report by handwritten note because of a "bullet-ripped gullet." No doubt he was yet another patient for Scrimger's hard-pressed staff at the ADS.

Stretcher-bearers attempted to collect the wounded, but after they incurred casualties from snipers this work was suspended until after dark. Many of the wounded were treated at Shell Trap Farm, both by Capt. Scrimger and also Capt. Haywood, MO of the 3rd Toronto Bn., who had set up his aid post in the stables of the farm. The wounded had to wait, many in the open courtyard, for the ambulances to come up after dark to collect them, then making their way back along the crowded roads, illuminated by the burning buildings of Ypres.

Shortly after 4:00 p.m. large bodies of Germans were seen moving southeastward from Kitchener's Wood and Oblong Farm, where they were heavily punished by guns of the 5th and 6th Batteries CFA, firing over open sights; one of the battery commanders, Maj. Harvey McLeod, was actually sitting on the roof of Shell Trap Farm directing fire. The Germans were stopped when the range was down to 900 yards. This was the last enemy attack of the day.

2/Lt. Bruce Bairnsfather, 1st Royal Warwicks, took part in an abortive attack early on April 25 and carried a wounded Canadian officer, probably to Scrimger's ADS. He described the scene: "Shells were crashing into the roof of the farm and exploding round it in great profusion." As Scrimger recorded in his personal diary:

April 25th. This has been a big day ... I got an hour's sleep this afternoon, the first for three days and nights ... About this time, lack of sleep and food, anxiety and the excitement of a vigorous cannonade, had worked me up to such an extent that I did not care what happened. I caught myself once out in the open cursing the Germans and all their works. I first now felt a personal hatred toward them. I was afraid, too, to speak for fear of breaking down.

In the late afternoon the farm was hit several times by heavy enemy artillery fire. Boxes of SAA exploded and some of the buildings caught fire; also burning was the straw in the courtyard, on which wounded men had been laid. Brig.-Gen. Turner and his staff evacuated the buildings, many of them having to wade through the moat, and the majority of the wounded were moved to relative safety. Turner's brigade captain, Capt. Harold MacDonald, was not so fortunate and in his own words, recounted by the *Montreal Star* on July 16, 1915:

> I was in the front of our Canadian headquarters staff on 25 April, which was the third day of the terrific St. Julien fighting, when I was hit on the neck and shoulder. I was dragged into a building where Capt. Scrimger dressed my wounds. A few minutes later German shells found the building and set it on fire. The staff were forced to abandon the building and left me there as an apparently hopeless case. But Capt. Scrimger carried me out and down to a moat, fifty feet in front, where we lay half in the water. Capt. Scrimger curled himself round my wounded head and shoulder to protect me from the heavy shellfire, at obvious peril of his own life. He stayed with me until the fire slackened, then got the stretcher-bearers and had me carried to the dressing-station. This, however, is only one of many incidents of Capt. Scrimger's heroism in those awful three days. No man ever better deserved the soldier's highest honour.

Capt. Francis Scrimger was recommended for the award of the Victoria Cross, the official announcement being published in the Supplement to the *London Gazette*, No. 29202, dated June 22, 1915. The citation read as follows:

> On the afternoon of 25th April 1915, in the neighbourhood of Ypres, when in charge of an advanced dressing station in farm buildings which were being heavily shelled by the enemy, he directed under heavy fire the removal of wounded, and he himself carried a severely wounded Officer out of a stable in search of a place of greater safety. When he was unable alone

to carry this Officer further, he remained with him under fire until help could be obtained. During the very heavy fighting between 22nd and 25th April, Captain Scrimger displayed continuously day and night the greatest devotion to duty among the wounded at the front.

He was decorated by King George V at Windsor on July 21, 1915. As a result of Capt. McDonald's wounds he lost an arm, but this did not prevent him from reaching the rank of brigadier-general, and after the war he became chairman of the Canadian Pension Commission in Ottawa.

Born in Montreal on February 10, 1881, Francis Alexander Caron Scrimger was the son of one of the leading Presbyterian ministers in Canada, principal of the Presbyterian College, the Rev. John Scrimger MA, DD, and Mrs. Scrimger. The family resided at 83 Redpath Crescent, and while living there Scrimger attended Montreal High School before going on to McGill University Medical School, graduating as an MD in 1905. He then spent some time on post-graduate studies in Europe. Returning to Canada he was commissioned captain in the Canadian Army Medical Corps (CAMC) on April 13, 1912, and appointed medical officer of the Montreal Heavy Brigade, Canadian Artillery. When war was declared, he became MO of the 14th Bn., CEF, on September 22, 1914. Sailing from Valcartier, Quebec, on October 3, 1914, the battalion was divided between two ships, half sailing on the *Alaunia* and the rest on the *Andania*. Disembarking at Plymouth, the battalion endured a wet English winter on Salisbury Plain before sailing from Avonmouth on the *Australind* on February 1, 1915. Scrimger was not with his battalion when it disembarked at St. Nazaire on February 15, as he was diagnosed with broncho-pneumonia and had been admitted to No. 1 General Hospital, Netheravon, Wiltshire, on January 8. After his medical discharge from hospital Scimger "pulled strings" to achieve the speedy posting to his unit in France, disembarking on March 16.

After gaining his VC, Scrimger carried on with his work as a surgeon at different hospitals and was invalided to England in

January 1916 following an injury to his left hand, which occured while operating on a patient at No. 1 General Hospital, Etaples. This injury became infected and necessitated the amputation of his middle finger. He was discharged from hospital at Ramsgate, Kent, in July 1916, and after postings to Brighton and London, Major Scrimger — he was promoted on December 5, 1916 — joined No. 3 Canadian CCS, Boulogne, in March 1917. With this unit, later stationed at Remy Sidngs near Poperinge, Scrimger served through the arduous conditions of the Third Battle of Ypres (later to be named the Battle of Passchendaele). During the winter of 1917–18 he developed a good working relationship and a strong friendship with Nursing Sister Carpenter, who had been posted to this CCS from an Etaples hospital in December and assisted him in the operating theatre.

When the major German offensive commenced in March 1918, enemy shells fell close to nurses quarters at the CCS and all nursing sisters were ordered back to Saint-Omer. Orders were received to send a surgical team to a hard-pressed British CCS near Roye, Somme (thirty miles southeast of Amiens), and Scrimger persuaded his CO to send him. Consequently Maj. Scrimger, together with an anaesthetist, two medical orderlies, and a batman were despatched to No. 50 CCS, collecting Nursing Sister Carpenter from Saint-Omer *en route*.

Wounded soldiers were arriving for treatment in large numbers at No. 50 CCS, and for three days and nights Scrimger and his team worked with little rest until the rapid enemy advance caused all nursing staff to be ordered to withdraw for their safety. Major Scrimger and the remaining staff continued treating the wounded until they too were ordered to fall back. It was not in Scrimger's nature to abandon his patients, so the remaining seriously wounded soldiers were carried to a nearby road busy with retreating wagons. It was not until all the wounded men had been found transport that Scrimger and his few helpers, which now included an Irish RAMC officer, departed the CCS. They did not leave empty-handed but loaded medical equipment on to wheeled stretchers with which they set off amongst the retreating soldiery. Around midnight they arrived at Montdidier, having walked over ten miles, to find Sister Carpenter there treating the wounded. The little group continued their journey to the rear, operating in makeshift situations, once even in an open field. By the end of March Scrimger was back again with No. 3 Canadian CCS, and around this time his engagement to Sister Carpenter was announced.

On September 5, 1918, he married Ellen Emerson Carpenter at St. Columba's Church, Pont Street, London. The service was performed by the Rev. Archibald Fleming DD and the Rev. J. Tudor Scrymgeour, Francis Scrimger's brother, who was also serving in France as a chaplain and working with the YMCA.

A 9,039-foot mountain in Kananaskis Park, on the Alberta/ British Columbia boundary in the Canadian Rockies, was named after him in 1918.

Promoted to lieutenant-colonel on April 21, 1919, Scrimger spent some months at the specialist plastic surgery at Sidcup, Kent, before he returned to Montreal with his wife. He was appointed assistant-surgeon at the Royal Victoria Hospital, and in 1936 was appointed surgeon-in-chief. Scrimger did not spare himself, and in addition to his work at the Royal Victoria Hospital he was consultant surgeon to a large pulp and paper company, and also published a large number of papers on medical subjects. He suffered a heart attack in November 1934, but after a few weeks rest he returned to work as hard as ever.

Francis Scrimger died suddenly after another heart attack on February 13, 1937, and was buried at the Mount Royal Cemetery, Montreal. On October 17, 2005, Lt.-Col. Scrimger's VC and campaign medals were presented to the Canadian War Museum, Ottawa, by his three daughters.

The site of Kitchener's Wood, Wijngaardstraat, Belgium, is now marked by a memorial to the memory of soldiers from 10th and 16th Bns. CEF killed during the night attack on April 22. This stone, seven-foot-high memorial symbolizing shattered oak trees and a gas cloud, was unveiled on March 22, 1997.

It is surprising that Francis Scrimger received no recognition for his extreme dedication when attached to No. 50 CCS, although his future wife, Nursing Sister Ellen Carpenter, was Mentioned in Despatches. This was published in the *London Gazette* dated May 28, 1918.

F.W. CAMPBELL

Givenchy, France, June 15

The fifth and last member of the Canadian Expeditionary Force to be awarded the VC in 1915 was also the oldest; Capt. Fredrick Campbell won the medal on his forty-eighth birthday. At the end of May, a provisional date of June 11 was fixed for simultaneous attacks north and south of the La Bassée Canal, with the objective of capturing La Bassée itself; this date allowed for sufficient artillery ammunition to be obtained, but even so insufficient artillery shells reduced the attack to a narrow frontage directed toward Violaines, northeast of Givenchy.

The southern sector of the attack was allotted to 1st Can. Bn. (Western Ontario Regt.), 1st CIB, with battalions from the British 21st Bde., 7 Div., on its left. The Canadians' direction of attack was against the German line at H2 to H3 (see map), held by 13th Regt. The date of the attack was postponed a number of times, but was finally fixed at 6:00 p.m. on June 15.

To conserve shells the supporting sixty-hour artillery bombardment was slow for the first forty-eight hours but early on June 15 it increased, and thirty minutes before the assault began it became intense. In addition, two 18-pounder guns were moved into the front line at the Duck's Bill, a semicircular embankment projecting forward opposite

H2; a third gun was positioned behind a ruined farmhouse 300 yards from H3. The two guns opposite H2 opened fire at 5:45 p.m. and destroyed three machine guns and part of the enemy embankment before they were put out of action by concentrated German artillery fire. The third gun did not fire as the officer in command was afraid of hitting Canadian infantry assembled in trenches in front of him; consequently the enemy redoubts at H3, containing several machine guns, were only slightly damaged. At 5:59 p.m. a mine that had been laid by men of 176th Tunnelling Company RE was exploded in front of the enemy strongpoint at H2; it was intended to explode under the German strongpoint, but the engineers had struck water in the gallery just short of their objective and the charge was therefore increased to 3,000 pounds of ammonal in the hope that it would totally destroy the strongpoint. When it was exploded the resulting crater was over forty yards wide; the German line was little damaged but many men in the Canadian front line were killed or injured. In addition, both stores of bombs in the 1st Bn.'s line were either destroyed or buried.

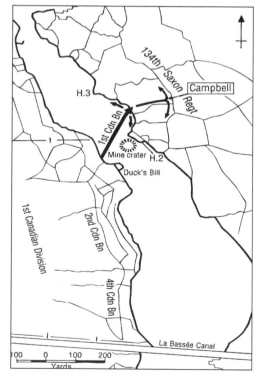

Near Givenchy, June 1915

The 1st Bn. attacked at 6:01 p.m. and within nine minutes the leading two companies were in the German second line, and the third company, No. 2, was in the front line. Capt. Campbell, the battalion machine-gun officer, crossed no man's land with No. 2 Company and took two Colt machine guns and their crews with him to the German front line.

Although the battalion captured the front-line trenches between points H2 and H3, lack of bombs meant that the strongpoint at H3 could not be taken; consequently, by 8:00 p.m., machine guns firing from H3 and I4 (450 yards north) controlled no man's land for a mile north from the Duck's Bill.

A German counterattack forced many of the battalion's men back toward the mine crater and at this point Campbell took one of his guns forward to meet the attack. Only one man, Pte. Howard Vincent, a lumberjack from Bracebridge, Ontario, remained from Campbell's original detachment, and he went forward with his captain. The tripod of the machine gun was damaged by shellfire so Campbell used Vincent's back as a support while he fired over 1,000 rounds, all the ammunition he had. He then ordered Vincent to retire, and although badly burned by the hot barrel of the gun, the private dragged it back to the Canadian line. Campbell was hit in the right thigh by a bullet and had started to crawl back when he was picked up by Company-Sgt.-Maj. C. Owen, in command of No. 1 Company, who carried him back for treatment. Campbell was passed down the medical chain of command and reached No. 7 Stationary Hospital at Boulogne on June 17. At noon on June 19 he became unconscious and died three hours later. In a letter to Mrs. Campbell the doctor explained that the wound was septic, "as all these cases are." Campbell was buried in Boulogne Eastern Cemetery, Plot II, Row A, Grave 24.

His commanding officer, Lt.-Col. F.W. Hill, also wrote to Campbell's wife and told her how much he would be missed. He continued, "I had twice before recommended him for promotion and honours, and have again done so. This time I feel his name will be found in the list." This was the case as the *London Gazette* of August 23, 1915, published the VC citation.

For most conspicuous bravery on 15th June, 1915, during the action at Givenchy. Lt. Campbell took two machine-guns over the parapet, arrived at the German first line with one gun, and maintained his position there, under very heavy rifle, machine-gun and bomb fire, notwithstanding the fact that almost the whole of his detachment had then been killed or wounded. When our supply of bombs had become exhausted, this Officer advanced his gun still further to an exposed position, and, by firing about 1,000 rounds, succeeded in holding back the enemy's counter-attack. This very gallant Officer was subsequently wounded, and has since died.

The medal was sent by the War Office to Canada on August 28, 1915, and subsequently given to his widow, Mrs. Margaret Campbell.

Frederick William Campbell was born at Mount Forest, Oxford County, Ontario, on June 15, 1867, and later that year moved with his parents, Ephraim B. and Esther A. Campbell, to a farm near Gleneden, Grey County. Educated at Mount Forest School, Campbell joined the local militia, the 30th Bn. Wellington Rifles, in 1885 when he was eighteen.

When the Boer War began he enlisted in the South African Contingent in London, Ontario, and served with the Royal Canadian Regt. Campbell was present at the actions at Johannesburg, Drenfontein, Paardeburg, and Cape Colony as part of a Maxim machine-gun crew and was mentioned in despatches for an incident at the Modder River. One wheel of his machine gun was damaged by shellfire so Campbell improvised, replacing the damaged spokes with legs from a table from a nearby house. (This wheel is held in the Citadel Museum in Quebec.) He was awarded the Queen's Medal and four clasps and returned home in 1900 with the rank of sergeant.

On November 25, 1903, he married Margaret Annie McGillivray and their three children, Arthur Clive, Jean Margaret, and Freda McGillivray, were all born at the farm he had purchased near his father's home, where he bred horses. In 1911 Campbell was present in London at the coronation of King George V. He was a public school trustee of a school at Normanby, his hometown, and a director of the Mount Forest Agricultural Society. Campbell remained in the militia and when war began immediately obtained permission to recruit in his local area. On August 17, 1914, he went to Valcartier Camp with a dozen volunteers. Assigned to 1st Bn., 1st Bde., with the rank of lieutenant, Campbell sailed on October 3 with the other 1,165 members of his battalion on the *Laurentic*. They disembarked at Plymouth on October 18 and proceeded to Salisbury Plain, Wiltshire, where they encamped at Bustard.

The battalion arrived at their billets in Merris, France, on February 14, 1915, and incurred heavy losses on April 23 in a counterattack northeast of Ypres, when the machine guns under Lt. Campbell were very effective.

A plaque was unveiled to Campbell's memory at the Royal Canadian Legion Hall, Mount Forest, by his daughter on June 20, 1965, and the branch is now named No. 134, Captain Fred Campbell VC. The whereabouts of Campbell's medals is unknown.

1916

In June 1916, Canadian troops were still in Flanders and heavily involved in fighting in the section of the Ypres Salient running in a southwesterly direction from Sanctuary Wood down to Hill 62, Hill 60, and Mount Sorrel. These actions were called the Battle of Mount Sorrel. By this time Arthur Currie had been promoted to command the 1st Canadian Division. Although at one point the enemy penetrated the line by 1,200 yards this lost ground was later recovered by Canadian troops and the pathway to Ypres was once again closed to the enemy.

A few weeks later, on July 1, the Newfoundland Regiment took part in the disastrous first day of the Battle of the Somme at Beaumont Hamel. They suffered 710 casualties out of 801 men who began the advance.

The 1st, 2nd, and 3rd Canadian Infantry divisions remained in the always-dangerous Ypres Salient in July and August, and at the end of the month the Canadian Corps was sent south to take part in the Battle of the Somme, in which the 1st Canadian Infantry Division was attached to the II Australian Army Corps. Between September 4 and 7, together with Australian infantry and artillery, they were involved in attacks on Mouquet Farm and other enemy positions to the north of Pozières, a village that had only recently fallen to Australian troops.

Cpl. Leo Clarke of the 2nd Battalion (Eastern Ontario) won his VC near Courcelette on the 9th, when the 1st Canadian Brigade attempted to capture German trenches in front of Martinpuich. His VC was the first won by a member of the CEF in 1916 on the Western Front.

A few days later Canadian troops were to play a more important role in the Somme campaign when they took part in the Battle of Flers-Courcelette on September 15, a battle famous for the first appearance of Allied tanks and which lasted a week. The 2nd Canadian Division began from positions astride the Albert-Bapaume Road, and the attack was part of a much larger British attack. After very heavy fighting the Canadians were able to capture the sugar refinery at Courcelette as well as the rest of the village. The day was a very successful one for the Canadian Corps. On the following day the 49th Battalion (Edmonton) and the Princess Pat's 7th Brigade had bombed Fabeck Garden near Courcelette and captured sixty prisoners. It was in this action that Pte. J.C. Kerr won his VC.

Three weeks later, on October 8, the 16th Battalion (Canadian Scottish) of the 3rd Canadian Brigade reached Regina Trench, having forced its way through thick enemy wire. However, they were unable to remain in these positions as the 3rd (Toronto) Battalion to their right was forced to withdraw. During this action Piper James Richardson won his VC, the last by a Canadian in the year.

By August 1916 the 4th Canadian Division had arrived in France, where it was to be heavily involved in the last weeks of the 1916 Somme battle in October and November.

T.O.L. WILKINSON

La Boiselle, Somme, July 5

In the early part of July 1916 the 57th Brigade, 19th (Western) Division, earned two VCs. On July 5 a member of the 7th (Service) Battalion, the Loyal North (LN) Lancashire Regiment who were part of the 56th Brigade, the 57th's sister brigade, was to also earn the nation's highest military honour. The man, Thomas Wilkinson, born of Irish parents in Shropshire, England, had enlisted in the CEF at Valcartier on September 23, 1914, and as soon as he reached England he was transferred as an officer to the 7th (Service) Battalion Loyal North Lancashire Regiment.

At the end of June 1916, on the eve of the battle of the Somme, the 7th LN Lancs were camped at Hénencourt Wood and on the 30th went forward to trenches to the northeast of Albert, the Tara–Usna Line, in support to the 8th Division on the following day. However, a planned attack on the village of Ovillers had been cancelled and when relieved on the 2nd, the North Lancs returned to the shelter of a railway cutting at Albert. At 3:00 a.m. on the 3rd the battalion was again on the move and resumed support positions in the Tara–Usna Line where it remained until nightfall. The 57th and 58th brigades had attacked La Boiselle during the day and the North Lancs were in support of the 7th (Service) Battalion, the King's Own (Royal Lancaster) Regiment, who were occupying a former German front-line trench. On July 4 at 1:00 a.m. the LN Lancs were ordered up to a trench line closer to the village. This trench was "very much knocked about and full of dead." Fighting was renewed at 8:00 a.m. and during the day forty to fifty German prisoners passed through their lines, and at dusk the fighting began to subside. At 2:00 p.m. on the 5th, the LN Lancs were detailed to help the 7th East Lancs with a bombing attack, although unfortunately the East Lancs lost ground and were forced to fall back to an original British front-line position, and in doing so left behind a machine gun. The LN Lancs were immediately ordered to recover both the lost ground and the gun, which they successfully accomplished in achieving. When a part of another unit retired, leaving a machine gun behind, and in order to repel an inevitable German advance Lt. Wilkinson rushed forward with two colleagues and set up a machine gun and held up a group of the enemy when they were advancing down a trench on the left of the position. His prompt action prevented a more determined rush by the enemy, and it was for this deed and for others carried out later in the day that he was recommended for a VC by Lt.-Col. Sherbrooke, CO of the 1st Sherwood Foresters. Tragically and soon after Wilkinson's acts of gallantry, he was killed when trying to rescue a wounded man who was lying forty yards in front of the position. The battalion was to remain in the trench line near the now-captured La Boisselle until late evening on the 7th, when it was relieved and left for bivouacs to the rear of the Tara–Usna Line.

Wilkinson's posthumous award was gazetted on September 26, 1916, and read as follows:

> For most conspicuous bravery. During an attack, when a party of another unit was retiring without their machine-gun, Lt. Wilkinson rushed forward, and, with two of his men, got the gun into action, and held up the enemy until they were relieved.
>
> Later, when the advance was checked during a bombing attack, he forced his way forward and found four or five men of different units stopped by a solid block of earth, over which the enemy were throwing bombs.

With great pluck and promptness he mounted a machine-gun on the top of a parapet and dispersed the enemy bombers. Subsequently he made two most gallant attempts to bring in a wounded man, but at the second attempt he was shot through the heart just before reaching the man.

Throughout the day he set a magnificent example of courage and self-sacrifice.

Thomas Orde Lawder Wilkinson was the second son of Edith and Charles Ernest Orde Wilkinson of Ardanoir, Foynes, County Limerick, and was born at the Lodge Farm, Dudmaston, Bridgnorth, Shropshire, on June 29, 1891, although the date given on his attestation papers was 1894. His father was in Comax, Vancouver, at the time of his younger son's birth. In 1908 Thomas attended Wellington College, where he was good academically as well as being athletic. In addition he joined the OTC and served with them for four years, during which time he became a colour sergeant and later company commander. He left college in November 1912, after four years, and in the following year visited his parents in Vancouver Island where they had immigrated. On September 23, 1914, Wilkinson enlisted at Valcartier as a private in the 16th Battalion, Canadian Scottish, with the service number of 28804. He was five feet eleven inches tall with brown hair. Valcartier, eighteen miles north of Quebec City, was a huge camp formed in the autumn of 1914 when troops were sent there well before the camp was even finished being built.

On November 30 Wilkinson applied for a commission with the 50th (Calgary) Battalion (CEF), but he wanted to speed up the process of reaching France and decided to apply for a commission in the Imperial Army, which was granted, and he left for England. Once there he got himself transferred to the 7th LN Lancs Regiment on January 31, 1915, and left for France with them as a gunnery officer. By taking this course he was to see action in France a month before he otherwise would have.

After his death his father was presented with his son's posthumous VC by the king at Buckingham Palace on November 29, 1916.

Wilkinson's body was never found and his name is listed on the Thiepval Memorial to the Missing, Pier 11, Face A, and on the Sandwick War Memorial, British Columbia. In 2004 a plaque to his memory was dedicated in St. Andrews Churchyard, Quatt, southeast of Bridgnorth and close to his place of birth in Shropshire. His regiment possesses his wallet, which contains two letters to his parents, and also the original citation written by Lt.-Col. Sherbrooke.

Wilkinson's file in the National Archives includes correspondence of 1927 from relatives in Ireland stating that the War Office has still not sent Thomas's war medals to them. At the present time his VC; 1914–15 Star, BWM, and VM are on loan for display in the Ashcroft VC collection in the Imperial War Museum.

In 2005 the Round Britain Rally paid tribute to his memory at a plaque that had been erected close to Lodge Farm, Dudmaston.

L. CLARKE

September 9

In the six days between September 3 and 9, 1916, Pozières Ridge had finally been taken by the Allies and there had been continuous fighting toward High Wood. Most of Leuze Wood toward Combles had also been taken, as had Faffemont Farm. Finally on September 9, the village of Ginchy was to fall into Allied hands after extremely hard fighting.

Back on the western side of the Somme battlefield the Australian and Canadian troops were trying to move toward Mouquet Farm as part of the plan to occupy the German stronghold of Thiepval. The position to the northwest of the Pozières OG trench lines was called Fabeck Graben, a section of which had been lost by the enemy in early September. Although Sir Douglas Haig wanted the Canadian Army to be allowed to "settle in" before they were committed to the fray, there was little chance as the enemy were not going to give up their positions in front of Mouquet Farm without a considerable fight.

In addition to relieving the Australians on the Mouquet Farm front, the Canadian Army, in the form of the 2nd (East Ontario) Canadian Infantry Battalion, were also ordered to attack on the south side of the Albert–Bapaume Road. Their objective was the German front trench astride the railway leading to Martinpuich.

The fighting continued on a front of 500 yards and more than sixty German prisoners were taken. However, the line was continuously bombarded by the enemy artillery and several German counterattacks were fought off. It was during this time that Cpl. L. Clarke of the 2nd Canadian Battalion won his VC. Armed with a revolver he attacked a party of about twenty of the enemy virtually on his own and routed them. After picking up a couple of German rifles he pursued five of the men, taking one of them prisoner. All this despite being seriously wounded in the leg by a German bayonet.

The Canadian attack had begun at 4:45 p.m. and three out of the four companies in the battalion made the assault. When they reached the enemy line they found that the Allied barrage had not been successful, and there were many Germans waiting for them.

Cpl. Clarke was then ordered by Lt. Hoey to take part of a bombing section and clear out some of the enemy on the left flank. He was then to join up with Sgt. W.H. Nicholls at a block that the latter was to build. Clarke was the first to enter what turned out to be a strongly fortified position and he and the rest of his group bombed the Germans out. A party of Germans had already seen enough of Clarke's methods and had to be urged to the attack. Clarke took them all on, firstly with the use of his revolver, and then seizing a German rifle he used that as well. The senior of the two German officers lunged at Clarke and wounded him severely just below the knee with his bayonet. It was the officer's last act as Clarke then shot him. The remaining five Germans turned and fled, and even then Clarke pursued them hard. One of the German soldiers, who spoke excellent English, surrendered and Clarke turned him over to Sgt. Nicholls who had managed to finish building the trench. Lt. Hoey had to order Clarke to have his wounds attended to; nevertheless, Clarke returned to his platoon in their billets the next day.

Despite his wounds, Clarke continued to take part in the fighting and on October 11 his battalion was instructed to secure the recently captured Regina Trench, which was still coming under heavy enemy artillery fire. When crouching down in the rear of a trench a shell exploded and the trench collapsed, burying him. He was trapped but his brother managed to dig him out. He was taken by ambulance train to Number One General Hospital at Étretat near Le Havre, but died of paraplegia the following day, on the 19th. He was buried in Étretat Churchyard, Plot II, Row C, Grave 3A.

The citation for his VC was published on October 26 and read as follows:

> For most conspicuous bravery. He was detailed with his section of bombers to clear the continuation of a newly-captured trench and cover the construction of a "block." After most of his party had become casualties, he was building a "block" when about twenty of the enemy with two officers counterattacked. He boldly advanced against them, emptied his revolver into them, and afterward two enemy rifles, which he picked up in the trench.
>
> One of the officers then attacked him with the bayonet, wounding him in the leg, but he shot him dead. The enemy then ran away, pursued by Acting Cpl. Clarke, who shot four more and captured a fifth.
>
> Later he was ordered to the dressing station, but returned next day to duty.

Clarke's father, Mr. H.T. Clarke, received his son's posthumous VC at a ceremony in Winnipeg in 1917 from the hands of the Governor General of Canada, the 9th Duke of Devonshire, in front of a crowd of 30,000 people.

Lionel Beaumaurice (Leo) Clarke was born on December 1, 1892, in Waterdown, Hamilton, Ontario. He was the son of Henry Trevelyan Clarke and Rossetta Caroline Nona Clarke, of 785 Pine Street, Winnipeg, Manitoba. His early years were spent in England, but his parents returned to Winnipeg in the period 1903–05. After leaving school Leo Clarke held a number of jobs, and when war broke out in August 1914 he was working for the Canadian National Railway in survey work in the Canadian north. He returned to Winnipeg and, giving his trade as a construction engineer, he attested and enlisted as a private with the 27th Battalion CEF on February 25, 1915. He was five foot seven and a half inches tall with dark-brown hair and his service number was 73132. He left with the battalion to sail to England on May 17 and arrived in France on September 18. Once there he transferred to the 2nd Canadian (Eastern Ontario) Regiment on October 13, in order to be near his brother, who was also serving with the battalion. Clarke was wounded for the first time on December 8. On April 25, 1916, he was admitted to hospital with influenza and returned to his unit on May 2.

On August 6, 1916, he was made an acting corporal and with his battalion moved south to the Somme battlefield at the beginning of September. The immediate goals were Mouquet Farm and the village of Courcelette, a mile behind the German front-line trenches.On September 18 he was back in hospital again, this time for six days.

After the war, in 1925, after some pressure from the Women's Canadian Club of Winnipeg, the city council agreed to a suggestion that Pine Street should be renamed Valour Road and commemorated the act with the erection of a bronze plaque on a lamppost at Portage Avenue. This plaque commemorates three winners of the Victoria Cross in the First World War who were all living in the same block when they joined the CEF: CSM Frederick Hall VC, 8th Bn. (WR), April 24, 1915, Ypres; Lt.-Sgt. Leo Clarke VC, 2nd Bn., September 9, 1916, Pozières; Capt. Robert Shankland VC, DCM, 43rd Bn. (CH of C), October 25, 1917, Passchendaele. There is also a large mural that shows images of the three local heroes.

At 2:00 p.m. on Sunday September 19, 1971, an historical plaque to the memory of Cpl. Leo Clarke was unveiled in front of the Royal Canadian Legion Building, Hamilton Street, Waterdown, Ontario. Relatives of his family attended the ceremony.

Apart from his posthumous VC Clarke's medals consist of the 1914-15 Star, BWM, and VM. They were donated to the Canadian War Museum in Ottawa in 2010. Together with those of Hall and Shankland, Clarke's decorations were lent to the Manitoba Museum for display between August and November 2014. Major O.M. Learmonth was a member of the same regiment as Clarke and he too was also awarded a posthumous VC.

J.C. KERR

September 16

Zollern Graben was a major German Second Line defensive position and stronghold on the crest of a ridge between Mouquet Farm to the southwest and Courcelette to the northeast. Attempts to capture the whole of it had been made by troops of the Canadian Army on September 15 and had only narrowly failed. In particular the much fought-for Sugar Refinery had at last fallen to the attackers. The Canadians had also overrun Mouquet Farm itself, but did not totally clear it and were subsequently driven out.

The enemy from the Zollern positions had a clear view of any attackers and could also enfilade adjoining trenches with machine-gun fire. The 3rd Canadian Division was given these positions to capture on the evening of the 16th. The division was made up of the 7th, 8th, and 9th Canadian brigades. The 7th were to strike at Fabeck Graben, which was part of a trench running from Courcelette to Mouquet Farm. If successful the 9th Brigade were to attack the Zollern from the east. The first part of the plan failed because the artillery overshot, but two bombing parties of the 7th Brigade were able to enter the Fabeck Trench from both ends, thus sealing off a party of the enemy, in a section of the trench that measured 250 yards. The defenders were in an impossible position as if they retreated they would be cut down by the Canadians to the left and right flanks. It was at this point that Private John Kerr of the 49th (Edmonton) Battalion was to win the VC. He moved forward as bayonet man in advance of his companions, he climbed over a "block" and moved thirty yards along the enemy position before being challenged. Eventually he was seen and a grenade thrown at him, and in defending himself with his arm he lost part of his right forefinger and his right side was also injured. A bomb fight ensued between the Canadians and the Germans, but Kerr grew impatient and wanted to hurry up the capture of the German position. He then ran along the top of the Fabeck Trench, firing down at its defenders killing several. The remaining sixty-two Germans surrendered. Although Kerr acted mostly on his own, the Germans probably thought that he was part of a large party of attackers. That night Mouquet Farm was attacked again and the British II Corps began to relieve the Canadian Division.

Kerr's VC citation was published on October 26, 1916, and read as follows:

> For most conspicuous bravery. During a bombing attack he was acting as a bayonet man, and, knowing that bombs were running short, he ran along the parados under heavy fire until he was in close contact with the enemy, when he opened fire on them at point-blank range, and inflicted heavy loss.
>
> The enemy, thinking they were surrounded, surrendered. Sixty-two prisoners were taken, and 250 yards of enemy trench captured.
>
> Before carrying out this very plucky act, one of Private Kerr's fingers had been blown off by a bomb.
>
> Later, with two other men, he escorted back the prisoners under fire, and then returned to report himself for duty before having his wound dressed.

He received his VC from the king on February 5, 1917.

John Chipman Kerr was born at Fox River, Nova Scotia, on January 11, 1887. Before the war he had moved northwest of his birth place in order to become a farmer when he purchased some virgin land at Spirit River, Alberta. Thirteen months after war was declared, Kerr and a small group of other homesteaders, including his brother Roland, walked fifty miles to the nearest railway and arrived at Edmonton, Alberta, where on September 25, 1915, they enlisted in the 66th Battalion. Kerr's service number was 101465. He was six feet tall, with dark brown hair. His next of kin was his mother, Mrs. Robert T. Kerr.

Kerr left for England on May 1, 1916, arriving six days later. At the beginning of June 1916, when being trained in England, 400 men of the 66th were transferred to the 49th (Edmonton) Battalion who were in Belgium in the area of Sanctuary Wood near Ypres. By then Kerr was a corporal with the 49th Battalion, which had arrived in France on June 8. The Canadians later went south to the Somme battlefield, arriving at Albert on September 13, 1916. Less than forty-eight hours later they took up positions at a point near the Sunken Road in front of and to the west of the village of Courcelette. Kerr was wounded on September 18, and suffered gunshot wounds, in particular to his right hand. He was returned to England, where he became a patient in the Military Hospital in Lewisham, and nine week later he went to Bromley for convalescence for a week, on December 1. He was never to return to active service. For a time he was a personnel orderly, and was later taken on the strength of the 224th Canadian Forestry Battalion. He was made acting corporal on May 26, 1917.

After the war, in which his brother Roland had died in the Ypres fighting in 1917, John Kerr returned to Canada. When the Second World War began he re-enlisted. Hoping to serve overseas he transferred to the Royal Canadian Air Force. Instead he ended up as a service policeman and sergeant-of-the-guard in Sea Island, British Columbia. He later returned to Port Moody and died there on February 19, 1963, at the age of seventy-six. He was buried in Mountain View Cemetery, Prince Edward Avenue, Vancouver.

His grave reference is Veteran's Division, Albray Section, Block 5, Plot 8, Lot 12.

Apart from his VC his other decorations included the BWM (1914–20), VM (1914–19), Canadian Volunteer Service Medal (1939–45), King George VI Coronation Medal (1937), Queen Elizabeth II Coronation Medal (1953), and Medaile de la Somme (France). They are held in the collection of the Canadian War Museum in Ottawa. His other commemorations include a plaque set up beside a ferry which he used to run in Dunvegan, Alberta, and in 1951 he was commemorated with Mount Kerr being named after him in the VC range at Jasper National Park, Alberta. His name is also on the Port Greville War Memorial, as well on a plaque there which tells his story. Finally, in 2006 the Chip Kerr Park in Port Moody in British Columbia was also dedicated to his memory.

Other holders of the VC with links with Edmonton include: Edmund De Wind, G.B. McKean, and C. Kinross.

J.C. RICHARDSON

October 8–9

In the four days that elapsed between Lt. H. Kelly of the Duke of Wellington's winning his VC at Le Sars and October 8, when Piper Richardson was to win his, there had been slight Allied progress in the battle. The British had advanced to the northwest of Eaucourt and the French Army had made progress to the northeast of Morval. On the 8th, the 1st Canadian Division were to advance to the Quadrilateral on the Le Sars Line, which was to the northwest of the village itself, and also reach Regina Trench, which ran across their lines in a southwesterly direction. Regina ran from the north of Courcelette to Stuff Trench, which in turn joined the Schwaben Redoubt.

The attack began at 4:50 a.m. on the 8th, when it was still dark and also raining. The two Canadian brigades under the leadership of Major General Currie were the 1st on the right and the 3rd on the left. The 3rd and 4th Canadian Infantry battalions of the 1st Brigade attacked the right-hand objectives, the Le Sars Line and the Quadrilateral. They reached the former but, owing to uncut wire, were held up at the second and also had to swerve to the left when looking for gaps in the wire. The two battalions therefore mingled together on the left. In the afternoon a threatened German counterattack was delayed by the intervention of the artillery, but the Canadians were forced back, being greatly outnumbered and also out of bombs. They ended the day at their jumping-off trenches.

On the left of 1st Canadian Brigade was the 16th Canadian Infantry Battalion (Canadian Scottish) and the 13th Canadian Infantry Battalion (Royal Highlanders), with the former battalion managing to enter Regina Trench after forcing its way through the wire. However, as the 3rd Battalion on its right fell back, the 16th found that it could not hang on. The Royal Highlanders on the left were also held up by uncut wire, and after suffering heavy casualties fell back before dark. It seems that the uncut wire was a huge problem all along the line, and one can only assume that the artillery should either have been more destructive or that over-optimistic reports allowed the attack to take place. In addition the Canadian lines were crescent-shaped and the Germans had a concave front on this sector, which gave them a distinct advantage over their attackers.

However, we are concerned here with the role of the 16th Battalion and in particular that of Piper James Cleland Richardson. To quote the diary of the battalion:

"When our barrage started," said Company Sergeant Major Mackie, who was advancing on the left flank of the leading wave Number 4 Company, "Major Lynch, Captain Bell, Piper Richardson and myself went out of the trench. After waiting for five minutes we bade goodbye to Captain Bell who was to take over the second line of the company, and Major Lynch gave the order to advance. The three of us walked in front of the leading line; Piper Richardson on the Major's left and I on his right. The going was easy as the ground was not cut up. About halfway over I commenced to wonder why the piper wasn't playing and crossed over by the side of him to ask the reason. He said he had been told not to play until ordered to do so by the major."

The party reached the wire, which they found to be uncut, and when they were searching for an opening the Germans began to open fire and throw bombs. Major Lynch fell mortally wounded. Richardson asked Mackie if he could play his pipes and was told to go ahead. The wire still slowed down the Canadian advance and many men from the first two waves became casualties because of the intense fire. Richardson, according to eyewitnesses, walked up and down in front of the wire for fully ten minutes, thereby inspiring about one hundred men of the Canadian/Scottish battalions to greater effort in their attack against Regina Trench. Richardson must have been leading a charmed life. He also helped with the bombing attack against the enemy. He later helped a wounded colleague back to safety and, on realizing that he had mislaid his pipes, he went back to recover them. He was never seen alive again, although his body was recovered from the battlefield.

Richardson's gallantry on October 8/9, 1916, inspired a great deal by the image of the lone piper walking up and down in no man's land under intense fire but seemingly untouched by it all. Much of this publicity was written up for reasons of propaganda and was of a *Boy's Own Paper* type. As late as September 1965 a comic-strip version of Richardson's bravery was published in a magazine called *The Victor*.

Richardson's posthumous award was not announced until October 22, 1916, owing to some administrative delay, and read as follows:

> For most conspicuous bravery and devotion to duty when, prior to attack, he obtained permission from his commanding officer to play his company "over the top."
>
> As the company approached the objective, it was held up by very strong wire, and came under intense fire, which caused heavy casualties and demoralised the formation for the moment. Realizing the situation, Piper Richardson strode up and down outside the wire, playing his pipes with the greatest coolness. The effect was instantaneous. Inspired by his splendid example, the company rushed the wire with such fury and determination that the obstacle was overcome and the position captured.

Later, after participating in bombing operations, he was detailed to take back a wounded comrade and prisoners.

After proceeding about 200 yards Piper Richardson remembered that he had left his pipes behind. Although strongly urged not to do so, he insisted on returning to recover his pipes. He has never been seen since, and death has been presumed accordingly, owing to lapse of time.

Clearly his remains were eventually found as his headstone is to be found in Adanac Military Cemetery. His VC was awarded to his father in December 1918 by the lieutenant-governor of Ontario.

James Cleland Richardson was born at Bellshill, Lanarkshire, Scotland, on November 25, 1895. He was the son of David Richardson and Mary Prosser who lived in Princess Avenue, Glasgow, and James attended school at Bellshill Academy; Auchinwraith Public School, Blantyre, and John Street Public School, Bridgeton, Glasgow. His family emigrated to Chilliwack in British Columbia in 1911/12 and by 1914 his father had become the town's chief of police.

Prior to the war Richardson had been a well-known piper and had worked as a driller for about six months. He also served in the cadets for six months prior to enlisting in the Canadian Forces in Valcartier on September 23, 1914, when he was eighteen years old. He had brown hair and blue eyes. His service number was 28930 and his regiment the 72nd (Seaforth Highlanders). He had served with the 72nd Seaforth Cadets prior to the war. He sailed for England in October, and when he left England for France on February 8, 1915, he was attached to the 16th Canadian Scottish and was with them in the famous Canadian stand at St. Julien in April 1915.

After Richardson's death in 1916 it was Major C.W. Peck who recommended that he should be awarded what would be a posthumous VC. Peck later became commander of the 16th Battalion (Canadian) Scottish and was to win VC himself at Cagnicourt in early September 1918.

The twenty-year-old John Richardson was buried at Adanac Military Cemetery, Plot III, Row F, Grave 36. His decorations, which apart from the VC are the 1914–15 Star, BWM, and VM, were left to his sister, Mrs. Charles A. Murray of Blackburn, White Rock, British Columbia, and are now in the Canadian War Museum in Ottawa.

Richardson's name is commemorated together with those of thirteen other VC holders on a Memorial Arch in Hamilton, Lanarkshire, and he is also remembered with the Richardson Chapter of OIDE in Chilliwack, British Columbia. In addition a bronze statue of him designed by John Weaver was unveiled on October 11, 2003, at the front of the grounds at Chilliwack Museum, and finally his famous bagpipes were rediscovered in Scotland in 2002 and sent back to Canada in November 2006. They are now on display in Canada at the British Columbia Legislature. Eight years later, on October 25, 2014, a musical based on his life entitled *The Piper* was first performed in British Columbia.

1917

On March 27, 1917, the next member of the CEF to win a VC, after Piper James Richardson won his on October 8, 1916, was Lt. Frederick Harvey of the Lord Strathcona's Horse (Canadian Cavalry) during operations to clear the enemy out of Guyencourt, a village to the southeast of Lagnicourt. He was the first of twenty-three men serving in the Canadian Forces to win the VC in 1917.

Twelve days later the week-long Battle of Arras began, on Easter Monday, April 9. As a consequence of meticulous planning by Arthur Currie of the 1st Canadian Division, the CEF took part in the very successful capture of Vimy Ridge overlooking the Douai Plain. Losing control of the ridge forced the enemy, who had lost 6,000 men as prisoners, to shorten his main defence line.

No fewer than four Canadians earned the VC in this victory: Capt. Thain MacDowell of the 38th Battalion (Eastern Ontario), Private William Milne of the 16th Battalion (Canadian Scottish), and Lance-Sgt. Ellis Sifton of the 18th Battalion (Western Ontario). Of these three only MacDowell survived the war. Although a Canadian triumph, there were still pockets of enemy resistance to clear up, especially on the eastern slopes of the ridge beyond Hill 145. In dealing with some of these the fourth man, Private John Pattison of the 50th Battalion (Alberta) lost his life when winning his VC.

On May 3rd Lt. Robert Combe of the 27th Battalion (City of Winnipeg) won a posthumous VC in a local action near the town of Lens whilst in the air. Capt. William Bishop won the VC in flying operations with 6 Squadron near the German-occupied town of Cambrai.

The remaining sixteen Canadian VCs for the second half of the year were mainly won in the battles of Hill 70 in August and Third Ypres from July 31 to October, shortly before the Allies finally took the village of Passchendaele in November. Mainly because of extremely poor weather, which led to impossible conditions to fight in, the campaign was called off in mid October. Haig planned to renew attempts to capture Passchendaele Ridge as soon as weather conditions improved. He gave Sir Arthur Currie and his Canadian Corps the task of finishing the operation. Currie agreed, but only if the weather would be suitable and for his corps to have adequate artillery protection.

German pillboxes were bombarded prior to the initial Canadian attack at 5:40 a.m. on October 26. Canadian Divisions systematically captured the enemy pillboxes, and by November 6th the Canadian Corps had managed to successfully capture the ridge before being replaced. It was the end of the Third Battle of Ypres. Canadian casualties were very high, having reached 12,401.

On November 20 the last Canadian VC of the year was won by Lt. Harcus Strachan of the Canadian Fort Garry Horse, on the first day of the Battle of Cambrai. What was to be only a temporary advance was led by Lt.-Gen. Sir Julian Byng in command of the Third Army.

On November 23 British troops attacked Bourlon Wood, but were unable to hold on to it.

F.M.W. HARVEY

Guyencourt, France, March 27

The Canadian Expeditionary Force went to Europe in 1915 and fought in the trenches during the autumn and winter of 1915/16. The cavalry brigade to which Lt. Frederick Harvey belonged was withdrawn from the line for training, and in March 1917 the Lord Strathcona's Horse was serving with XV Corps north of Péronne on the Somme. Other cavalry regiments in the brigade included the Royal Canadian Dragoons, the Fort Garry Horse, and the Royal Canadian Horse Artillery, along with a machine-gun squadron and a field ambulance.

On March 24 the brigade was ordered to form a front that was to extend for twelve miles with Nurlu in its centre. This village is northeast of Péronne, east of the Canal du Nord, and south of Equancourt. The orders were for the cavalry to advance beyond the British infantry positions. By evening the Dragoons were occupying former enemy positions, including the woods to the southwest of Liéramont. The Fort Garry Horse had captured the villages of Etricourt and Ytres to the northwest. In the afternoon of the next day the Fort Garrys captured two more woods and launched an attack on a third and more strongly held wood. This clearance was carried out at the gallop and had the effect of emptying the wood of the enemy. This was the first time in two years of warfare that the cavalry had ridden successfully at a position strongly held by rifles and machine guns.

On the following day the Lord Strathconas were ordered to capture a wood south of Equancourt and the village itself, to the north and south of the railway line. Harvey and Lt. Gordon Flowerdew, of the same regiment, who was to win the VC a year later, were sent to reconnoitre the enemy positions. The wood was taken and the enemy were driven back into the village. The Lord Strathconas dismounted, advanced on foot, and captured the village at the point of the bayonet. At the same time the Fort Garry Horse, attacking from a northerly direction, captured their objectives, despite machine-gun fire.

During the evening of March 26 and the next morning Dragoons occupied Longavesnes and Liéramont; they then handed the defence of the former over to the infantry, while remaining themselves in Liéramont. The next targets were the village of Guyencourt and Saulcourt. The Fort Garrys and the Lord Strathconas attacked in the evening of September 27, but a heavy snowstorm delayed the beginning of the attack until 5:15 p.m. Visibility was adequate and the Fort Garrys galloped forwards to Hill 140; there they established two machine guns in commanding positions. They then went around the hill to Grebaussart Wood, Jean Copse, and Chauffeurs Wood, and managed to post three more machine guns. Other squadrons from the brigade rode straight at the village of Saulcourt and reached its outskirts. Canadian machine gunners caught the retiring German infantry. The Lord Strathconas moved on to a ridge on the left side of Guyencourt and, on reaching the northwest corner of the village, they were able to take some shelter in the lee of its walls.

It was at this point that Harvey won his VC. He was in command of the leading troop (Second Troop, C Squadron) and rode well to the front of his men. His citation, gazetted on June 8, 1917, tells what happened:

During an attack by his regiment on a village, a party of the enemy ran forward to a wired trench just in front of the village, and opened rapid fire and machine-gun fire at a very close range, causing heavy casualties in the leading troop. At this critical moment, when the enemy showed no intention whatever of retiring, and fire was still intense, Lieut. Harvey, who was in command of the leading troops, ran forward well ahead of his men and dashed at the trench, still fully manned, jumped the wire, shot the machine-gunner and captured the gun. His most courageous act undoubtedly had a decisive effect on the success of the operations.

Not surprisingly, the German machine gunner was overwhelmed with the speed of events and did not live long. The trench was captured and the village of Guyencourt fell to the Lord Strathconas.

Harvey was at first awarded a DSO by Sir Douglas Haig, and for two weeks wore the ribbon. Then he received the news that it had been made up to the nation's highest honour. On June 7, 1917, Brig.-Gen. the Hon. J.B. Seely, commander of the Canadian Cavalry Brigade, inspected the Canadian Cavalry Brigade in Devizes in Wiltshire and presented various military awards including the VC ribbon to Lt. F.M.W. Harvey for his gallantry at Guyencourt in March 1917. He was later decorated with the VC by the king at Buckingham Palace on July 21. About a year later Harvey again distinguished himself when Brig.-Gen. Seely of the Canadian Cavalry Brigade instructed him to reconnoitre Fontaine-sous-Montdidier. In a brilliant manoeuvre he attacked and captured the village, a few miles to the south of Moreuil. Shortly afterward, on March 30, 1918, he won the MC when involved with Lt. Gordon Flowerdew, also of Lord Strathcona's Horse, at the Bois de Moreuil. Flowerdew was mortally wounded in a cavalry charge and died the next day.

Harvey was awarded his MC on July 10, 1919, by the king.

Frederick Maurice Watson Harvey was born in Athboy, County Meath, Ireland, on September 1, 1888. He was one of seven brothers born to the Rev. and Mrs. Alfred Harvey. He attended the Portora Royal School at Enniskillen and Ellesmere College. As a young man he excelled as a rugby footballer, and was also proficient in boxing and athletics. At one time he lived for a short period in Dublin at

8 Woodstock Gardens, and played rugby for the Dublin team called the Wanderers, and also for Ireland. Other VC holders who played for the Wanderers team included Robert Johnston and Thomas Crean.

Harvey moved to Canada in 1908 and lived for three years in Fort Macleod, Alberta, when he worked as a surveyor. He enlisted in the Canadian Mounted Rifles at Fort Macleod in 1915, was commissioned in 1916, and went overseas with the Rifles. Soon he was transferred to the Lord Strathcona's Horse. This regiment had been raised during the Boer War and originally consisted mainly of recruits from the North-West Mounted Police. The regiment distinguished itself during the South African War and afterward became a permanent part of the Canadian Militia.

Harvey married Winifred Lillian Patterson in 1914. She was a daughter of Superintendent Patterson of the North-West Mounted Police and had been born on the family farm. She went to England during the First World War, following her husband there, and worked in an ammunition factory. When the war was over Harvey trained for a time as a physical-education instructor and in 1927 was sent to Kingston, Ontario. In 1938 he was made a lieutenant-colonel and took command of the Lord Strathcona's Horse; as commanding officer he was responsible for A Squadron at Winnipeg and B Squadron in Calgary. During this pre-war period he went to England for a six-month course for senior officers at Sheerness. Soon after the Second World War began he was promoted to brigadier, and on November 5, 1940, was appointed district officer commanding Military District Number 13, one of the most important Canadian military commands. During this time his wife lived again in Britain, helping with the wounded.

In 1943 Harvey "blotted his copybook" and upset a great number of people when he was quoted in the press as being severely critical of teaching methods, Canadian home life, and of the boys themselves. The young men they had grown into were seemingly "selfish and lacking in Canadian ideals." With hindsight, Harvey may have been correct with his criticism but, nevertheless, it seemed to be an inappropriate time to state such views. In 1944 Harvey went to Britain for a two-and-a-half-month tour of the Canadian

Army and returned to Canada with many ideas for training, which he used in his command at Currie Barracks. In 1945 Harvey's only son, Lt. Dennis Harvey, was killed in action in northern Europe. In December Harvey retired from the army and a large dinner dance was organized as a tribute to the popular officer. In 1956 he was a member of the Canadian contingent to the VC review at Hyde Park. Harvey was honorary colonel of the Lord Strathcona's Horse from 1958 to 1966, and in 1968 he led a contingent of 109 men to Ottawa for a wreath-laying ceremony on Remembrance Day.

Harvey was described by Lt. Col. Ian McNabb of the Lord Strathcona's Horse in the following way:

> He came here an immigrant, married locally, went to war and came back a hero. He has really been the father of the regiment. He was an excellent example of officer-like qualities, had a tremendous sense of humour and loyalty to the military.

Harvey was a tall man, quiet but also very determined, and always seeking perfection in his command. Being a soldier was his career, but horses were his hobby and he often served as a judge of hunter and jumper divisions. His wife, too, shared his love of horses. After he retired from the army Harvey travelled to Australia, New Zealand, and Ireland, as well as to Britain, attending various horse shows or races.

Harvey died on August 24, 1980, at the age of ninety-one. A service was held at St. Stephen's (Anglican) Church on August 25, followed by burial at Union Cemetery, Fort Macleod, Alberta. He had lived in Calgary for a very long time, the home of the Lord Strathcona's Horse, and for the last eighteen months of his life he lived at Trinity Lodge, Glenmore Trail, Calgary, where he died. A service of full military honours was held at St. Stephen's on September 13, and at the parade ground at Sarcee Barracks a service was held in driving rain in front of 150 people. The service included a riderless horse with a pair of riding boots reversed in the stirrups to symbolize a fallen soldier, alongside marched a troop of brass-helmeted soldiers dressed in scarlet tunics with lances at their sides. Other soldiers carried the colours of the regiment. The pipes and drums of the Calgary Highlanders were on parade and an eleven-gun salute was fired. Harvey's wife, Winifred, who was born two years after her husband, lived until August 9, 1989.

Harvey's name is commemorated in Calgary, where there is a barracks named after him and a mountain in Jasper National Park, Alberta, which was named after him in 1949. Apart from his VC, his decorations include the MC, BWM (1914–20), VM (1914–1919), Defence Medal (1939–45), Canadian Volunteer Silver Medal (1939–45) and "Maple Leaf" Clasp, War Medal (1939–45), King George V Silver Jubilee Medal (1935), King George VI Coronation Medal (1937), Queen Elizabeth II Coronation Medal (1953), Queen Elizabeth II Silver Jubilee Medal (1977), Canadian Forces Decoration (CD) and two clasps, Croix de Guerre (France), and CBE. They are on display in the Museum of Regiments in Calgary, Alberta.

T.W. MACDOWELL

Vimy Ridge, France, April 9

Despite the Canadian Army's eventual success in capturing Vimy Ridge in April 1917, the fighting did not initially go according to plan in all the parts of the operation. For example, the 4th Canadian Division, on the extreme left of the line, had the shortest distance to cover but the hardest task to accomplish. Indeed, the high ground known as the "Pimple" to the north of Hill 145 and south of the Souchez River did not fall to the Canadians until the 12th.

Capt. Thain MacDowell was OC B Company of the 38th (Ottawa) Battalion, which had been reorganized after the Somme battle of 1916 and had moved up to the Vimy Trenches soon after Christmas Day. Thus the battalion was positioned in front of the ridge for three months before April 1917. On the 9th, and with two runners, Ptes. Hay and Kebus, MacDowell was looking for a suitable place for use as a command post. Ahead of them were some German machine guns and MacDowell promptly knocked out one of the machine gunners by throwing a bomb that killed him. The German's colleague decided to make himself scarce and disappeared into a hole in the ground. The Canadians quickly followed the vanishing German and discovered that they had come across a major enemy fortification.

MacDowell called on the "unseen" to surrender and there was no reply, so with his two runners posted at the two entrances, he began to investigate. He descended a stairway. After fifty-two steps he rounded a corner into the main room of the underground fortress and was suddenly confronted by a large group of the enemy. He quickly decided on a course of action and called back up the steps, using a voice full of great authority, to supposed colleagues waiting at the head of the tunnel. The Germans were seemingly convinced and immediately raised their hands in a gesture of mass surrender; they even piled arms in the centre of the room when ordered to do so. MacDowell was then able to send them out of the tunnel in small groups of about ten at a time.

Very soon the process stopped and MacDowell later found out that his runners had shot the first ten men to emerge as they did not know that they were not armed. MacDowell sternly commanded the remaining Germans to move out of the tunnel and they did so in groups of twelve. At one point things looked bad for MacDowell, when a German snatched up a rifle, but he did not have time to use it. It turned out that the men were mainly Prussian Guardsmen, and the final total of prisoners came to seventy-seven.

Although he was wounded in the hand, MacDowell continued to hold the position for five days and had to endure some heavy shellfire. Eventually he was relieved by his battalion.

MacDowell received his VC, together with a DSO won earlier on the Somme, during the investiture in the forecourt of Buckingham Palace on July 21, 1917. The king was accompanied by Field Marshal the Duke of Connaught and Admiral the Marquess of Milford Haven. The parade was witnessed by the queen, together with Princess Mary, from the balcony in front of the palace. All told, twenty-three men received the VC at this investiture and eight families received the medal as the recipient's next of kin.

In the War Diary for the 38th Canadian Infantry Battalion of April 9 are four reports that were written by MacDowell; three of them are reproduced below. He gave his location as "Dugout approximately Junction of Cyrus and Clutch" and the first report was timed at 8:00 a.m. The reports were addressed to the commanding officer of the 38th Battalion.

Objective reached but I am afraid is not fully consolidated. The mud is very bad and our machine guns are filled with mud. I have about 15 men near here and can see others around and am getting them in hand slowly. Could D Company come up in support if they have stopped in the front line? The runner with your message for A Company has just come in and says he cannot find any of A Company officers. I don't know where my officers and men are but I am getting them together. There is not an NCO here. I have one machine-gunner here but he has lost his cocking piece off the gun and the gun is covered with mud. The men's rifles are a mess of mud and they are cleaning them. My three runners and I came to what I had selected previously as my company headquarters. We chucked a few bombs down and then came down. The dugout is 75 feet down and is very large. We explored it and sent out 75 prisoners and two officers. This is not exaggerated as I counted them myself. We had to send them out in batches of 12 so they would not see how few men we were. I am afraid that a few of them got back as I caught one man shooting one of our men after he had given himself up. He did not last long, and I am afraid we could not take any back except a few who were good dodgers as the men chased them back with rifle shots. The dugout is a very large one and will hold a couple of hundred. The men were 11th Regiment R.I.R. I cannot give you an estimate of our casualties but believe they are severe. Will send one back as soon as possible. There is a field of fire of 400 yards or more and if there were a couple of brigade machine guns we could keep them back easily as the ground is almost impassable - horrible mess. There are lots of dead Bosche, and he evidently held well. I can see 72nd men on our left. The 78th have gone through after we reached here. The barrage was good, but men did not keep close to it enough and held back. There are no shovels found yet so we will just get our rifles ready. No wire is here and cannot spare men to send out. The line is obliterated. Nothing but shell holes, so wire couldn't be of much use. Men are pretty well under pressure. There is no artillery officer left here. His fire is very weak and suppose he is going back. This is all I can think of at present. Please excuse writing.

The next report was at 10:30 a.m.:

Have been along the line. The dugout we occupy is at the corner of Cyrus and Baby. It has three entrances well distant from each other and will hold easily 250 men at the very least. The tunnel leads down toward our line which I did not explore. It has a winch and cable for hoisting. There are only 15 men with me of whom two are stretcher-bearers. The rifles are one mass of mud. I have two Lewis guns and only four pans. Both guns are out of action on account of the mud. We have a very few bombs as we had to bomb several dugouts.

The 78th I have no trace of but there are two German machine guns just in front of us. They are firing constantly. Snipers are also busy. We cannot locate them as yet. The 72nd are on the left and seem to be spread along fairly well. The ground is practicably impassable. His aeroplanes came over and saw a few of my men at the dugout entrance and now we are getting his heavies from our right on his left.

I have no subalterns or NCOs and unless I get a few more men with serviceable rifles I have to admit it, we may be driven out. Three of my men are wounded as it is so I might as well tell you the facts of the case.

The runner has just come in with your message. We are in BABY trench slightly to the right of Cyrus. I was wrong in my other message as to my location. I had just arrived. I will try to get in touch with Major Howland D Company 38th but don't like to leave here as I mentioned above have not an officer or NCO. There are a lot of wounded out of here as I can see by the rifles standing up. The heavy battery from the right is working very well at present.

Then at 2:45 p.m.:

While exploring this dugout Kelty and I discovered a large store of what we believe to be explosives in a room. There is also an old sap leading away down underground in the direction of No. 7 Crater. This was explored down to a car but no further as it may be wired. Would you get in touch with brigade as quickly as possible and ask that a party of either 176th or 182nd Tunnelling Company come up and explore these. We have cut all wires for fear of possible destructive posts. The dugout has three entries and will accommodate easily 250 or 300 men with the sap to spare. It is 75 feet underground and very comfortable. The cigars are very choice and my supply of Perrier water is very large.

If I might I would suggest that you take it up with the brigade that this place be occupied in strength as there is a great field of fire to the north and west as well as to the east. This you see makes it a very strong supporting post to our left flank and I would strongly recommend that it ought to be occupied by brigade machine guns. I cannot locate them. I have no NCOs to leave in charge here to look out for them myself.

It is quite all right for any one to come up here. They are firing at us all the time with their heavy guns from the southeast but I have no casualties to report since coming in here except being half scared to death myself by a "big brute."

I cannot impress upon you too much the strength of the position and the value of it as a strong supporting point to the left flank by which they will undoubtedly make their counterattack. Observation is good here on the side of Lens and other villages and battery positions can be seen. We have taken two machine guns that I know of and a third and possibly a fourth will be taken to-night. This post was a machine-gun post and held by a machine-gun company.

I believe they are Prussian Guards. All big strong men who came in last night. They had plenty of rations but we had a great time taking them prisoner.

It is a great story. My two runners Kebus and Hay did invaluable work in getting me out of the dugout as we had to conceal the fact we were only three in number. I don't think they all got back though.

Please have these Engineers sent up at once to examine wire further as this is a great dugout and should not be destroyed. I believe the sap runs into No. 7 Crater and might help in being an underground CT.

There are a large number of wounded in front of here, as I can see by the rifles stuck in the ground. We are using German rifles as ours are out of business. I now have three Lewis guns but only about 15 pans of ammunition. Kelty is here with me. I have no NCOs. Please point out the value of this as a supporting point on our left flank.

I cannot think of anything further. Tell Ken to come up for tea to-morrow if it is quiet. Sorry to hear of the CO and Hill and the others.

MacDowell's citation for his VC was gazetted on June 8, 1917:

For most conspicuous bravery and indomitable resolution in face of heavy machine-gun and shellfire. By his initiative and courage this officer, with the assistance of two runners, was enabled, in the face of great difficulties, to capture two machine guns, besides two officers and seventy-five men. Although wounded in the hand, he continued for five days to hold the position gained, in spite of heavy shellfire, until eventually relieved by his battalion. By his bravery and prompt action he undoubtedly succeeded in rounding up a very strong enemy machine-gun post.

Thain Wendell MacDowell was born in the parsonage in Lachute, Quebec, on September 16, 1890. His parents were living at Carp,

Ontario, but his mother, Eleanor Elizabeth Richardson, went to her grandparents' home in Lachute for Thain's birth. His father was the Rev. J.V. MacDowell and soon the family moved to Lyn, Ontario, where his father served as a Methodist minister until his death in 1894. The family consisted of four boys and one girl. After Mrs. MacDowell remarried, the family moved in 1897 into the home of her new husband in Maitland, Ontario. Thain MacDowell, who was to become a first-class athlete, grew up in the Brockville area and was educated at Maitland Public School, Brockville Collegiate Institute, and Victoria College, University of Toronto, where he received his BA early on in the First World War. Prior to the war he served with the 41st Regiment for twelve months and for four months with the Queen's Own. Soon after graduation he attested on February 1, 1915, in Ottawa. He was five foot nine inches tall, with dark-brown hair. He became an officer with the 38th (Ottawa) Canadian Infantry Battalion (later perpetuated as the Cameron Highlanders of Ottawa). After intensive training in London, Ontario, he was promoted to captain on August 1, 1915, and a week later left for Bermuda, where he served in garrison duties. In May 1916 he left for England, where he trained for three months before leaving for France on August 3. He was awarded a DSO on November 18, 1916 (*London Gazette*, January 1917), on the Somme near Petit Miraumont in an attack against Desire Trench and Desire Support Trench. "He led his B Company against the German trenches and, advancing to within throwing distance, he bombed three German machine guns which had been holding up the advance. After severe hand-to-hand fighting he captured three officers and fifty men." The following day he was wounded in action and returned to England and was discharged on November 30.

By January 1917 he had recovered; he returned to his battalion and was promoted to major on February 28. After winning his VC at Vimy Ridge in April he became a patient in No. 7 Stationary Hospital Boulogne, and then at Hospital in Etaples. He was invalided to hospitals in England, and in July he was given permission to return to Canada on sick leave, which he did on August 4. Once there he spent time at Brockville Hospital, where he was treated for a nervous breakdown and exhaustion. His sick leave was followed by ordinary leave, and he left Canada for England on February 5, 1918. He was back in England on March 1, 1918, He worked until the end of the war at Headquarters, Overseas Military Forces of Canada, and the Canadian Training School. He was promoted to temporary major on October 25, and of the four Vimy Canadian winners of the VC he was the only one to survive the war. He was struck off the strength of the CEF on October 14, 1919, and in the same year he received an honorary master's degree at the University of Toronto as the member of the university who had won the highest military honour during the war.

On May 1, 1920, he became lieutenant and brevet major with the Ottawa Regiment (the Duke of Cornwall's Own), and seven years later he was transferred to the Reserve of Officers. Postwar he became interested in mining and worked as a director with a number of mining and chemical companies. For five years, between 1923 and 1928, he acted as private secretary to the minister of national defence at Ottawa. In 1921 he attended the VC dinner in London and the similar dinner that took place in the House of Lords in 1929. Also in 1929 he married Norah Jean Hodgson of Montreal, and was placed on the retired list as a lieutenant-colonel in July of the same year. He and his wife first lived in Toronto but two years later moved to Montreal. They were to have two sons. In 1933 he was appointed honorary lieutenant-colonel, Frontenac Regiment. He also attended the 1956 VC/GC review in Hyde Park.

In 1937 and 1938 MacDowell had an impostor (not unusual for the holder of a VC), who paraded under "false colours" in Sydney, Australia, with a miniature medal of the VC. MacDowell himself has been described as a "big burly Canadian" who later wore rimless spectacles and was proficient at golf. During the Second World War he gave lectures to the Canadian Army.

MacDowell died at Nassau in the Bahamas on March 27, 1960, and was buried at Oakland Cemetery, Brockville, Ontario. On September 2, 1970, a plaque to his memory was unveiled by MacDowell's widow, who lived on until 1983, at the intersection of Maitland Road at Highway 2, Maitland. It was one of a series of plaques being erected by the Ontario Department of Public Records and Archives. It was dedicated by the Rev. Vernon Macpherson, padre of the Brockville Rifles. This particular ceremony was sponsored and arranged by the Brockville Rifles, and Lt.-Col. W.S. Watson acted as programme chairman. Various dignitaries attended the ceremony.

In a memorial room in the Soldiers' Tower Memorial, University of Toronto, is a Maxim MG08 that Capt. (later Lt.-Col.) Thain MacDowell "captured" on Vimy Ridge in an incident that led to the award of the Victoria Cross. His name is also listed on the Great War Memorial Screen. The tower commemorates those who died in the Great War who had belonged to the university community. It was dedicated in 1924. Other commemorations to his memory include a range named after him by the director of national defence called the Connaught Range and Primary Training centre in Ottawa. It is marked with a cairn and plaque.

MacDowell's portrait is in the Canadian War Museum, and the Royal Canadian Legion, Branch 96 in Brockville dedicated its auditorium to his memory on November 5, 2009. Apart from his VC and DSO his medals include the BWM, VM and MiD Oakleaf, King George VI Coronation Medal (1937), and the Queen Elizabeth II Coronation Medal (1953). They are held by Victoria College, University of Toronto.

W.J. MILNE

Near Thélus, France, April 9

By April 1917 Vimy Ridge had been in German hands for three years, and during this time they had turned it into a seemingly impregnable position. In 1915 there was an attempt by the French to take the ridge, which failed at a cost of 130,000 casualties, and a year later the British also made an unsuccessful assault. However, in the spring of 1917 a new attack was planned by the Allies to capture this very important ridge, and extremely careful and elaborate plans were drawn up. These included an extension to the tunnels that ran toward the ridge, which would give considerable protection to the attackers as they moved up to the front line. The Canadian Corps was assigned the task of taking the ridge, although the commanding heights of Hill 135 to the west and Hill 145 to the east of the point where the Arras–Lens road angled across the ridge had to be taken first.

On April 9, 1917, Easter Monday, the assault began at 5:30 a.m. in appalling conditions of sleet and snow. The advance began after a bombardment that had lasted for five days — representing a gun for every eight yards over a twelve-mile front. In front of Vimy, from right to left, were the four Canadian divisions, and we are concerned here with the role of the 16th Battalion, Manitoba Battalion, 1st

(Canadian Scottish) Division, and Canadian Expeditionary Force in the initial fighting.

The division's first objective was the German line known as Zwolle Graben (Black Line), which was close to the Arras–Lens road; it was also the last trench belonging to the enemy front-line system. Once taken, the Canadians were to remain there for forty minutes. The second line was the Zwischen Stellung (Red Line), where they were to remain for up to three-and-a-quarter hours before moving on to the third or Blue Line; here they were to stay for one hour thirty-six minutes. The fourth and final line to be captured was the Brown Line, which lay to the east of the main ridge and had belts of wire. Here, the barrage was to continue for twelve minutes, giving time for the Canadians to catch up with it. The next enemy position after the village of Thélus was Farbus, in front of which was a wood where the enemy had a considerable number of gun positions.

As it happened, the 1st Division was extremely successful and reached its final objective, the Brown Line, at about 1:10 p.m., or nearly seven-and-three-quarter hours after the attack began. It became quite clear that the effort put into the very detailed planning of the attack had paid off as the Canadians were well prepared and knew the ground. In addition, once the final objective was reached, it was clear that the enemy guns in Farbus Wood would be out of action.

No. 1 Company of the 16th Battalion had assembled and the men were able to complete their journey to the start line by use of the Bentata Tunnel, which was shellproof and thus allowed the troops considerable protection as they moved up toward the front line. By 4:20 a.m. on April 9, at dawn, all companies were in position and forty minutes later their flanking units were also in place, namely the 14th Battalion to the right and the 18th Battalion to the left. When the barrage ceased, the Canadians went forward over land that was full of mine craters blown by the French during their efforts to capture the ridge in 1915, as well as by the British and Germans in 1916. These craters were as much as twenty feet deep and had steep or greasy chalk sides down to six or seven feet of slimy water. To add to this hazard, the enemy, who had been taking shelter from the Canadian barrage, now emerged and machine gunners were waiting on the far lips of these craters. The attackers dashed forward in small groups, taking on some of these craters and quickly overcoming several of them. However, other enemy machine guns were also placed in zigzag positions and the Canadians were fired on from both the front and the flanks, and men kept falling. In addition, one enemy line had escaped the attention of the Canadian barrage and the Germans put up a stiff resistance before succumbing to the bayonet.

The right-hand company of the 16th Battalion became held up after the Visener Graben Line was taken, and from a position to their half-left an enemy machine gun was causing many casualties. The dead from the 16th Battalion lay in front of this strongpoint and soon a series of explosions could be heard in the direction of the enemy machine-gun position. This was the result of the actions of Pte. William Milne, who had leapt from a shell hole close to the position while signalling his comrades to advance. He crawled on his hands and knees to within bombing distance of the machine-gun crew and with hand grenades put the whole position out of action. Later he did the same for another hostile machine-gun point between the Black and Red Lines; concealed in a haystack near Terry Trench, this position was also holding up the advance. Sadly Milne was killed before the day's end.

The Black Line fell as planned and after a pause the advance continued toward the Red Line. It was at the Red Line that the enemy's morale began to give way despite the protection of deep dugouts, and many of them turned and ran, a number being shot down as they did so. Once the Canadians had reached the Red Line they could see both to the left and right just how successful the day had been, and they moved forward over the previously impregnable ground as if they were on manoeuvres.

The men of the 16th Battalion were spectators for the rest of the day as they had reached their objective; their colleagues continued their advance and the 1st Brigade passed through them. By the end of the day the 1st Brigade had even reached the far side of Farbus village, a tremendous achievement.

Milne was awarded a posthumous VC and his name is listed on the Vimy Memorial. His citation was gazetted on June 8, 1917:

For most conspicuous bravery and devotion to duty in attack. On approaching the first objective, Private Milne observed an enemy machine-gun firing on our advancing troops. Crawling on hands and knees, he succeeded in reaching the gun, killing the crew with bombs, and capturing the gun. On the line reforming, he again located a machine-gun in the support line, and stalking this second gun as he had done the first, he succeeded in putting the crew out of action and capturing the gun. His wonderful bravery and resource on these two occasions undoubtedly saved the lives of many of his comrades. Private Milne was killed shortly after capturing the second gun.

William Johnstone Milne was born on December 21, 1891, at 10 (not 8) Anderson Street, Wishaw, Cambusnethan, Lanarkarkshire, Scotland. He was the son of David and Agnes Milne. In 1910 he emigrated to Canada, where he worked on the land at Moose Jaw in south-central Saskatchewan. He later enlisted there on September 11, 1915, and was allocated the service number 427586. His papers state that he was five foot five and a half inches tall with dark-brown hair. He embarked for England on October 23, 1915, with the 46th (Saskatchewan) Battalion, where apart from training he was twice treated for Gonnorrhoea at the Connaught Military Hospital in Aldershot in March and June. He joined the 16th (Canadian Scottish) Battalion in Belgium in the trenches in the Ypres Salient. In August 1916 the 16th Battalion took over from the 1st Anzac Corps and became responsible for 3,000 yards of front line trench along Pozières Ridge. Milne's battalion took part in a joint attack with the 52nd and 49th battalions on the Fabeck Graben Line on September 4, and a few weeks later, on October 8, 1916, they also took part in an attack on Regina Trench. This was the occasion when Piper Richardson won his VC. In late October the 16th Battalion, as part of the 1st Canadian Division, was relieved and went north to take over in the Vimy sector to the north of Arras. At the end of November/beginning of December Milne was in hospital with influenza.

Milne's VC, British War Medal, and Victory Medal became the property of his sister, Ellen Milne, who lived in Wishaw. They were later sold to a Scottish medal collector and subsequently purchased by a Canadian collector, Jack Stenabach. In July 1989 the decorations, which included the VC, VM, and WM together with the next-of-kin bronze plaque, were sold for 94,000 Canadian dollars. At the present time they are on loan from the Canadian War Museum, Ottawa, to the Canadian Museum of Civilization in Hull, Quebec. In recent years Milne has been commemorated together with thirteen other VC holders with Lanarkshire connections. The design of the memorial uses blocks of marble in a horseshoe shape and is to be found in the centre of Hamilton, Lanarkshire. He is also remembered with the Milne Channel named after him in northeast Saskatchewan and he is commemorated on the Saskatchewan War Memorial. Also in the province there is a plaque to his memory at "NW114 Section 30 Township 16 Range 29 west of 2nd Meridian."

E.W. SIFTON

Near Neuville-St-Vaast, France, April 9

On April 9, 1917, the 18th Battalion of the 4th Canadian Infantry Brigade of the 2nd Canadian Division was opposite Hill 135 and the village of Thélus, which were their objectives for the day. On their right was the 16th (Canadian Scottish) Battalion and to their left was the 19th (Central Ontario) Battalion. At the beginning of the long-planned attack to capture Vimy Ridge the weather was very cold with a mixture of snow, sleet, and driving rain. When the Canadian artillery barrage moved forward from the German first line, the 18th Battalion began their attack with a three-platoon frontage in four waves at 5:30 a.m. They had to face a tenacious enemy who in many cases had been sheltering in strong concrete dugouts or underground fortresses, some of which were large enough to contain a whole battalion.

Lt.-Sgt. Ellis W. Sifton was a member of C Company of the 18th Battalion on the right of the 4th Brigade. The German first line was quickly taken with very few casualties, but the Canadians were held up in the fight for possession of the second line. As they advanced, enemy machine gunners enfiladed them and they began to suffer casualties. Two machine guns in particular began to take a toll on the Canadians and several of Sifton's colleagues became casualties.

He was the first to spot the position of one of these machine-gun nests and he leapt up and rushed the trench, quickly overcoming the enemy position. He used his bayonet, killing the crew and knocking over their gun; they were simply overwhelmed by the speed and ferocity of his attack. His colleagues quickly came to his aid and together they took on another party of Germans who were rapidly advancing down a trench. Sifton even resorted to using his rifle as a club. However, one wounded German who had survived took careful aim at Sifton and shot him dead.

Sifton was awarded a posthumous VC, which was presented to his father, Mr. S.J. Sifton, in Canada by the Governor General, His Excellency the Duke of Devonshire, in 1917. His citation was gazetted on June 8, 1917, was as follows:

> For most conspicuous bravery and devotion to duty. During the attack on enemy trenches, Sergt. Sifton's company was held up by machine-gun fire, which inflicted many casualties. Having located the gun, he charged it single-handed, killing all the crew. A small enemy party advanced down the trench, but he succeeded in keeping these off till our men had gained the position. In carrying out this gallant act he was killed, but his conspicuous valour undoubtedly saved many lives and contributed largely to the success of the operation.

Sifton had made a major contribution to the capture of this part of the German defences of the supposedly impregnable Vimy Ridge, most of which was captured by the end of the day.

He is buried in the Lichfield Crater Cemetery, whose original name was CB 2, and which is situated close to the N17 Arras–Lens road, about half a mile to the east of Neuville-Saint-Vaast. The cemetery is enclosed by a circular rubble and flint wall; fifty-eight men (mainly Canadians) are buried there. The CWGC Grave Registration Form indicates that at first Sifton was commemorated with a unique grave marker that featured the VC in its design. Together with the nearby Zivy Crater (CB 1), it is a very moving place to visit and the names of the dead are listed on panels.

Ellis Welwood Sifton was born in the settlement or farm of Wallacetown, Ontario, in Canada on October 12, 1891. He was one of three children of John James Sifton and his companion Amelia Bobier. John had become a farmer, and prior to the war had served with the Wallacetown Rifles for a few years. He volunteered in St. Thomas, Ontario, and was attested on on October 23, 1914. He was five foot seven and three quarters inches tall with fair hair and grey eyes. He became a member of the 18th Battalion of the Canadian Expeditionary Force. His next of kin was his sister Ella. After initial training he sailed from Halifax to Bristol, landing on April 29, 1915. From there the battalion moved to Shorncliffe for further training prior sailing to France on September 14. After he arrived in France, Sifton was to become excellent NCO rising to the rank of lance-sergeant on March 11, 1917.

His family used to worship at St. Peter's Church, Tyrconnell, and on May 21, 1961, an historical plaque commemorating Sifton's life and career was unveiled there. The church is southeast of Wallacetown on County Road 15, near the John E. Pearce Provincial Park. Tyrconnell is a hamlet by Lake Erie and the cemetery is the burial place of many members of the Sifton family. The plaque itself was commissioned by the Ontario Department of Travel and Publicity with the help of the Archaeological and Historic Sites Board, also of Ontario. The ceremony of unveiling was sponsored by the London Branch of the 18th Battalion Association and was carried out by two of Sifton's sisters, Miss Ella and Miss Lila. The president of the Battalion Branch acted as programme chairman and the plaque was dedicated by the Rev. John Graham, recorder of St. Peter's. Around a hundred members of the former 18th Battalion attended the ceremony, together with their families and around a thousand spectators.

Sifton's decorations apart from the VC are the 1914–14 Star; BWM, and VM and they are held at Elgin County Pioneer Museum, St. Thomas, Ontario. In 2007 the original VC was lent to the museum. In 2013 the museum staged a further special display in which a replica VC was featured.

J.G. PATTISON

Vimy Ridge, France, April 10

On the left of the Canadian line on April 10, 1917, the second day of the battle of Arras, the Canadian Army was still engaged in clearing a few parts of Vimy Ridge that had not been taken the day before. In particular, the enemy was tenaciously hanging on to an outpost line on the eastern slope of Vimy Ridge beyond Hill 145.

Maj.-Gen. Watson, commander of the 4th Canadian Division, decided that as the 11th Canadian Brigade was exhausted the battalions of the 10th Canadian Brigade should carry out the attack on the 11th Brigade's final objectives. The task was given to the 44th (Manitoba) Battalion and the 50th (Alberta) Battalion, who were to start from Hill 145. Soon after midday the two battalions crossed the Zouave Valley in artillery formation and then deployed along the road near the side of the hill. After a fifteen-minute barrage, they left their positions at zero hour, 3:15 p.m. Having not been involved in the first day's fighting, the two battalions went forward with great determination; they charged down the slope and entered the German Hangstellung Trench very soon after the barrage had lifted.

At first progress was very slow and casualties mounted; the main reason for this was that the German defenders had a clear field of fire for their machine guns. One strongpoint in particular stood in the way of the men of A Company who, with the assistance of B Company, made several attempts to take it out. It was at this stage that Pte. John Pattison of the 50th Battalion moved forward alone from shell hole to shell hole, keeping as close to the ground as he could in order to avoid the fire from the machine guns. He finally reached a position from which he could throw bombs with some degree of accuracy and lobbed three grenades on to the German position, managing to knock out the machine guns, killing or wounding several of the crew. He then rushed the strongpoint and finished off the surviving Germans with his bayonet. Twenty minutes later all the enemy objectives had been taken and the Canadians consolidated the captured line.

The operation was a success, but the 50th Battalion had nearly 240 casualties. While mopping up the enemy dugouts the Canadians came across 150 unwounded prisoners who were subsequently released. They also claimed a number of enemy machine guns. When the 44th Battalion moved forward to the north side of the Bois de la Folie they were able to link up with the left flank of the 3rd Division, and by the next day the whole of the main section of Vimy Ridge was in Canadian hands: a front of 7,000 yards and up to 400 yards in depth.

Pattison survived the day's fighting and also remained unscathed after the next day's successful attack on the position known as the Pimple. He had been informed that he had been recommended for the VC, but he did not live to wear it. He died on June 3, 1917, during the attack on Lens electric-generating station. His last hours were described in a letter from his son Henry to Canon Lummis:

> The attack proved a very heavy loss to the 50th Battalion, which required all available men to be used from Base Headquarters, where my Father was recuperating from a foot injury sustained in a previous engagement. He was sent back in the line and put on outpost duty when a direct shell-hit wiped out all those in that position. This position was taken over by the enemy and my Dad was reported missing for three months. It was not until a wooden cross, erected

by the enemy, was found, that his death was confirmed. No personal possessions were ever recovered.

Pattison was killed at Callons Trench and when his body was found it was taken to La Chaudière Military Cemetery on the western side of the Lens–Arras road, for burial in Plot VI, Row C, Grave 14. The cemetery, which is three kilometres south of Lens and can be seen from the top of Vimy Ridge, was begun next to a house that used to contain a German gun position. Pattison's grave has the inscription "'Lest we Forget' mother, wife and family." The cemetery contains the graves of 638 Canadians and 268 Britons. Originally it was very small. Later it became known as Vimy Canadian Cemetery No. 1 when other burials from small cemeteries and isolated graves near the ridge were brought into it.

Pattison's VC was gazetted on August 2, 1917:

For most conspicuous bravery in attack. When the advance of our troops was held up by an enemy machine-gun, which was inflicting severe casualties, Private Pattison, with utter disregard of his own safety, sprang forward, and, jumping from shell hole to shell hole, reached cover within thirty yards of the enemy gun. From this point, in face of heavy fire, he hurled bombs, killing and wounding some of the crew, then rushed forward, overcoming and bayoneting the surviving five gunners. His valour and initiative undoubtedly saved the situation and made possible the further advance to the objective.

John George Pattison was born in Woolwich, London, on September 8, 1875. His attestation forms note that he was born in Sandwich, Kent. He was the son of railwayman Henry Alfred Pattison and Mary Ann Pattison, and the only child to survive from a family of three. In 1879 the family moved to New Cross, Deptford, where John attended school at Clifton Hill County School, a London County Council School.

After leaving school Pattison trained as a platelayer in the shipyards. At some point he married Sophia Louise Ann Allen and they had four children: two sons and two daughters. In June 1906 the family emigrated to Canada, at first living in Rapid City, Manitoba, and later moving to Calgary, where Pattison worked as a labourer in the operation and construction department of the Canadian Western Natural Gas Company. The family address was 1622, 1st Avenue, Westmount, Calgary.

On March 6, 1916, although aged forty, Pattison enlisted in Calgary with the service number of 808887, and became member of the 137th Battalion. On his papers he stated that he was five foot two and a half inches tall with brown eyes and brown hair. In addition he gave his job as labourer. He had tried to join his son Henry's battalion, the 82nd, but without success. Henry, however, managed to obtain a transfer to the 137th and the two men were able to go overseas together.

John Pattison left for England on August 21 and arrived in Liverpool for further traning eight days later. On November 24 he made his military will. He left for France in January 1917 and had been transferred to the 50th Battalion (Alberta). Henry was left behind as he was too young and he did not join his father's battalion until August. Meanwhile John had been wounded and was badly concussed in early May, and had been transferred to the care of No. 1 Canadian Field Ambulance. He rejoined his battalion four days later but in the following month was reported missing and on the third reported as killed. Later in the year Henry was allowed to wear a miniature VC medal and ribbon in honour of his father's deed in the capture of Vimy Ridge. Initially, he was to due to go to England to attend a VC presentation, but this arrangement was changed and instead the decoration was presented by Lt. Gov. Brett to Henry's mother, Sophia Pattison, in Victory Park, Calgary, at a public ceremony on April 10, 1918, the decoration having been sent on to Canada by the War Office. However in October 1918, Henry did have his moment of glory at a special ceremony at the town hall in New Cross, when Deptford Borough Council presented him with an illuminated scroll that told of his father's valour. He was also invited to sign the Borough's Roll of Honour.

On June 3, 1939, Mrs. Sophia Pattison was introduced to King George VI during his state visit to Canada. She had worked for the same department as her husband and she retired on May 2, 1940, living on until March 25, 1947.

Pattison is remembered with one of the peaks named after holders of the Victoria Cross by the Geographical Society of Alberta in the Victoria Cross Range in Jasper Park. His name is also one of eight holders of the VC with local connections on display in Lewisham Civic Centre; and his portrait by Ethel Wright used to hang on the walls of the Canadian Western's boardroom. In 1967 a bridge over the River Elbow was also named to commemorate him, as he used to live in the district of the bridge and had also trained in the local barracks. His name is also listed on the St. James's War Memorial in Hatcham, southeast London, where before the war he had been a member of the Church Lads Brigade. In 1920 his name was also listed on a stone tablet in an oak frame that was erected in St. Michael Church, Knoyle Road, Deptford. However, the church was destroyed in the enemy blitz of 1941 and presumably the memorial was destroyed as well. Lewisham, being so close to London, was on a direct route for enemy bombers. Lastly Pattison's name is featured on a mural in the Lewisham shopping centre.

At some point Pattison's decorations were acquired by the Glenbow Museum, where they remain. Apart from his VC they include the BWM and VM. The museum also owns the colours of the 137th Battalion of the Canadian Expeditionary Force, raised in Calgary in 1916.

R.G. COMBE

South of Acheville, France, May 3

Just over three weeks after the main part of Vimy Ridge had been captured by the Canadians on April 9, 1917, they were still involved in local actions in the area of the town of Lens, due north of Arras. This time the target was a group of small villages incorporated in the German third line in the plains of Douai. The names of the villages, from right to left, were Fresnoy, Acheville, Méricourt, and Avion.

The 1st Canadian Brigade had three battalions in front of Fresnoy, and on the brigade's left was the 27th (City of Winnipeg) Canadian Infantry Battalion and then the 31st (Alberta), both of the 6th Canadian Infantry Brigade. We are concerned here with the part of the line at Acheville where the 27th Battalion was under orders to capture the northern part of the Arleux Loop and Oppy–Méricourt Line. Arleux, another small village, which had only recently fallen to the Canadians.

Soon after 3:45 a.m. on May 3, the 27th Battalion attack had only gone forward around 200 yards before the enemy barrage was suddenly shortened. This had a disastrous effect on the Canadians, who suffered considerable initial casualties making the operation a very costly one. On the left of the 27th Battalion, the men of the 31st

Battalion were held up by dense wire on their front. As a result they were unable to advance on the 27th Battalion's flank.

In the right company of the 27th Battalion, Lt. Robert Combe was soon the only surviving officer. Signalling to the small number of men who were still with him, he continued through the German barrage. However, he found that if his small party were to reach the German line, they would have to run the gauntlet of the British guns as well. He steadied his men, but in the end only five men survived to reach the enemy line. When they entered the German trench they were accompanied by a few men from another company (from the 1st [Western Ontario] Battalion) whom they had picked up along the way.

The mixed group began to bomb the trench alongside the road between Fresnoy and Acheville, using German bombs as their own supply had dried up some time before. In all, eighty Germans were captured and 250 yards of trench line taken. Combe's men charged the enemy several times with great courage. Combe was always the first man to round the traverse and into dugouts until a German sniper killed him, just as a party of reinforcements arrived to assist him. His citation was published in the *London Gazette* of June 27, 1917:

> For most conspicuous bravery and example. He steadied his company under intense fire, and led them through the enemy barrage, reaching the objective with only five men. With great coolness and courage, Lieut. Combe proceeded to bomb the enemy, and inflicted heavy casualties. He collected small groups of men, and succeeded in capturing the company objective, together with eighty prisoners. He repeatedly charged the enemy, driving them before him, and whilst personally leading his bombers, was killed by an enemy sniper. His conduct inspired all ranks, and it was entirely due to his magnificent courage that the position was carried, secured and held.

Although the Canadians had fought to a standstill, they were handicapped by their lack of numbers, and by late evening they were relieved by the 29th (British Columbia) Battalion. There had been 270 casualties during the day but, to offset this figure, 120 Germans had been taken prisoner and 400 yards of enemy trench had also been captured.

Combe was first buried at Acheville, close to where he had been fighting, but unfortunately his grave was later lost so his name is listed on the Vimy Memorial.

Robert Grierson Combe was born on August 5, 1880, in Aberdeen, Scotland. He was the youngest of six children of James and Elizabeth Combe of 2 Millburn Street; later, around 1892, the family moved to 24 Ferryhill Place. Combe's father was a hotel waiter and two of Robert's elder sisters became schoolteachers. Robert was first a pupil at Ferryhill School, but in 1894 he joined the local grammar school, where his name appears on the Board of Bursary and Foundation Winners. After leaving school in 1897 he served an apprenticeship as a chemist in Aberdeen with William E. Hay, but then decided to emigrate to Canada, probably in 1906. He joined the staff of a drugstore in Moosomin, Saskatchewan, but later ran his own business for several years in Melville, Saskatchewan. In 1909 he

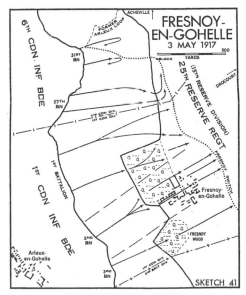

married Jean Taquair Donald of Moosomin. Her family had moved to Moosomin in 1889 and, after spending her school years there, she took up teaching at Riga, Coverdale, and Moosomin.

Robert Combe had two years military service prior to the war, first with the V.B. Royal Fusiliers for one year and then with the 16th Light Horse. In the second year of the war he attested on

Fresnoy-en-Gohelle, May 3, 1917

April 1, 1915, in Prince Albert, had a medical in Sewell Camp, and was granted a commission. He was five foot ten inches tall with brown eyes and black hair. He was posted to the 53rd Battalion in Prince Albert, but actually went overseas with the 27th (City of Winnipeg) Battalion. He was in France in mid March 1916, and three months later he was invalided back to England, medically unfit for active service suffering with rheumatism and lumbago. He became a patient in Miss Pollock's Hospital in Weymouth Street, London, from June 29 to July 18. However he needed more treatment and was sent to Bath for convasescence. At a medical board held in London on July 18 it was noted that his recovery was very slow and he was granted two months home service and a month's leave. After he was declared fit again he was put in charge of physical training. In this post he eventually rose to the rank of major. However, at his own request, he reverted to the rank of lieutenant as he wished to return to active service and left for France with the 27th Battalion.

In early January 1915, three months before he enlisted, he had written home to his former school at Aberdeen:

> I hope to call on you when the third Canadian contingent gets over in the spring and to become a Life Member. Training conditions here are sublime. I had fifty recruits out the other morning for a route march with the thermometer at 18 degrees below zero. I froze my chin and one cheek. Several of the men had frozen noses and cheeks. We all feel very fit, however, and the cold is most invigorating. We are all very anxious to get over. Many men like myself have not been home for nine or ten years, while others have never seen "the old country." We expect to concentrate at Regina or Winnipeg any day now, and after a short course there, hope to embark. I have a lieutenancy in the 95th Saskatchewan Rifles. I have been trying to get back for a visit to the old country for two or three years, but being a married man now it is not so easy to pick up one's traps and march. My wife has never been in Scotland, and one of the things she is most anxious to see is "the old school." I hope it will come up to

my boastful accounts. I just notice one of my old class in the first list of volunteers — Hugh F. Mackenzie, Glasgow. I hope I shall meet many more and that we have a chance to have a little reunion — preferably at Potsdam.

After the couple married in 1909, Jean Donald Combe followed her husband to Europe where she trained with the British Red Cross for a year. She was posted to Aboyne Castle Hospital, where she later became quartermaster. She was then posted to Edinburgh War Hospital, working with the Voluntary Aid Detachment.

After her husband was killed in May 1917, Jean returned to Canada where she trained as a physiotherapist at Hart House, Toronto. On the completion of her training, she was posted to Tuxedo Military Hospital in Winnipeg. When the war finished she was demobilized and then joined the staff of Dr. Galloway's Clinic in Winnipeg. While working there she was summoned to Regina in order to receive her husband's VC from the hands of the Prince of Wales at the Regina Legislative Assembly. Owing to ill health she had not been able to attend a previously arranged investiture at Buckingham Palace during the time she was in Britain.

In 1925 Mrs. Combe moved to Victoria, where she set up home. In 1942 she was appointed supervisor of Blur Triangle Leave Center, a position that she held until 1946 when the center was closed. In February 1963 she was back in Victoria, but a short time later she became ill and died in hospital on April 12. Members of the 27th Battalion, her husband's former unit, acted as her pallbearers at her funeral. It was generally felt that she had lived a very Christian and useful life.

A life-size oil painting of her husband was hung in the Ottawa's Peace Tower and he is also remembered in Melville Museum. In addition the government of Saskatchewan named a northern lake in the province after him. There is also an historical plaque to his memory at 217 Main Street, Melville, and the Melville Branch of the Royal Canadian Legion is named in his memory.

Apart from the VC Robert's decorations include the BWM and VM. All are held in the Saskatchewan Archives in Regina and are put on display on special occasions. His name is also listed on the Aberdeen War Memorial and on the family headstone in Allen Vale Cemetery, Aberdeen.

W.A. BISHOP

Near Cambrai, France, June 2

During the early months of 1917, Allied casualties among both aircraft and crew had been very heavy, particularly after the start of the Battle of Arras in early April when the ground forces' need for air cooperation was at its height, culminating in "Bloody April" when German aircraft were much in the ascendency. The combining of more than one Jasta to make large formations of Fokker aircraft, such as that headed by Manfred von Richtoven, the Red Baron, was a very successful German tactic, and it was not until the Arras offensive was over in May that the tide began to turn again in favour of the RFC.

Canadian born T/Capt. William A. Bishop was the commander of B Flight, No. 60 Squadron, RFC, and he had returned to France on May 22, after spending two weeks' leave in England. Since late March he had accumulated some sixteen victories over enemy aircraft and had been nominated for a Military Cross (gazetted on May 26). The squadron was based at Filescamp Farm, near Izel-lès-Hameau about thirteen miles northwest of Arras, and equipped with Nieuport 17 Scouts. This small rotary-engined biplane was very manoeuvrable, with sensitive controls, and armed with a Lewis gun firing above the propeller arc.

Four days after his return Bishop shot down a German Albatros, and the following day a two-seater Aviatik. The enemy tactics had recently changed and their two-seater reconnaissance aircraft often flew in threes and would fly over their own anti-aircraft guns. When British machines appeared, these decoy two-seater machines would dive away and the enemy anti-aircraft guns would open fire on the British aircraft. Bishop proposed to his commanding officer Major A.J.L. Scott that an attack on aircraft on the ground at an enemy aerodrome would be a suitable retaliatory action, and he was given outline permission for carrying out such an action.

The initial idea had been for two aircraft to make an attack and was suggested to Bishop by Capt. Albert Ball whose feats and very impressive number of victories had made him an inspiration for the Canadian. The two had discussed the possibilities of such a raid when Ball visited the squadron during the first few days of May, but after Ball had been killed on the 7th, Bishop was unable to persuade any of the rest of the squadron pilots to accompany him.

Not to be outdone, Bishop was more than usually careful in preparations for his flight, and with his mechanic, ensured that the aircraft engine and his Lewis gun were in particularly good working order. Bishop took off at 3:57 a.m. on June 2, 1917, flying Nieuport B1566, and headed toward Arras and the Cambrai road, but after nearly half an hour he lost his bearings and found himself well inside enemy-held territory. He descended through the clouds and spotted an enemy airfield, but as this appeared deserted he flew on southeast for a further three miles before locating another aerodrome near Cambrai. He could see activity below him as six Albatros Scouts and a two-seater aircraft had been run out of their hangars and were being prepared for flying.

Bishop dived down low and, amidst heavy ground fire, attacked the line of aircraft firing as he passed over the machines. He then turned for an attack from the opposite direction and spotted that one Albatros had begun to taxi. It was about ten feet from the ground when Bishop fired a short burst that caused it to hit the grass and break up as it slid along the field. A second Albatros was also attempting to take off. Bishop's fire missed the aircraft but the enemy pilot swerved and crashed into a tree at the edge of the airfield, ripping off its starboard wings. Bishop now turned to fly home, but as he climbed away to 1,000 feet two more aircraft took off in opposite directions, a difficult tactic to oppose, and he was left with little alternative than to fight.

One Albatros climbed and closed in behind the Nieuport while the other waited at some distance. Bishop turned and fired before beginning to circle, a manoeuvre that eventually placed him under the tail of the Albatros. As it came into view he fired a complete drum into the machine and the enemy fell away to crash near the airfield perimeter.

In his hurry to get back to his home airfield, Bishop had overlooked the other Albatros and was suddenly made aware of its presence as it dived in with guns firing. He returned fire and expended a complete drum from his Lewis gun before the enemy machine dived down toward the airfield. Bishop now headed west at full speed and flew low to avoid a formation of four enemy aircraft near Cambrai. He crossed the front lines near Bapaume when his aircraft received further damage from enemy anti-aircraft fire before he arrived back at Filescamp Farm airfield at 5:40 a.m.

Bishop circled over the airfield and fired several very lights before he landed. As he taxied in he held up three fingers to his mechanics to indicate his latest victories. The Nieuport was "full of holes caused by machine gun fire" and had torn fabric on the wings and fuselage. Shortly after he landed Bishop made his combat report, in which he stated that the airfield he had attacked was either Esnes or Awoignt, both not far from Cambrai. Major Scott reported the sortie to the RFC Wing HQ and the news rapidly spread, which resulted in many messages of congratulation for Bishop, including one from Maj.-Gen. Hugh Trenchard, GOC RFC, who described the sortie as "the greatest single show of the war."

Bishop continued with the normal duties of a scout pilot, and his victory tally continued to increase. When flying one of the newly issued SE5 Scouts on June 28 he attacked two enemy two-seater machines over Monchy-le-Preux and his engine was hit by anti-aircraft fire. He attempted to fly back to Filescamp Farm, but the engine caught fire and he crashed into poplar trees while attempting to land. He was left unconscious, hanging upside down, while his machine was on fire, but fortunately some nearby infantry rescued him. This experience was his closest brush with death.

On August 9 Trenchard informed Bishop, by telephone, that he was to receive the Victoria Cross for his raid on June 2, and two days later the Supplement to the *London Gazette* No. 30228 of August 11, 1917, published the citation:

Captain Bishop, who had been sent out to work independently, flew first of all to an enemy aerodrome. Finding no machine about, he flew on to another aerodrome about 3 miles south-east, which was at least 12 miles the other side of the line. Seven machines, some with their engines running, were on the ground. He attacked these from about 50ft, and a mechanic, who was starting one of the engines, was seen to fall. One of the machines got off the ground, but at a height of 60ft Captain Bishop fired fifteen rounds into it at very close range, and it crashed to the ground.

A second machine got off the ground, into which he fired thirty rounds at 150yds range, and it fell into a tree.

Two more machines then rose from the aerodrome. One of these he engaged at the height of 1,000ft, emptying the rest of his drum of ammunition. This machine crashed 300yds from the aerodrome, after which Captain Bishop emptied a whole drum into a fourth hostile machine, and then flew back to his station.

Four hostile scouts were about 1,000ft above him for about a mile of his return journey, but they would not attack. His machine was badly shot about by machine gun fire from the ground.

Bishop left No. 60 Squadron for England late in August, and on the 28th was promoted to major. The following day he was invested with his VC by the king at Buckingham Palace.

Bishop was disappointed when news of his home-based posting had reached him earlier in the month, as he had become slightly obsessed with the number of his victories and wanted to be the top "ace" in the RFC. From his return to No. 60 Squadron in May to his departure in August, his accredited score of victories was twenty-eight. Bishop's new posting was as chief instructor at the School of Aerial Gunnery, but he was granted two months' extended leave in Canada from September 15 before taking up this new post.

Following his investiture and many celebrations in London, Bishop was granted extended home leave and sailed for Canada, but not before the award of a bar to his DSO, the citation appearing in the *London Gazette* No. 30388 of September 25:

> For conspicuous gallantry and devotion to duty when engaging hostile aircraft. His consistent dash and great fearlessness have set a magnificent example to the pilots of his squadron. He has destroyed not fewer than forty-five hostile machines within the past five months, frequently attacking enemy formations single-handed, and on all occasions displaying a fighting spirit and determination to get to close quarters with his opponents, which have earned the admiration of all in contact with him.

Bishop arrived in Montreal where he was greeted by large crowds and much front-page press coverage. He had arrived home in Owen Sound by October 6, and on the 17th he married his fiancée, Margaret Eaton Burden, at Timothy Eaton Memorial Church, Toronto (named in memory of Margaret's grandfather, the department store founder), where thousands of people lined the streets to catch a glimpse of the couple.

Bishop was attached to the British War Mission in Washington, and with his new wife travelled across North America on a number of very successful public-relations tours. Canada was dealing with a crisis on conscription and the ever-present long casualty lists, so the appearance of Bishop, the VC and multi award-winning airman, was a tonic much needed and recognized by the Department of Militia and Defence. They, along with the Office of Public information, encouraged Bishop in the writing of his autobiography, which was published under the title *Winged Warfare*. The book's introduction was worded as a thinly veiled recruitment drive and also includes a fictional combat with von Richtofen, "The Red Baron."

Bishop was promoted to major on March 13, 1918, and returned to England with his wife, where he expected to be appointed to the School of Aerial Fighting at Loch Don, Scotland. Instead he was given the command of No. 85 Squadron at Hounslow, Middlesex. This new squadron was initially equipped with Sopwith Dolphin aircraft, but these were replaced by the SE5a Scout. Bishop was given virtually a free hand in the selection of his pilots and over 200 applications were received.

The RAF was formed on April 1 when the RFC and the RNAS combined, so it was No. 85 Squadron RAF that flew to France on May 22, 1918. The squadron was based at Petite-Synthe, near Dunkirk, and five days later Bishop recorded his forty-eighth victory with the destruction of an enemy two-seater over Passchendaele. The following day, when on patrol near Ypres, he made a lone attack on a formation of nine enemy Albatros and shot down two of them.

By the following month Bishop had added a further five victories, and on June 4 he was credited with four more. Four days later the squadron moved to Saint-Omer and it was not until June 15 that Bishop achieved another victory. This was a Pfalz D.III destroyed near Estaires, and was followed the next day by victories over two more Pfalz machines near Amentières. Three more enemy aircraft were added to list of victories on June 17, and claims for another two the next day.

The rapid increase in Bishop's rate of victories since his return to operational flying was not unconnected with his ambition to become the highest-scoring British flyer. Although he had exceeded Albert Ball's final total of forty-four, the flyer with the most victories was then Capt. James McCudden, with fifty-seven. Bishop was also aware that the Canadian government and Military High Command wanted to withdraw him from operational flying as he was much more useful for propaganda purposes. Bishop's fears were realized on June 18, when orders were received at Saint-Omer for his return to England by midday the next day. On the 19th Bishop decided to have "one last look at the war" and took off on a lone mid-morning sortie. It took no more than fifteen minutes of combat for him to bring down four more Pfalz D.III aircraft and an LVG two-seater, only three of which were officially credited to him, but it still brought his official total to seventy-two.

In recognition of his last tour of duty, in which he had twenty-five victories in twelve days of actual combat, the *London Gazette* of August 3 announced the award of the Distinguished Flying Cross.

On August 5, Bishop was promoted to the rank of lieutenant-colonel in the Canadian Cavalry and posted to Canadian Forces HQ in England. Here his work was to supervise the formation of the Canadian Corps Wing (later to become the Royal Canadian Air Force), but by the end of September this wing was not ready for operations and Bishop travelled to Canada on October 3 to update the Canadian prime minister. Bishop arrived back in England on November 17, having heard the news of the Armistice when on board ship.

Before the war ended he had received recognition of the French government in the form of Croix de Guerre with palms and Croix de Chevalier, legion of Honour. Both honours were gazetted on November 2.

William Avery Bishop was the third of four children of William A. Bishop and his wife, Margaret Louise (Green). He was born on February 8, 1894, at Owen Sound, Grey County, Ontario, where his father, a lawyer, was the county registrar.

Bishop could not achieve the entrance requirements for university so he followed in the footsteps of one his brothers, Worth, who had earlier graduated from the Royal Military College (RMC), Kingston, and entered the college on August 28, 1911. The treatment meted out to first-year cadets by their seniors, who abused their position of authority, was at times brutal and sadistic, so it is unsurprising that Bishop was involved in a number of episodes resulting in disciplinary procedures, which included rustication at the end of his first year for failing examinations. Three years later, when the outbreak of war was announced, Bishop had commenced his final year at the RMC and been promoted to corporal. Like many of his contemporaries he did not want to miss the expected excitement and adventure of a European war. Consequently, on September 30, No. 943, Gentleman Cadet William Avery Bishop was granted a discharge from the RMC. His RMC discharge paper records that he was five feet six inches tall and that his conduct had been "good."

He was commissioned in the 9th Mississauga Horse with the rank of lieutenant, but was in hospital suffering from pneumonia when his regiment embarked for England in October 1914. After he recovered he was transferred to 7th Canadian Mounted Rifles (CMR) stationed in London, Ontario, and on January 9, 1915, he was commissioned as a lieutenant. Bishop's shooting skills served him well and in particular he excelled with the machine gun. He was admitted to Victoria Hospital, London, Ontario, on April 6 for less than a week, with injuries to his eye, wrist, and hand after a horseback-riding accident.

Before he was posted overseas, Bishop became engaged to his long-time girlfriend, Margaret Beattie Eaton Burden, whom he had met at Owen Sound where her wealthy parents took their summer holidays.

"A" Squadron, 7/CMR, designated as 2nd Canadian Division Mounted Troops, embarked on the SS *Caledonia* and sailed for England on June 9, 1915. On a rough crossing that caused the death of some of the 700 horses on board, the convoy came under U-boat attack off the coast of Ireland. Two of the ships were sunk, with the loss of Canadian lives, but the *Caledonia* arrived safely and Bishop disembarked at Plymouth, Devon, on June 23.

The 7/CMR were based at Shorncliffe, Kent, for training camp. In July, after Bishop had witnessed an RFC machine land and later take off from a nearby field, he wrote "... the only way to fight a war; up there above the mud and the mist ..." He was hospitalized again on July 24, this time with pleurisy and, following his discharge from the Helena Hospital at Shorncliffe on August 1, Bishop began his efforts to transfer into the RFC.

Bishop had learnt from acquaintances in the RFC that Lord Hugh Cecil at the War Office could facilitate transfers to the RFC, and on his next leave Bishop presented himself there. He was able to put in a transfer request but was informed that a wait of six months was to be expected for pilot training. On the other hand an immediate transfer would be available to an observer trainee. After talking this over with his CO, Bishop put in his application for a transfer, and on September 1, 1915, he was accepted into the RFC and posted to No. 21 (training) Squadron at Netheravon, near Salisbury, Wiltshire.

His training continued until the beginning of 1916 and his skill at aerial photography was such that he soon trained others in this task. No. 21 Squadron was posted to France and arrived at Boisdinghem airfield near Saint-Omer on January 18, 1916. The squadron was equipped with RE7 machines and the daily work was reconnaissance, aerial photography, artillery spotting, and bombing sorties. The flying conditions for the crews in these early aircraft were hard and Bishop was admitted to No. 10 Stationery Hospital at Saint-Omer for a few days in February, suffering with slight frostbite to his face.

Bishop appears to have been accident prone, as in the first few months of his time in France he was involved in an accident in a truck, injured when part of an aircraft fell on him, and later suffered a knee injury when his regular pilot, Roger Neville, made a crash landing. Despite the pain from his knee he continued on sorties until May 2, when he proceeded to London on leave. The injury to his knee did not improve and on May 11, the last day of his leave, he was admitted to Lady Carnarvon's Hospital for Officers at 48 Bryanston Square, London, diagnosed as suffering with synovitis. While there he met and was befriended by the philanthropic Lady Susan St. Helier, widow of Baron St. Helier, who was a socialite with a circle of very influential friends.

When discharged from hospital Lady St. Helier arranged for Bishop to convalesce at her house, 52 Portland Place, and later, when his father suffered a minor stroke, she used her influence to have Bishop returned to Canada to complete his recuperation. In so doing he missed his squadron's activity in the Battle of the Somme when their casualties were very high. Bishop returned to England in September 1916, but a medical board did not pass him as fit for pilot training as he had a heart murmur, his knee still troubled him, and he had been affected by an earlier bout of pneumonia. It would seem likely that Lady St. Helier's influence enabled Bishop to have a subsequent, less stringent medical examination when he was passed fit and on October 1 he reported to Brasenose College, Oxford, for initial ground training. On November 15 he was posted to the Central Flying School at Upavon, Wiltshire, to begin flying instruction.

At Upavon his instructor was a Norwegian pioneer aviator, Capt. Trygve Gran, and it was due to his perseverance that Bishop, whose training was interspersed by more than the usual number of crashes and heavy landings, finally gained his pilot's brevet. His first solo flight was in a Maurice Farman "Shorthorn" and he was appointed a flying officer in the RFC on December 8, 1916. Following night flying training at Northolt, Bishop was posted to No. 37 (Home Defence) Squadron at Sutton's Farm, Hornchurch, Essex, for advanced training in night flying and patrols attempting to locate enemy airships. Bishop missed the activity of the operational squadron and applied for a transfer back to the Western Front.

On March 7, 1917, he was posted to No. 60 Squadron, which was equipped with Nieuport 17 Scouts and based at Filescamp Farm airfield near Arras where his commanding officer, Major A. J. Scott, allotted him to B Flight.

Bishop's first patrol was on March 22 when he had difficulty coping with the sensitive controls of his machine and became separated from the remainder of the patrol. His next flight, two days later, concluded with an especially heavy-handed landing of his Nieuport, which was witnessed, at close hand, by a group of important visiting officers including the brigade commander. Bishop was later informed he would be sent back to England for further flying instruction, but that he would remain with the squadron until a replacement pilot arrived.

The following day, Bishop was on patrol in Nieuport A306 with three other aircraft, between Saint-Léger and Arras, when they engaged three Albatros D.III scouts, one of which attempted to fly under the tail of the leading Nieuport and in so doing came into Bishop's view. He fired about fifteen rounds and hit the enemy aircraft in the cockpit. The Albatros dived down and Bishop followed for about 7,000 feet, his guns still firing at about twenty yards range. The

Albatros flattened out and Bishop did likewise and fired a series of long bursts that sent the other machine down to crash on the ground. After he had pulled up out of his dive his engine stalled at 1,500 feet above the ground, but he managed to glide down and surprisingly made a good landing close to the front lines. He was unsure where he had landed and relieved when the soldiers who appeared were British. Bishop had to wait until the following day before he could fly his aircraft back to Filescamp Farm, where he discovered that the action, his first victory, had been confirmed by a number of witnesses and this had saved him from being posted back to England.

His second victory was on March 31, at 7:30 a.m., flying Nieuport A6769 with two other aircraft, on escort duty for six FE2bs of No. 11 Squadron which was on an important photographic reconnaissance well inside enemy-held territory. Bishop later described the event when the Nieuports were flying about 1,000 feet above the FE2bs and six Albatros scouts were spotted climbing up to attack the reconnaissance machines, and a further two diving down to attack the British scouts. The three Nieuports dived down and Bishop "managed to frighten off two of the Boches" and then spotted a British machine being attacked by one of the Albatros and "... forgetting everything else, I turned back to his assistance." Bishop attacked this Albatros and opened fire twice at fifty yards range, striking the enemy machine in the centre section. Immediately it fell out of control into a spin behind enemy lines. He then "rejoined the photography machines, which unfortunately in the meantime had lost one of their number."

Although his normal flying technique was still "ham-fisted," once Bishop went into attack he had adapted his flying tactics to gain the upper hand over the enemy through height, surprise, and by attacking out of the sun. Furthermore his excellent shooting abilities combined with a very keen sense of situational awareness made him a formidable fighter pilot.

Bishop, in addition to leading his flight on patrols, was increasingly flying solo sorties. These lone patrols hunting enemy machines were much in the manner of Albert Ball, who had earlier flown with 60 Squadron and was then the top British ace. Bishop was intent on bettering this victory total and, like Ball, he was never completely happy with having the responsibility of other pilots' lives, preferring a role in combat with only himself to consider.

The following month, known as Bloody April by the RFC pilots due to the ascendancy of the German Fokker aircraft and the subsequent crippling casualties to both RFC crew and aircraft, Bishop was in his element. He regarded the increased number of enemy aircraft as more targets for his guns, but his squadron was less fortunate and had a high loss rate for the month: thirteen of the original eighteen pilots were shot down, along with seven of their replacements. However, the squadron did have thirty-five confirmed victories during April, of which a third were Bishop's.

In the first week of April, all-out efforts were made to attack enemy observation balloons in readiness for the forthcoming British offensive, and Bishop was credited with the destruction of one kite balloon, together with its attendant scout, on April 7. For this action he was awarded a Military Cross (gazetted on May 26) and on the following day, Easter Sunday, the day before the start of the Battle of Arras, he claimed his fifth victim, but returned to base sobered by a near miss when a bullet had pierced the aircraft's windscreen, narrowly missing him. He celebrated his new status of "ace" by having the nose of his aircraft painted blue.

On April 25 Bishop was promoted to captain and made flight commander of C Flight, and by the end of the month he had been credited with twelve victories and the destruction of an observation balloon. During the first week of May, Bishop increased his number of victories by four, including two on the 2nd, before he returned to England for two weeks' leave on May 7.

In London, Bishop, the latest protégé of Lady St. Helier, was introduced to all her society friends who included members of the royal family, many senior politicians, and personages such as Max Aitken, the influential Canadian newspaper magnate. Bishop much enjoyed his new-found celebrity status during this period of leave.

He returned to France on May 22 and within two weeks had taken part in the action for which he was awarded the VC. On June 18 the Supplement to the *London Gazette* No. 30235 published the citation for the award of his DSO, for destroying two enemy aircraft in the action on May 2. Consequently at his VC investiture he was also presented with his DSO and MC awards.

By the end of 1918 Bishop had been demobilized and had returned to Canada where he had been offered the opportunity of a year-long lecture tour in the U.S.

This tour, which was well paid, did not meet with approval in all quarters and Bishop was compared to Piper Lindlater, a nineteenth-century recipient of the VC who had appeared in music halls wearing his full uniform, much to the outrage of many senior military figures. During December 1918 David Henderson, one of the founding fathers of the RFC, then based at the British Embassy in Washington D.C., was contacted on this matter and this letter in Bishop's file has the handwritten annotation, "Spoke to Col. Henderson. H.E. does not mind."

Bishop left the U.S. lecture tour after a few months and in July 1919, together with another Canadian VC recipient, William Barker (see page 392), set up an aviation business, BBAL, a charter airline. Unfortunately the business struggled with financial difficulties and the partnership was later dissolved. The difficulties both men suffered in their attempts to acclimatize themselves to civilian life, and their "hell-raising" lifestyle, did little to aid their airline business.

Nineteen twenty was not a good year for the Bishop family, as not only did William suffer serious head injuries and blurred vision in an aircraft crash, and the subsequent loss of his pilot's licence, but his wife gave birth to a daughter who tragically only survived for a few weeks.

In late 1921 Bishop and his wife came to live in England where, using his many contacts including Lady St. Helier, he was very successful in particular with sales of a new type of pipe patented by a French company. The couple's first child to survive was born at 139 Wigmore Street, London, on June 13, 1923, and was named Arthur Christian William Avery Bishop. His godparents were Prince Arthur of Connaught and Princess Louise. Bishop's occupation on the birth certificate was given as "Lieut. Colonel Canadian General Staff (Reserve) V.C. — Company Director of Stanmore." The family was then living at Brockley Hill House, Stanmore, Middlesex. A daughter, Margaret Marise, was born at 27 Welbeck Street, London, on February 15, 1926. On this occasion Bishop's occupation was described as "Financier of St. Pancras" and the family address was 18 Chester Terrace, St. Pancras, London.

The Wall Street Crash of 1929 hit Bishop's finances hard and he and his family later returned to Canada, but he was still living in London in March 1930 when his good friend William Barker VC was tragically killed in a flying accident. British newspapers reported Bishop's great distress on hearing this news.

Bishop was appointed vice president of the McColl-Frontenac Oil Company, but from 1931 his work and connections were increasingly with the RCAF in which he was promoted to air vice-marshal in 1936. Also in this year he became an honorary, and the only non-German, member of the German Aces Association and he was photographed in Berlin, seated between Goering and Udet.

In 1938 he was appointed air marshal, head of the Air Advisory Committee, and was made director of recruiting two years later in January 1940. The RCAF used Bishop's status as Canada's premier ace of the First World War to encourage recruits. He was a tireless campaigner and so successful that some applicants were turned away. He was so enthusiastic in his efforts selling war bonds and conducting numerous inspection tours that the pace, together with his increasing intemperance, led to his exhaustion and at his own request he was relieved of his official duties in 1944.

In recognition of his military service in two world wars Bishop was awarded the Commander of the Order of the Bath in the king's birthday honours list on June 1, 1944, and in the same year he received the Canadian Efficiency Decoration.

Bishop worked part time as an executive for the oil industry from 1945 until his retirement to Montreal in 1952, where he and his wife Margaret led a very active social life. He attempted to enlist in the RCAF at the outbreak of the Korean War, but his request was turned down.

Four years later, on September 11, 1956, and at only sixty-two years of age, William Bishop died at his winter home in Palm Beach, Florida. He was cremated at St. James's Crematorium, Toronto. His ashes were buried in Greenwood Cemetery, Owen Sound, Ontario.

Bishop's only son, Arthur William Bishop, enlisted in the RAF as a fighter pilot and survived the Second World War. He was a journalist and author of a number of books on Canadian military history, including *Courage of the Early Morning*, a biography of his father, published in 1965.

Bishop's life had always been eventful and he was not shy, on occasion, about embroidering the truth. He had always had his detractors, but the greatest controversies began after his death. In 1978 a stage musical of his life and career, *Billy Bishop Goes to War*, was first produced in Vancouver. Based on Arthur's biography, it was subsequently staged in over fifty cities in Canada, the U.S., and Great Britain, where it was presented in August 1980. Two years later the Canadian National Film Board released a drama-documentary, *The Kid Who Couldn't Miss*, which cast doubt not only on the veracity of Bishop's winning VC action, but also on the validity of many of his other victories.

This production was not well received and was even described as second-rate by one of Bishop's detractors. The findings of a subsequent Canadian Senate investigation regarding this film were not conclusive, but did question various points in connection with the German airfield raid near Cambrai.

Thousands of words have since been written about Bishop's "victories," but his detractors have not been completely successful in proving their case. It is a fact that in his autobiography and in many subsequent articles published in the 1920s and '30s, the description of Bishop's exploits was comparable to such writers as W.E. Johns, the creator of Biggles, the boy's own fictional flying ace. Even Bishop, in later life, referred to these stories, and was quoted as saying, "It is so terrible that I cannot read it today ... it was headline stuff ... Yet the public loved it."

The citation of his VC gained in June 1917 was only based on details Bishop related and these were not witnessed. This lack of evidence is one of the major bones of contention. Details of recommended awards were supposed to be kept confidential, but in 60 Squadron at least these rules had been relaxed as shown by details in a letter of June 1, 1917, to Margaret. Bishop wrote he had just learned that "when I got my DSO, I was recommended for the VC." Existing documents confirm that he was recommended for the DSO on May 7, but no papers exist to prove that Scott had originally asked for a VC. After Major Scott's recommendation for the VC on June 2, as was the usual practice, corroboration of the action was then sought, but no reliable witnesses could be found.

However, rumours had begun as early as June 19 regarding "a young British pilot" who had smashed four machines on an enemy airfield, and by the beginning of August stories circulated that an unnamed "colonial" airman had been recommended for a VC. One plausible theory is that the awards process had developed its own momentum and to arrest its progress at this late stage with the possibility of unfavourable newspaper reports would have been problematic, particularly as the final major Allied advance of the war had just begun.

Bishop is commemorated in Canada in many ways: in Ontario there is the Owen Sound Billy Bishop Regional Airport, and also at Owen Sound the Billy Bishop Home and Museum, and the 167 Air Marshal Bishop Squadron, Royal Canadian Air Cadets. Toronto has Billy Bishop Way near Downsview Airport and also Billy Bishop Toronto City Airport. Pearson International Airport was originally named Bishop Field Toronto Airport, Malton. In Hamilton the Memorial School has a Billy Bishop entrance. In 2009 the name of Air Vice-Marshal William Avery "Billy" Bishop was added to the wall of honour at the Royal Military College at Kingston. A hazardous materials training school is named CFB Borden Billy Bishop Centre and at the Brampton Flying Club there is the Billy Bishop Hangar. Ottawa Airport has the "Billy Bishop Room" for VIPs and a roadway on private land here is named Billy Bishop Private.

In Winnipeg the Bishop Building is to be found at the 1st Canadian Air Division and the Canadian NORAD Region Headquarters. On the Alberta–British Columbia border, Mount Bishop (Canada) is a 9,350-foot-high mountain. Vancouver has the Billy Bishop legion Branch 176. One of the prestige awards for aviation in the

Air Force Association of Canada is the Air Marshal W.A. Bishop Memorial Trophy.

In Greenwood Cemetery at Owen Sound, Bishop is commemorated not only on his own stone, but his name is also engraved on his grandparents' headstone. Two other VC winners are also buried in this cemetery, Thomas Holmes and David Vivian Currie.

Bishop's medal entitlement was: VC, CB, DSO + Bar, MC, DFC, BWM, VM (MiD), 1939–45 War Medal, Canadian Efficiency Medal, Silver Jubilee Medal 1935, Coronation Medals 1937 and 1953, GVI Efficiency Decoration, Croix de Guerre avec 2 Palmes, Legion d'honneur First Class, and the Aero Club of America Medal of Merit. His medals are held at the Canadian War Museum, Ottawa. Bishop's name, together with the other VC recipients of the RAF, appears on the roll of honour left of the altar in St. Clement Dane's Church, the Strand, London.

M.J. O'ROURKE, F. HOBSON, H. BROWN, and O.M. LEARMONTH

Hill 70 near Loos, August 15–18

During Canadian operations northwest of Lens and the capture of Hill 70 in mid-August 1917 no fewer than six Victoria Crosses were won.

In July Sir Douglas Haig informed General Sir Henry Horne of the First Army that he wanted the coal-mining area of Lens captured. In turn Horne asked the Canadian Corps under Lt.-Gen. Sir A.W. Currie to carry out the task. Currie was unhappy with the objectives given him by First Army, and as Lens was dominated by Hill 70 to the north and from the southeast by Sallaumines Hill he considered that the two heights were tactically more important than Lens itself. To occupy the latter while leaving the high ground in the hands of the enemy was not sensible. Deployment of artillery in the open plain would also be difficult.

At a meeting of corps commanders Currie was able to persuade Gen. Horne to allow Hill 70 to become the immediate main objective. He reasoned that Canadian possession of the hill with the resulting observation deep into enemy-held territory would force the Germans to make counterattacks that could then be effectively dealt with by artillery. An earlier plan to occupy the railway was also altered to one of "raid and withdraw," and was to be carried out by the 3rd Division.

On August 14 the 1st Corps "staged demonstration attacks with dummy tanks directly west of Lens." The treeless Hill 70 was of chalk downland at the end of one of the spurs running northeast from the Artois plateau, which dominated Lens and gave views of the Douai plain beyond. In September 1915 it had been taken by the British, who were unable to hold on to it. The La Bassée–Lens road climbed over its western slopes, short of the bare crest. In the north it fell away toward the Loos valley. The descent was interrupted on the south side by the Cité Spur, over which spread four northern suburbs of Lens, which were brick-built company towns of miners' houses. Most of these had been reduced to ruins by shellfire. When fighting among these ruins the enemy were to have the advantage and they also gave a special challenge to the artillery. The final Canadian objective was a series of former enemy trenches that formed an arc around the eastern slope of Hill 70. As far as possible, Hill 70 was to be "a killing by artillery."

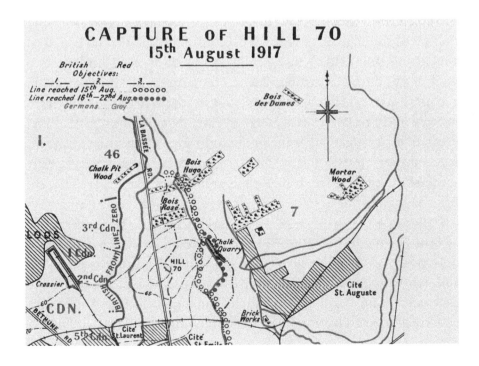

Nine field brigades were to give support to the main assault, four with the 2nd Division on the right and five with the 1st Division on the left. The barrage would be supported in turn by 160 machine guns. The infantry divisions had two brigades forward from north to south, the 3rd, 2nd, 5th and 4th, giving ten battalions. Their objectives were marked out in three stages and the assault began as dawn was breaking at 4:25 a.m. on August 15. The engineers began to fire drums of burning oil into Cité Ste. Elizabeth and other targets to supplement artillery fire and provide a smoke screen.

It is clear that the enemy were expecting an attack, so that even as troops moved up and into their assembly positions they were met with gas shells. Despite this the speed and strength of the Canadian attack quickly overwhelmed the trench garrisons, and according to the official history, "... within twenty minutes the first objective beyond the Lens–La Bassée highway, an average advance of 600 yards, had been reached by the two divisions." To the right the 4th and 5th brigades of the 2nd Canadian Division moved through the ruins of the mining villages of Cité St. Laurent and Cité St. Edouard, and after a pause of half an hour the 4th Brigade followed through the village of Cité Ste. Elizabeth and then formed a defensive flank that faced the edge of Lens town. According to the official history it was at this point that Sgt. Frederick Hobson of the 20th Battalion won a VC during a strong enemy counterattack. However, other accounts say that it happened on August 18, three days later, which is more likely to be the case. The 5th Brigade pushed on further and pressed on through Cité Saint-Émileto the final objective, which was reached soon after 6:00 a.m. The 1st Canadian Division was equally successful and the 5th and 10th battalions of the 2nd Canadian Brigade gained the top of Hill 70, and the 16th, 13th, and 15th battalions of the 3rd Canadian Brigade occupied the western side of Bois Hugo and Bois Rase. The brigade then moved on to its final objective. On the front of the 2nd Canadian Brigade the fresh 7th and 8th battalions "reached their intermediate objective along the German Second Position." Enemy machine guns in Bois Hugo were quickly dealt with by bombing parties moving round the flanks.

By 6:00 a.m. the operation had been completed except for a further advance down the eastern slope of Hill 70 by the 2nd Brigade. The necessary pause to allow for the artillery timetable gave the enemy a brief respite, which they made full use of, having "steadied along the front of Cité St. Auguste." The 7th and 8th battalions now met intense machine-gun and rifle fire that swept the slope, slowing the impetus of the Canadian attack. Casualties mounted as the artillery barrage lost its protectiveness. The 7th Battalion left a group of fifty men to hold the northern end of the Chalk Quarry and returned to their previous objective, and the 8th Battalion conformed.

On the following day the forward-artillery observers were able to look over the Douai plain to the east and to the northeast of Lens. As the ground was being consolidated local enemy counterattacks were carried out against the "new front from Bois Hugo, from the wood near the Chalk Quarry, from the Brick Works and from Lens...." However, these were broken up by artillery fire, followed by machine-gun and rifle fire. Later in the morning the enemy advanced en masse in extended order on a front behind Cité St. Auguste. The Canadians, from their positions on the hill, witnessed the casualties and disorganizinion caused by their artillery barrages.

At 12:45 p.m. further enemy counterattacks developed against the new Canadian line, and waves of German attackers against the 3rd Canadian Brigade were checked and virtually destroyed by artillery and machine-gun fire. An attack against the 2nd Brigade from the Cité St. Auguste also made no headway, but the 7th and 8th battalions (the two battalions involved) had suffered heavy losses and were exhausted. The order to advance, due to take place firstly at 4:00 p.m. and then post-to 6:00 p.m., was therefore cancelled.

Of the sixteen stretcher-bearers with the 7th British Columbia Regiment (2nd Canadian Brigade), 1st Division, two were killed and eleven were wounded, most by German snipers. Of the remaining three, Pte. Michael O'Rourke began his heroic and tireless work in which he was to save the lives of at least forty men over the next three days when, often under very heavy fire, he not only attended to their wounds but also brought them food and water. Several times he was knocked down by shell bursts and sometimes partially buried. For his work he was later awarded the VC, and the citation below (*London Gazette*, November 8, 1917) gives full details of his heroism. With an Irish brogue he remarked to the press in later years about his VC: "Shure I 'dint know what it was all about. It was me job, you see, to take out the wounded. There was a lot o' snipin' and machine-gunnin' around but I couldn't do anything else but keep on goin', you know what I mean?"

> Michael James O'Rourke, No. 428545, 7th Battalion. Canadian Infantry. For most conspicuous bravery and devotion to duty during prolonged operations. For three days and nights Private O'Rourke, who is a stretcher-bearer, worked unceasingly in bringing the wounded into safety, dressing them and getting them food and water. During the whole of this period the area in which he worked was subjected to very severe shelling, and swept by heavy-machine-gun and rifle fire. On several occasions he was knocked down and partially buried by enemy shells. Seeing a comrade who had been blinded stumbling around ahead of our trench, in full view of the enemy, who were sniping him, Private O'Rourke jumped out of his trench and brought the man back, being himself heavily sniped at while doing so. Again he went forward about 50 yards in front of our barrage, under very heavy and accurate fire from enemy machine guns and snipers and brought in a comrade. On a subsequent occasion, when the line of advanced posts was retired to the line to be consolidated, he went forward under very heavy enemy fire of every description, and brought back a wounded man who had been left behind. He showed throughout an absolute disregard for his own safety, going wherever there were wounded to succour, and his magnificent courage and devotion in continuing his rescue work, in spite of exhaustion and the incessant enemy fire of every description, inspired all ranks and undoubtedly saved many lives.

The capture of the final objective in front of Cité St. Auguste was to take place on August 17 at 4:00 p.m. using two fresh battalions, the 5th (Saskatchewan) and 10th (Alberta). After an intense bombardment, and under a rolling barrage, the attack advanced by short rushes down the 400-yard slope. The objective was gained, but not without heavy loss of life as the enemy themselves were in force, massing for a counterattack. Fierce close fighting took place, especially at the Chalk Quarry, where the Germans left behind a hundred dead, in addition to a hundred wounded and thirty prisoners.

In Norman Trench the 5th Battalion took fifty prisoners and captured eight machine guns, but by 5:30 p.m. the battalion had run out of ammunition and was forced to fall back. On the right flank the 10th Battalion grimly hung on. Communication between the 10th Battalion HQ and Company HQ had broken down because all wires had been cut. Artillery support was desperately needed. Two runners then attempted to take back messages from the front line: one was killed, but the other, Pte. Harry Brown, with his arm shattered, kept on going through an intense barrage until he arrived at the "close support line," where he looked for an officer at a company HQ in order to deliver his message. All the time an intense enemy barrage was going on. He was so exhausted that he fell down the dugout steps but retained consciousness long enough to hand over his message, saying "important message" and collapsing. The message received allowed the Canadian artillery to save the situation. Brown died of his wounds a few hours later at a dressing station near Hill 70 and was buried in the same cemetery as Maj. Learmonth (see below) in Plot II of Noeux-les-Mines Communal Cemetery, Row J, Grave 29. The battalion war diary mentions Brown in Appendix B: "This man displayed courage and self-control seldom witnessed. His devotion to duty was of the highest possible degree imaginable, his action undoubtedly saved the loss of the position, at least temporarily and saved many casualties to our troops."

Brown's citation was published in the *London Gazette* of October 17, 1917:

Harry Brown, Private, No. 226353, late Canadian Infantry Batt. For most conspicuous bravery, courage and devotion to duty. After the capture of a position, the enemy massed in force and counterattacked. The situation became very critical, all wires being cut. It was of the utmost importance to get word back to Headquarters. This soldier and one other were given the message with orders to deliver the same at all costs. The other messenger was killed. Private Brown had his arm shattered, but continued on through an intense barrage until he arrived at the close support lines and found an officer. He was so spent that he fell down the dugout steps, but retained consciousness long enough to hand over his message, saying, "important message." He then became unconscious, and died in the dressing station a few hours later. His devotion to duty was of the highest possible degree imaginable, and his successful delivery of the message undoubtedly saved the loss of the position for the time and prevented many casualties.

A series of unsuccessful counterattacks then took place. With the assistance of artillery and machine-gun fire the line of the quarry was held. However, to the south the 5th Battalion was "much reduced in strength and short of ammunition, and had to fall back to a shell hole position about 200 yards short of the final objective where the 2nd Canadian Division had been established." During the night the 1st Brigade took over from the 3rd Brigade on the left of the division and on the following night took over the 2nd Brigade's sector as well.

The minor Canadian actions on August 17 met with "varying success" and determined German counterattacks continued. A series of attacks were made against the quarry and many Canadian gunners were put out of action as a result of gas shells. Late the same day large numbers of the enemy reached within a hundred yards of the quarry before being stopped by Lewis guns and rifles of the 4th Battalion. German planes were very active and a gas alert was also on. Another attempt was made three hours later, and a third at 4:15 the next morning. This third attack coincided with an attack against Chicory Trench on the right flank of the 2nd Division. Only one German company managed to close with the defences of Chicory Trench and was quickly dealt with by a Boer War veteran, Sgt. Frederick

Hobson of the 20th (1st Central Ontario) Battalion (4th Brigade), who played a major role in repulsing a German attack. His battalion had by then been in the line for three days, with the 18th Battalion to the right and 21st in the centre, and on the first day he, together with members of A Company, had seen action at Nabob Alley when they bombed along it, pushing back the enemy who were only retreating very slowly, and having captured about seventy yards of trench the Canadians established a post.

On August 18, however, on seeing an important Lewis gun post wiped out, Hobson rushed forward and dug the gun out, together with a surviving member of the crew, and proceeded to engage the enemy at short range until the gun jammed. Not being a trained Lewis gunner he ordered the wounded survivor of the gun crew to "remedy the stoppage." Hobson, now also wounded, rushed forward to attack the enemy with bayonet and clubbed rifle. He was laid low by a rifle shot but by then the Lewis gun was back in action and reinforcements were on their way up. The Lewis gun enfiladed the enemy advance and caused many casualties.

Hobson's VC was published in the *London Gazette* of October 17, 1917:

No. 57113, Frederick Hobson, Sergeant, late 20th Battalion. Canadian Infantry. During a strong enemy counterattack a Lewis gun in a forward post in a communication trench leading to the enemy lines was buried by a shell, and the crew, with the exception of one man, killed. Sergeant Hobson, though not a gunner, grasped the great importance of the post, rushed from his trench, dug out the gun, and got it into action against the enemy, who were now advancing down the trench and across the open. A jam caused the gun to stop firing. Though wounded he left the gunner to correct the stoppage, rushed forward at the advancing enemy, and with bayonet and clubbed rifle, single-handed held them back until he himself was killed by a rifle shot. By this time, however, the Lewis gun was again in action, and, reinforcements shortly afterward arriving, the enemy was beaten off. The valour and devotion to duty displayed by this non-commissioned officer gave the gunner the time required to again get the gun into action, and saved a most serious situation.

Some fairly lurid accounts survive about Hobson's deed. Here is an example:

When he engaged the enemy in no man's land he bayoneted or club rifled fourteen of them. When men of the company went out after him he was hit by a stick bomb and his middle was torn away ... the rescuers found the fourteen dead Germans in a semicircle around him.

The 4th Brigade's war diary mentions that the brigade had received a request from the 20th Battalion for a Lewis gun to be sent to it because one had been destroyed in a hostile bombardment. The battalion war diary notes that "our Lewis Gun posts in Nabob Trench did splendid service until wiped out." It also states that when a large number of troops came over the fighting "was of a most desperate nature."

After Hobson's death the enemy staged another counterattack, at 5:00 a.m. on August 18, to the north of the Chalk Quarry, which mainly affected two companies of the 2nd Battalion (Eastern Ontario Battalion) astride Bois Hugo. Penetrating the more northerly position the German bombers, who were using Flammenwerfer and bombs, were soon driven out. Both company commanders, Maj. Spence and Maj. O.M. Learmonth, whose company was south of the wood, died of wounds, Maj. Learmonth winning the Victoria Cross. Although mortally wounded he stood on the parapet and still directed the defence and hurled grenades at the approaching enemy. He even caught some of the enemy bombs and threw them back at them with good effect. When no longer able to do this he instructed his junior officers in running the battle. The battalion held its ground and further attacks were dealt with by artillery fire. They were relieved by the 3rd Battalion between 10:00 p.m. and 1:15 a.m.

According to the Skeffingtons' *Thirty Canadian VCs*:

He saw a number of the Germans, after their advance had been checked within a few yards of our trenches, had found shelter to some extent in a small wood; and to rout them out of the wood a bombing party from No. 3 Company was sent forward. They bombed the Germans out of the wood and down a trench called Horse Alley, driving them into the open, where our snipers and machine gunners engaged them and cleaned them up. Throughout the whole of the attack Learmonth showed what his Commanding Officer, Major R. Vanderwater, DSO, had named a "wonderful spirit." Absolutely fearless, he so conducted himself that he imbued those with whom he came into contact with some of his personality. When the barrage started he was continuously with his men and officers, encouraging them and making sure that no loophole was left through which the enemy could gain a footing. When the attack was launched against the thin Canadian line, Learmonth seemed to be everywhere at once. When the situation was critical, he took his turn at throwing bombs. He was wounded twice, but carried on as if he were perfectly fit and whole. He was wounded a third time, his leg this time being broken, but still he showed the same indomitable spirit. Lying in a trench, he continued to direct his men, encouraging them, cheering them, advising them. At a quarter past six that morning the battalion headquarters received word that Learmonth was badly wounded and was being carried out of the line on a stretcher; but the enemy attack had been repulsed. He had waited till he saw the finish. They brought him down to headquarters, and, lying on a stretcher, he gave valuable information to the officers there before he was taken to hospital. He died shortly afterward — the man who would not give in.

Learmonth later died of his wounds, and at 11:00 a.m. on August 22 the battalion moved from huts at Mazingarbe to Noeux-les-Mines, northwest of Lens, where he was buried in the Communal Cemetery, II, K, 9, quite near the grave of Pte. Harry Brown. According to figures mentioned in the 2nd Canadian Brigade War Diary, O'Rourke's 7th Battalion suffered casualties of thirteen officers and 416 other ranks during the three-day operation, and Brown's 10th Battalion had lost eleven officers and also 416 other ranks. Hobson's 20th Battalion of the 4th Brigade had suffered 182 casualties during operations from August 15 to 21.

Learmonth's VC citation was published in the *London Gazette* of November 8, 1917:

> For most conspicuous bravery and exceptional devotion to duty. During a determined counterattack on our new positions, this officer, when his company was momentarily surprised, instantly charged and personally disposed of the attackers. Later, he carried on a tremendous fight with the advancing enemy. Although under intense barrage fire and mortally wounded, he stood on the parapet of the trench, bombed the enemy continuously and directed the defence in such a manner as to infuse a spirit of utmost resistance into his men. On several occasions this very brave officer actually caught bombs thrown at him by the enemy and threw them back. When he was unable by reason of his wounds to carry on the fight, he still refused to be carried out of the line, and continued to give instructions and invaluable advice to his junior officers, finally handing over all his duties before he was evacuated from the front line to the hospital where he died.

Michael James O'Rourke was the son of James O'Rourke and Catherine (*née* Baker), and was born in Limerick on March 3, 1874. Michael and his siblings were orphaned in 1885 and prior to the year he worked as a miner and tunneller. In his attestation papers, dated March 23, 1915, he stated that he had been born several years after 1874, in Limerick, in March 1878. If the 1874 date is indeed correct O'Rourke was able to maintain the deception until his death, when obituaries gave conflicting dates of birth, making his gravestone incorrect as well. Giving his age as thirty-seven he would have underestimated it by four years. He also stated that he had served in the Royal Munster Fusiliers for seven years. A Roman Catholic and a former miner, O'Rourke applied for enlistment and was passed fit for service abroad at his interview in New Westminster, British Columbia. He was five feet and five and three quarter inches tall, with dark hair. He gave his next of kin as his sister, Mrs. K. Mack. His service number was 428545.

His address in 1915 was at 2564 Broadway, Montreal. He joined the 30th Battalion 1st Reinforcement Draft at New Westminster on March 23, 1915. A few weeks later he was transferred to the 1st Draft of 47th Battalion on May 1, 1915. He travelled to England, where he arrived on May 6, transferring to the 30th, and was camped at the Canadian base at Shorncliffe in June. While there he fell foul of the authorities for the first time and had seven days' pay deducted as a result of being drunk and using abusive language. On August 21 O'Rourke left the 30th Battalion for the 7th and arrived in France the following day. He was to spend the whole of his military service as a stretcher-bearer. On December 11 he was attached to the 1st Canadian Division.

O'Rourke was a temperamental Irishman with periods of great gallantry coupled with bouts of drunkenness. In May 1916 he was awarded nine days' leave and at the end of June he was in trouble again, and this time was given fourteen days' field punishment No. 1 for drunkenness. On October 6 he received the MM "for bravery in the field" from Lt.-Gen. Julian Byng, which was gazetted on December 9, 1916. On November 20, 1916, he was attached to 1st Canadian Division Train until February 2, 1917.

On winning his VC during the fighting for Hill 70 in August 1917, O'Rourke was granted ten days' leave in early October before his VC was gazetted on November 8, 1917, in the *London Gazette*. Returning from France on December 2, he received his decoration three days later from the king, at Buckingham Palace. During the same investiture as Cadet Hanna, Cpl. Konowal, Sgt. James Ockenden, PO Ernest Pitcher, and Cpl. Ernest Egerton were each awarded their VCs. Soon after he was granted fourteen days' leave, which was extended to a ten-week furlough in Canada between December 23 and the end of March 1918.

From his medical records O'Rourke was clearly no longer fit for foreign service, and in Vancouver he was discharged from service with the 11th Battalion Canadian Garrison Regiment CEF on July 16, 1918, "having become medically unfit for further service overseas by reason of disabilities incurred on active service." His medical records state he was unfit because of "exposure to cold and wet & strain of service." He showed a "fairly marked degree of debility, is nervous and tremulous — somewhat anaemic. The left sciatic is somewhat tender — and there is pain on full extension of leg flexed on abdomen. Can walk 3 or 4 miles at an easy gait; is somewhat dyspnoeac on such exertion as running, climbing hills & c. The sciatica is of slight grade." He was graded as Class C3 permanent. But despite his bouts of drinking, papers in the file housed in Ottawa described his conduct and character as "very good." He was discharged in Vancouver on July 7, 1918, after he had been declared medically unfit. He then resided for a short time at the Georgian Hotel, 4th Avenue, Seattle.

After the war three of his medals were stolen from his home and he was given assistance by the Prince of Wales in acquiring replacements for them. When working as a stevedore in Vancouver in 1929 he was invited to London for the House of Lords' dinner in November. In the crush he was unable to get near the prince before the grand dinner, but the prince did manage to talk to him later. In 1935, on the waterfront, O'Rourke led a strike of a thousand longshoremen.

After the Second World War, O'Rourke visited London in the summer of 1956 for the VC centenary. He died in the following year at his sister's home, 3410 Point Gray Road, Vancouver, on December 6. Four days later he was given a full military funeral in Holy Rosary Cathedral, with seven holders of the VC acting as pallbearers, including Robert Hanna and Harcus Strachan. A large congregation of servicemen attended the service and afterward he was buried at Forest Lawn Burial Park, North Burnaby, British Columbia.

His decorations were once in the Officers' Mess of the British Columbian Regiment but are now kept in the Regimental Museum. As noted O'Rourke's decorations, including his VC, DCM, MM,

1914–15 Star, King George VI Coronation medal (1937), and Queen Elizabeth II (1953) had been stolen in the 1920s and, therefore, any medals apart from the two Coronation medals, which are displayed, will be copies. In 2014 a new gravestone was dedicated. His memory is also commemorated by a painting in the Canadian War Museum, Ottawa. Together with Robert Hanna he also has a plaque in France close to the former Loos battlefield.

 John Henry (Harry) Brown was born to a Roman Catholic family in Ganonoque, Frontenac, Ontario, on May 9, 1898. This is the date on his Baptism certificate at St. John's Church. He was the son of Henry Brown and Adelaide Henry Ledger. After her husband's death Adelaide married Patrick McAuliffe and became known as Helen.

Ganonoque is a small town on the St. Lawrence River. After leaving school Harry became a farmer, but after the war began he worked as a storeman in a factory in London, Ontario.

At the age of eighteen he enlisted in the Canadian Mounted Rifles in London, Ontario, on August 18, 1916, and was given the service number of 226353. He was five foot six and a half inches tall with dark brown hair. His mother's home address at this time was at East Emily, R.R. No. 1, Ontario, and Harry's own address was 164 Bruce Street in Hamilton, Ontario, where his wife, Louise, lived. His mother was his next of kin. When he was about to go overseas with the Canadian Mounted Rifles he made a will, on October 10, 1916, in favour of his mother, and embarked for England on October 25, arriving there on the 31st. He camped at Shorncliffe, became a member of the 11th Battalion, and was briefly transferred to the 4th Canadian Training Brigade.

Brown had a brief spell in hospital from November 23 to December 10 with tonsillitis. On May 27, 1916, he arrived in France when he was assigned to the 10th (Quebec) Battalion and left for the trenches a fortnight later.

On August 17 he was admitted to No. 7 CCS dangerously wounded with gunshot wounds and died soon after his shattered arm had been amputated. He was buried at Noeux-les-Mines Communal Cemetery, II, J, 29, in the same cemetery as Okill Learmonth.

Brown's posthumous VC was presented to his mother Helen McAuliffe by the Duke of Devonshire, Governor General, at a ceremony infront of the Parlimentary Buildings in Ottawa on January 22, 1918. She was to die of cancer a year later, on September 3. Brown's decorations apart from the VC include the BWM and VM and are held in the Canadian War Museum in Ottawa, which also holds a painting of him.

In recent years Brown has been commemorated in Gananoque with the Canadian Legion naming their branch after him. In August 2007 his VC was put on display there and in the same year on August 16, ninety years after he won his VC, he was also honoured with a commemorative cairn built in his name close to the town cenotaph. His name is listed on the the Galt War Memorial in Queen's Square, the Omemer Cenotaph, the Peterborough War Memorial, and on an historical plaque ouside the Armoury in Galt.

Frederick Hobson was born in Norwood, South London, on September 23, 1873. He joined the Regular Army and served with the 2nd Wiltshire Regiment from 1897 and took part in the Boer War (1899–1902). He was discharged in the following year with the rank of corporal and shortly afterward met Louise Moses. In 1904 the couple emigrated to Canada and once there they soon married. The couple were to have five children, four sons and one daughter: George (1905), Frederick (1909), Albert (1911), Florence (1913), and John (1915).

Hobson was employed by Dominion Canners, and in 1913 the family were living in Galt at 69 South Street. He then became a storekeeper employed by the city authorities. Despite being in his early forties and having the responsibility of a pregnant wife, Hobson was determined to return to the army after the war began, a decision much against his wife's wishes.

Hobson's attestation papers note that he was just short of six feet tall, with blue eyes and a scar on the back of his head. He appears to have joined the Norfolk Rifles at the end of October 1914 and then tried to enlist in Galt several times, without success. But he then decided to try again, this time in Toronto, from his sister Florence's home, who lived at 1381 Lansdowne Avenue. He was successful: on November 10, 1914, he enlisted as a member of the 20th 1st Central Ontario Regiment, CEF, and was confirmed with the rank of sergeant from New Year's Day 1915. His service number was 57113.

On May 15 Hobson left Canada and arrived in England on May 24, and after nearly eight months' training he sailed from Folkestone for Boulogne on January 1, 1916. He was to spend two years in France and Flanders. In early February 1916 he was given seven days' leave, and on June 30 was promoted to sergeant. On September 16 he was badly wounded by gunshot in his right hip and admitted to No. 4 Canadian Field Ambulance before being released to his unit. He was briefly attached to the 255th Tunnelling Company, from October 20 until December 15, and in July 1917 was given ten days' leave before returning to the 20th Battalion. He was killed in action while serving in the fighting northwest of Lens on Hill 70 near the La Bassée–Lens road, where he won the VC on August 18.

Back in Canada, and even while Hobson was still living, Louise seems to have taken up with a widowed neighbour, who was keen to marry her. His name was Thomas George Thorn of Stafford, Ontario, and the couple married on April 1, 1918. He provided for Louise and her five children, and the children, who remembered their father, were forbidden ever to refer to him again. The State provided a pension toward their upkeep.

On May 8, 1918, Hobson's VC was presented to his sister Florence Brown in Toronto by the Governor General of Canada, the Duke of Devonshire, on the steps of the Legislature. Hobson's name was later commemorated on the panels of the Vimy Memorial on the inside side wall. In 1959 Florence Brown presented her late brother's medals to the Fort Malden National Historic Park, and they were later acquired by the Canadian War Museum in Ottawa. His medals included his Boer War medals, the Queen's South African Medal together with three clasps (1899–1902), and the King's South African Medal with two clasps (1901–02). Those awarded for his service in the First World War include a 1914–15 Star, BWM, and VM.

In 1995 in Valour Place beside the Sgt. F. Hobson Armoury in Cambridge (formerly the city of Galt), a Heritage Foundation plaque to Frederick Hobson was unveiled by his grandson Albert Hobson. The armoury holds a replica VC and a copy of his VC Citation. There is also a Cambridge street named after him. Other plaques to VCs in Galt were also unveiled — those to Lt. Samuel Lewis Honey and Capt. George Fraser Kerr. Another reminder of Frederick Hobson VC was the naming of the Simcoe branch of the Legion after him and finally but also in Simcoe there is a road named Frederick Hobson VC Drive.

Okill Massey Learmonth was born in St. Louis Road, Quebec, on February 22, 1894 (the 20th according to his attestation papers), the only son of William Learmonth and Martha Jane (*née* Richardson). His father was deputy lieutenant-governor of the province of Quebec and the family was Presbyterian. Learmonth was educated at St. George's School and Quebec High School. After he graduated he joined the Union Bank of Canada and worked later on Anticosti Island on a private estate. From there he joined the staff of the Provincial Treasurer's Department, part of the Canadian Government Service. The family address was 48 Murray Avenue, Quebec.

Prior to the war Learmonth served in the militia for two years with the 90th C.H. and enlisted in the Canadian Forces in Valcartier on September 29, 1914. He was five foot eight inches tall with blue eyes and fair hair. He was mobilized for service with the 84th Regiment Royal Rifles and left Canada for England on 3 October as a member of the 12th Battalion. After his arrival in England in mid-October he was transferred to the 2nd (Eastern Ontario) Battalion, with whom he was to serve with great distinction. After training in Salisbury Plain he left for France on February 6, 1915. Two weeks later he made a will in favour of his mother. In mid-June he was made a lance corporal. In the last few weeks of the year he was being treated for gonorrhea, and returned to his unit on December 25, 1915, after several weeks' treatment. Learmonth was awarded eight days' leave between April 10 and 18, 1916. On May 7 he was promoted to corporal and commissioned as second lieutenant on June 15. While serving on the Somme in mid June he was wounded by a gunshot to his hand and right leg. After a day in 7 Stationary Hospital he was invalided to England, where he became a patient in the Royal Free Hospital, Grays Inn Road, London, on June 15. On June 30 he went before the medical board, although his wounds were not yet healed. The form notes that Learmonth "is suffering from the strain of constant duty and this board recommend that he be permitted to spend his leave in Canada." He was therefore granted leave to Canada from June 30 until September 14 and, after a two-week extension, was awarded another medical board on September 28 at 86 the Strand in London. In the same month he suffered from a shrapnel wound to his right index finger, and after it had healed he was found to be fit for service. At the time he was attached to the 12th Reserve Battalion at Shorncliffe.

On October 9 he was made acting temporary lieutenant and on the 18th was taken on the strength of the 2nd Battalion once again and joined them in the field on the 20th. On December 10 he went on a Lewis gun course, returning a week later.

On April 15, 1917, he was promoted to acting major while in command of a company. In the following month he was allowed to go on leave to Paris for ten days from May 25. He was promoted to lieutenant and was awarded the MC, which was published in the *London Gazette* in mid-August 1917.

Finding himself the senior officer of his battalion present after reaching the final objective of an attack, he showed great skill in handling the situation, directing the consolidation and making daring personal reconnaissances under heavy fire. His resource and coolness were responsible for repulsing a strong counterattack, and he set a splendid example throughout.

On March 21, 1917, Learmonth made another will to replace the one made in favour of his mother earlier in the war. This time it was in favour of a nursing sister whom he might well have met during some of the spells he had spent in hospital. Her name was Irene Winifred Lamarche, and at one point she may have served in the Canadian Nursing Service at No. 8 Canadian General Hospital. The couple arranged to marry in Paris, but never did so as Learmonth visited the Consulate-General and postponed the ceremony. In his will he also set aside £10 to be awarded to his batman Pte. E.A. Insley. During 1917 Nursing Sister Lamarche was released on medical grounds and returned to North Bay.

On July 25, 1917, Learmonth was granted four days' leave. He was promoted to captain and acting major and won his posthumous VC at Hill 70 near Lens on August 18, 1917, dying of his wounds the following day at 7 CCS. He was buried four miles southeast of Bethune at Noeux-les-Mines Communal Cemetery, II, K, 9. Harry Brown VC is buried close by.

In The Victoria Cross 1856–1920 by Creagh and Humphris, an entry on Learmonth quotes a misleading newspaper account from November 9, 1917:

There is a poignant romance connected with the late Capt. Learmonth, of the Canadian Forces, who came from Quebec, and whose award of the Victoria Cross was in the *Gazette* published yesterday. Capt. Learmonth went to France as a ranker with the Canadians, and was promoted a non-com. on the field. He received his commission just over twelve months ago, and about the same time married Miss S.W. Tamarche [*sic*], who belonged to his province, and was attached to the Canadian Nursing Service. Mrs. Learmonth was invalided back to Canada some time back, and her gallant husband died of wounds three months ago.

Learmonth's next of kin was his mother, Martha Learmonth. She was sent her son's decorations, plaque, and scroll in 1921/2 at her home address at 65 Murray Avenue, Quebec City.

In 1920 Okill Learmonth was commemorated in Quebec City by the naming of Learmonth Avenue; with a painting by James Quinn at the Canadian War Museum; and at the Okill Learmonth Chapter of the Imperial Order of the Daughters of the Empire. His VC is with the Governor General's Foot Guards. Apart from the VC and MC his medals included the 1914–15 Star, BWM, and VM. He was the second man from the 2nd Battalion (Eastern Ontario) to win a VC in the war, Leo Clarke being the other.

R.H. HANNA and
F. KONOWAL

Lens, France, August 21–23

The first three days of the Canadian operations against Hill 70 and Lens yielded no fewer than four winners of the Victoria Cross, and before the operations were completed six days later there were to be two more, won by CSM Robert Hanna on the 21st and Acting/Cpl. Filip Konowal between the 22nd and 23rd.

Lt.-Gen. Currie, in charge of the Canadian operations at Hill 70 and Lens, was keen to clear up the situation in front of the town on the lower half of the southern slope of the hill. The plan was now to close in from the north and west by occupying the enemy front line on a 3,000-yard frontage from Eleu (on the Arras–Lens road) to the east of Cité St. Emile. The attack was scheduled to begin at 4:35 a.m. on the 21st and would be carried out by the 10th and 6th Brigades of the 4th and 2nd Divisions respectively.

However, the enemy was very active from 4:00 a.m. and dropped shells all along the front line and assembly area, causing casualties. The shelling then increased and the left flank of the 29th Battalion (6th Brigade) suffered particularly badly. In addition, the Canadian artillery was dropping short close to the junction of Commotion and Carfax Trenches. At 4:30 the enemy opened up a heavy bombardment with "fishtails" and trench mortars on the left flank of the 29th Battalion. The enemy also used what was described as "a square box bomb which on bursting emitted large flame and dense smoke."

It was still dark when the Canadian attack began, and it happened to coincide with a German counterattack. The 2nd Division found the enemy either advancing or about to advance. After fierce hand-to-hand fighting in the western environs of Lens the 10th Brigade retained most of its objectives. However, north of the Lens–Bethune road the 27th (City of Winnipeg) and 29th (Vancouver) battalions of the 6th Brigade had been caught by enemy artillery and became involved in difficult fighting in a triangle between the Lens–Bethune and Lens–La Bassée roads. The 29th Battalion, south of Cité St. Emilie, met a strong force of enemy infantry who were without rifles but were loaded with bombs, and were about to attack. In fifteen minutes, using their bayonets in the dim light and ground mist, the 29th forced back members of the 1st Foot Guard Regiment beyond the trench that was the battalion objective. The left company of the 29th Battalion, when held up, requested artillery support. Fighting for possession of Cinnabar Trench continued for the rest of the morning and it was during this fighting that 75631 CSM Robert Hanna of B Company won his VC.

When all the officers had been either killed or wounded, quoting Nicholson's book on the history of the Canadian Expeditionary Force 1914–18, he "assumed command and led a party against a German strongpoint that three assaults had failed to capture. He personally killed four of the defenders, seizing the position and silencing its machine-gun. He then made good a portion of Cinnabar Trench and held it against repeated counterattacks." The 2nd Division's war diary notes that Cinnabar Trench was continuously fought for and that Hanna's B Company held part of it with a block and ninety men, together with some members of A Company as well. The enemy had been pushed back to the section of Cinnabar Trench which was close to a water tower, and later they captured the right flank of the trench. Casualties were very heavy.

It appears from the 6th Canadian Brigade's war diary that "The enemy reinforced his line and continuously from C.T.s and houses from Cité du Grand Condé and houses along Auguste Cité road, men appeared to pour in from every direction." "Enemy snipers from positions in this area caused heavy casualties as well and the houses along the Auguste Cité road were full of machine guns."

Part of the account in the Skeffingtons' *Thirty Canadian VCs* notes that after Hanna had assumed command he saw

> ... that the crux of the position was a German post protected by a heavy wire and armed with a machine-gun. He collected a party of his men and led them against the post amid a hail of rifle and machine-gun fire. Rushing through the wire he bayoneted three of the Germans, brained a fourth, and overthrew the machine-gun. The redoubt was captured. The Germans arrived in force, and counterattacked. Hanna, who was now short of bombs, built a block. Again and again the enemy tried to rush his position; but he and his handful of men held it until they were relieved later that day ...

Despite Hanna's heroism the enemy still held nearly 500 yards of Cinnabar Trench and several other smaller trenches, which made the Canadian position in this sector precarious, and so the 27th and 29th later withdrew to their original line. The two battalions were relieved in the line on the night of August 22/23 by the 52nd Canadian Battalion, and then proceeded to Fosse 10.

Hanna's citation was published in the *London Gazette* of November 8, 1917:

> Robert Hanna, Company Sergeant-Major, No. 75361, 29th Battalion. Canadian Infantry. For most conspicuous bravery in attack, when his company met with most severe enemy resistance and all the company officers became casualties. A strong point, heavily protected by wire and held by a machine-gun, had beaten off three assaults of the company with heavy casualties. This Warrant Officer, under heavy machine-gun and rifle fire, coolly collected a party of men, and leading them against this strong point, rushed through the wire and personally bayoneted three of the enemy and brained the fourth, capturing the position and silencing the machine-gun.

This most courageous action displaying courage and personal bravery of the highest order at this most critical moment of the attack, was responsible for the capture of a most important tactical point, and but for his daring action and determined handling of a desperate situation, the attack would not have succeeded. Company Sergeant-Major Hanna's outstanding gallantry, personal courage and determined leading of his company is deserving of the highest possible award.

The sixth member of the Canadian Forces to win the VC in the Hill 70/Lens operations in August 1917 was Acting/Cpl. Filip Konowal, a Ukrainian in the Canadian Army. He was a member of the 47th Battalion (10th Brigade), 4th Division, and he gained his award over August 22/23. Some accounts say August 22/24, but he was being treated for his wounds on the 23rd at a CCS.

On August 21 three battalions of the Canadian 10th Brigade were also as deeply involved in the fighting as the 6th Brigade, and the brigade orders were to capture Green Crassier, a large heap of mine refuse between the railway station and the Lens Canal 350 yards beyond the 10th Brigade's right. The brigade gained and held on to all its objectives in the western environs of Lens after bitter hand-to-hand fighting in the ruined houses. One section on the left had not been captured by the 50th Battalion to the south of the Lens–Bethune road, where they had been caught in a barrage thirty minutes before zero hour at 4:35 a.m. and suffered a hundred casualties. Therefore, it became necessary to alter the movements of the assaulting companies. A feint attack, halfway to the objective at Aloof Trench, had put the enemy on the alert. Only small groups of men managed to reach the objective, which was the junction of the La Bassée–Bethune road. After retiring, most of these men did not reach their own lines.

The 46th Battalion in the centre had suffered heavily from German shelling the previous night, and their forward company officers became casualties and had to be replaced. In spite of this and the failure of the 50th Battalion, the 46th managed to reach its objective. They were now in Aconite Trench and positioned in a row of houses to its east. The 47th to their right had escaped the shelling but carried out bitter fighting all day through the Cité du Moulin toward the Lens–Arras road and Alpaca Trench, from which the enemy machine gunners took a heavy toll. By evening one company had reached the Arras road and by 10:00 p.m. all the battalion objectives had been gained. Advance posts were set up a little way out in front. It was during the extremely fierce fighting that Cpl. Konowal of the 47th Battalion was heavily involved in the mopping-up of cellars, craters, and machine guns, gaining the Victoria Cross for two specific deeds in the period August 22/23.

The battalion war diary notes:

> Later, during the day, we assisted the 44th Battalion on their attack on the Green Crassier by raiding a Machine Gun nest in a tunnel in the vicinity of Fosse 4. The party under leadership of Captain D.B. Wedon destroyed part of the tunnel with two ammonal charges, and Cpl. Konowal single-handed killed the entire Machine Gun crew and captured one gun, establishing a post in the tunnel, but was forced to withdraw late under heavy enemy counterattack, the enemy counterattacked our positions on the Lens–Arras Road no less than six times during the day ...

Konowal single-handedly took on two further attacks in which he killed several Germans, and on the following day, when involved in a minor operation, he destroyed another machine gun. All told he killed sixteen men. The battalion war diary noted in chilling fashion, "The situation made it unwise to take many prisoners."

Cpl. Konowal's deeds were written up in Skeffingtons' *Thirty Canadian VCs*, in which a colourful account is painted:

> The buildings about the Lens–Arras road proved difficult enough to clear. The main body of our troops had passed through and continued to the objectives beyond, but a couple of buildings still held Germans and German machine guns, and there was heavy fighting upon the rear of our advancing

men. Entering one of these houses Konowal searched for the Germans, and finding no living traces of their occupation, dropped daringly into the cellar. Three men fired at him as he landed, but this he escaped unharmed. Then ensued a sanguinary battle in the dark, a mêlée of rifle fire and bayonet, with the odds three to one. Finally the scuffling ceased and Konowal emerged into the daylight — he had bayoneted the whole crew of the gun! But this is all taken for granted in the business of mopping-up, and the corporal and his section continued their way along the road, every sense alert to locate the close rifle-crack that might betray the wily sniper. There was a large crater to the east of the road, and from the bodies of our good men before the edge it seemed obvious that a German machine-gun had been in position there. Halting his men Konowal advanced alone. Upon reaching the lip of the crater he saw seven Germans endeavouring to move the ubiquitous machine-gun into a dugout. He opened fire at once, killing three, and then, charging down upon them, accounted for the rest with the bayonet. These drastic methods rapidly concluded the clearing of their section of the line, and the corporal and his men moved on up to our new front, where the enemy was delivering heavy and incessant counterattacks. Heavy fighting continued throughout the night, and in the morning troops of the 44th Battalion, who were making an attack upon the Green Crassier, requested the aid of a party of the 47th in a raid upon a machine-gun emplacement in a tunnel about Fosse 4. Corpl. Konowal was an expert in this subterranean fighting, and his party succeeded in entering the tunnel. Two charges of ammonal, successfully exploded, somewhat demoralized the German garrison and then Konowal, dashing forward in the darkness with utter disregard of his own safety he had displayed all through the fighting, engaged the machine-gun crew with the bayonet, overcoming and killing them all. Altogether this good fighting man killed sixteen men in the two days of the actual battle, and continued his splendid work until he was severely wounded.

The 10th Brigade war diary notes than on the 23rd the 47th repelled several bombing attacks on their right flank and inflicted heavy losses on the enemy. On the 24th the battalion "consolidated on the right flank." On the 26th the 47th Battalion returned to Niagara Camp, Château de la Haie, for a "hot breakfast." Their casualties during August totalled 242 and those of the 10th Brigade were 1,081, although many of these were for the slightly wounded. The battalion had captured fifty-three Germans, including twelve wounded, as well as three machine guns and the destruction of two more.

The following extract also comes from *Thirty Canadian VCs*:

The fighting about Lens in Aug 1917 called for more individual dash and initiative on the part of the troops engaged than had been required before. The house-to-house fighting, the repeatedly isolated and difficult positions, the many knotty problems which required instant solution — all these combined to make leadership, whether of a section or a battalion, more arduous and responsible ...

Konowal's citation was published in the *London Gazette* of November 26, 1917:

Filip Konowal, Acting Corpl., 47th Infantry Battalion. Canadian Expeditionary Force. For most conspicuous bravery and leadership when in charge of a section in attack. His section had the difficult task of mopping up cellars, craters and machine-gun emplacements. Under his able direction all resistance was overcome successfully, and heavy casualties were inflicted on the enemy. In one cellar he himself bayoneted three enemy and attacked single-handed seven others in a crater, killing them all. On reaching the objective, a machine-gun was holding up the right flank, causing many casualties. Corpl. Konowal rushed forward and entered the emplacement, killed the crew, and brought the gun back to our lines. The next day he again attacked single-handed another machine-gun emplacement, killed three of the crew, and destroyed the gun and emplacement with explosives. This non-commissioned officer alone killed at least 16 of the enemy, and during the two days' actual fighting carried on continuously until severely wounded.

Robert Hill Hanna was the son of Robert, a farmer, and Sarah Hanna and was born in Aughnahoory, Kilkeel, County Down, Northern Ireland, on August 6, 1887. He was brought up as a Presbyterian and educated at Balliran's School. He emigrated to Canada in 1905 and settled in British Columbia to work in the forests as a lumberman.

At the age of twenty-eight, on November 7, 1914, Hanna enlisted in the Canadian Infantry, in Valcartier, Quebec. He was five foot three inches tall. He was posted as a private to the 29th (Vancouver) Battalion British Columbia Regiment, CEF, with a service number of 75361. Sarah, his mother, whose address was Aughnahoory, Kilkeel, Co. Down, was his next of kin.

On completing his training Hanna left for England at the end of August 1915, and from there embarked for France on September 17, arriving in Boulogne the following day. After six months' active service he caught German measles and was admitted to Number 7 General Hospital at Saint-Omer on April 1, 1916. He was discharged on the 13th. On June 24 he was slightly wounded on the cheek by shrapnel, from which he quickly recovered.

Judging from his promotions in rank Hanna was a good soldier. On August 20 he was appointed lance corporal and made up to sergeant in the field on October 9. Shortly afterward he was granted a week's leave of absence. On August 21, 1917, the day he won the Victoria Cross, he was appointed acting CSM, and six days later he was promoted in the field.

Hanna's winning of the VC led to his being considered for a commission, and he returned to England for officer training on September 22. Although he would of course not have known it at the time, he was never to return to active service in France.

Following the announcement of his VC in November he attended an investiture at Buckingham Palace on December 5. Other men who had also won the VC were present, including William Butler, Ernest Egerton, Filip Konowal, James Ockenden, Michael O'Rourke, and Ernest Pitcher. Hanna then returned to Northern Ireland for a brief visit to his family home at Kilkeel where he was given a hero's welcome. Returning to England for officer training, he was commissioned on January 26, 1918, and appointed a temporary lieutenant on February 12, 1918, serving with the 1st Canadian Reserve Battalion.

When the war was over he returned to Canada, sailing on May 10, 1919, and was demobilized in Ottawa on the 24th. Once home he returned to the lumber industry and managed a logging camp. In the 1930s he got married and had at least one son, and at the end of the decade he decided to give up managing a logging camp and return to farming. In June 1956 he attended the VC centenary celebrations in London, and according to one witness was seen to be "a great big, fine chap, always smiling." The following year he was one of seven VC pallbearers at the funeral of, and attended the requiem Mass for, the late Michael O'Rourke on December 10. Harcus Strachan was another of the VC pallbearers.

Hanna died in his eightieth year on June 15, 1967, at Mount Lehman, British Columbia, and was buried in the Masonic Cemetery, Burnaby Plot 49, Section C, Grave 2. The inscription on his gravestone is "Life's work well done." The grave gives his date of birth as 1887.

Hanna was a Mason and a member of the Orange Order, and is commemorated by a wooden bench at Helen's Tower, Thiepval, on the Somme, together with four other VC winners, members of the Orange Order. Apart from the VC he was entitled to a 1914-15 Star; BWM, VM, King George VI Coronation Medal (1937), and Queen Elizabeth II Coronation Medal (1953). They are in private hands and his personal sword is on the wall of Kilkeel Royal Canadian Legion Club. Together with Michael O'Rourke VC he has a plaque in his memory close to the former Loos battlefield in France.

Filip Konowal was born in Kutkiw, but in his service records it is noted as Kutcowce, Podolskoy. Many accounts say that he was born on September 15, 1888, but on his attestation papers he wrote down the date of March 25, 1887.

Konowal was the son of a Russian farmer, Miron, and his wife, Eudkice, and grew up as a Greek Catholic. On July 25, 1909, when he was twenty-two, he married Anna Stanka, of Russian parentage, and the couple had one daughter, Maria, born in 1909. Also in 1909 he was conscripted into the Imperial Russian Army and became an expert in close-quarter combat. He remained with the army for four years before emigrating to Canada, arriving in Vancouver in April 1913. He left his wife and daughter behind while he sought to make his fortune.

Seeking employment Konowal became a lumberjack in Western Canada before moving, after a few months, to Eastern Ontario, where he worked in the Ottawa Valley. On July 12, 1915, he enlisted in Ottawa, giving up his job as a labourer to join the Canadian Expeditionary Force as a member of the 77th Battalion. His service number was 144039. Also on his attestation papers Konowal spelt his Christian name as Filip and for the rest of his life was sometimes known as Philip and at other times Filip. At five foot six inches he was on the small side, with brown eyes and brown hair. He trained in Canada until leaving Halifax for Liverpool on June 19, 1916. At Bramshott Camp he was transferred to the 47th British Columbia Battalion on July 6 and made a lance corporal sixteen days later. On the same day he made his will in favour of his wife, although he had first written down his mother's name before changing his mind.

Konowal left for France on August 10, 1916, arriving there the following day. He took part in the Battle of the Somme and in mid-September became a casualty when a tendon in his right hand was severed. He spent a brief period in hospital, and when released on the 18th was attached to No. 4 Canadian Sanitary Section for five weeks.

In February 1917 he was in hospital again, this time for eight days with diarrhea and dysentery. On April 6 he was promoted to acting corporal, and took part in Vimy Ridge fighting. Later in the summer he went further north to the Loos area, where he was to win a VC on August 22/23. In carrying out his VC actions he was seriously wounded by gunshots to his face and neck and was admitted to 6th CCS on the 23rd and invalided back to hospital in England on the 27th. Once there he was taken to Beaufort Hospital, Bristol, before being transferred to a convalescent hospital in Wokingham, where he was a patient for ten days, being discharged on September 22.

On November 1 he was taken on the strength of the 16th Reserve Battalion and on December 6 he proceeded on command for duty with the Military Attaché in the Russian Embassy, London. On the 30th he was appointed to acting sergeant. A few days later he was decorated with his VC at Buckingham Palace on December 5, 1917, in the same investiture as six other holders of the VC: William Butler, Ernest Egerton, Robert Hanna, James Ockenden, Michael O'Rourke, and Ernest Pitcher.

On January 19 Konowal was granted permission to wear a Russian medal, the Cross of St. George, 4th Class. On February 15 he was transferred to the 1st Canadian Reserve Battalion. He returned from working at the Russian Embassy on July 8, 1918, and his rank reverted to corporal. For a short period from August 1 he served with the Canadian Forestry Corps. A few weeks later he left for Canada and was taken on the strength of the Canadian Siberian Expeditionary Force on September 18. He was appointed acting sergeant on October 1, 1918.

Leaving Vancouver on October 11, he disembarked at Vladivostok. In rank he reverted to corporal on December 16, 1918, after he had been absent without leave for less than twenty-four hours, and his pay was docked for a day. He served on command to Omsk from March 28 to June 1, 1919. He embarked for return to Canada on June 5, 1919, arriving on June 20.

When the Russian campaign was over he was demobilized (July 4, 1919) with the rank of corporal, but before he left the army he was medically examined and was clearly still affected by his wounds, both mental and physical. He suffered from partial paralysis of a facial muscle on the left side as a result of bullet wounds at Lens and his left hand was partly crippled as a result of wounds received at Ypres. He also suffered from fluttering of the heart and periodic pains on exertion.

He clearly had a "short fuse," for in Hull, Quebec, in the same month that he left the army, he killed a man, an Austrian called William Artich, who had either insulted Canada or its national flag. Using his war wounds as an excuse, Konowal pleaded insanity. Two years later he was brought before the Court of the King's Bench, Crown Side, District of Hull, and on April 20 the jury returned a verdict of "Not Guilty," accepting the plea of insanity as a result of war wounds. Nevertheless, the court ordered that he should be kept strictly in custody until the "pleasure of the Lieutenant-Governor was known." There was no other indictment against him.

Altogether Konowal spent nine years in various hospitals, including Saint-Jean-de-Dieu Hospital in Quebec, and from around 1927 he was confined in the hospital for the criminally insane in Bordeaux, Quebec. On release he found it very difficult to get employment, but he was able to enlist as one of the Governor General's Foot Guards in Ottawa in 1928. He was well enough to travel to London in 1929 for the House of Lords' dinner in November. He was unemployed in the early 1930s but in 1936 he did manage to get a job in the Canadian House of Commons as a junior caretaker, probably owing to the assistance of Milton Gregg VC, who was sergeant-at-arms from 1934 to 1944. One of his duties was to keep the floor of the Hall of Fame clean, and at this time he was spotted by Prime Minister William Mackenzie King. He was then promoted and allowed to take charge of Room 16, the prime minister's office.

Konowal's first wife, Anna, died of starvation in the Ukraine and his daughter disappeared in Russia, probably dying in a Soviet work camp, and he later married a widow, Juliette Leduc-Auger, in 1934. In 1939 he was invited to attend a garden party for King George VI and Queen Elizabeth, when the royal couple were visiting Canada. The party took place at the Rideau Hall in Ottawa, and the king shook hands with Konowal during the dedication of the National War Memorial.

After the end of the Second World War, when he was too old

to serve, Konowal became a member of the Quebec branch of the Canadian Legion of the British Empire Service in December 1945. In 1953 the Toronto branch of the Royal Canadian Legion number 360 invited him to be their patron. This honour was confirmed during a Remembrance Day dinner held on 7 November in Toronto. The Royal Canadian Legion also established a scholarship in his memory toward the cost of a grant to the Royal Military College of Canada.

When the VC centenary celebrations in London were being planned, Konowal knew that he would be unable to raise the amount of money needed for the trip. In order to assist with his expenses he asked the Ukrainian branches to contribute, despite the Ottawa War Museum saying that they would help with his transport costs. He duly attended the VC centenary celebrations, which included a tea party at Westminster Hall on June 25, hosted by the prime minister, Sir Anthony Eden, the Hyde Park review on the 26th and the subsequent garden party at Marlborough House.

Back once more in Canada, Konowal continued with his cleaning job at the House of Commons and his income was also helped by a small disability allowance. When asked by a reporter of the *Ottawa Citizen* about his job as a janitor he replied, "I mopped overseas with a rifle, and here I must mop up with a mop." Of his VC he remarked, "I was so fed up standing in the trench with water to my waist that I said the hell with it and started after the German Army. My captain tried to shoot me because he figured I was deserting."

Konowal, who in his later years must have been "a bit of a character," died in Ottawa on June 3, 1959, in the Veterans Pavilion, Civic Hospital, Ottawa. He was given a funeral with full military honours, which took place at St. John the Baptist Ukrainian Catholic Church. He was buried in Lot 502, Section A, at Notre Dame Cemetery in Ottawa. His widow died in 1987 and is buried beside him. Initially the grave was marked with a small tablet, and thirty-six years later this was replaced by a standard Commonwealth War Graves stone at a wreath-laying ceremony on December 6, 1995.

On Konowal's death his decorations, including two Coronation Medals, were entrusted to a Ukrainian Canadian Veteran, Mr. G.R. Bohdan Panchuk, who served with the RCAF in the Second World War and became a leading light in the Ukrainian Canadian

Veterans' Association. It appeared that the medals were later acquired by the Canadian War Museum in Ottawa. Since his death at least five historical plaques have been set up in the Ukrainian's memory, mostly in the mid-nineties: one in Ottawa at Cartier Square, a second at the Drill Hall of the Governor General's Foot Guards (July 15, 1996), a third at the Royal Canadian Legion Branch 360 in Toronto on Queen Street West (August 21, 1996) (the branch also sponsored a small booklet on Konowal's life, in three languages), and a fourth in the armoury of the Royal Westminster Regiment, New Westminster, British Columbia (1997). This regiment emerged from the 47th Battalion. The plaques are written in English, French, and Ukrainian. A further tribute to his memory was the issue of a new 46 cent postage stamp featuring his portrait, issued in July 2000.

These commemorative memorials were not confined to Canada, as on August 21, 2000, a plaque and statue of Konowal (prepared by Petro Kulyk) was unveiled in his home village of Kutkiw in Ukraine. In addition a nine-foot-high bust, as well as a trilingual plaque commemorating his bravery, was unveiled. A dual ceremony took place in Ottawa, where he was posthumously awarded the National Council of Veteran Associations Order of Merit, which was presented to Claudette Wright, his grand-daughter. The Canadian War Museum in Ottawa has a painting of Konowal and should still have his medals, which at one point were mislaid. The story is that the museum bought them from a dealer in 1969 and displayed them until 1972, and between 1972 and 1974 they went missing. In fact, Konowal's VC was stolen and later rediscovered in an antique shop when an approach to an auction house was made in 2004. The Police recovered it and it was back on display in the Canadian War Museum on August 23, 2004. His medal entitlement also includes the BWM, VM.King George VI Coronation Medal (1937), Queen Elizabeth II Coronation Medal (1953), and Cross of Saint George (4th Class (Russia)).

The Ukrainian community contributed a great number of men to the Canadian Expeditionary Force in the First World War, and probably feel that this fact has been insufficiently acknowledged. In this context Filip Konowal VC has become a great hero to the community.

C.P.J. O'KELLY, T.W. HOLMES, and R. SHANKLAND

Wolf Copse and Bellevue Spur, October 26

By mid-October the brooding spectre of Bellevue Spur, with its seemingly impregnable fortifications, hung like a dark, menacing cloud over Haig's diminishing ambitions. A cordon of pillboxes, varying in shape and size and protected by thickets of barbed wire, straddled the slight rise, less than 1,500 yards from the outskirts of Passchendaele. Twice in the space of three days these grim defences, forming part of the enemy's Flanders I barrier, had dealt crushing blows to British hopes. Following the repulse of the New Zealand Division and the consequent defeat of the Australians on October 12, Haig's misguided optimism had finally given way to realism. In turning to the Canadian Corps to salvage something from the wreckage of his plans, he lowered his sights. The talk was no longer of breakthroughs but of securing a defensible winter position and diverting attention away from new plans for an armoured strike at Cambrai. Thus was a campaign born of extravagant designs subverted into little more than a costly distraction.

The Canadians arrived from the Lens sector to find an army wallowing in mud. Almost half the area in front of Passchendaele was either under water or reduced to swamp. The Ravebeek valley, cutting through the British line below Bellevue, was all but impenetrable. But at least Gen. Sir Arthur Currie, GOC Canadian Corps, was given time to prepare. As planked roads stretched across the wasteland, the artillery ranged with far greater accuracy on the notorious barbed-wire entanglements strung across the spur. By October 25 clearer weather revealed gaps torn in the wire, but as the infantrymen filed toward their jumping-off position, observers noted bleakly that the pillboxes lining the crest were still largely intact.

The Canadian plan was reminiscent of Plumer's original approach. Currie intended to carry Passchendaele in three bounds, each attack separated by at least three days. In the first, the Canadian 4th Division was to advance south of the flooded Ravebeck valley with the 3rd Division employing two brigades against Bellevue and Wallemollen spurs.

Once again the weather proved an implacable foe. The attack was launched at 5:40 a.m. on October 26 in driving rain. The northern assault was led by the 4th Canadian Mounted Rifles of the 8th Brigade, the 43rd Battalion (Cameron Highlanders of Canada), and the 58th Battalion, both of the 9th Brigade. At first all appeared to go well. Despite losing a number of men to enemy shells on the start line, the Canadians made ground quickly over the broken wire. The 43rd's war diarist recorded: "When dawn broke sufficiently our men could be clearly seen moving slowly over the skyline and round the two formidable-looking pillboxes on the crest of the ridge overlooking Bn. HQ."

The 4th CMR, advancing on the left, enjoyed similar success. With C and D companies leading and A and B companies in close support, the Canadians soon overcame the first belt of blockhouses. Their objectives were Woodland Copse and Source Farm, but having battled with bomb and bayonet through the concentrated fire sweeping across the lower slopes they suffered a serious check northeast of Wolf Copse. Fire from two machine guns either side of a pillbox thinned their ranks, forcing them to seek cover. A Company had overtaken D Company, and mixed parties attempted to rush the position, although none got closer than fifty yards. Suddenly, nineteen-year-old Pte. Tommy Holmes, described as a "frail, delicate youth with a contagious smile," leapt from a shell hole and headed for the pillbox. The unit historian recorded:

Before those around him realized what he was about to do [he] rushed for-ward and tossed a bomb so accurately into the trench of the machine-gun crew that they and their guns were put out of action. He then returned to his companions for more bombs, which by this time were getting scarce, but he succeeded in getting one from Pte. Dunphy. Again he dashed for-ward, this time going directly up to the pillbox, and threw his bomb into the entrance where it exploded; those who were not killed or wounded came out and surrendered.

Nineteen prisoners were taken and an officer who observed the action sent a runner forward to identify the youngster so that he could recommend him for a bravery award. Before the runner returned the officer was killed, but fortunately there were other witnesses to ensure that Holmes' courage did not go unrecognized. His daring had relieved a critical situation but, even as the Canadian riflemen pressed on, a greater disaster threatened to overwhelm 9th Brigade's operation.

By 7:00 a.m. early optimism had evaporated. Through the rain and drifting smoke officers at 43rd Battalion HQ at Waterloo Farm could see that the 58th Battalion's attack had stalled on the right. Wounded began drifting back followed by the remainder of the battalion, fleeing in some disorder back to the original start line. For a while chaos reigned across the 9th Brigade front. Of most concern was the fate of the Canadian Highlanders. Since dawn, when groups of men were seen pushing on toward the crest, little definite news had been received. It was known that all of the officers in B and C companies, leading the attack, were out of action, but no one knew the whereabouts of D Company or its two senior officers Capt. D.A. Galt and Lt. Bob Shankland DCM. As close supports, it was their job to capture and consolidate the final objective, for which purpose they had the assistance of a small party of the 9th Canadian Machine-Gun Company. Equally uncertain was the location of A Company, tasked with holding the support line.

Each assault battalion had a company of the 52nd Battalion in reserve, and it was decided to push them forward while runners searched for the "missing" companies. A Company was soon found on the left, held up by an enemy trench 250 yards beyond two pillboxes. But by 9:30 a.m. there was still no word of D Company. At that moment, another panic, this time among the 52nd's companies, saw large numbers of Canadians streaming back. Some rallied near the start line, but others did not stop until they reached 43rd Battalion HQ across the Ravebeek. Worse news followed. Due to the precipitate retirement, the 4th CMR had been forced to pull back.

It was at this bleak moment, around 10:00 a.m., that Lt. Shankland, who had been virtually given up as dead, made a startling appearance at Battalion HQ. His coat was torn with bullets and spattered with mud. No stage entrance could have been more dramatic. And the news he brought with him was no less electrifying. The 43rd diarist noted:

Lt. Shankland reported ... that he was holding the ridge about 40yd forward of the two pillboxes with about forty men including men of the 9th MG Company with two of their guns which were in action. He stated that provided his ammunition held out he could hold his position against any attack as he had already dispersed one counterattack which was forming up in the low ground 500yd forward on his front. He did not know where Capt. Galt, his Company Commander, was as he had last seen him during the attack attempting with 5 ORs to capture a strongpoint on the right of the position he now held, suffering considerable annoyance from snipers half left on his frontage and also from the direction of the strongpoint Capt. Galt had tried to capture. His men were, however, using their rifles with great effect upon isolated Germans who were seen going back and also along with the Brigade guns against the enemy assembling.

What he neglected to say was that he had been the leading figure in the brave stand. After silencing two pillboxes and capturing two half-completed strongpoints, only twenty men and one machine gun had made it on to the crest. It was Shankland, joining them shortly afterward, who inspired them to cling on. Gradually more men trickled forward in support, including another machine-gun detachment that helped them beat off a flank attack. One machine gun was knocked out, but every enemy attack was driven off. Their defiance was typified by the machine-gun subaltern whom Shankland left in command while he made his perilous dash to HQ to plead for reinforcements. According to Shankland, Lt. Ellis "though wounded ... refused to go out while his guns remained in action."

News of the resolute defence by a few men on Bellevue Spur marked the turning point in Canadian fortunes, revitalizing the attack just as it seemed that a repetition of the previous reverses was inevitable. Fresh orders were issued. A makeshift company, including many men who had fled back to Battalion HQ, was led back up the slope to form a defensive flank on the right of Shankland's isolated party. At the same time, another company of the 52nd Battalion was pushed forward to fill the gap between the Canadian Highlanders and the 4th CMRs. This was A Company, commanded by Acting Capt. Christopher O'Kelly MC, and with his arrival the battle entered its final decisive phase.

O'Kelly's company had begun the day in brigade reserve at Abraham Heights. At 8:30 a.m., amid alarming reports of the "reverse" suffered by the 43rd and 58th battalions, A and B companies of the 52nd Battalion, had been warned to "hold themselves in readiness to move at a moment's notice." That order arrived an hour later, O'Kelly's men advancing to Waterloo Farm to await further instructions. They were still there when Shankland burst in.

By 11:30 a.m. O'Kelly's company was moving up the bare, northern slopes, through an enemy barrage pounding the spur. They advanced without artillery support and without knowing what opposition faced them. All they knew was that Shankland's party was pinned down in front of enemy blockhouses and totally exposed on both flanks. In fact, the slopes were freckled with pillboxes. Some were loopholed while others were simply concrete shells with platforms built over the doorways, enabling machine gunners to fire over the top. O'Kelly lost a few men to these and to the shelling, but the majority swept over the brow to find an enemy attack threatening the Highlanders' left flank. Scarcely pausing, O'Kelly led his company in a charge that drove the enemy off with heavy loss. But any elation was short-lived as they quickly became the target for a hail of fire from the pillboxes confronting Shankland's party.

The struggle resolved itself into a series of small-scale actions as O'Kelly led his men against one pillbox after another. These posts housed anything up to five machine guns and thirty or more men, supported by riflemen and bombers. O'Kelly's method of attack was simple and effective. It involved edging to within rifle-grenade range, creating a diversion by firing off a shower of grenades and peppering it with machine-gun fire while a small party, often only three or four strong, made a dash for the blind side from where they tossed in bombs as a signal for the place to be rushed. O'Kelly had already cleared two pillboxes by noon when B Company, led by Lt. H.M. Grant MC, arrived to join the attack. By then Shankland himself, although slightly wounded in the face and neck, had rejoined his men. Two battalion scouts who accompanied him later returned with three prisoners, including a German officer who spoke good English. He explained that he had expected to find his company on the ridge and had simply blundered into the Canadian position. An incongruous interlude in the midst of battle ended with him nonchalantly pulling out a silver case and lighting a cigarette.

Across the front, the impetus of the 52nd proved irresistible. The two companies "took out" nine pillboxes and the fortified Bellevue Farm in succession, capturing almost 200 officers and men in the process. O'Kelly's men's share was six pillboxes, one hundred prisoners, and ten machine guns. One unexpected result of the advance was the sudden re-emergence of Capt. Galt, Shankland's company commander, who had been missing since early in the day. It transpired he had led a party into an enemy strongpoint only to find their path blocked by a tangle of wire shielding a sniper's nest. As they attempted to return whence they came, heavy machine-gun fire killed two men and forced the remainder to shelter in a shell hole until liberated by the 52nd's attack. His return, at around 1:25 p.m., enabled the exhausted Shankland to retire and have his wounds dressed.

The main battle was over but sporadic fighting continued. During the afternoon O'Kelly's men were instrumental in defeating an enemy counterattack, described as "heavy" in his VC citation and "faint" by the 52nd's war diarist. As darkness fell, the offensively minded O'Kelly led his men in another foray, during which he captured an enemy raiding party consisting of an officer, ten men, and a machine gun, thus swelling the number of prisoners taken by the 52nd to 275, together with twenty-one machine guns. By 7:25 p.m., despite shelling and minor clashes across the ridge, it was clear that the Canadians were there to stay. Capt. Galt reported: "The situation looks OK as far as I can judge. The 52nd are 100yd in front of us and in fair strength. It has to be regretted we did not get further but it was not possible ... conditions considered we are OK."

The 3rd Division had advanced an average of 500 yards, driving the enemy from the Flanders I Line between the Ravebeek and Wolf Copse. But the price of establishing a foothold on the main Passchendaele ridge had been dear. By the end of October 26 the 4th CMR had only four officers out of twenty-one unhurt. In all, the unit lost 321 officers and men killed, wounded, missing, or evacuated suffering from exposure. The 43rd, meanwhile, sustained 339 casualties, and their wounded were still being recovered from the battlefield two days later.

Perhaps in atonement for this, as well as in recognition of the great courage displayed, honours were distributed with a degree of largesse unusual among Commonwealth forces. The 43rd received no fewer than thirty-two gallantry awards, while the 4th CMR's list of twenty-one honours included ten Distinguished Conduct Medals, surely something of a record for a single action. The decorations were headed by three Victoria Crosses. Bob Shankland's was the first to be announced, on December 18. It prompted a wave of congratulatory letters, including one from a chaplain who had been present during the fighting. George Taylor informed Shankland's father: "Everyone who knows agrees that the man who was the means of saving the day and bringing in a brilliant victory was your son ... We all agree that the VC should be given him."

Three weeks later the *London Gazette* of January 11 announced the awards to No. 838301 Pte. Thomas Holmes and Lt. (Acting Captain) Christopher O'Kelly "for most conspicuous bravery."

A college student at the outbreak of war, Christopher Patrick John O'Kelly was only twenty-one when he won his Victoria Cross. It was the high point of a life that promised much yet ended in tragedy three days short of his twenty-seventh birthday.

Born in Winnipeg, Manitoba, on November 18, 1895, he was the son of Christopher and Cecilia O'Kelly, who lived on Yale Avenue. Educated at public schools in Winnipeg, Chris O'Kelly was an undergraduate at St. John's College when he decided break his studies to enlist on February 22, 1916. He joined the 144th Battalion (Winnipeg Rifles), known as the Little Black Devils, and proceeded overseas as a lieutenant with his unit on September 18, 1916. Shortly after arriving in Liverpool on the 26th, he was transferred from the 144th, then being used as a reinforcement unit, to the 52nd Battalion. He reached the trenches in March 1917, and soon made a name for himself as a daring leader with D Company.

In the aftermath of the Vimy operations, O'Kelly, who was commanding No. 9 Platoon in C Company, played a distinguished part in a minor action in the Avion-Mericourt sector. In the early hours of June 28, the 52nd launched an attack on Avion Trench. Dashing across no man's land, they were confronted by uncut wire and a machine-gun post. Covered by a Lewis gunner, the men scrambled into the trench, with O'Kelly leading a bombing section against the gun. Capt. E.R.C. Wilcox, C Company commander, recorded:

As [O'Kelly] climbed the eastern side of Toronto Road he threw a bomb. One of the gun crew threw a stick bomb at practically the same moment ... Lt. O'Kelly's bomb exploding [*sic*] killed the machine-gun crew. He at once shouldered the gun and brought it in and superintended placing the block.

The enemy grenade fatally wounded one of O'Kelly's men, but he escaped unharmed to receive the Military Cross (*London Gazette*, September 26, 1917). Promoted acting captain on August 28 and given command of A Company, O'Kelly seemed destined for glory, provided he lived long enough. Fortune continued to smile on him and he came through his greatest test on Bellevue Spur without injury. But the fighting had left some scars: Capt. Theodore Roberts of the Canadian War Records Department, who met him shortly after the 52nd came out of the line, subsequently edited a volume on his country's VC winners, in which he noted: "He was very young. His manner was quiet and somewhat grim, as if he had looked too closely into a hundred faces of death." Unaware that he had been put up for the VC, O'Kelly applied for leave to return home on account of his mother falling seriously ill. This was granted, but not before he had been offered and had declined a staff appointment.

One of ten Winnipeggers to win the VC in the First World War, he was the first to make it home, his return on April 9, 1918, sparking huge celebrations. Civic and military dignitaries met him at the Canadian Pacific Railway depot and thousands lined the streets to cheer him as a procession of automobiles and bands made for the Fort Garry Hotel and a private reception. Five days later O'Kelly, described as a "rather retiring, modest youth," was feted at the Columbus Hall in a gathering organized by the city's Catholic Club.

Returning to England in the summer, he headed back to France in August and rejoined the 52nd Battalion on September 8, in the midst of the Allies' war-winning offensive. Barely three weeks later, on September 28, he was badly wounded leading A Company in an attack toward the heavily fortified Canal du Nord, near Cambrai. Hit in the left groin by machine-gun fire, he was unable to move and, while "lying out," was injured again by shrapnel in the left leg. Initially treated at 30 Casualty Clearing Station, he was transferred to 20 General Hospital before being evacuated to the Prince of Wales' Hospital in Marylebone Road, London. His wounds healed quickly and he moved to a convalescence hospital in Matlock Bath three days before the end of the war. Transferred to the 18th (Reserve) Battalion on November 19, his recovery was almost complete when he suffered a setback. While out riding on Boxing Day, his horse slipped and fell on an icy road, crushing his right foot and necessitating further medical treatment. It was not until March 17, 1919, that he was fit enough to embark on the SS *Olympic* bound for Canada and demobilization.

In 1921 O'Kelly rejoined the Winnipeg Rifles, a militia unit, as a major. The following autumn, together with a business partner, he ventured to Lac Seul in northern Ontario to prospect some gold-mining sites. They were last seen alive on November 18, 1922, taking their motor-powered canoe across the lake. That day a storm blew up and when it was over, material from the boat was washed ashore. Nothing more of the two men was seen until the spring thaw released the body of O'Kelly's companion. There was no sign of the ill starred war hero.

A wooden cross was raised on Goose Island in 1927, close to where he disappeared. Submerged when a dam was built at Lower Ear Falls, it was eventually recovered ten years later and presented to the local branch of the Royal Canadian Legion. To mark the forty-third anniversary of his death, a provincial plaque was unveiled at the Legion Hall in Red Lake, Ontario, in honour of Chris O'Kelly VC, MC. His decorations are at the Canadian War Museum in Ottawa and also include the British War Medal (1914–20) and Victory Medal (1914–19).

At the time of his award Thomas William Holmes was the youngest winner of the Victoria Cross in the Canadian forces. He was born in Montreal, Quebec, on August 17, 1898, the second son of John and Edith Scarfe Holmes, who originally came from Owen Sound, Ontario. In 1903, after six years in Montreal, the Holmes family returned to Owen Sound. Tommy Holmes was then aged four and he went on to attend several schools, the last years of his education being spent at Ryerson School, where he was remembered for his high-spirited daring.

He was working as a poulterer on a farm at Annan when he decided to enlist in the 147th Battalion, a Grey County unit, on December 12, 1915. Holmes was only seventeen, and looked even younger, but he advanced his age by a year and was accepted. His elder brother, Roy, was serving with the 58th Battalion at the time. The 147th, known as the 1st Grey Battalion, trained at Niagara and Camp Borden. A diptheria outbreak delayed their passage overseas and they eventually arrived in England on November 20, 1916. Transferred initially to the 8th Reserve Battalion, Holmes was sent as part of a draft to the 4th Canadian Mounted Rifles. Two months after arriving in France, he went into action with his machine-gun section at Vimy Ridge. Two days later, on April 11, 1917, he was wounded in the left arm. Evacuated to England, he met his brother who had been blinded in one eye at Sanctuary Wood the previous June and was working at Hastings Hospital.

After a spell with the 8th Reserve Battalion at Shorncliffe, Holmes rejoined his unit in October, shortly before the Canadian Corps' introduction to the Passchendaele campaign. In letters home Holmes made no mention of his gallantry. His only reference came in a note to his parents in December when he said some of his comrades had told him he had been recommended for "a decoration."

Holmes was the second Owen Sounder to be awarded the Victoria Cross, the first being the legendary Canadian air ace, Billy Bishop. Discharged at the end of the war as a sergeant, he arrived home to a hero's welcome in the spring of 1919. Crowds turned out to greet him and a round of parades, receptions, and speeches followed. Not long afterward, he left Owen Sound for Toronto, where for the next fourteen years he worked as a chauffeur for the Harbour Commission. The good fortune that marked his war career appeared to desert him in peacetime. In 1935 a burglar ransacked his Toronto home and stole his prized VC. It was never recovered and a replacement was sent to him. The theft was not his only problem. The months spent in the trenches had undermined his health. It emerged that the teenage hero, whose boyish grin had provided Canadians with one of their abiding images of the conflict, had contracted tuberculosis. Only after a fight with several federal government departments, however, was he granted a pension. Holmes overcame his bout of TB only to be stricken by cancer. Ill health had already forced him to quit his job, and for the last ten years of his life he fought a losing battle against the disease. He died in Toronto on January 4, 1950, and was buried in Greenwood Cemetery, Owen Sound. The inscription on his headstone simply reads "Rest in Peace."

Nine years later his sister, Annie King, unveiled a commemorative plaque in Queen's Park, Owen Sound. However, the chequered history of Holmes' VC continued even after his death. In August 1978 the replacement cross that had been presented to the Owen Sound Branch of the Royal Canadian Legion by his daughter was stolen. This theft, however, at least had a happy ending as Tommy

Holmes' second VC minus a piece of its ribbon was recovered. It is once more on display in Owen Sound Royal Canadian Legion. Holmes's other medals incuded the BWM, VM, and King George VI Coronation Medal (1937).

In memory of Thomas Holmes one of Ontario's Historical Plaque was erected in Owen Sound, in a park on the northeast corner of 1st Avenue West and 8th Street West.

Robert Shankland was born at 68 Church Street, Ayr, Scotland, on October 10, 1887, the only son of William Shankland, a railway guard who had spent forty years working for the Glasgow & South Western Railway Company. Educated at Smith's Institution and Russell Street School, Ayr, he enjoyed a distinguished academic record, winning a string of medals. A member of the 2nd Ayr (Parish Church) Company, of the Boys' Brigade, he spent two years in John T. Scott's accountant's office in Newmarket Street before following his father into the G&SW Railway Company, working as a clerk in the stationmaster's office at Ayr. At the time, he was living with his parents, but, like many adventurous young Scots in the early years of the century, he sought wider horizons. In 1911 he decided to quit his job and seek his fortune in Canada.

He settled in Winnipeg, joined the Crescent Creamery Company, and rapidly worked his way up to assistant cashier. A popular figure, Bob Shankland was a keen sportsman, playing baseball for the works' team and serving as secretary for the provincial soccer champions. When war broke out, he was living at 733 Pine Street, where his fellow residents included two more future winners of the Victoria Cross, Frederick William Hall and Leo Clarke.

Shankland enlisted as a private (No. 420933) in the 43rd Battalion (Cameron Highlanders of Canada) on December 18, 1914. Initially, his skills as a bookkeeper and organizer marked him down for deskbound duties and he was made orderly sergeant while the unit was quartered at the city's Minto Street barracks. The 43rd sailed for

England in June 1915, but it was not until the following February that Shankland, still a sergeant, arrived at the front. Promotion followed swiftly. He was made company sergeant-major and was serving as acting regimental sergeant-major at Sanctuary Wood in June 1916 when he earned the Distinguished Conduct Medal (*London Gazette*, August 19, 1916). The citation read: "For conspicuous gallantry in volunteering to lead a party of stretcher-bearers, under very heavy shellfire, and bringing in some wounded and partially buried men. His courage and devotion were most marked."

He went through the bitter fighting on the Somme and during the autumn was commissioned a second lieutenant in the 43rd. The following year he saw service at Vimy Ridge. Although slightly wounded during his unit's epic struggle on Bellevue Spur during which he won his VC, Shankland enjoyed numerous narrow escapes. On one occasion a bullet struck a tin box of fudge in his breast pocket before emerging through the bottom without touching him.

He was on leave, staying with his parents in Ayr, when his VC was announced. Naturally quiet and retiring, he had neither written nor spoken of his actions. The only hint his parents had of his bravery was from the Canadian chaplain, George Taylor. When confronted with the chaplain's comments, however, he dismissed them, saying "Ministers can write anything." A journalist who visited Shankland's parents received much the same response. His mother recalled how his "ire had been roused" when his photograph appeared in the press following his award of the DCM. "There's to be no more advertisement, he says," declared Mrs. Shankland, "and if he was here just now you would get nothing out of him."

Reluctant hero or not, Ayr's first VC winner, remembered by his former workmates at the railway station as "a game yin," could not entirely escape the attentions of the local citizenry. On December 31, in front of a packed town hall chamber bedecked with flags, the "Auld Toun" conferred on him the honour of becoming the youngest Freeman of the Royal Burgh. At the same ceremony, he was presented with a gold wristwatch by the Boys' Brigade Company in which he had served. In a modest reply, he studiously avoided any mention of his actions except to note, with a smile, that he had learned more about his fight on Bellevue Spur during the civic reception than he ever knew before.

By the end of the war he had been promoted captain but before returning to Canada he had one last appointment in Scotland — his wedding. In April 1920 the local press in Ayr proudly announced that Capt. Robert Shankland VC, DCM, had married Anna Stobo Haining, daughter of the stationmaster at Prestwick, in St. Nicholas' parish church, Prestwick, with hundreds of people waiting outside to catch a glimpse of the couple. They sailed for Canada on May 1. The couple had two sons, and during the interwar years Bob Shankland served as secretary-manager with a number of Winnipeg firms.

Five years after his return, the city staged its own unique tribute. In a series of articles on Canadian VC winners, Carolyn Cornell, librarian at the *Winnipeg Tribune*, suggested that in recognition of the honour won by three former residents of Pine Street, the road should be renamed. The Women's Canadian Club of Winnipeg agreed and after much lobbying the city council decided in favour of the new name — Valour Road. A plaque displayed on a lamppost in the street paid tribute to Fred Hall, Leo Clarke, and Bob Shankland. Eighty years later, the gallant triumvirate were further honoured by the opening of Valour Plaza, with a monument in the shape of the Victoria Cross as its centrepiece, five blocks north of where they lived.

By 1939 Shankland had moved to Vancouver where, in June, he was one of six VC holders presented to King George VI and Queen Elizabeth during their Canadian tour. They were destined to meet again four years later in England, by which time Shankland would be back in uniform.

At the outbreak of the Second World War, Shankland, by then aged fifty-one, re-enlisted in the Queen's Own Cameron Highlanders of Canada. Promoted major in January 1940, he was subsequently appointed camp commandant of the Canadian HQ in England with the rank of lieutenant-colonel. However, he was denied the chance to serve in France on account of his age. In 1946 he left the army to take a post as secretary of a securities corporation in Vancouver. Ten years later Shankland, who had been a widower for four years, returned to Britain to attend the Victoria Cross centenary celebrations in Hyde Park.

Bob Shankland died on January 20, 1968, in Shaughnessy

Hospital, Vancouver. His body was cremated and his ashes scattered in the grounds of Mountain View Cemetery. To the very end, he sought to play down his role in the capture of Bellevue Spur. When pushed on the subject during a visit to his hometown of Ayr, he simply remarked: "All I did was play poker with the Hun!" That others knew better was evidenced in the C\$240,000 paid by the Canadian War Museum in May 2009 to ensure his outstanding medal group was saved for the nation as a lasting memorial to courage in adversity. Apart from the VC and DCM they include the British War Medal (1914–20), Victory Medal (1914–20), Defence Medal (1939–45), Canadian Volunteer Service Medal (1939–45), plus Overseas Clasp War Medal (1939–45), King George VI Coronation Medal (1937), and Queen Elizabeth II Coronation Medal (1953). His battlefield blouse and a set of his decorations as miniatures are on display in the Queens' Own Cameron Highlanders Museum in Minto Armoury, Winnipeg.

H. MCKENZIE, C.J. KINROSS, and G.H. MULLIN

Near Furst Farm and Meetcheele Spur, October 30

It was a clear moonlit night and as the freezing wind whipped across the exposed heights of Bellevue Spur shadowy figures lay huddled, numb with cold, waiting for the first grey streaks of dawn and the roar of heavy artillery that would send them on their way. Near Furst Farm, two green flares shot into the sky. Shells had been falling among the leading companies of the Princess Patricia's Canadian Light Infantry and the 49th Edmontons most of the night, but now the bombardment grew more intense. It was a little after 4:30 a.m. on October 30, the day selected by General Currie for the second stage of his advance on Passchendaele.

The men of the 7th Brigade were taking over where the 9th Brigade had left off. The Princess Pats, on the right, and the 49th, on the left, were to clear the pillboxes scattered across the narrow spur, carrying the line beyond Meetcheele Spur and Furst Farm to the northwestern fringes of Passchendaele, an advance varying in depth from 850 to 1,100 yards. On their left, the 5th Canadian Mounted Rifles (8th Brigade) were to seize the strongpoints from Source Farm to Vine Cottage, thus securing a foothold on Goudberg Spur.

Day broke cold and stormy. The gusting wind had done little to dry the drenched ground. According to Lt.-Col. Agar Adamson, the Princess Pats' CO, although it did not rain heavily in the early morning "it might just as well as done so far as the ground was concerned." Not for the first time, the British barrage scheduled for 5:50 a.m. was less than effective. Lt.-Col. R.H. Palmer, commanding the 49th Edmontons, described it as "very light" and inaccurate with "shorts" falling on his right flank. Worse still, he complained, it was two minutes early, an error that had tragic consequences for the men of B and C companies. Even before they clambered out of their shell holes, a counter-barrage broke around them, machine guns quickly joining in. Palmer bitterly noted: "The line slowly advanced at Zero but suffered casualties immediately ... My right front company lost practically all its effective strength before it crossed the road." The road, running from Wallemolen to Bellevue, was barely thirty-five yards beyond the 49th's start line.

The barrage was timed to creep forward in fifty yards bounds at four-minute intervals, but even this proved too much for the Canadians, battered by wind and pelted by machine-gun fire. At 5:52 a.m., A and D companies, forming the second and third waves, moved off, "suffering heavy casualties." The attacking waves split into smaller parties, advancing in short rushes. Eventually even these tactics became impossible in the face of fierce resistance from machine guns near Furst Farm. Around 6:30 a.m. the remnants of B Company lay trapped in shell holes in front of a well-sited pillbox firing into them at almost point-blank range. Any forward movement appeared suicidal. But Private Cec Kinross, an unorthodox individual from No. 15 Platoon, who was known throughout the battalion by his nickname "Hoodoo," saw things differently. The young D Company runner, whose reputation as a fighting soldier was matched only by his unruly behaviour out of the line, decided to put his own plan into action.

It meant stripping off anything that might impede him. The men going into action that day were weighed down by up to 170 rounds of ammunition, three sandbags, two rifle grenades, an aeroplane flare, two iron rations, one day's fresh rations, one or two waterbottles, a Tommy cooker or a tin of solidified alcohol, and, in certain cases, a shovel. But Hoodoo Kinross had little use for any of these for what he had in mind. Lt. Alfred E. McKay of D Company later reported that the men were being machine-gunned, sniped, and shelled, when he suddenly saw a lone figure dart toward the strongpoint. In an account written on November 6, he stated:

> Private Kinross ... threw off his equipment and advanced single-handed, with a rifle and bandolier to attack the gun. On reaching their position he jumped into the Post, shot and clubbed all the crew and destroyed the machine-gun ...

None of the six men manning the gun survived Kinross' ruthless assault. According to McKay, this single act of heroism transformed the battle, allowing the company to advance 300 yards.

While the 49th Edmontons were engaged in their bitter struggle, the Princess Pats, on the right, were also being severely tested. Their line of advance led past the strongpoint at Duck Lodge and on to the crest of Meetcheele Spur, where a large pillbox dominated all approaches. Col. Adamson wrote: "It was useless to lay down any

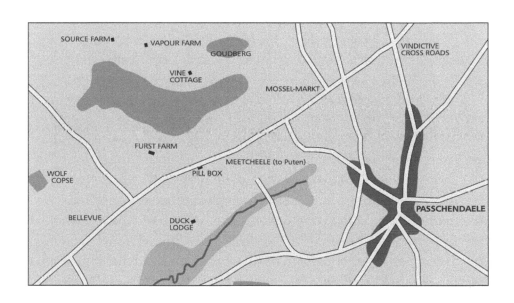

mode of attack to troops going over unknown and swamped lands, pitted with shell holes filled with water." Much would depend on the initiative of section leaders and individual soldiers.

The Princess Pats attacked with No. 2 Company on the right and No. 3 on the left. Behind them came two platoons of moppers-up with No. 4 and No. 1 companies, forming a third wave. Accompanying the infantry was a small detachment of the 7th Canadian Machine-Gun Company, under the command of thirty-one-year-old Lt. Hugh McKenzie DCM, who had served more than two years in the ranks of the Princess Pats. He knew many of the infantrymen personally, particularly those in No. 3 Company with whom he had served.

McKenzie had four Vickers guns and a force of twenty-seven men, divided between the 49th Edmontons and the Princess Pats. Their orders were to move forward with the infantry at zero hour, advancing 200 to 300 yards at a time and pausing for ten to fifteen minutes between each bound. Few plans, however, survive contact with the enemy and this was no exception.

Like the 49th the Princess Pats suffered fearful losses at the opening of the assault. Caught by the enemy's counter-bombardment, they then waded into a hail of fire from machine guns at Duck Lodge and the pillbox on Meetcheele Spur. By 7:00 a.m. almost every subaltern was either dead or wounded. Numbers 3 and 1 companies, on the left, had only two surviving officers between them. The losses among NCOs was almost as severe. To make matters worse, the battle was fought for long periods in a vacuum. Enemy shelling had ripped up telephone cables, leaving runners to brave galling fire to maintain communication with headquarters.

Despite the confusion, however, progress was made. Duck Lodge fell after a sharp struggle and the advance along the Bellevue–Mosselmarkt road carried the Canadians remorselessly toward what the Princess Pats' historian called "the most dramatic and fateful incident of the day." Numbers 3 and 1 companies had already been roughly treated. Only forty men survived in No. 3, and they had been led, in turn, by a company sergeant-major and an acting sergeant. Now they faced their greatest test. Directly ahead, bordering the road on the right, lay the massive fortification dominating Meetcheele

Spur, a modest eminence little more than fifty feet high. Machine guns firing from the pillbox swept the entire ridge, inflicting casualties among troops advancing almost half a mile away. Mixed parties of numbers 3 and 1 companies succeeded in reaching the foot of the slope, but could get no further. Casualties began to mount and it seemed only a matter of time before the Canadians would be compelled to give ground. It was at this critical moment that Lt. McKenzie made his way forward, accompanied by Lt. J.M. Christie DCM and Sgt. Harry Mullin MM, a twenty-five-year-old American-born scout who was one of the Princess Pats' snipers.

McKenzie's passage across the ridge had been a difficult one. Only one man had been lost in the early stages, but thereafter his two gun teams had taken a hammering. As they approached the huge pillbox, however, McKenzie realized that someone needed to kickstart the stalled attack. Cpl. T. Hampson, second-in-command of the machine-gun detachment, recorded:

> There seemed to be a lull or complete stop. Mac was a lieutenant and I was a corporal. We talked the situation over for seemingly some time. I suggested something had to be done. A minute or so after, Mac got out of the shell hole that we were resting in, got what men we had left going again (I won't mention how) but sorry to have to say he hadn't gone more than 200 yards or so when he was hit through the head with a bullet.

McKenzie's death, however, was not in vain. With Christie providing accurate covering fire, the machine-gun subaltern had rallied the survivors, in some cases by forcible means, and organized them for one last effort. Whether by design or not, and his subsequent VC citation claimed it was, the desperate frontal attack which McKenzie led took the form of a forlorn hope, diverting attention away from a flank attack. If this was McKenzie's plan, it worked, though only at the cost of his own life and as a result of the fearlessness of Sgt. Mullin.

Taking advantage of McKenzie's gallant charge, Mullin crawled close to an enemy post beside the pillbox. A well-placed grenade disposed of the occupants and then Mullin jumped up and raced for the pillbox. Capt. Theodore Roberts, of the Canadian War Records Office, described the climax of the fight:

> Mullin climbed to the top of the pillbox. Crawling to the centre, he fired down upon the German machine gunners inside, laying them out across their weapons. Then, sliding down the roof, he landed beside the entrance in time to receive the surrender of the thoroughly demoralised garrison.

Ten prisoners were taken by the sergeant armed only with a revolver. Mullin's action had been widely witnessed and, miraculously, although his clothes were riddled by bullets, he was unharmed. Just as Kinross' action had influenced the outcome of the 49th's battle, so Mullin's feat of daring galvanized the Princess Pats.

First news of the vital capture did not reach Battalion HQ until 9:25 a.m. The message simply read: "Crest of hill taken. Large pillbox surrendered. Our machine guns established." A little over an hour later, Mullin reported personally to Col. Adamson, giving him full and accurate details of the location of the blockhouse, the extent of the advance and the strength of the unit, which he estimated fairly accurately at 225 from the 600 men who had set out less than five hours earlier.

By the time Mullin returned to the fray, two counterattacks had been repulsed; a third, from the direction of Vindictive Crossroads, was similarly dealt with before noon and brought a slackening of enemy fire. A line of shell-hole posts running roughly level with the blockhouse was established and consolidated, the Princess Pats making contact with the right flank of the 49th Edmontons. It was not until midnight on the following day that the two shattered battalions were able to quit the gruesome battlefield. Even then the Germans made it difficult, drenching the Gravenstafel ridge with poison gas.

The 7th Brigade's assault, like that of the 9th Brigade four days earlier, had failed to achieve all its objectives, but it had edged the Canadians closer to their main goal. Once again, the casualty lists made harrowing reading. The Princess Pats lost twenty out of twenty-five officers, nine of them killed, and 343 men, of whom 150 were either killed, reported "missing believed killed" or died of wounds. The 49th's losses were still greater. They had suffered 443 casualties, including 126 dead. The loss among Lt. McKenzie's small party from the 7th Canadian Machine-Gun Corps was proportionately grim: seventeen casualties out of twenty-eight who had started.

Almost ten weeks later, the *London Gazette* of January 11, 1918, announced the awards of the Victoria Cross to No. 437793 Pte. Cecil Kinross and No. 51339 Sgt. Harry Mullin. Kinross, who had been seriously wounded in the arm and head toward the end of the day's fighting, was said to have fought "with the utmost aggressiveness against heavy odds." It was no overstatement, although the official dates of his award, October 28–29 until October 31–November 1, are misleading, for he ended his greatest day in a Casualty Clearing Station. The long list of honours for the battle also included MCs for Lt. McKay of the 49th and Christie of the Princess Pats. Unaccountably, the posthumous award to Lt. Hugh McKenzie (erroneously spelt MacKenzie) was delayed until February 13. He had received gun shot wounds to the head inflicyed by an enemy sniper and been buried close by the pillbox he died attacking, although his grave was later destroyed. His death made a deep impression on the pitifully few men of his detachment who survived the fight. Many years later, Cpl. Hampson remembered:

We put a cross up where we buried him. Came up after we were relieved and did this. Just showing how much we thought of him. You know, it was 6 miles of duckboards to do this. Seems crazy but we did it. Yes, Mac was blunt, said little, meant what he said, have a good laugh after. A man among men.

Although often claimed as a Scottish-born VC winner, Hugh McKenzie was actually born in Liverpool on December 5, 1885, the second son of James and Jane McKenzie, both of whom came originally from

Inverness. His father, a sugar boiler in a confectionery factory, had moved south in search of work, eventually joining the Merchant Navy as an engineer. McKenzie spent the first two years of his life on Merseyside, but in 1905 moved back to Inverness with his mother, three brothers, and three sisters in 1887 when his father was lost at sea. His mother, Jane, died in Dundee on April 28, 1919.

Educated at Leachkin School, he joined the Highland Railway Company as a cleaner. Around 1905 the family uprooted again and moved to Dundee, although they maintained their connections with Inverness, spending their annual holidays there. McKenzie found work with Messrs Watson & Sons of Seagate, and then the Caledonian Railway Company as a carter. A noted sportsman, he was a fine athlete and a founder member of the Dundee Amateur Boxing and Wrestling Club. As a wrestler, he was crowned North Scotland champion, won a clutch of trophies and became a club instructor.

He emigrated to Montreal in 1912, and around this time married Marjory McGuigan, who came from Dundee. They had two children, Alexander born on February 15, 1913, and Elizabeth born in 1909. She was born out of wedlock and remained in Scotland with relatives, presumably until her parents were settled in Canada. By 1914 the McKenzies were living at 297 Gertrude Avenue, Verdun. McKenzie may have carried out work on the railways, although on joining the army he gave his trade as machinist.

McKenzie enlisted on August 21, 1914, as a private with the service number of 1158 in the Princess Patricia's Canadian Light Infantry. On his attestation papers he was described as being five foot seven inches tall, with grey eyes, brown hair, and a fresh complexion. His only identifying mark was a tattoo in the form of a heart on his right wrist. Two days after his enlistment, in a display rich in imperial pageantry, Pat's Pets, as they were soon dubbed, were presented with their Colours in front of a huge crowd in Lansdowne Park, Ottawa. McKenzie was a member of No. 3 Company, which proceeded to England arriving there in October. No. 3 Company was selected to become the first Canadian unit to serve on the Western Front, arriving in France before Christmas as reinforcements for the British 80th Brigade (27th Division). They took their places in the line near

St. Eloi mound, the scene of much fighting in the winter of 1914–15. Hugh McKenzie's war, however, was soon interrupted by a bout of dysentery. He was admitted to hospital on January 22, returning to his unit eleven days later.

April found the Pats in the Salient, south of the Canadian Division. They missed the first poison gas attack, but the following month at Bellewaarde Spur fought a costly defensive action that has become enshrined in regimental legend. McKenzie, by then a corporal in the machine-gun section, figured prominently in the four-day battle. His numerous acts of gallantry began on May 4 when the Pats' crude trenches were pounded by shells, which wiped out his gun team and went on until May 8 when he led fresh troops to their relief. In twenty-five days, the Pats had lost 700 men. McKenzie was awarded the Distinguished Conduct Medal (*London Gazette*, January 14, 1916):

> For conspicuous gallantry. His machine-gun having been blown up by a shell and the whole crew killed or wounded, Cpl. McKenzie displayed the utmost coolness in stripping the wrecked gun of all undamaged parts and bringing them safely out of the trench, which by then had been absolutely demolished. Having no machine-gun, he volunteered to carry messages to and from Brigade Headquarters under terrific fire and succeeded. His devotion to duty has always been most marked.

The same list of awards featured the DCM to Lt.-Cpl. J.M. Christie, who as the unit's sniping officer, would play a key role in McKenzie's final action.

The following month, McKenzie, who had been promoted sergeant on September 11, was awarded the French Croix de Guerre (*London Gazette*, February 24) "for gallant and distinguished service in the field." His active service with the Princess Pats ended in September 1916 when, as a result of his machine-gun experience, he was transferred to the 7th Canadian Machine-Gun Company as company sergeant-major, a rank confirmed on November 18. Almost his entire military service had been spent with machine guns, and his proficiency, already recognized in his selection for a special course at Saint-Omer, was further reflected in his being promoted temporary lieutenant in the field on January 28, 1917. Although commissioned into the Princess Pats, he never served as an officer with them, being immediately seconded to the 7th Brigade's machine gunners.

While his army career went from strength to strength, his private life was a mess. His marriage had hit trouble and on February 6, 1917, he applied to stop his monthly twenty-dollar payments to his wife on the grounds of her "infidelity." Around this time, he asked a friend, Clement Hayward, to "look into his family." What Hayward found was shocking, and he referred to it years later as a "sordid story." He discovered that his wife had placed their son in a Montreal infants' home for young Protestant children. Hayward wrote back but could not bring himself to mention this, and after McKenzie's death travelled back to Montreal only to find that his estranged wife had reclaimed her son.

Whether or not any of this was known to McKenzie is not clear, although it may be significant that he left both his DCM and his Croix de Guerre with his mother, who was still living in Dundee. At that time, his elder brother Robert was serving in the Army Service Corps and a younger brother Alexander, a reservist in the Cameron Highlanders, was a prisoner of war. Throughout the war, McKenzie had paid several visits to his relatives in Scotland, the last time during a ten-day spell of leave in October 1917. Rejoining his unit on October 17, he was killed in action thirteen days later.

On November 5 a telegram informed his widow, then living at 1021 Clarke Street, Montreal, that he was reported "missing, believed killed." A second wire confirming his death followed a week later. In his will, scribbled out while in Flanders on March 14, 1915, and apparently unaltered before his death, he left all his back pay and wristwatch to his mother and the remainder of his personal effects to his wife. His widow later received his Victoria Cross and other campaign medals, but it would not be for another fifty-two years before his complete group was brought together in unusual circumstances.

Marjory McKenzie, who had settled in North Bay, Ontario, remarried on January 6, 1920. According to a regimental account, her daughter came out to Canada after her husband's death and stayed with her until she died. Their son, Alex, later served in the Canadian Army during the Second World War, and was killed in a road accident shortly after being demobbed.

Tragedy continued to stalk the McKenzies. In May 1955 a fire ripped through the daughter's house in Amherstburg, on the shores of Lake Erie, killing her sister-in-law and three children. All her possessions were destroyed in the blaze, including her father's VC. Unaware of the medal's fate, staff at the Princess Pats' regimental museum embarked on a quest to locate the McKenzie VC and any surviving relatives. Appeals were published in Canada and Scotland, which eventually resulted with contact being made with his daughter Elizabeth in 1970. She had just returned from Scotland, bringing with her the DCM and Croix de Guerre that her father had left with relatives during the First World War. Fifty years before, in December 1920, she had unveiled a plaque to her father in Rosebank Primary School, Dundee where she was a pupil at the time. On learning about the loss of the VC, the regiment organized an official replacement to be presented that she in turn donated to the Canadian War Museum.

Today, the VC, DCM, 1914–15 Star, BWM, VM, and Croix de Guerre (France) medals are on extended loan to the PPCLI museum in Calgary from the Canadian War Museum, a fitting memorial to one of the bravest of Princess Pat's "originals."

McKenzie is one of sixteen VC holders with links with Liverpool to be commemorated at Edge Hill, Liverpool.

One of the war's most unconventional heroes, Cecil John Kinross, was born on February 17, 1896, at Dews Farm, Harefield, near Uxbridge in Middlesex, the third of five children to James Stirling Kinross and his wife Emily (*née* Hull). His father was a Scot from Ardoch in Perthshire and, according to family records, had led him as a teenager to the United States where he was said to have worked as a cowboy in Texas. Returning to England to run a farm in Hurley, Warwickshire, owned by his brother, he met his wife-to-be before heading south to Dews Farm. At some point, the family decided to move back to Warwickshire and it was there Cecil Kinross was educated, at Hurley School and Lea Marston Boys School before progressing to Coleshill Grammar School.

In 1912 James Kinross uprooted his family again and travelled once more across the Atlantic, only this time he chose to settle not in the United States but in Canada at the year-old township of Lougheed, Alberta. Situated south of the Iron River valley and some ninety miles east of Edmonton, Lougheed lay astride the Canadian Pacific Railway and was ideal country for growing cereal crops. The small prairie town remained Cec Kinross' home for the rest of his life. He was working as a farmer when war broke out and the following year he travelled to Calgary where he enlisted on October 21, 1914, as a private in the 51st Battalion, Canadian Expeditionary Force. His army papers show him to have been almost six feet tall, with blue eyes, dark brown hair, and scars on both shins caused by a ploughing accident.

He embarked for England on December 18, 1915, as a member of the 3rd Reinforcing Draft. Posted, on landing, to the 9th Reserve Battalion at Shorncliffe, he proceeded to France to join the 49th (Edmontons) Battalion on March 6, 1916, reaching his new unit, which was in divisional reserve near Kemmel, ten days later. Piper J.C.Richardson was also a member of the same Battalion. Kinross quickly became known as something of an oddball character and proved a hard man to control. A former sergeant-major in the unit later insisted no officer ever got the better of him:

His appearance on parade, even after several days in reserve and at rest was, as often told him by his platoon officer, "a disgrace to the platoon, Kinross," which always brought forth a queer smirk on his dial, only not enough for a charge of dumb insolence. Of course, the next parade he would be good-and-spruced-up, by reason of a chunk or two of trench mud having fallen off his clothes while moving around, and to that extent he was regarded as incorrigible.

As time went by, the young private, who was made runner of "Steady D" Company, acquired a reputation as being something of a jinx for his officers, resulting in his nickname Hoodoo, by which he would forever be remembered by veterans of the 49th. A comrade recalled:

> He had in the short space of a few months about umpteen officers pass through his hands. All the shells, etc, that Fritz threw round him and his follow-the-leader seemed to have the other fellow's moniker on them, and never his "Hoodooship's." It happened so often in this manner that when he was given charge of another "Puppy" to follow his trail, the boys used to start betting as to how long the new tourist would last … It never struck them that if only one came back from a line trip it would be any other than Hoodoo.

His legendary cussedness allied to his reputation for being a harbinger of misfortune may account for two spells away from the battalion. From May 23 to August 25, 1916, he was attached to the 7th Canadian Trench Mortar Battery and the following year from May 18 to July 24 he served with the 7th Field Company, Canadian Engineers. In between, he went through the fighting on the Somme, being wounded during the disastrous attack on Regina Trench on October 8, 1916, when the 49th suffered 50 percent losses. Admitted to No. 3 Canadian General Hospital in Boulogne on October 10 with shrapnel wounds to his right arm and body, he was discharged to a convalescent depot three days later, rejoining his unit on November 6.

He took part in the attack on Vimy Ridge, where the Canadian Corps gained its greatest victory, and after an interlude with the brigade engineers rejoined the 49th Battalion in time for the August fighting around Lens. His next major action on the outskirts of Passchendaele was also his last. The shrapnel wounds to his head, left arm, and body resulted in him being hospitalized for three months. Evacuated to England, he was a patient at No. 16 Canadian General Hospital in Orpington when a photographer visited his ward to take his picture. The young Canadian only discovered the reason when he read of his VC award in a newspaper a few days later. According to a medical report, his wound was "progressing satisfactorily" and on February 15, 1918, he was posted to the 21st (Reserve) Battalion at the Alberta Regimental Depot in Bramshott.

Trouble, however, never seemed far away when Kinross was around. Within hours of receiving his Cross at Buckingham Palace on April 6, 1918, he was arrested by military policemen who accused him of wearing a VC ribbon to which they thought he was not entitled. They were only convinced after Kinross had taken his medal from his pocket and showed them the inscription on the back. As a tribute to his heroism, on July 14, 1918, Maj. C.Y. Weaver, commanding the 49th Battalion, ordered that Hoodoo Kinross' old platoon would be renamed No. 15 (Kinross) Platoon.

Ruled medically unfit in December 1918, he returned to Canada the following month, still suffering from the legacy of his injuries sustained in the fighting near Passchendaele. A medical examination carried out at Edmonton on January 27, 1919, found that he had lost all sensation in two fingers on his left hand and had only partial feeling in his left arm, which made it difficult to hold farm implements such as forks and spades. The subsequent report also noted that since being wounded he suffered "headaches about once a month which last two or three days." It concluded that he might take up to a year to recover from his partial paralysis and was unable to fully resume his old job in farming. On the 19th of the following month he was honourably discharged from the army.

At a civic reception in Edmonton, he was presented with a purse of gold and granted 160 acres of prime farmland some eight miles west of Lougheed. Perhaps as a result of his injuries, he appears not to have worked the land, preferring instead to rent it out while taking jobs with neighbouring farms. Variously described as "wild and crazy," "happy go lucky," and "everybody's friend," Cec Kinross was a gregarious man noted for his eccentricities. People recalled the time in 1934 he went into hospital to have his tonsils removed and refused to have anaesthetic. And they remembered his reaction to being teased about which required the greater courage: charging a

German machine post single handed or jumping into a frozen stream. He settled the argument by taking off his coat, walking over to a hole in the icebound stream, and plunging in!

A confirmed bachelor, Kinross travelled to Britain in 1929 to attend the Prince of Wales banquet for VC holders and again twenty-seven years later for the Victoria Cross centenary celebrations. Having taken early retirement, he moved into the Lougheed Hotel, which had long been his second home, and lived there cheerfully on his army pension until his sudden death on June 21, 1957.

Such was his popularity, people turned out in their droves to witness the passing of a great, albeit thoroughly unorthodox, Albertan. In the largest funeral ever seen in Lougheed, the community hall was filled to overflowing with hundreds more listening to the service relayed over a public address system. Among the pallbearers were a holder of the DCM, three Military Medallists, and another Albertan VC holder, Alex Brereton. Cec Kinross was buried with military honours in the soldiers' plot of Lougheed cemetery with pipers playing a lament.

Kinross was entitled to the VC, BWM, VM, King George VI Coronation Medal (1937), and Queen Elizabeth II (1953) Coronation Medal. Their whereabouts is unknown but the Loyal Edmonton Regimental Museum in Edmonton does have a set of his decorations as miniatures.

More than six decades on, he is still proudly remembered on both sides of the Atlantic. In his hometown, both the local branch of the Royal Canadian Legion and a children's playground bear his name, while in his English birthplace a blue plaque unveiled on February 17, 2011, off Harvil Road, Harefield, near Uxbridge commemorates his association with the borough of Hillingdon. Together with Robert Ryder VC he also had a plaque laid in his honour on November 4, 2014, at the Harefield War Memorial at a ceremony arranged by Hillingdon Council. But his most spectacular memorial resides in Jasper National Park, in the Rockies, in the shape of a 2,731 metre peak overlooking Pyramid Lake and named after him in 1951. Mount Kinross stands as a towering salute to a towering personality.

As fellow Lougheed farmer Thomas Barton once remarked: "You couldn't get him to talk about the VC or what happened. He was a very proud man. But he didn't give a damn for anything."

One of a handful of American-born winners of the Victoria Cross, George Harry Mullin was born in Portland, Oregon, on August 15, 1891, the son of Harry and Effie Mullin. The family moved to Canada when he was two years old and homesteaded at Moosomin, Saskatchewan. Mullin attended the Moosomin Public School and later the Moosomin Collegiate. At the outbreak of war, he was farming at Kamloops, British Columbia, where he lived with his mother.

He enlisted in the 32nd Battalion at Winnipeg on December 14, 1914, and was one of a draft transferred to the Princess Patricia's Canadian Light Infantry in February 1915. He became a battalion sniper and was wounded at Sanctuary Wood in June 1916. Evacuated to England for hospital treatment, he rejoined the unit in September 1916 on the Somme, where his brother Roy was killed.

He joined the battalion's sniper section and was awarded a Military Medal (gazetted February 19, 1917) for an act of gallantry carried out on December 16, 1916, opposite Vimy Ridge. The recommendation stated:

In the La Folie Sector as a sniper [he] assisted Sgt. Dow in his reconnaissance of an enemy post. At 3.20 a.m. [he] accompanied Lt. McDougall's party to the same spot, killed the sentry, threw bombs down the communication trench to block the enemy supports and assisted in carrying his officer out of the crater. He has on many occasions examined enemy wire after an artillery bombardment under very dangerous circumstances and his reports have always been accurate.

Sgt. N.D. Dow received a Military Medal and Lt. A.A. McDougall a Military Cross for this action.

Mullin was promoted corporal in the field on March 16, made acting sergeant on April 9, the day of the assault on Vimy Ridge, and by July was a full sergeant, commanding the battalion's scouts and snipers. It was while serving in this role that he won his Victoria Cross at Meetcheele Spur. He left the Princess Pats in March 1918 and was attached to the 6th Reserve Battalion prior to attending the Canadian Officers' Training School at Bexhill. Commissioned temporary lieutenant on August 6, 1918, he was posted to the 6th Reserve Battalion and saw out the rest of the war as battalion bombing instructor.

He had married in April 1918 and before returning to Canada in June 1919 he helped to coach and lead the 6th Reserve Battalion baseball team. After the war he returned to farming, but maintained his military associations. He served in the 4th South Saskatchewan Regiment, the 1st Assiniboia Militia, and 110 Field Battery (Howitzers). During the Second World War, he again volunteered for service and spent six years as an officer in the Veterans' Guard of Canada, including a spell in command of an internment camp.

The war interrupted his ceremonial duties as sergeant-of-arms at the Saskatchewan Legislature, a post he had held since 1934. But in 1953 he donned full regalia as one of Saskatchewan's representatives at the coronation of Queen Elizabeth II.

Major Harry Mullin died in Regina, Saskatchewan, on April 5, 1963, aged seventy, and was buried in the South Cemetery Legion Plot, at Moosomin, where his parents had first settled in Canada over sixty years earlier. He is commemorated with the name of a lake in northern Saskatchewan and a plaque at reference SW114 Section 18 Township 14 Range 30 west of 1st Meridian.

His Victoria Cross group, including the Military Medal, is now displayed alongside Hugh McKenzie's awards in the Princess Patricia's Canadian Light Infantry Museum at Calgary, having been purchased by the Canadian War Museum for an undisclosed sum in 1975.

The complete list of medals awarded to Mullin apart from his VC and MM are: the BWM (1914–20), VM + MiD Oakleaf, Canadian Volunteer Service Medal (1939–45), War Medal (1939–45), King George VI Coronation Medal (1937), and the Queen Elizebeth II Coronation Medal (1953).

In the display Room of the Arlington Amphitheatre, in November 2014, Princess Anne unveiled a memorial in George Harry Mullin's honour as well as those three other Americans who served in the CEF, Bellenden Hutcheson, William Metcalf, and Raphael Zengel who had won the Victoria Cross Canada's highest decoration.

G.R. PEARKES

Vapour Farm, October 30–31

 As Maj. George Pearkes clambered out of his muddy shell hole at around 5:54 a.m. on October 30, he could barely make out the dark shapes of his men, indistinct in the dim early morning light. Flares and rockets shot through the grey gloom, followed by the enemy counter-bombardment, shattering in its intensity as it exploded around them. Pearkes, OC C Company, 5th Canadian Mounted Rifles, would remember that moment well. Many years later, he said:

We'd hardly got out ... when that barrage came down. At that time I was hit in the thigh [by shrapnel] and was knocked down. I rather thought: "Now I've got it!" There seemed to be a little uncertainty among the men immediately alongside me, whether they should go on when I'd been hit. For a moment I had visions of going back wounded and I said to myself: "This can't be. I've got to go on for a while anyway, wounded or not." So I clambered to my feet and I found a stiffness in my left thigh but I was able to move forward and then the rest of the company all came forward.

The ground fell away toward a swamp speckled with the stumps of Woodland Plantation. Beyond it, roughly 1,000 yards from the start line, lay their objective, the fortified Vapour Farm strongpoint on the edge of Goudberg Spur. Parallel to his company, and skirting the other side of the mire, was A Company, headed for the strongpoint at Vine Cottage. Behind came D and B companies to consolidate the ground won. Together, they represented 8th Canadian Brigade's attacking force, squeezed, because of the dreadful nature of the ground, into a two-platoon front between the 49th Edmontons and the 28th Londons (Artists' Rifles). As we have seen, the enemy's barrage took a fearful toll of the 49th. The 5th CMR were similarly hard hit. Worst affected of all, however, were the Artists' Rifles. Caught in the open, they suffered crippling losses which stopped their advance on Source Farm almost before it had begun. Ignorant of the disaster which had befallen their flanking unit, C Company pushed on. It soon became clear something was wrong. As well as fire from the strongpoints in front, they found themselves exposed to fire from untouched pillboxes on the left. Pearkes began losing men at an alarming rate:

> We found that the barrage ran away from us; we couldn't begin to keep up with it [even though] it was moving at the rate of 100 yards every eight minutes ... I was carrying a rifle and I remember turning around and helping men who were not wounded but who had got stuck in shell holes. I'm certain that there were men who, wounded, fell into the shell holes and were drowned. If you got in you just couldn't climb out by yourself ... because the sides all kept oozing down if you reached out to help yourself.

Despite everything, C Company had reached its intermediate objective by 6:30 a.m. During a lull in the barrage, the German defenders were seen scurrying back toward their main defences around Vapour and Source Farms. During that last effort, the Canadians were assailed by machine guns ranged to the left and to the front. Yet Pearkes managed to maintain some semblance of order.

Realizing the danger represented by the Source Farm strongpoint, he sent a platoon to take it, while pressing on toward Vapour Farm with just thirty-six men.

At 7:55 a.m. Pearkes signalled his success. The fate of A Company's advance was more obscure. A pall of smoke blotted out much of the battlefield. Observers thought they had seen A Company on the intermediate objective. Later, flares were reported on the right and were taken to mean they too had reached their final objective. But it was not so. So heavy were their losses that they were unable to make an attempt on Vine Cottage. Instead, they veered left, reinforcing Pearkes' small garrison. It was not until 8:30 a.m. that a message from Pearkes, scribbled forty-five minutes earlier, apprised Battalion HQ of the true position. It read: "We hold source, vapour and vanity, both flanks in the air. Have about 50 men from 'C' and 'D.' We must have help from both sides. Hun about 100 yards away."

Attempts to support them were hampered by enfilading fire and heavy shelling. Pearkes' men had achieved the near-impossible. But their grip was tenuous. Almost a mile ahead of the 28th Londons, they had advanced way beyond any other unit. But without support it seemed their sacrifices would be in vain. Pearkes sent off another urgent appeal for help, this time via one of the company's two pigeons. The man carrying the message clips had been killed, so Pearkes ingeniously attached his note to the bird's leg using a strand of sandbag fibre. In the hours that followed, a trickle of reinforcements, including men sent up from the 2nd CMR, arrived, but they were still all too few in number. An attempt to take Vine Cottage was driven off and the swaying fortunes were revealed in a brief report sent by Pearkes at 10:50 a.m.:

Am holding line of shell holes ... Vapour and Source farms inclusive. Have about 30 men and Lts Andrews, Gifford and Otty, 5th CMR Bn. Strong counterattack by enemy en masse successfully beaten back. 50 men 2nd CMR arrived. Both my flanks in the air. Bde. on left must endeavour to come up. Am short SAA but will hold on. Vanity house now held by enemy.

The garrison's two Lewis guns exacted a heavy toll, but on the debit side the party sent against Vine Cottage was overwhelmed. Later, around eight to ten men of the 2nd CMR, all that remained of a company of reinforcements, staggered in. Throughout, Pearkes had been the life and soul of the defence. Although in great discomfort from his leg wound, he seemed to be everywhere, crawling from shell hole to shell hole, cracking jokes, directing fire, even taking a few potshots at the enemy. But after nearly eight hours of continuous fighting exhaustion was setting in. At 1:45 p.m., he informed Battalion HQ: "Germans are digging in on top of ridge about 200 yards away. Are in force. I have 8 2nd CMR and 19 5th CMR. All very much exhausted. Ammunition running short. Do not think we can hold out much longer without being relieved. Both flanks still in the air."

Years later he admitted, "it looked a pretty hopeless position." But there was nothing for it but to stand and fight. Pearkes recalled: "To have gone back and given up everything we had gained that morning didn't seemed very sensible as, if we had started to drift back there would have been more casualties." A British unit was ordered to form a defensive flank toward Source Farm, but unaccountably it never budged, leaving Pearkes to form his own fragile perimeter. In a message which reached Battalion HQ at 5:45 p.m. via a wounded officer, he reported:

> About 10 men "A" Company 2nd CMR Bn. have got through. Huns counterattacking again. We have had some more casualties. Have formed a defensive flank on the left and continued a short distance past Source Farm with right flank resting on Woodland Plantation. Reinforcements might get through after dark. They are most urgently needed, also SAA. Men of 5th CMR Bn. all in. Do not think I can hold out until morning.

But as darkness fell, first ammunition and then relief reached the defiant Canadians in the form of two companies of the 2nd CMR. Of all the attacking units, only the 5th CMR had captured and held any of its final objectives. Fewer than forty men struggled back from

Vapour Farm and Source Farm. The last to leave was George Pearkes, his trouser leg caked in blood and mud. In his post-battle report, the Battalion CO, Lt.-Col. D.C. Draper, recorded:

> The boldness, initiative and skill displayed by Maj. G.R. Pearkes cannot be too highly commented upon. It was entirely due to his leadership that the operation of this battalion was so successful. For a considerable time he held Vapour and Source Farms with a mere handful of men, beating off the first German counterattack without any other assistance. His appreciation of the situation was most accurate and his reports at all times were clear, concise and invaluable.

Pearkes' own assessment, recorded years later, was more prosaic: "We had got on when nobody else had got on; we had survived ... and we were all thankful." There can have been little surprise when, on January 11, 1918, the *London Gazette* announced the award of the Victoria Cross to Maj. George Pearkes "for most conspicuous bravery."

George Randolph Pearkes, destined to become the most distinguished Canadian holder of the Victoria Cross, was born in Watford, Hertfordshire, on February 26, 1888, the eldest son of George and Louise Pearkes. After a spell being taught by governesses, he went to Berkhamsted School where he remained for the next ten years. Although an intelligent boy, academic study took second place to outdoor pursuits, most notably horse riding. A member of the school cadet force, his ambition was to become a cavalry officer. But all that changed when his father's business slumped.

Instead of joining the army, Pearkes emigrated to Canada, and in May 1906 he headed west for Red Deer, Alberta, where his ex-headmaster owned a farm. It was nicknamed Baby Farm because it served as a kind of practical agricultural college, teaching youngsters the way of the land. At twenty-one, Pearkes, who was a Roman Catholic, had his own homestead, consisting of 160 acres of untamed Albertan wilderness on which he built his own makeshift shelter.

Within a little over a year, he had been joined by his brother (who in true pioneering spirit helped build a log cabin), his mother, who had separated from her husband, and his sister.

In 1913, having already ventured to the far north as a member of a land survey expedition, he joined the Royal North-West Mounted Police, being stationed at White Horse while his brother looked after the farm. At the outbreak of war, he immediately applied to buy himself out to enlist. But it was not until early 1915 that the authorities relented and on March 2, 1915, he joined the 2nd Canadian Mounted Rifles at Victoria, British Columbia, as a trooper. He gave his mother, Mrs. Louise Pearkes, as his next of kin and her address was 1213 Stanley Avenue, Victoria. His service number was 107473. His skills as a horseman brought him swift promotion. He was made a rough-riding corporal but when they sailed for France in September 1915 it was as a dismounted cavalry unit later to be fully converted to infantrymen.

Pearkes was among the first party from the 2nd CMR to go into the trenches. He later recalled his tour of the line near Ploegsteert: "There was a sort of strangeness to it all which, at the same time, keyed one up and I was excited." His first brush with the enemy came near Messines in December. Selected for specialist bombing training, he was kept on as an instructor. By the time he returned it was as sergeant of the bombing platoon. Shortly afterward, he was wounded during a fight near Hooge on March 26, 1916. He was quickly back with his unit and on April 30, his platoon officer having been wounded, he was commissioned in the field.

His career had begun to assume a pattern that would continue for the rest of the war. Astoundingly successful and blessed with good fortune, it was punctuated by promotions, injuries and awards for gallantry. Wounded and temporarily blinded on May 20, he lied about the extent of his wounds in order to return to his unit. Within a matter of a few weeks he had won his first award, a Mention in Despatches, for destroying an enemy listening post. An appointment as 8th Brigade bombing officer proved short-lived. On September 27 he was transferred to the 5th CMR to take command of C Company. Four days later, he led them in an attack on Regina Trench on the Somme. Wounded again, his fearless leadership resulted in his award of the Military Cross (*London Gazette*, December 21, 1916): "He led a bombing party with great courage and determination, clearing 600 yards of trench and capturing 18 prisoners." That same month and within the space of two days he rose from lieutenant to acting major.

The unit, and his company in particular, came to represent his universe. By the close of the Passchendaele campaign, he had made up his mind to make the army his life. The injury sustained at Vapour Farm quickly healed and by mid-November he was back with the "Fighting Fifth." His stay, however, was brief. Posted as senior major to the 116th Battalion, he was promoted lieutenant-colonel in command of the unit in January 1918. During the Allied offensive at Amiens on August 8, his new unit featured prominently, resulting in his third decoration. The citation for his DSO noted:

> He handled his battalion in a masterly manner and with an enveloping movement completely baffled and overcame the enemy, who were in a very strong position. He then captured a wood, the final objective, which was about 5,000 yards from the start. Before this, however, the men were becoming exhausted, on observing which he at once went into the attack himself, and by his splendid and fearless example, put new life into the whole attack, which went forward with a rush and captured 16 enemy guns of all calibres up to eight inches.

Pearkes' outstanding war record ended on September 17 at Guemappe, France. During a bombardment of his unit's billets, he was seriously wounded in the arm and side. His life hung in the balance, and it was only the surgeons' skill that saved him. He was convalescing in London when the war ended. On New Year's Eve he was mentioned in despatches again and shortly afterward awarded the French Croix de Guerre.

After he was demobilized he returned to Canada in March 1919 and for the next nine years served as a staff officer in the western provinces. In August 1925 he married Constance Blytha Copeman, whose family originally came from Norfolk. They had two children. A daughter, Priscilla Edith, born in 1928 died in childhood, and a son, John Andre, was born in 1931. Pearkes' career continued to flourish. By 1935 he was serving as director of military training and staff duties, and in 1938 he took command of Military District No. 13 based at Calgary on promotion to brigadier. Shortly after the outbreak of the Second World War, he was appointed to command the 2nd Brigade, 1st Canadian Division, and proceeded with it to England in December 1939. Two months later, following a visit to the BEF in France, he was struck down by spinal meningitis. Despite fears that he might not survive, he pulled through and in the aftermath of Dunkirk was promoted major-general in command of 1st Canadian Division.

Pearkes proved an excellent commander. Thoroughly professional and greatly respected, he brought the division up to a high level of efficiency. But there was friction with other commanders, and in the wake of the Dieppe debacle, in which his division was not involved but that he had strongly opposed, he was sent back to Canada to take over Pacific Command, with responsibility for protecting the western provinces in the unlikely event of a Japanese attack. He held the post until 1945, retiring from the army with a Companion of the Most Honourable Order of the Bath (CB) and the U.S.'s Order of Merit.

In June 1945 he embarked on a new career as a politician. He was elected a Progressive Conservative MP for Nanaimo, British Columbia, and when his party was returned to office in 1957, Pearkes was appointed minister of defence and became a Canadian privy councillor. At the time, he was the only cabinet minister in the Commonwealth to hold a VC. He eventually stepped down in 1960 to become one of the most popular lieutenant-governors in the history of British Columbia. During his eight years in office, he also served as grand president of the Royal Canadian Legion, retiring from the post in its golden anniversary year of 1976.

A man revered by ex-servicemen and respected by politicians and ordinary citizens alike, he retained a desire to serve his fellow Canadians. "I took an interest in my soldiers and in the Legion," he once said. "I have concern for people rather than just the favoured few." George Pearkes, whose extraordinary life took him from cadet to major-general and from homesteader to lieutenant-governor, died in a Victoria rest home on May 30, 1984, aged ninety-six, after suffering a stroke. The man of whom it was said he merited the phrase "Chevalier sans peur et sans reproche" was given a state and military funeral as befitted his dual career. The funeral parade was led by thirty-two Mounties followed by units of the Princess Pat's, a guard of the Canadian Scottish and a black, riderless horse with saddle draped in black and riding boots reversed in the stirrups. He was buried in Holy Trinity Cemetery, West Saanich, Sidney, Victoria, section 4, west.

Apart from the VC his considerable number of decorations include the Companion of Canada; Companion Order of the Bath, DSO, MC, Knight of Grace, Order of St. John of Jerusalem, 1914–15 Star, BWM (1914–20), VM (1914–19) and MiD Oakleaf, Defence Medal (1939–45), Canadian Volunteer Service Medal (1939–45) "Maple Leaf" clasp, War Medal (1939–45), King George V Silver Jubilee Medal(1935), King George VI Coronation Medal (1937), Queen Elizabeth II Coronation Medal (1953), Queen Elizabeth II Silver Jubilee Medal (1967), Canadian Forces Decoration & 3 Bars, Canadian Centennial Medal (1967), Croix de Guerre (France), and Commander, Legion of Merit (United States). They are in the care of the Canadian War Museum in Ottawa.

The Hon. George Pearkes is remembered in a number of ways:

- A plaque at the RCMP Museum Centennial Training Dept. in Regina.
- Two Canadian Legion Posts in Summerside, Prince Edward Island, and Princeton, British Columbia.
- The main building in the Canadian Department National Defence HQ in Ottawa is named after him.
- George R. Pearkes Arena in Saanich, British Columbia.
- Mount Pearkes, along the mainland of the British Columbia south coast.
- The George R. Pearkes Children's Foundation.
- The George R. Pearkes Centre for Children, a treatent facility for

children with cerebral palsy, later part of Queen Alexandra Centre for Children's Health in Victoria.

- General George R. Pearkes Elementary School in Hudson's Hope, British Columbia.
- In his memory a ceremonial sword is presented in Berkhamstead School to be awarded each year to the school's best senior NCO cadet.
- A lake in north Saskatchewan.
- CCGS *George R.Pearkes*, a Canadian Coast Guard icebreaker.
- Numerous streets.

C.F. BARRON and
J.P. ROBERTSON

Vine Cottage and Passchendaele, November 6

On the morning of November 6 Philip Gibbs, the distinguished British
war correspondent, picked his way toward a line of captured pillboxes
on the approaches to the Steenbeek. From there, "through the smoke
of gun-fire and the wet mist" he saw Passchendaele. Or what was left
of it. As he scanned the crest of the ridge that "curved round black
and grim below the clouds, right round to Polygon Wood and the
heights of Broodseinde," he could see only one ruin poking through
the murk. It was the church, "a black mass of slaughtered masonry."

No more than a speck on any but the most detailed of maps,
Passchendaele and its formidable ridge, an objective in the early
stages of a campaign designed to break the deadlock of three
years' fighting, had become the vainglorious raison d'être for the
continuation of a struggle in which hope of a breakthrough had long
since vanished. The Germans, however, had no intention of giving
up the ridge without a fight. As Gibbs looked on, the damp air was
filled with "the savage whine" of the enemy's artillery "and all below
the Passchendaele Ridge monstrous shells were flinging up masses
of earth and water." After four months of fighting, the village that
would give its name to the campaign and all its futile carnage had
become the day's main target. It was not, however, the only one.

On the left, the Canadians of the 1st Division had the task of clearing the enemy strongpoints along the spurs feeding on to the main ridge northwest of Passchendaele. As always, the lines of attack were governed by the swamp. The entire divisional frontage was constricted into the 380 yards width of the Bellevue-Meetcheele Spur, along which the 1st (Western Ontario) and 2nd (Eastern Ontario) battalions were to advance in conjunction with a flank attack by the 3rd (Toronto) Battalion to the east astride the Goudberg Spur. The latter operation was a continuation of the efforts made by the 5th Canadian Mounted Rifles to capture the Vine Cottage strongpoint. The ruined farmhouse sheltered one of the largest pillboxes in the sector, with walls reckoned to be eighteen inches thick and machine guns covering every conceivable approach. The defenders also had another ally — the mud. The rain and relentless shelling had created a glutinous barrier guaranteed to restrict any assault.

Conscious of the difficulties, Lt.-Col. J.B. "Bart" Rogers DSO, MC, drew up a plan that concentrated on dealing with Vine Cottage. His attacking force consisted of C and D companies and two platoons from A Company, under the command of Maj. D.H.C. Mason DSO. The spearhead, led by Capt. J.K. Crawford, comprised C Company and the elements of A Company, attacking on a three-platoon front with three platoons in close support. Lt. H.T. Lord's platoon was given the job of seizing Vine Cottage. At 6:00 a.m., the two most northerly platoons of Crawford's force slipped out of their shell holes near Vanity House and crept as close to the barrage as they dared. An anxious ten-minute pause followed before the bombardment ranged on to their objective, and then they moved off. The swampy ground made it impossible to approach Vine Cottage due eastwards from the jumping-off line. Lord had no choice but to attack southeastwards, maintaining shape and direction under trying conditions, before swinging left to reach the battalion's final objective facing due north. Hardly surprisingly, the attack did not run smoothly.

It was soon apparent that the barrage had made little impression. The defences consisted of two intact pillboxes, of which the largest was at Vine Cottage, and "a multitude of two or three man 'funk holes' dug into the side of deep shell holes." From these burst a withering fire that combined with the mud to delay both Crawford's and Lord's advance. Each machine gun had to be assaulted in turn, leading to heavy losses. Retribution, however, was severe. Lt.-Col. Rogers candidly reported:

> When our men got to within about 20 yards of them they ceased firing and the crews attempted to surrender but in the majority of cases they were given no quarter and the bayonet was used to good effect as our men were infuriated at the casualties which had been caused by them.

Slowly, and at considerable loss, Lord's depleted platoon closed in on Vine Cottage and the outlying posts. A persistent drizzle was falling as they divided into smaller parties, hoping to confuse the defenders by rushing from three directions at once. But every time they were driven back before they could get within bombing range. As casualties mounted in proportion to the number of failures, it appeared as though Lord's attack would go much the same way as that of 5th CMR on October 30. That it did not do so was due to the resolution and initiative of Cpl. Colin Barron, a Scots-Canadian member of D Company.

Barron, who was commanding one of the battalion's Lewis gun sections, had grown frustrated by the repeated reverses. So he decided to show the way. Worming his way round the flank, lugging his weapon with him, he somehow managed to reach a position close by the strongpoint without being seen. Then, he opened fire at "point-blank range" with devastating results. Two of Vine Cottage's three machine-gun crews were annihilated one after the other by his deadly fire. According to Rogers, they were put "absolutely out of action." The third gun, blocked from Barron's view, continued to fire, but even before the pillbox's startled garrison had time to react, their nemesis was among them, followed by the remnants of his platoon bent on revenge. According to one account: "There was a wild melee in the confined space ... for a few moments, with Barron using the bayonet and clubbed butt of an old rifle he had picked up, with terrible effect."

Four men fell to Barron and the remainder, according to his VC citation, were taken prisoner, although given Rogers' earlier comments this must be a matter for some conjecture. In his own account, he makes no mention of prisoners, merely stating that "at least a dozen of the enemy" were bayoneted in the final assault. Barron, meanwhile, rounded off his whirlwind attack by turning one of the captured machine guns on to those members of the garrison who had escaped his frenzied charge.

Much behind time and greatly reduced in number, Lord's platoon had nevertheless accomplished their mission, and succeeded in linking up with Capt. Crawford's force. Enemy machine guns continued to play havoc along the Canadian lines of communications and, although reports of Vine Cottage's capture had been made shortly after 11:00 a.m., it was not until 12:30 p.m. that Battalion HQ received confirmation of their success.

Eventually, at 6:52 p.m., after an afternoon spent consolidating and recovering the wounded, a fuller report arrived from Maj. Mason in which he stated that "C Company continue to hold objectives … and are digging in … Estimated strength of C Company 150 … 40 prisoners taken and are being held at Vine Cottages [sic] until dusk, so they can take stretcher cases out." All told, Crawford's platoons had taken fifty-nine prisoners, including one officer, and captured five machine guns, three of them taken by Cpl. Barron at Vine Cottage. The price, as always, was a heavy one: sixty-four men, including three officers, dead, 154 wounded and twenty-two missing. Among the wounded were Capt. Crawford, whose leadership was recognized by the award of the DSO, and Lt. Lord who received a Bar to his MC. According to Lt.-Col. Rogers, only the determination of his men had saved the day and prevented the "serious stumbling blocks" around Vine Cottage from defeating his attack. And of them all none had displayed greater determination than Colin Barron.

While the 3rd (Toronto) Battalion had been slugging it out across the Goudberg Spur, the main effort had been focused 1,500 yards further southeast on the high ground from which the 2nd Division, employing the 6th Brigade, launched its attack on Passchendaele. Behind a creeping barrage, described as "splendid" by the Canadians, the 27th (City of Winnipeg), 31st (Alberta), and 28th (North West) battalions advanced at a rapid rate. The 27th's objective was the village itself, and so swiftly did they follow the barrage on to their first objective that the enemy scarcely had a chance to resist. It was textbook stuff, but the nearer they came to the village the fiercer the opposition grew.

By adopting the newly devised tactics of single file sections leapfrogging one another on to the strongpoints, they gradually whittled away the enemy defences. But one machine gun, on the left, proved particularly stubborn. Barring the Canadians' entry into the main street, the position was ringed by uncut wire and broken, reinforced walls. Three times the 27th's flanking platoon had charged it, only to be driven back by point-blank fire and a shower of bullets from marksmen hidden in nearby houses. It was at this cheerless moment, with the toll of casualties mounting and hopes fading, that Pte. Peter Robertson intervened.

Standing six feet three inches tall, Robertson, a locomotive engineer known as "Singing Pete," was a good-humoured giant of a man who had refused all offers of promotion. He was highly regarded as a fighting soldier, but few could have anticipated that one man could succeed where an entire platoon had failed, not once but on three occasions. Robertson, however, was apparently undaunted by the odds. A man noted for his willingness to take risks was about to take one of the greatest gambles of his life. While his comrades blazed away at the machine-gun post with Lewis guns and rifles, he leapt up and sprinted alone across the line of fire. With the bullets from marksmen kicking the ground around his feet, he dashed round the flank, hurdled the barbed-wire fence, and set about the gun team with his bayonet. It was all over within seconds. Four men lay dead around the gun and as the remainder bolted back toward the houses Robertson turned their own gun on them. Few survived to reach the sanctuary of the ruins.

By 7:10 a.m. the Canadians "were streaming through and either side of Passchendaele in large numbers, bayoneting Germans in the ruins and along the main street." Foremost among them was Peter Robertson. Not content with merely capturing the machine gun, he had decided to employ it against its former owners. With his comrades trailing after him, he advanced through the village, setting up his captured weapon and using it to great effect whenever targets presented themselves. House-to-house fighting continued until 7:40 a.m. when the 27th reported Passchendaele cleared. A little over an hour later, the eastern crest of the ridge beyond the village had been secured. The rest of the day was spent consolidating the ground so spectacularly won. The Germans retaliated with sporadic shelling and a few disorganized counterattacks that were easily beaten back. But minor firefights amid the ruined village continued throughout the day. It was during one of these that Robertson, displaying courage in a different cause, lost his life. From his position on the eastern edge of the village, he saw two snipers from his battalion lying wounded well in advance of the Canadian line. Without hesitation, he set out across the open to bring them in. He rescued one, but the enemy were closing in, infiltrating more men forward, raising the stakes considerably. Robertson, however, ignored the risks. Capt. Theodore Roberts, of the Canadian War Records Office, wrote:

> In spite of a veritable storm of bullets, Robertson went out again. He fell before reaching the second man — he was probably hit — but picking himself up, he continued on his way, and secured his second comrade. Slipping on the sticky mud, nearly exhausted, he stuck to his man, and had put him down close to our line, when an unlucky shell exploded near by, killing him instantly.

In the gathering darkness, a heavy bombardment fell on the Canadian positions. Enemy patrols were sighted, but an anticipated German counterattack never materialized. It had taken Haig's army ninety-nine days to cover five miles, but now, at least, the fight for Passchendaele was over.

Nine weeks later, the *London Gazette* of January 11, 1918, announced the award of Victoria Crosses to Cpl. Colin Barron and Pte. Peter Robertson, the latter sadly posthumously. His grave is in Tyne Cot Cemetery in Belgium Plot L. III, D. 26.

Colin Fraser Barron was born at Baldavie, Boyndie in Banffshire, Scotland, on September 20, 1893, the son of Joseph Barron, a farmer. He was educated at Blairmaud, Boyndie, and emigrated to Canada in March 1910. Settling in Toronto, he became a railway worker. In keeping with his Scottish roots, he enlisted in the 48th Highlanders, a militia unit, on May 16, 1913, and was posted to H Company.

It is unclear if he was still serving with this unit at the outbreak of war, but his attestation papers have him volunteering for the Canadian Expeditionary Force on January 11, 1915, giving his occupation as teamster and his father, living in Mill of Boynde, Banffshire, as next of kin. A medical examination revealed that a shoulder bone, broken in an accident in 1913, had still not set, but this was not deemed sufficient to reject him for military service and he was posted to D Company, 35th Battalion. Shortly before heading out to France in July 1915, he forfeited a day's pay for going absent without leave. On July 31, he joined the 3rd (Toronto) Battalion, the unit with which he was to remain throughout the rest of the war. Promoted lance-corporal on April 9, 1917, the day the Canadian Corps captured Vimy Ridge, and was confirmed in the rank of corporal on January 11, 1918, the same day his VC was gazetted. The following month he was made acting sergeant and assigned to the Canadian Corps Lewis Gun School as an instructor. It was from there, in March 1918, he returned to his native Scotland to attend a ceremony at which the Duke of Richmond and Gordon presented him with a gold watch and a wallet of treasury notes raised by public appeal. Given an extension to his leave to deal with family affairs, he eventually returned to his training duties in May.

He returned to Canada a sergeant and was demobilized on April 23, 1919. Between the wars he continued to soldier in the militia, re-enlisting in the 48th Highlanders of Canada on November 4, 1921. He served until May 22, 1931, rising to CSM. He married and had two daughters, but like many veterans he was forced to endure an uphill struggle to support his family. For a time, he served with the Provincial Police at Kitchener, Orangeville, and Niagara Falls. According to his daughter, Marjory Thompson, he had been rejected by the national force as he was not tall enough. In between running his own transport business, working for the Ontario Department of Highways, and a job at Don Jail, there were periodic bouts of unemployment. During the depression he was out of work for two years, eventually finding work as a guide at the provincial government building before transferring to the staff at Don Jail.

When the Second World War broke out he enlisted again in the Royal Regiment of Canada, successors of the Toronto Regiment. Described at the time as being "still powerful and built for hand-to-hand fighting," Colin Barron was the first Canadian holder of the Victoria Cross who was not a member of the Permanent Force to be sent on active service. He was a member of the Canadian force that took part in the occupation of Iceland and was later made provost sergeant-major at 1st Division HQ in England.

After the war, he returned to his job as a security guard at the Don Jail and later joined the Toronto Corps of Commissionaires, serving at the CBC television studios, Hester How School, and Sunnybrook Hospital. He attended Davenport Presbyterian church and was an honorary member of many Toronto military clubs. His daughter Marjory recalled: "He enjoyed going to the Legion and he would go on all the parades, but he would never talk about his experiences. He could be quite fearsome when his temper was up, but even now I find it hard to think about what he did." Barron was among the Commonwealth holders of the Victoria Cross who attended the Coronation of Queen Elizabeth II, reportedly saying he wished he were young enough "to be in her service as I was in her grandfather's."

Colin Fraser Barron VC died in Sunnybrook Hospital on August 15, 1958, and was buried in the Veterans' Plot, Prospect Cemetery, in Toronto. His VC group was later sold.

His daughter Marjory said of him: "He was a very proud man; proud of his roots and his award. As a young man, he was a bit of a devil. And he was a fighter too."

James Peter Robertson, who won the only VC awarded for the fighting in Passchendaele itself, was born at Albion Mines, Pictou, Nova Scotia, on October 26, 1883, the son of Scottish-born parents Alexander and Janet Robertson. One of eleven children, he was educated at Springall, Nova Scotia, where the family moved when he was four. During their time there, one of his brothers was presented with a gold cross for saving an injured man after a colliery explosion, despite having been injured himself. In 1898 the family relocated to Medicine Hat, Alberta, and it was there that Pete, as he was known, joined the Canadian Pacific Railway. He worked his way up to fireman and was transferred to Lethbridge as a locomotive engineer. A happy-go-lucky character forever telling jokes and with a song for all occasions, he was reputedly known throughout Alberta as "Singing Pete."

He enlisted in Alberta on June 14, 1915, and given the service number of 552665 and before heading overseas he wrote to "the best mother in the world": "The empire needs the very best that's in us." Her address was 656 5th St. South East, Medicine Hat. Joining the 13th Canadian Mounted Rifles, he was based for a time in Medicine Hat, where a delay in being shipped to Europe sparked a mutiny. It also led, on one occasion, to Robertson coming to blows with a civilian who had insulted members of the unit for their lack of action.

He eventually embarked for England on June 29, 1916. Posted initially to the Lord Strathcona's Horse, he served briefly with the 11th Battalion at Shorncliffe before being transferred to the 27th Battalion and proceeding to France on September 27. His early service with his new unit was blighted by illness. A bout of influenza was followed by treatment for influenza and the more serious matter of a sexually transmitted disease that resulted in him forfeiting allowances and pay during nearly two months spent in hospital. He rejoined the 27th Battalion in February 1917 and in the months that followed he saw a considerable amount of action in which he enjoyed a number of narrow escapes. Once, he and two comrades had to be rescued after surviving almost a day buried in the wreckage of their collapsed dugout, and on another occasion he was given up for dead after a disastrous attack. However, his fighting qualities and cheery optimism never flagged. Following his final gallant action at Passchendaele, one of his officers wrote of him: "He was a dandy soldier ... he kept the boys in good spirits under the most trying conditions."

On April 25, 1918, the citizens of Medicine Hat, Alberta, turned out in great numbers to see Janet Robertson receive her son's Victoria Cross from the lieutenant-governor, Robert G. Brett. In his address, he declared: "This cross is only a small thing, its cost is very little, but it has engraved on it the words 'For Valour,' which mean a great deal. Money can do much — with money titles can be bought, but money cannot buy the Victoria Cross. It must be won by valour and service." Tributes poured in for Canada's first "Locomotive engineer VC." In Cleveland, Ohio, 77,000 delegates at an international railway convention saluted his courage. As a mark of respect, the Canadian Pacific Railway displayed his photograph in Montreal station and almost twenty years after his death, the people of Medicine Hat dedicated the Robertson Memorial Park in his honour. Since then, a swimming pool, a street, and the local branch of the Royal Canadian Legion together with a "Hero Class" coastguard vessel have all been named after him. It is not known what happened to his VC and service medals.

H. STRACHAN

Masnières, France, November 20

On November 20, the opening day of the Battle of Cambrai, Maj.-Gen. J.E.B. Seely, in command of the Canadian Brigade (5th Cavalry Division), was waiting for a chance to follow in the wake of the day's successful tank sorties, which stretched across a four-mile front. The brigade had started out at Gouzeaucourt and before 2:00 p.m. had arrived at Les Rues Vertes, close to the canal crossing at Masnières. After conferring with Brig.-Gen. H. Nelson (88th Brigade), who informed him that he thought the tanks had already crossed the canal, Seely, whose squadrons were halted south of Les Rues Vertes, decided to send his leading regiment, the Fort Garry Horse, to continue the advance across the canal. He then went forward with his brigade major, Geoffrey Brooke, and his aide-de-camp, Prince Antoine d'Orleans, together with six orderlies. The group was close behind a tank that was making for the canal bridge. In his memoir *Adventure* Seely wrote this version of events:

> My instructions were, as soon as the tank had crossed the bridge, to take my Brigade over and gallop toward and beyond Cambrai. As the event proved, had the bridge remained intact, this we could easily have done. With the thousands of

horsemen and machine guns supporting us, the results might well have spelt a disaster of the first magnitude to the German Army. The tank rumbled along the street leading straight to the bridge, I, on my faithful *Warrior*, cantering along behind it. It got on to the middle of the bridge, but then there was a loud bang and crash, and down went the tank and bridge together into the canal. At the same moment there was a burst of rifle fire from the opposite side of the canal, and one or two of my orderlies were hit. I sent back a message at once reporting this disaster, saying that I would endeavour to bridge the canal elsewhere. At the same time I sent for my Brigade to come to the outskirts of Masnières. One squadron was sent to try to find a means of bridging the canal further to the south. That redoubtable soldier, Tiny Walker, my machine-gun officer ... took on the job. He managed to find two baulks of timber near a demolished lock, and, under cover of continuous rifle fire directed on every nook and cranny in the buildings opposite, got this narrow structure

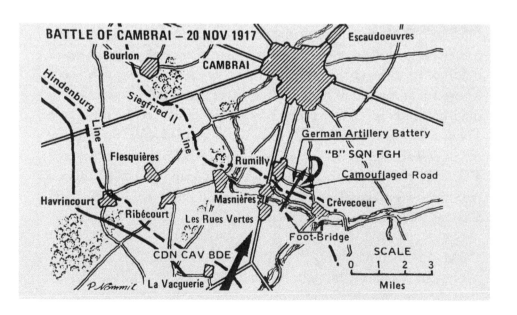

into position. The squadron, commanded by Strachan [sic, Capt. Duncan Campbell], of Fort Garry Horse, led their horses across and galloped into the open country, with the intention of silencing a German battery that was firing at us at about eight hundred yards' range.

Following an infantry advance into Masnières, there were still a number of the enemy holding out in the northern part of the village. Just beyond the village and still on the main Cambrai road stood the village of Rumilly and part of the Beaurevoir–Masnières line to the south of it. Having already travelled ten and a half miles, the advance guard of the Fort Garry Horse had entered Masnières with the intention of moving forward to Rumilly and attacking the enemy lines, including a battery that was being a nuisance, as well as hoping to capture the German Corps Command Post at Escaudoeuvres. The Canadians crossed the river bridge before reaching the canal bridge and found the latter had already been damaged by German demolition, although it could be used by infantry, until it collapsed owing to the weight of the tank *Flying Fox II* of F Battalion. Under heavy fire an alternative bridge was found to the southeast at the De-Saint-Quentin Ecluse de Masnières Lock, a few hundred yards from the main bridge, and the cavalry began to cross a twenty inch bridge under heavy fire at about 3:45 p.m. Two companies of the Hampshire Regiment had already used it, and with the help of machine-gun detachments and French civilians the bridge was made suitable for the passage of horses. It seems that those on the spot were unaware of the existence of a second and much more suitable bridge close to Mon Plaisir Farm, which was 1,600 yards southeast of the main bridge and hidden from fire, although its map reference was clearly marked on the divisional operation order, which clearly did not reach Cavalry Corps HQ.

Capt. Duncan Campbell was in command of B Squadron and moved off toward the Rumilly-Niergries ridge and attacked the enemy lines. They came under heavy machine-gun fire and "were hard put to it on the marshy ground about the canal." A gap had been previously cut in the enemy wire and they charged through this from the swampy ground near the canal. It was at this point that Campbell was mortally wounded and Lt. Harcus Strachan took his place. In an interview fifty years later Strachan stated:

> As I rode up Dunc was coming riding slowly back crouched in the front arch of his saddle and I thought he was wounded, but I just shouted "Okay" and galloped up to the head of the squadron. And the time I saw him was early the next morning when the small party was returning over the narrow bridge and we came on Dunc's body. Right at the bridge where we had crossed. I buried him there.

Southeast of Rumilly the Fort Garrys came across a mile-long camouflaged road that was used as a German supply route. In an interview with the author John Gardam, published in *Seventy Years After 1914–1984*, Strachan said:

> We got up to this narrow road along the crest and found the Germans had been using it for their supply route and they had it camouflaged, shutting it off from the side of our people. Well, you know it's awkward, we had to dismount there and cut our way through it and open it up and make arrangements for the rest of the Regiment to come through. The order was that when we got through the hedge we were able to dribble through, we would form in line of troop columns, no squadron front, not to present a good target. Then I told each troop commander, "Let your troops straggle. I don't care if they don't look well, let them straggle. Don't give the enemy machine guns a good target." I also said, "Now every troop commander has full authority to proceed in any way he likes suitable to the opposition and the ground, but he must not get out of touch with the squadron ..." We then thought, "well, we're over the worst of it" and lo and behold we saw a cavalry man's dream of heaven, an unprotected battery of guns. So we got up over the hill and lo there was our dream, four 77 mm guns. They are lined roughly with gun teams all

behind and the crews congratulating each other about the fine shooting they were doing. Boy, they did not know what was going to happen! Well, we didn't need an order. We just were riding with swords drawn that way and we went in with swords. The Germans made a grave mistake, I think. I don't know how they were trained in foot fighting, but they all left their guns. For me, I would have crept under a gun and sat down and hid. They all straggled away and were sitting ducks. There was no opposition from them whatsoever, and it was all over in a moment.

Strachan then gathered together his remaining men and continued his move toward Rumilly. They came under fire from blockhouses on the outskirts of Masnières and then halted in a sunken road half a mile to the east of the town. Realizing that they were now alone, with no other cavalry, let alone infantry troops, in sight, and in failing light, Strachan had to decide what action to take. The slight pause allowed the enemy to recoup, and soon the remaining cavalrymen became almost surrounded. By now the squadron was down to fewer than fifty men, and two troopers were sent back to HQ in Masnières with messages. Simultaneously, in order to cause greater confusion, Strachan set his men to cut three main telephone cables that ran along the edge of the sunken road. The light was still just strong enough for Rumilly church tower to be seen, and Strachan took a compass bearing and made the decision to gather up the remaining horses and deliberately try to cause them to stampede and thereby cause confusion in the enemy's mind as they fired at the riderless horses, although in reality, far from stampeding, the horses simply wandered off into the darkness. He then decided to lead his men back to Masnières on foot by using the straightest possible route in the growing darkness. At least four groups of Germans were encountered during the return journey to brigade, but each time the dismounted cavalrymen routed their foe and also collected a few prisoners while doing it. The remaining members of the squadron, now in two groups, reached the makeshift bridge of wooden beams carried up on tanks where their adventure had all started, in the early hours of the night.

However, Strachan's troubles were not yet over, for when making his way across one of the two tanks which supported the wooden structure he fell off it into ten feet of canal water. Presumably still damp, he then reported to Col. Patterson, who promptly burst into tears as he had assumed the worst and that the whole of B squadron had been "scuppered." When it had been decided earlier in the afternoon to call off the cavalry action, Patterson had in fact crossed the canal and ridden for half a mile in a vain search for B Squadron in order to recall them, but had failed to find them.

Capt. Campbell's body was later recovered from the lock and reburied at Flesquières Hill British Cemetery.

Strachan was awarded a VC for his gallantry and leadership, which was published in the *London Gazette* of December 18, 1917:

> Harcus Strachan, M.C., Fort Garry Horse, Canadian Cavalry. For most conspicuous bravery and leadership during operations. He took command of the squadron of his regiment when the squadron leader, approaching the enemy front line at a gallop, was killed. Lieutenant Strachan led the squadron through the enemy line of machine-gun posts, and then, with the surviving men, led the charge on the enemy battery, killing seven gunners with his sword. All the gunners having been killed and the battery silenced, he rallied his men and fought his way back at night through the enemy's line, bringing all unwounded men safely in, together with fifteen prisoners. The operation — which resulted in the silencing of an enemy battery, the killing of the whole battery personnel and many infantry, and the cutting of three main lines of telephone communications two miles in rear of the enemy's front line — was only rendered possible by the outstanding gallantry of this officer.

A second announcement was made in the *London Gazette* of March 23, 1918, when his Christian name was altered. Strachan was presented with his VC as well as MC by the king at Buckingham Palace on January 16 in the same investiture as that of Frederick

Booth, William Hewitt, and Arthur Hutt. While in London he gave several sittings for "a portrait in oils" commissioned by the Canadian government, which now hangs in the Canadian Parliament House in Ottawa.

A few days after his investiture he returned to his birthplace and was given a public reception by the Bo'ness Town Council at the Town Hall. After sitting through a long speech given by the Provost, Strachan was presented with a sword of honour on behalf of the Burgh. After the presentation "a distinguished baritone" gave a rendering of "Scots Wha Hae." Strachan then gave a brief response and was followed by a speech from Lord Rosebery and others.

On January 17, 1918, Strachan was given a month's leave and was later allowed compassionate leave to Canada for two months between February 23 and April 24, which was later extended to May 23. He left France for England on April 18, 1919. At one point when he had been visiting his hometown he had been invited to join the Freemasons, into which he was initiated. The ceremony was completed over a year later when he was once more visiting his hometown in May. He kept in touch with the Lodge in the ensuing years, and a portrait of him hangs in a room of the Douglas Lodge.

By the end of the war Strachan held the rank of temporary major, serving with the 19th Dragoons, and on November 30 he was given four days' leave in the United Kingdom. He was discharged on April 30, 1919, and returned to Canada with 2,000 other soldiers in May.

Harcus Strachan (pronounced Strawn) was born in Hollywood, a large house in Dean Road, Borrowstounnes (Bo'ness), West Lothian, Scotland, on November 7, 1884. He was the third son of William Strachan, a solicitor and sheriff-clerk of the County of Linlithgowshire and of Isabelle Thomson (*née* Veitch). He was educated at Bo'ness Academy and at Royal High School, Edinburgh, and then Edinburgh University in 1903, where he studied medicine. He "was considered a good all round sport," especially in rugby and cricket. He left his home in Scotland for Canada in 1908, accompanied by his brother Alexander. Together they had decided to emigrate and take up as homesteaders, and they purchased a ranch in Chauvin, Alberta. Later Strachan left the farm in the hands of his brother, mother, and two sisters. His next of kin was his mother

In the summer of 1915 when he was thirty years old Strachan enlisted in the Canadian Army, leaving for England on June 9, 1915, as a member of the 7th Canadian Mounted Rifles: his service number was 15585. His service records are confusing as they state that he enlisted in Canterbury, Kent, on July 15, 1915. He had dark hair and was five foot eleven inches tall. He left for France in February, arriving there on the 25th. He was promoted to lance corporal on May 7 and transfered as a trooper to the Fort Garry Horse. He was quickly promoted to corporal and later to lance sergeant by the end of July. As a trooper he had quickly made his mark, and was commissioned as a second -lieutenant in the field in September 1916. In early March he had ten days' leave and, a month later, was able to spend a few days in Paris. On May 1 of the same year he won an MC, which was published in the *London Gazette* of August 16, 1917:

> For conspicuous gallantry and devotion to duty. In command of a party which attacked the enemy's outposts (south of Saint-Quentin). He handled his men with great ability and dash, capturing eight prisoners and killing many more. The operation was carried out without a single casualty to the party.

On July 8 Strachan took part in a raid in which he was wounded by gunshot wounds to his right arm and thigh and also gassed. He was admitted to 55 CCS and then the 34th. He was later transferred to No. 12 Stationary Hospital at Etaples and on to No. 8 General Hospital in Rouen, followed by a period of convalescence in Dieppe, until he was discharged on the 22nd. He rejoined his unit in the field on August 30. He was able to return to Canada in September for ten days' leave and convalesce at the family home. In late September 1917 he returned to France and took part in the Battle of Cambrai in November.

After the war, when he returned to Canada, Strachan changed careers, joining the Canadian Bank of Commerce to become a bank manager after trying his hand at farming. He was also an officer in the militia with the 19th Alberta Dragoons, and by April 1922 was a major, second-in-command. The year before he attempted to enter federal politics on behalf of the Liberal Party for the Wainwright constituency, but was defeated by "the tide that swept the United Farmers of Alberta to power."

He later said in an interview, "Not a damn soul voted for me."

In 1926 he transferred from the Dragoons to the 15th Canadian Light Horse, and a year later went on reserve. In November 1929, together with two VCs from Edmonton's 49th Battalion, John Kerr and Cecil Kinross, he attended the VC dinner at the House of Lords hosted by the Prince of Wales.

Moving to Calgary in the late twenties, he married a Calgary woman, Betsy Stirling, who worked in the bank in Chauvin. The couple were to have one daughter, Jean. Strachan, together with six other VC holders from Alberta, was presented to the king and queen during ceremonies in the Alberta Legislature during the Royal couple's visit to the province in 1939. Strachan was by now ADC to the Governor General. After the Second World War broke out he returned to active service, becoming lieutenant-colonel of the 15th Alberta Light Horse. In early 1940 he accepted an appointment as major in the South Alberta Regiment, and in July he became lieutenant-colonel commanding of the former Edmonton Fusiliers and served in Europe for a time. Toward the end of 1944, when he had turned sixty, he returned to reserve status in Canada, and in July 1946 went on the retired list. He had rejoined the bank in 1945, and retired to Vancouver with his wife Bess in 1950.

He was invited to London as part of the Canadian contingent for the VC centenary celebrations in June 1956, and on December 10, 1957, was one of seven VC pallbearers at Michael O'Rourke's funeral at Mount Lehman, British Columbia. On November 19, 1959, he attended a dinner in Toronto at the Royal Canadian Military Institute.

Strachan's wife predeceased him, and he was proud of being able to cope by himself without "being a nuisance to anybody." His main hobbies were golf and the study of military subjects. He survived to an advanced age, dying in his ninety-fifth year at the University of British Columbia Hospital, Vancouver, on May 1, 1982, after a long illness. A Freemason since 1917, he requested that he should be given no funeral service, and was cremated at North Vancouver Crematorium with his ashes being scattered in the Rose Garden.

Strachan was a strong character and an excellent leader of men. A friend whose father served with him during the Second World War described him as "a real fine person around here." He could also bristle if someone dared to address him as "Strachan," as opposed to "Strawn." According to an article in the *Star Weekly* of September 3, 1966, he had a new enemy to upset him, the "permissive welfare society." "I live out here in this paradise on earth, Vancouver, and I spend a lot of my time chewing tobacco, spitting on the lawn and disagreeing with a great deal of what I hear." He is commemorated with Mount Strachan, part of the High Rock Range in Alberta, and his decorations are not publicly held. Apart from the VC and MC they include the BWM (1914–19), VM (1914–19), Canadian Volunteer Medal (1939–45), War Medal (1939–45), King George VI Coronation Medal (1937), Queen Elizabeth II Coronation Medal (1953), Queen Elizabeth II Silver Jubilee Medal (1967), and Canadian Centennial Medal (1967).

In recent years Strachan has been remembered in a number of ways. Firstly with a monument on the banks of the Saint-Quentin canal at Masnières, southwest of Cambrai at a point where the Fort Garry crossed toward Rumilly on November 20, 1917. The memorial was dedicated on June 11, 2014, in the presence of members of the Fort Garry Horse. In 2013 one of the lakes eight-five kilometres east of Thompson was named after him. On August 15, 2014, a plaque was set up and a time capsule in a plastic jerry can was left there, protected by a rock cairns. Third, and finally, in November 2014 a new memorial board in memory of pupils of the Royal High School in Edinburgh was unveiled which includes his name as a former pupil.

1918

Prior to the German March Offensive in March/April 1918, the last Canadian serviceman to receive the VC was Lt. Harcus Strachan on November 20th, the first day of the Battle of Cambrai.

In 1918, a year that turned out to be the last of the war, no fewer than thirty-five VCs were awarded to men serving with the Canadian Expeditionary Force. The first man serving with the CEF to earn the VC in the year was Lt. Gordon Flowerdew of the Lord Strathcona's Horse on March 30, northeast of Moreuil Wood. The wood was part of the defence of the city of Amiens.

The man behind what was to be the Canadian Army's finest year of the war was its Canadian Corps Commander Arthur (now Sir Arthur) Currie and he issued his "advance or fall" proclamation to his troops on the eve of the Battle of Lys in April 1917, when he appealed to his Canadian troops to stand firm and stem the tide against an expected great German offensive. He had already made a successful plea to General Horne to keep the whole of the Canadian Corps together and to prevent any of his divisions being taken from him. In the end the whole of the Canadian Corps was concentrated in the line from April 11, but not used in actual battle. Currie appeared to be in Field Marshal Haig's good books and, possibly through their non-appearance as a single fighting unit, an unknown quantity to the German Army.

Only one Canadian VC was won in this period on April 27/28, and that was by Lt. George McKean of the 14th Battalion (Royal Montreal) in the Gavrelle sector northeast of Arras. Six weeks later, to the southeast of Arras at Neuville-Vitasse, Cpl. Joseph Kaeble of the 22nd Battalion (French Canadian) won his on June 8/9.

By mid July the enemy advance that began in March finally ran out of steam. This was when the Allies seized the initiative, and the beginning of August marked what has become known as the Last Hundred Days. The Allies began what was to be a series of spectacular victories over the German Army, leading to the end of hostilities on November 11. Dominion troops played a very significant role in these victories, especially the Canadian Corps and the Australian Army, who became the spearhead of the Allied victory.

In conditions of great secrecy the Canadian Army moved southward. Their role was to support the British and French armies in a major planned advance against enemy lines. This move was actually what the enemy was expecting, but the Canadians Corps wanted to give the impression they were remaining in Flanders so they sent two battalions further north. At the same time the rest of the corps moved south. The deception seemed to have worked.

On August 8, in conditions of thick fog, the Allied action began at 4:20 a.m. with a barrage that was followed by advance of Australian and Canadian infantry accompanied by 430 tanks. Enemy positions were quickly captured and the Allied troops, Australians and Canadians in particular, were able to advance several miles and capture several thousand prisoners and a considerable number of enemy guns. Within a period of forty-eight hours the Canadians had won no fewer than eight VCs. Two more were won to the northwest of Roye at Parvillers-le-Quesnoy a few days later.

At the end of August, back in the Arras sector, two more Canadian troops won the VC in the renewed Arras Offensive, or Second Battle of Arras, one at Monchy-le-Preux to the east of Arras and one at Wancourt. The enemy had fallen back toward the Hindenburg Defence Line, which consisted of several well-defended trench systems. A vital section of it was the Drocourt-Quéant Line, which linked the 1914 enemy frontline with the enormously strong Hindenburg defence line. Currie was only given a couple of days in which to plan how his Canadian Corps would break the Drocourt-Quéant Line.

At the beginning of September the first of three attacks began against the Hindenburg Line on September 2, and the Canadian Corps were to be very much a part of it. Lt.-Gen. Sir Arthur Currie, the Canadian Corps commander, together with British troops, were to break their way through the Drocourt-Quéant Switch; a task they seemingly achieved with considerable ease. The Switch ran in front of Buissy and Villers-lès-Cagnicourt in a southeasterly direction. In two days the Canadians won no fewer than seven VCs. Soon the enemy was forced to make a general retreat to the line of the Canal du Nord, in front of Cambrai. On September 2 Currie's corps broke through it, in an operation that he considered more of a triumph for his men than events of August 8.

The Second Battle of Cambrai began on September 26. On the 27th Currie planned to stage the next part of the operations in two parts: first to cross a dry section of the Canal du Nord and capture Bourlon Wood to the east of Cambrai and the high ground close to the Arras-Cambrai road. The wood was an important part of the final section of the German Hindenburg Line and one that protected Cambrai. The second part of the operation was to capture the bridges over the Canal de l'Escaut to the northeast of Cambrai.

Together with British and New Zealand troops, Currie's men managed to cross a dry section of the Canal du Nord with comparative ease, and then the Canadians moved north toward Bourlon. Assisted by a tank battalion, they closed on the wood from two sides and captured no fewer than 10,000 prisoners together with 200 guns. Three Canadians won the VC during this successful battle.

The main section of the Hindenburg Line had been attacked as part of the overall British advance, and specially adapted Mark V tanks were preceded by a heavy artillery barrage. The much vaunted Line was broken — forty miles quickly fell.

In these operations to the east, northeast, and north of the Cambrai the Canadian Corps won another five VCs. After the city had been captured on October 5 the Allied armies moved forward in a northeastern direction toward Belgium.

The first VC of the war to be gained by a member of the 1st Royal Newfoundland Regiment was won at Ledegem, nine miles east of the city of Ypres, on October 14, when a section of the enemy frontline was captured. Nearly three weeks later the Allied army reached the outskirts of Valenciennes on November 1, and after very heavy fighting the city was captured within the next few days. It was in this fighting that the last Canadian VC of the war was earned.

The way was now open eastward, to the city of Mons in Belgium, where the war had begun four years earlier. The Canadian Corps reached Mons when it was already known that the end of the war was only days away. However, German troops were not going to give up that easily and they took up positions in the city and street. House-to-house fighting ensued. The Canadians fought their way into the centre of the city by November 11, the day that the Armistice was declared. Inevitably there were Canadian casualties during this final fighting, which would become a stain on Currie's considerable reputation as an excellent general.

During the final day of fighting the last Canadian casualty of the war was Private George Lawrence Price.

During the war the German Army was wary of fighting against Currie's Canadian Corps. He was also extremely popular with his troops. They called him "Guts and Gaiters." His strengths included very brief and meticulous battle plans, the use of engineers to build pontoon bridges, a considerable use of gas, and the use of creeping barrages as well as hurricane bombardments.

King George V, who knighted him in 1917, also admired Currie and invited him to lunch with him and the queen before he returned to Canada in August 1919. Sadly the reception on his homecoming was decidedly frosty, as on reaching Halifax he didn't even receive an official welcome. In 1920 he was appointed inspector general of the Canadian Militia. Currie died prematurely on November 30, 1933, at the age of fifty-seven.

E. DE WIND

Racecourse Redoubt near Grugies, France, March 21

On March 21, 1918, 2nd Lt. Edmund De Wind was one of seven men to win the VC, which he earned when in charge of the defence of a position called Racecourse Redoubt, southeast of Grugies. He was a member of the 15th (S) Battalion, North Belfast Royal Irish Rifles (RIR) (107th Brigade, 36th [Ulster] Division). The 108th Brigade was to their right and 109th Brigade to their left. The Ulster Division was to the southwest of the German-held town of Saint-Quentin, where, by March 17, it was obvious to the Ulstermen that there was a huge increase in German activity. The much-anticipated German offensive was surely close at hand.

Racecourse Redoubt straddled a railway line that led into St. Quentin and was one of fourteen redoubts in the area. They had been established because of the thinness of the defensive line; in fact, there was a group of three in this forward zone, each held by one of the three divisional brigades. Racecourse Redoubt was in the middle of the three and the 15th RIR occupied it, together with the 1st RIR.

At 4:35 a.m. on March 21 the German artillery opened fire and the enemy assault on the Ulsters began at 9:40 a.m. The attackers were helped by a thick mist and they quickly reached the line of redoubts, which were immediately surrounded and cut off. The one known as Jeanne d'Arc was overrun first as it was the most easterly. The mist then began to clear, which helped the defence of the two remaining redoubts to hold out; however, as each trench line was fought for and eventually overrun, it was only a question of time before the inevitable surrender. Finally only a small part of the redoubt around the railway cutting remained and this fell soon after De Wind had collapsed, mortally wounded. The time was just before 6:00 p.m. and he had gained a posthumous VC for his bravery and self-sacrifice. Immediately after he was killed the remaining men in the garrison surrendered. De Wind's citation published in the *London Gazette* of May 15, 1919, tells the story:

> For seven hours he held this most important post, and, though twice wounded and practically single-handed, he maintained his position until another section could be got to his help. On two occasions with two NCOs [non-commissioned officers] only he got out on top under heavy machine-gun and rifle fire, and cleared the enemy out of the trench, killing many. He continued to repel attack after attack, until he was mortally wounded and collapsed. His valour, self-sacrifice and example were of the highest order.

Thirty or so survivors (including HQ staff) were ordered by the Germans to remove their boots and were marched off, barefoot, into captivity.

De Wind was officially listed as missing, and a cable dated April 19, 1918, was sent to his mother by the War Office, who remained reluctant to authorize a death certificate despite his death becoming increasingly obvious as the months went by. Then, in September, a report from a rifleman arrived at the War Office via the German Red Cross Society; it was given by Rifleman A. Wright of D Company, supported by an unnamed officer in De Wind's battalion, who confirmed that De Wind had been killed. According to Wright, a trench mortar shell landed close to De Wind at about noon on March 21, 1918, and killed him outright.

Edmund De Wind was born in Comber, County Down in Northern Ireland on December 11, 1883. He was the youngest son of Arthur Hughes De Wind, chief engineer of the Belfast and County Down Railway, who died in 1917, and Margaret Jane De Wind. In 1900 the family lived at 32 and 32a Bridge Street, Comber, and then they moved to 31 Castle Street, which was later demolished. In 1908–09 Arthur De Wind built a house which he called "Kinvara" in Killinchy Road, and the family took up residence there in 1909. Arthur De Wind worshipped at the St. Mary's Church for more than forty years and was organist and choirmaster there. Edmund began school at Campbell College in Belfast in May 1895 and left five years later in December 1900 when he was seventeen. He joined the Bank of Ireland and worked in Belfast and Cavan. In 1911 he left for Canada, working in the Canadian Bank of Commerce and holding positions in several of its branches, including Toronto. He had served as a private for six months in 1912 with the 2nd Regt. of Queen's Own Toronto Rifles of Canada, and on November 6, 1914, he enlisted in the 31st Bn. (Calgary Regt.) in Edmonton, Alberta. He was five feet six inches tall with blue eyes and dark brown hair. His service number was 79152. The 31st Bn. was in 6th Bde., 2nd Canadian Div., which was part of the Canadian Corps under First, Second, Fourth, and Reserve (Fifth) Armies. He sailed for England with his battalion on May 29, 1915, and, after further training, left for France on September 15 in the same year.

Between September 1915 and April 1917 he served in the machine-gun section of his battalion, and on November 1 he wrote home describing the sections' rest in a farmhouse for a week. During his front line service he was at Thiepval, on July 1, 1916, at Courcelette in September 1916 and at Vimy Ridge, Messines Ridge and Cambrai in 1917. After Vimy Ridge he was sent to an officer cadet school, and was discharged from the 31st Battalion on September 25 and granted a commission the following day with the 15th Bn. Royal Irish Rifles. He had first applied for a commission with this regiment when still in Canada. In December he returned to the front with them, before being involved in the German offensive of March 21, 1918, when he became one of three soldiers from his regiment to win a VC in the Great War. At the time of his death he was engaged, and played hockey and cricket when at home in Ireland. He was also keen on sailing, shooting, fishing, and tennis.

De Wind's VC was not gazetted until the much later, on May 15, 1919, because details of his extreme bravery were only revealed after the Armistice, when former occupants of Racecourse Redoubt returned from prisoner-of-war (POW) camps. It was presented to his mother, Mrs. Margaret J. De Wind, in the Quadrangle at Buckingham Palace on June 21, 1919; although over eighty years of age she travelled from Belfast with her daughter to accept the award. While waiting in the palace anteroom, the king noticed Mrs. De Wind and gave instructions to an equerry to arrange for a private audience, which took place and saved the elderly woman from a long wait. Mrs. De Wind died in 1922. After De Wind's death the gross value of his will was £1020 15s 7d and his executor was his sister, Catherine Anne.

De Wind's name is listed on the Pozières Memorial to the Missing, as he has no known grave, and after the war a captured German field gun was presented to the town of Comber as a memorial to him. It was placed in the town square, and details of his action in winning the VC were included on a commemorative plate. The gun disappeared in the Second World War in the drive for scrap metal toward the war effort, but the plate was saved and is now in the porch of the St. Mary's Church in Comber. A memorial plaque to De Wind is also in the church itself.

In 1948, Mount De Wind was named after him in Jasper National Park, Alberta, and in Ulster one of the entrance pillars in St. Anne's Cathedral, Belfast, is dedicated to De Wind's memory with an inscription. A road in Comber is called De Wind Drive and is part of a housing estate built in 1961. In 1985, De Wind's name was also included in the stone memorial to Ulster VCs in the approach to the Ulster Tower at Thiepval, France.

De Wind's name is also remembered by the Ulster History Circle with a blue plaque in Bridge Street, Comber, which was unveiled on September 14, 2007. His name is included on the local war memorial, and a photograph of him hangs in the central hall of Campbell

College, Belfast, which also contains a photograph of his memorial plaque. A school building is also named after him and his name is also listed on the school war memorial.

On 17 Broadway Street E., Yorkton, Saskatchewan, is a plaque to his memory placed there as the building was one of the branches he worked for when with the Canadian Bank of Commerce. In addition a lake in north Saskatchewan has been named after him.

De Wind's decorations, apart from the VC, include the 1914–15 Star, BWM, and VM. They are in private hands but the Royal Irish Ulster Rifles Regimental Museum does have a medal display.

Keith Haines, a head of history at Campbell College, De Wind's former college, has privately published a short biography of De Wind.

A.A. MCLEOD

Over Albert, Somme, France, March 27

As the war entered what was to be its last year it was long known that the enemy was planning a major attack on the Western Front, and it was also expected that they would attack the Allied lines at their weakest points. The role of the RFC was outlined by its commander Major-General Hugh Trenchard: his squadrons were to carry out extensive bombing attacks on enemy-held road and rail networks, their artillery positions and reserves.

No. 2 Squadron RFC, based at Hesdigneul-lès-Béthune on the outskirts of Béthune, and equipped with Armstrong Whitworth FK8 aircraft, had undertaken numerous reconnaissance and bombing missions since their deployment to this airfield on June 30, 1915. After a short but intense artillery bombardment, the long-expected German offensive began on March 21 on a fifty-mile front from south of Arras to the River Oise below Saint-Quentin. Many British infantry battalions were overwhelmed with the ferocity of the enemy attack and were forced to fall back rapidly in the face of superior numbers. As a consequence the workload on No. 2 Squadron soon increased and many crews flew up to three sorties a day when the weather allowed. As enemy ground troops moved forward, so their aircraft units did likewise and occupied airfields from which the RFC had departed when enemy artillery had moved within range.

Six days after the great offensive began, the enemy was still making forward progress and, despite stubborn resistance, British troops were still falling back. In the Amiens sector, concentrations of enemy troops had been reported south of Albert, the ruins of which had been abandoned by the British during the night, and new defensive positions taken up on higher ground to the west of the town. The weather was overcast and misty. Despite this aircraft from No. 2 Squadron were ordered to find and attack the enemy troop concentrations reported to be in the Bray-sur-Somme area. Six aircraft, each with a full bomb load, were detailed for this morning sortie and included pilot Second Lt. Alan McLeod accompanied by Lt. Arthur Hammond his observer who were flying in FK8 No. B5773.

The six aircraft took off at 9:40 a.m. as a group, but McLeod soon became separated in the thick cloud and after nearly two hours' flying and unable to locate his objectives, McLeod now needed to refuel. Eventually he found the landing-ground of No. 43 Squadron at Avesnes-le-Comte, ten miles east of Arras, and badly damaged his machine's tail skid when he landed the heavily loaded aircraft. It was not until 1:00 p.m. that McLeod took off again, in the direction of Albert, after the FK8 had been fuelled and repaired.

After a further two hours' flying the weather did improve, but there was still no sign of the reported troop concentrations and so McLeod decided to return to base. However, an observation balloon was then spotted beneath them. McLeod immediately began a shallow dive in its direction, but before the balloon was in range of either guns or bombs, Hammond pointed upward to a Fokker flying at 3,000 feet, probably part of the customary protection for the balloon. McLeod immediately changed direction and began a very steep climb toward the enemy aircraft, and when close enough he manoeuvred in such a way that enabled Hammond to fire a burst from his Lewis gun at the enemy triplane, which was not expecting to be attacked by the British two-seater. The enemy aircraft fell into a spin and crashed on German-held ground near Albert.

Unfortunately for McLeod, this attack had been seen by a further eight Fokker triplanes, which emerged from cloud and dived down in line to attack the AW FK8. The first enemy machine attacked with its guns firing, but Hammond waited until it was within his range and with a long burst set it on fire and it fell away. The next attacker, Lt. Hans Kirschstein, flew under McLeod's aircraft and raked the big aircraft from nose to tail, wounding Hammond in two places. At the same time another Fokker attacked from a different direction and Hammond was again wounded, as was McLeod, in his leg. Despite his nauseating pain Hammond fired at the closest enemy machine, which quickly burst into flames and exploded. Kirschstein then came in for another attack and on this occasion some of his bullets hit McLeod's fuel tank in front of the cockpit, which then caught fire. The flames, fanned by the wind, quickly burned away the cockpit floor. McLeod's boots and leather flying coat were on fire and parts of the aircraft controls were smouldering. Kirschstein, convinced that McLeod's aircraft was doomed, broke off the engagement and went off in search of other victims. He later recorded the time of the attack as 1520 hours and the position three kilometres southwest of Albert.

Meanwhile Hammond, with no floor to support him, had climbed out to sit on the fuselage and held on to the Scarff ring Lewis gun mounting with his feet "on the bracing wires at the side of the fuselage." McLeod had swung one leg out of the cockpit on to the lower left wing. With one foot on the rudder pedal and a hand on the control column he attempted to fly the machine crab-like to keep the flames from Hammond. Another of the enemy aircraft flew in for a final look at the burning machine but came too close, and Hammond, despite his injuries and precarious position, fired a burst from the Lewis gun. The Fokker heeled over and fell to the ground.

McLeod did not release his bomb load as he was unsure of his whereabouts and did not know if he was above Allied positions. Amazingly he managed to control his aircraft well enough to crash-land, and although he was then under enemy fire from ground troops, the crash site was not far from friendly positions. McLeod was thrown clear when the aircraft hit the ground, but Hammond was trapped in the burning wreck. Under hostile machine-gun and shellfire he dragged Hammond from the burning aircraft and attempted to carry him away, but in his wounded state he was unable to do so. Consequently he half rolled and half dragged Hammond toward a shell hole. While doing this his aircraft's bombs exploded and McLeod was wounded by shrapnel. Once the two men had reached shelter McLeod collapsed from exhaustion and loss of blood. During the whole event Hammond had been wounded six times and McLeod five.

It was some time before the nearest friendly troops, men of the South African Scottish regiment, rescued the flyers and carried them to their trenches where their wounds were dressed. McLeod and Hammond spent several hours there under enemy bombardment until, under cover of darkness, stretcher-bearers carried them more than a mile to a dressing station. One of the airmen's rescuers later said that "the observer was too bad to talk; both smelt terribly of burnt flesh."

The two airmen were taken by ambulance to a CCS at Amiens for further treatment, and the following morning by hospital train to Étaples. On March 31 McLeod was then sent via Boulogne to the Prince of Wales Hospital in London.

Initially McLeod and Hammond had been reported missing, and in a letter to Dr. McLeod, Major Snow, the commanding officer of 2 Squadron, wrote, "... I have to advise you that your son, Lieut. A.A. McLeod has been missing since yesterday morning.... Without exaggeration he was the most gallant and fearless officer I have ever met in the flying corps...."

Meanwhile it was not long before McLeod attempted to reassure his father that he was not badly hurt, and in a letter written before the end of March he wrote that his wounds were not causing him pain and there was no need for his father to worry. Major Snow was soon to write again with the much better news that, "he is on our side of the lines and not ... a prisoner of war ..." and finished by writing that he hoped McLeod's action would be rewarded as it deserved.

Despite McLeod's subsequent protestations in the days that followed that he was "as fit as a fiddle," his wounds were more serious than he knew, or was told, and his father travelled to England to be with him and helped in his convalescence. McLeod's mother and sisters were kept informed of his progress by frequent telegrams.

As Major Snow had hinted in correspondence to McLeod's father, the two airmen were rewarded for the action of March 27, McLeod with a VC in particular for his heroics in saving his observer's life and Hammond with a bar to his MC.

The Supplement to the *London Gazette* No. 30663 dated May 1, 1918, published the citation for the award of the VC:

2nd Lt. Alan Arnett McLeod, Royal Air Force.

While flying with his observer (Lt. A.W. Hammond, M.C.), attacking hostile formations by bombs and machine gun fire, he was assailed at a height of 5,000 feet by eight enemy triplanes, which dived at him from all directions, firing their front guns. By skilful manoeuvring, he enabled his observer to fire bursts at each machine in turn, shooting three of them down out of control. By this time, Lt. McLeod had received five wounds, and while continuing the engagement, a bullet penetrated the petrol tank and set the machine on fire.

He then climbed out onto the left bottom plane, controlling his machine from the side of the fuselage, and by side-slipping steeply kept the flames to one side, thus enabling the observer to continue firing until the ground was reached. The observer had been wounded six times when the machine crashed in "No Man's Land," and 2nd Lt. McLeod, notwithstanding his own wounds, dragged him away from the burning wreckage at great personal risk from heavy machine gun fire from the enemy's lines. This very gallant pilot was again wounded by a bomb while engaged in the act of rescue, but he persevered until he had placed Lt. Hammond in comparative safety, before falling himself from exhaustion and loss of blood.

The citation for the award of a bar to his Military Cross to Lt. Arthur William Hammond, one of whose legs had been amputated after their rescue, was gazetted on July 26, 1918.

It was not for over five months that McLeod was sufficiently recovered to receive his award, and on September 4, using two sticks and accompanied by his father, he was invested with his VC by the king at Buckingham Palace. Later that month McLeod and his father returned to Canada.

Alan Arnett McLeod was born on April 20, 1899, to Alexander Neil McLeod and his wife Margaret Lilian (Arnett) at 292 Main Street, Stonewall, twenty-one miles north of Winnipeg. Alexander was a previous mayor of Stonewall where he had a medical practice. Alan had two younger sisters, Margaret Helen and Frances Marion.

At the age of fourteen, Alan joined a summer training camp of the 34th Fort Garry Horse at Fort Sewell in June 1913 where "mostly he groomed horses, shovelled manure and the like. But he was thrilled, they even let him wear a uniform."

On the outbreak of war in the following year, McLeod attempted to join the cadet wing of the Royal Flying Corps, but he had to wait until after his eighteenth birthday before the RFC would accept him. His training began on April 23, 1917, at the University of Toronto where he satisfactorily completed the course by early June and was then sent to Long Branch, just west of Toronto. He had his initiation flight on June 4 in a Curtis JN4 and after a little over two hours of instruction, made his first solo flight five days later. By June 16 he had been posted to Camp Borden for advanced training. McLeod's first impressions of the camp were not favourable, as he wrote home shortly after he arrived: "it's an awful hole here ... just a mass of sand and tents ... I just hate this place." Despite these initial misgivings he qualified as a pilot at Camp Borden by the end of July.

Further training at the School of Aerial Gunnery followed and his letters written at that time showed his eagerness to go overseas as rumours concerning such a move circulated in the camp. On August 9 he wrote that he would be "going over in the next draft, whenever that is."

Following home leave, Second lieutenant Alan McLeod travelled to Montreal and on August 20 embarked on board the SS *Metagama* for England. This was exactly four months after he had left school and after he had five hours solo flying in his logbook. The sea journey took longer than anticipated due to a U-Boat threat when the ship was forced to put into port in Ireland for safety, but it eventually docked on September 1.

After ten days' leave in London, during which he wrote that there had been a bombing raid every night, he was sent to Hursley Park, Winchester, where he received further training including the Wireless and Observers' Course before a posting to No. 82 Squadron at Waddington, Lincolnshire. This squadron was equipped with Armstrong Whitworth FK8 (AWFK8) two-seater aircraft, which McLeod described as "having the aerodynamics of a cow." No. 82 Squadron was soon to be sent to France, but McLeod, as he was not yet nineteen, had been transferred to No. 51 (Home Defence) Squadron which flew FE2b two-seater bi-planes and was based at Marham, Norfolk. He served with this unit for two months and frequently flew on night patrols.

Possibly due to the shortage of trained pilots McLeod was posted overseas before his nineteenth birthday, and in late November he arrived at the RFC Pilot's Pool at Saint-Omer. On the 29th he was assigned to No. 2 Squadron RFC based at Hesdigneul-lès-Béthune, on the southwest outskirts of Béthune. He was assigned to B Flight of this squadron which flew AWFK8s on army co-operation work in addition to day and night bombing sorties. He wrote home reassuring his parents, "Just to let you know how safe I am ... the Squadron I'm in has only had 1 man killed in the last 6 months ... the casualties in the RFC in France are a great deal less than they are in England & in Canada ... at Borden 6 were killed in one week."

After two weeks McLeod began flying artillery spotting missions and on December 19, in FK8 B5782 with Lieutenant Comber as observer/gunner, he attacked a formation of eight yellow and green Albatros scouts. Comber shot one down out of control with his Lewis gun.

In the new year, on January 14, with Lt. Reginald Key as observer, McLeod took off, ordered to attack a kite balloon at Bauvin, ten miles southwest of Lille. Enemy observation balloons were well protected, with experienced anti-aircraft gunners and fighter aircraft often in attendance. Consequently it was not an easy target. McLeod climbed above the balloon under considerable anti-aircraft fire and began to dive toward it when three enemy Albatros were spotted diving in his direction. He continued the dive down to the balloon, which was at 3,000 feet, and when level he pulled up, enabling Key to rake it with fire from his Lewis gun and set it aflame. McLeod banked to avoid the burning debris and as an Albatros attempted to manoeuvre under the British aircraft, Key fired, shattering part of the enemy aircraft's upper wing, and the machine broke up. After some exchanges of fire with the two remaining enemy aircraft, McLeod returned to base.

Two days later, on another artillery co-operation flight near la Bassée, again with Lt. Key, McLeod came under accurate fire from an anti-aircraft battery and also small-arms fire from nearby buildings. He dived on the battery, raked it with machine-gun fire, and followed this attack with bombs. He then strafed a column of troops before a return to his work with the artillery.

On January 14 his commanding officer, Major W.R. Snow, sent details of McLeod's actions at Bauvin and la Bassée to OC No. 1 Wing, who in turn submitted McLeod's name for the award of a Military Cross. This award was not confirmed, but McLeod was mentioned in Despatches.

On January 27 McLeod began two weeks' leave in England and stayed at the Savoy Hotel on the Strand. On the night of January 28 Gotha aircraft bombed London and over one hundred people were killed and injured in an air-raid shelter at nearby Longacre when Odhams Printing Works was hit by a large bomb.

McLeod returned to France from his leave and in the following weeks, with the other airmen of his squadron, was kept busy in patrols and sorties over a wide area of the front.

After winning a VC when flying in operations over Albert, and a subsequent six months in hospital, he returned to Canada with his father. Alan McLeod received an official welcome home when he arrived with his father at Winnipeg railway station on September 30, which was later followed by a public reception in Stonewall. He told the crowds that he was only home on leave and would be rejoining the RAF in January. By now the RNAS and RFC had combined to form the RAF on April 1.

Tragically, just four weeks later, McLeod contracted a very virulent strain of Spanish influenza and died in Winnipeg General Hospital on November 6, 1918. His funeral was three days later and large crowds paid their respects as the cortège, where a gun carriage carried his flag-draped coffin, made its way to the Old Kildonan

Presbyterian Cemetery where he was buried in Grave 238 with full military honours.

At the Highlanders' Memorial Church, Glasgow, a memorial tablet to McLeod was unveiled on January 27, 1924, by Colonel Sir John Lorne McLeod, ex-Lord Provost of Edinburgh. It was reported that "all the McLeods of the Highland light infantry and the Argyll and Sutherland Highlanders" were present at this ceremony.

Alan McLeod is commemorated in Stonewall by a plaque in his former home at 292 Main Street and also a bust at Stonewall Collegiate in the high school library. Alan McLeod VC Avenue in the town was named in his honour.

In 1940 the RCAF authorized a booklet, *Canada's Air Heritage*, which was distributed throughout the service. The book profiled only four men, Bishop, Barker, Collishaw, and McLeod, and, in addition, the RCAF commissioned oil paintings of these men, copies of which were sent to schools and air bases across Canada.

Alan McLeod was inducted into the Canadian Aviation Hall of Fame in 1973. An acrylic painting by George Tanner was commissioned by the Heritage Department of Air Command in 1994 to become part of the visual display of the McLeod display held in the Air Command Museum. The aircraft are depicted to be from Jasta 11 of JG 1, being all red, but in fact Hans Kirschstein flew with Jasta 6 so it is likely they attacked McLeod and Hammond. This Jasta had their aircraft striped like zebras, and were not red at all.

On April 3, 2004, the eightieth anniversary of the RCAF, Hangar 11, a First World War building at Canadian Forces Base Borden Museum and now the Air Force Annex, was dedicated to the memory of McLeod.

In St. Clement Dane's Church, the Strand, London, his name appears with those other VC recipients of the flying services on the wall left of the altar. McLeod's medal entitlement was: VC, BWM, Victory Medal + MiD oak leaf. In 1967 McLeod's medals and personal letters were donated to the Canadian War Museum in Ottawa by his sister, Mrs. Helen Arnett, but at the time of writing the medals are on loan and displayed in the Bishop Building, Headquarters of Canadian Air Division, Winnipeg.

G.M. FLOWERDEW

Northeast of Bois de Moreuil, France, March 30

No fewer than twenty-nine servicemen who won the VC gained the award in a period of only weeks beginning on March 21, an indication of the heroism shown when tackling the might of the German Army in what was to be the enemy's final attempt to break the stalemate of the Western Front. On March 23, a few miles to the southeast of Amiens, a mounted detachment numbering about 500 men was formed from what was left of the 3rd Cavalry Div. Brig.

General J.E.B. Seely (Canadian Cavalry Bde) provided 200 cavalrymen, and his brigade staff and the British provided two brigades of 150 men each. For the next few days they helped to re-establish infantry lines that had been destroyed, and on occasions carried out small counterattacks on enemy positions.

On March 27, the Canadian Brigade was put under the control of the 2nd Cavalry Division and on the 28th the Anglo-Canadian Cavalry passed under the control of the French First Army. The French then linked up with the right flank of the British Army.

On the 29th, the 2nd Cavalry Division was once more put under British command, where it joined up with the left of the French Army. Units of the German 243rd Division began to occupy Moreuil

Ridge, a very commanding position, and were beginning to move into the Bois de Moreuil on the Amiens side of the ridge. The position commanded the right embankment of the River Avre.

Brig.-Gen. Seely had learnt the bad news of the German progress from the GOC 2nd Cavalry Div., Brig.-Gen. T.T. Pitman. In his book *Adventure*, Seely recalls galloping forward to the village of Castel, leaving his brigade two miles behind. He found the village to be very close to the enemy, and when he rode down the main street, it was being spattered with bullets. Seely was accompanied by Major Connolly, commander of Lord Strathcona's Horse, and his aide-de-camp. At a crossroads he saw the Allied line spread out in front of him at a distance of about 600 yards, just beyond the River Luce. The enemy fire was coming from the lower part of the Bois de Moreuil, some 1,400 yards away. However, as Seely turned a corner he found himself shielded from the enemy fire and was able to converse with a French general (unnamed in Seely's book). It appeared to the Frenchman that to take the ridge was just not possible with Seely's small force against perhaps a whole German division. Seely, however, was keen to make the attempt and wrote later that this was a "big moment" in the war for him. It was agreed between the two men that the French should take the town of Moreuil to the south of the wood and that Seely's force should capture the wood itself. The two Allied armies would then link up and the German advance on Amiens would be halted. Seely gave his orders to Major Connolly for the capture of the ridge.

The plan was for three mounted squadrons of the Royal Canadian Dragoons to attack initially, to be followed up by attacks from mounted and unmounted men from Lord Strathcona's Horse. The Canadian brigade was to attack in three separate but converging thrusts. Seely had a few words with Lt. Flowerdew and told him he was confident that he would succeed in taking the wood. "With his gentle smile he turned to me and said: 'I know, sir, I know, it is a splendid moment. I will try not to fail you.'" With orders to take the wood, Lt. Gordon Flowerdew (who had been made C Squadron commander in January) began his gallant charge, with men from Lord Strathcona's Horse and they rode for about a mile, over the River Luce and around the northeastern part of the Bois de Moreuil.

In coping with the cavalry, the German infantry put up a strong resistance and there was a lot of hand-to-hand fighting, but by 11:00 a.m. the northern section of the wood had been captured by the Canadians. It was at this point that Flowerdew, with sword raised, led his men to almost certain death in a suicidal attack on two lines of the enemy, each with about sixty men and three machine guns. Flowerdew had ordered one troop, under Lt. Frederick Harvey VC, to dismount while he led the remaining three troops in the charge. Harvey had won his VC at Guyencourt on March 27, 1917.

By midday the wood was clear of the enemy, but they soon counterattacked and after continuous fighting three improvised battalions from the 8th Division relieved the cavalry during the night. By a coincidence this group was under the command of Brig.-Gen. G.W. St. G. Grogan, who himself was to win a VC a couple of months later in the third Battle of the Aisne. However, by March 31, most of the wood, together with Rifle Wood to the north, had been retaken by the enemy but the following day Rifle Wood was back in Allied hands, as was most of the Bois de Moreuil.

During the fierce fighting Flowerdew himself had been cut down by bullets that hit his chest and legs. He was mortally wounded and taken to a field hospital near Moreuil, where he was operated on and one of his legs amputated. His life could not be saved, however, and he succumbed the next day and was buried in Namps-au-Val British Cemetery, Plot 1, Row H, Grave 1. His age on the headstone installed after the war was given as thirty-two instead of thirty-three. The cemetery, designed by Sir Reginald Blomfield, is eleven miles southwest of Amiens and was made at the end of March 1918, when the German advance was beginning to fade. The casualties were mostly brought from the 41st, 50th, and 55th Casualty Clearing Stations. Also in the cemetery are the remains of twenty-four members of the Canadian Forces, most of whom were cavalrymen, almost certainly Flowerdew's colleagues in the famous charge.

Moreuil Wood is on the top of a high ridge and close to the road is a French war memorial, which, according to the inscription, was destroyed by "Hitler's Soldiers" in the Second World War. The area again came into the limelight on August 8, 1918, the beginning of the end of the German Army, and in Moreuil there is a street commemorating this date.

The citation for Flowerdew's posthumous VC was published in the *London Gazette* of April 24, 1918, as follows:

> For most conspicuous bravery and dash when in command of a squadron detailed for special service of a very important nature. On reaching the first objective, Lieut. Flowerdew saw two lines of the enemy, each about sixty strong, with machine guns in the centre and flanks, one line being about two hundred yards behind the other. Realizing the critical nature of the operation, and how much depended upon it, Lieut. Flowerdew ordered a troop under Lieut. Harvey, V.C., to dismount and carry out a special movement while he led the remaining three troops to the charge. The squadron (less one troop) passed over the lines, killing many of the enemy with the sword, and, wheeling about, galloped at them again. Although the squadron had then lost about seventy percent of its numbers, killed and wounded, from rifle and machine-gun fire directed on it from the front and both flanks, the enemy broke and retired. The survivors of the squadron then established themselves in a position where they were joined, after much hand-to-hand fighting, by Lieut. Harvey's party. Lieut. Flowerdew was dangerously wounded through both thighs during the operations, but continued to cheer on his men. There can be no doubt that this officer's great valour was the prime factor in the capture of the position.

Two months later Gordon's mother, accompanied by her daughters Eleanor and Florence, was presented with her son's VC by the king in the Quadrangle at Buckingham Palace on June 29.

Gordon Muriel Flowerdew was born at Billingford Hall, a farm in Billingford, near Scole in Norfolk, on January 2, 1885, and baptized in St. Leonard's, the village church. He was the eighth son of ten boys and four girls who were the children of Arthur John Blomfield Flowerdew and Hannah Flowerdew (*née* Symonds).

The main part of the village of Billingford, including a fine windmill, is adjacent to the main road running from Scole to Great Yarmouth. The Hall, though, is off the road and has to be approached up a track that rises through fields to the summit of a ridge. There are three main buildings in the area: the Hall, whose origins are several hundred years old, and from where the farming in the area has been organized for generations; the small church of St. Leonard's, which lost its tower in the early part of the nineteenth century; and beyond the church, the former rectory. These three buildings dominate the ridge and appear almost to "keep an eye" on what is happening below in the rest of the village, situated in the Waveney Valley, which also separates Suffolk from Norfolk.

Flowerdew attended Framlingham College between 1894 and 1899, and at the age of seventeen emigrated to Canada in 1903 and lived on a homestead to the north of Duck Lake, where he took up work as a cowboy and later worked in various occupations including that of a farmer. In 1910 he moved to British Columbia and in the following year became a member of the Regiment of Cavalry (31st Regt., British Columbia Horse). Three years later, when war broke out, he enlisted at Valcartier, Quebec, on September 24, 1914. He was five foot seven inches tall with brown eyes and brown hair, and his mother was his next of kin. His service number was 2505 and he joined Lord Strathcona's Horse (Royal Canadians). He was made a corporal at the end of October, and became an acting sergeant and sailed for England on May 4, 1915. After further training in England he embarked for France as part of the Canadian Cavalry Brigade. He was later promoted to full sergeant in July 1916 and was to become very popular with his men. On May 25, 1917, he was slightly wounded, and on June 9 was awarded a ten-day leave of absence. In fact, from his papers he seemed to have spells of leave quite often.

After the action at Moreuil Wood, Alfred Munnings, a fellow pupil at Framingham College for a short time, painted the famous charge of the Canadian horsemen, the original of which hangs in the Canadian War Memorial in Ottawa. A copy of the picture, *The Flowerdew Charge*, was presented to the College in 1991 at a special ceremony. Guests included officials from the Canadian High Commission and also Lord Strathcona, the great-grandson of the founder of the regiment.

Flowerdew's decorations were owned by Framlingham College and originally presented by one of his brothers and sisters, who each kept a miniature cross. Apart from the VC the decorations included the 1914–15 Star, BWM, and VM. The VC itself was later collected from the college by a Canadian official for display in Canada, where Flowerdew had become quite a folk hero, and was then displayed at the Lord Strathcona's Horse Museum (1990–2003).

In the college chapel is displayed the wooden cross from Flowerdew's original grave in France, and citations of the three men from Framlingham who won the VC in the Great War are also on display. The other two men are William Hewitt (1894–1900) and Augustine Agar. The citations are displayed on the chapel wall together with replicas of the medals. At the entrance to the college is an anteroom with displays of various aspects of the history of the college, which was founded as a memorial to Prince Albert. In addition to a copy of Munnings' painting of the charge is a second painting of the Canadian Cavalry during the war and copies of newspaper articles, etc.

The man who had recommended Flowerdew for the VC was Brig.-Gen. J.E.B. Seely, later a friend of Alfred Munnings, who went to France in 1918 to carry out commissions for the Canadian government. In St. Leonard's Church, Billingford, there is a memorial to the men from the village who died in the Great War, and Flowerdew's name is the first one listed. There is also a second memorial that lists the names of the men who served in the war but who survived, and on this list there are no fewer that four Flowerdews. There is also a brass plaque to Arthur Blomfield Flowerdew, one of Flowerdew's brothers, who died in the Boer War; and lastly there is a brass plaque, erected by her then surviving children, to Hannah Flowerdew (1850–1930), who lived at the hall for fifty years. By 1970, of the original fourteen Flowerdew children only three were still living.

Flowerdew's VC, returned to the college during a special presentation on February 3, 2003, and his deeds have always attracted a lot of interest. He was even written up as "the man who won the war" on one occasion, surely something of an exaggeration? Certainly what he and his colleagues achieved thoroughly surprised the German attackers, who were only eleven miles from the outskirts of Amiens. The Bois de Moreuil was in a very commanding position and perhaps the enemy didn't really appreciate just how important it was to hold onto this last real objective, and of the advantage to gain by driving a wedge between the French and the British armies before moving on to reach the vitally important city of Amiens. On the other hand, the enemy, which had been on the offensive for nine continuous days, was surely beginning to run out of steam. The possibility of the German Army losing the war was already apparent to the Allies by the beginning of April, as by then the enemy had clearly overstretched itself while the Allied armies had absorbed whatever had been thrown at them. A final reason for the attraction of the Flowerdew story may be that it was because his VC action was a cavalry charge, which in 1918 surely belonged to another age? Even so, the charge will forever have a romantic appeal.

In April 2004 Framingham College presented Flowerdew's VC, together with Lance Corporal William Hewitt's, to the Imperial War Museum where they joined that of Lt. Augustine Agar RN. On June 9, 2004, a memorial to commemorate Flowerdew and the famous charge of the Fort Garry Horse was dedicated at Moreul/Rifle Wood. It can be found next to a new highway underpass at corner of the D23 and D934 north of Moreuil. In recent years Flowerdew has become even more of a folk hero, and also in 2004 a popular play was written about him and his famous charge by Stephen Massicotte, called *Mary's Wedding*. He is also remembered with a marker to the northwest of Hara Lake at his former homestead north of Duck Lake. He also has a lake named after him in north Saskatchewan.

Back in England a commemorative paving stone in his memory will be placed in his home village of Billingford in March 2018.

G.B. MCKEAN

Gavrelle Sector, France, April 27/28

Lt. George McKean 14th Bn. (Quebec Regt.) CEF, 1st Canadian Div. won his VC in the Gavrelle Sector, seven miles northeast of Arras, on April 27/28, 1918, when the Battle of Lys was continuing to the north. Details of the raid which led to McKean winning the VC was written up and a copy of the report is kept with the TWO 95/3778 War Diary:

A group led by Lieut. G.B. McKean had the hardest task of all. The occupants of this trench, Hussar, were hemmed in by the barrage and had to fight or surrender. They decided to fight and so obstinately did they fight that Lieut. McKean was forced to send to the front line company for bombs. This exchange of bombs went on for several minutes and as there was considerable wire in front of the block things seemed shaky for a minute or so. Lieut. McKean set an example by making a flying dive over the block, landing "Head on," striking the stomach of a Hun. The Hun was considerably startled — Lieut. McKean's revolver was in his hand ready for use when he dived — exit Hun. The rest of the group at once tumbled over and this block gave no further trouble. The second block fought for a few minutes and on being rushed the garrison ran to the dugout at H 5d 87.07. A mobile charge was thrown down by Sergeant Jones which exploded almost at once, not giving the Sergeant time to get clear and he was killed. A machine gun was destroyed with this dugout. Too much cannot be said of the excellent leadership and personal courage of Lieut. McKean.

His VC citation was published in the *London Gazette* of June 28, which tells the extraordinary story as follows:

... Lieut. McKean's party which was operating on the right flank, was held up in a block in the communication trench by most intense fire from hand grenades and machine guns. The block, which was too close to our trenches to have been engaged by the preliminary bombardment, was well protected by wire and covered by a well-protected machine gun thirty yards behind it. Realizing if this block were not destroyed the success of the whole operation might be marred, he ran into the open to the right flank of the block, and with utter disregard of danger, leaped over the block head first on top of the enemy. Whilst lying on the ground on top of one of the enemy, another rushed at him with fixed bayonet. Lieut. McKean shot him through the body and then shot the enemy underneath him, who was struggling violently. This very gallant action enabled this position to be captured. Lieut. McKean's supply of bombs ran out at this time, and he sent back to our front line for a fresh supply. Whilst waiting for them, he engaged the enemy single-handed. When the bombs arrived, he fearlessly rushed the second block, killing two of the enemy, captured four others, and drove the remaining garrison, including a hostile machine-gun section, into a dugout. The dugout, with its occupants and machine gun, was destroyed. This officer's splendid bravery and dash undoubtedly saved many lives, for had not this position been captured the whole of the raiding party would have been exposed to dangerous enfilading fire during the withdrawal. His leadership at all times has been beyond praise.

A few months later, on September 2, McKean won the MC at Cagnicourt, eleven miles southeast of Arras, during which time he was also severely wounded. The citation read:

> As scout officer during two days' heavy fighting, he with his scouts led the battalion forward and sent in accurate reports and rallied men who had lost their officers. He was wounded early but pressed forward and entered Cagnicourt with three men, and observing a party of the enemy over 100 strong retiring from the village he dashed to a flank and headed them off and caused them all to surrender. Had these enemy troops been allowed to gain the high ground east of the village they would have inflicted heavy casualties on our troops. He continued to send in reports until exhausted by loss of blood. His conduct throughout was magnificent.

He was taken to the Red Cross Hospital at Le Tréport and was soon invalided back to England and was unable to return to his regiment as during his convalescence he was also suffering from shell shock.

George Burdon McKean was the son of James McKean, a merchant, and his wife, Jane Ann (*née* Henderson). He was born in Willington, Bishop Auckland, Co. Durham on July 4, 1888. He attended Bishop Barrington School, which had been endowed and erected in 1810, which appears to have been a school for boys from poor homes who were bright enough to deserve a good education. After leaving school McKean served an apprenticeship as a cabinet-maker with Messrs T. Thompson's Exors. of Newgate Street. However, his future was elsewhere and he left Bishop Auckland in 1902 at the age of fourteen in order to join his brother who was farming near Lethbridge, Alberta, who had gone on ahead. On arrival in Canada George initially worked on a cattle ranch and later on a farm owned by his brother. In 1911 he entered Robertson College and later enrolled in the University of Alberta, where he took an arts course. During his time there he became a keen sportsman and football player, and played for the college. He also found time to be scoutmaster of a troop attached to the Robertson Presbyterian Church in Edmonton, and during the summers acted as a student missionary at Hardieville and Athabasca Landing (Athabasca). His studies were interrupted when war was declared.

McKean attempted to enlist in 1915 in Calgary. By coincidence the woman he was to soon marry was Isabel Hall, who worked as secretary to the Calgary military registrar. On his attestation papers McKean gave his job as school teacher. He had considerable difficulty in passing the medical examinations. Having been rejected (possibly owing to his small size, he was five foot six inches) on three occasions, he was finally successful in Edmonton on January 22, 1915. His service number with the 14th (Quebec) Regiment) was 436568. His address at this time was 121 13th Avenue West, Calgary, Alberta.

He embarked for England on April 18, 1916, as a sergeant of the 51st Infantry Bn. and arrived in Liverpool six days later. He was then transferred to the 14th Bn. the Quebec Regt. (CEF), and in mid June sent to France as a private witht eh 19th Bn. On the 22nd he was promoted to corporal in the field, and later lance sergeant, but at his own request reverted to being a private on August 7. However, his rank reverted to corporal on October 11. He was wounded for the first time with gunshot wounds to the scalp at the end of November, and was in hospital until mid December. On March 2, 1917, McKean won his first medal, the MM, at Bully Grenay close to the town of Lens (*LG* April 26). He was recommended for a commission and left for England in order to take an officers course. He passed the tests and was made a temporary lieutenant on April 28, 1917, before being made a scout officer and later a full lieutenant, and in 1919 he became a captain.

After his VC citation was published in the *London Gazette* of June 28 he was honoured in his hometown of Bishop Auckland in mid-July in a ceremony at King's Hall when he was presented with an illuminated address and a gold watch by Mr. G.W. Jennings and

Mrs. Deans, members of the town council. Other council officials also took part in the ceremonies. McKean particularly appreciated the welcome from his old hometown, as he had moved to Canada. On July 31 at an investiture he received his VC from the king in the Quadrangle of Buckingham Palace. He won the MC when taking part in a scout patrol at Cagnicourt in September 1918. He was wounded on September 4 and became a patient in the Kitchener Hospital in October 1918, with gunshot wounds to the leg. He was granted ten days' convalescence in Matlock, Derbyshire, and finally released from hospital in February 1919. He was placed in charge of the Bureau of Information in the Khaki University of Canada in London. It was an educational scheme run by the YMCA of Canada with the aim of preparing soldiers for civilian life. In 1920, when still in the army, he attended the VC reception at Buckingham Palace. McKean served in Egypt until September 1925, and left the army when working in the Corps of Military Accounts on March 17, 1926, with the rank of captain.

After the war he wrote up his experiences in a book called *Scouting Thrills* (Macmillan, 1919) and also wrote books for boys in Canada.

He decided not to return to Canada and settled down in Brighton and in the mid 1920s he ran a sawmill in Cuffley, Hertfordshire, where on November 26, 1926, he was severely injured in an accident when splitting logs. He was struck by pieces of a broken circular saw and died in Potters Bar Cottage Hospital without regaining consciousness. After an inquest in the hospital he was buried at Brighton Extra-Mural Cemetery, reference 41624. His gravestone is of the type used by the Commonwealth War Graves Commission. However, his date of death is given as November 16, 1926, instead of November 28, and his age as being thirty-seven.

This dreadful accident left Constance, his widow, in severe financial difficulties but even so it wasn't until 1979 that she sold her late husband's VC and medals, a decision that was not popular with some other members of the family. They were sold at Sothebys in March 1979 and purchased by Mr. J.B. Hayward for £17,000 (C$40,000). At the time the price was a record. Later they were acquired by the Canadian War Museum, Ottawa, where a painting of McKean by the Canadian war artist Frederick Horsman Varley is also on display.

McKean is also commemorated in the Jasper National Park where he has a mount named after him, and on September 6, 2003, a commemoration to him was unveiled in Cagnicourt near Arras in the presence of a group of members of his family, including his daughter Pat Stanley, who was born two days after her father's death in November 1926 and wore her father's decorations. The place in front of the village church has been renamed "Place du Lieutenant George Burdon McKean." The village can be found slightly to the south of the D 939 Arras-Cambrai road and is where he won his MC on September 2, 1918. The IWM in London holds a portrait of him dated 1919 by Leon Underwood. Apart from his VC, MC, and MM his medals include the BWM and VM and are on display in the Canadian War Museum in Ottawa. He will be allocated a commemorative paving stone in Co. Durham in April 2017.

J. KAEBLE

Neuville-Vitasse, France, June 8/9

Nearly two miles to the southeast of Arras, at Neuville-Vitasse, in an area where the German Army had made very little progress since the start of their Spring Offensive in March, they began a barrage on the night of June 8, 1918, which began to lift off the Allied front line at 9:50 p.m. Three German raiding parties, each numbering about fifty men, then rushed forward immediately and entered the Allied line in a number of places.

However, the attackers were quickly repulsed before they reached the line of the 22nd Bn. Quebec Regt. (5th Bde) 2nd Canadian Div. (CEF) and the Canadians turned the tables on their foe by rushing forward, using bombs and Lewis guns, and capturing a German prisoner. A few Germans from their attacking party managed to reach the Canadian parapet but were then immediately repulsed. Cpl. Joseph Kaeble was in charge of one of the Lewis gun sections and at this point was largely responsible for keeping the enemy raiders at bay. In spite of being mortally wounded he continued operating his Lewis gun, until through total exhaustion he fell back down into the trench. He had suffered compound fractures of both legs and other wounds and died the following day at 2/1st London Field Ambulance in Neuville-Vitasse, and was buried seven miles west of

Arras in Wanquertin Communal Cemetery Extension, Plot II, Row 8, Grave 8. Three months later he became the first French Canadian to win the VC when he was awarded a posthumous one (*London Gazette* September 16, 1918) and the citation read:

> For most conspicuous bravery and extraordinary devotion to duty when in charge of a Lewis-gun section in the front-line trenches, on which a strong enemy raid was attempted. During an intense bombardment Corpl. Kaeble remained at the parapet with his Lewis gun shouldered ready for action, the field of fire being very short. As soon as the barrage lifted from the front line, about fifty of the enemy advanced toward his post. By this time the whole of his section except one had become casualties. Corpl. Kaeble jumped over the parapet, and holding his Lewis gun at the hip, emptied one magazine after another into the advancing enemy, and, although wounded several times by fragments of shells and bombs, he continued to fire, and entirely blocked the enemy by his determined stand. Finally, firing all the time, he fell backwards into the trench, mortally wounded. While lying on his back in the trench he fired his last cartridges over the parapet at the retreating Germans, and before losing consciousness shouted to the wounded about him "Keep it up, boys; do not let them get through! We must stop them!" The complete repulse of the enemy attack at this point was due to the remarkable personal bravery and self-sacrifice of this gallant non-commissioned officer, who died of his wounds shortly afterward.

Joseph Kaeble was born in St. Moise, Mantane County, Quebec, on May 5, 1892, the son of a farmer, Joseph Kaeble, and his wife, Marie Ducas. Joseph Junior was one of three children as well as a half-brother. After their father died, when they were living in Gaspé, the family moved to the village of Sayabec. When Joseph left school he trained to be a mechanic and worked at a local sawmill.

He was one of ten volunteers who enlisted in Sayabec. He joined up on March 20, 1916, and gave his date of birth as May 5, 1893, and his job as a merchant. He was French Canadian and Roman Catholic. His family name was Keable but it was later changed to Kaeble. He spent six months training in Valcartier before leaving for England on September 27 with the 189th Battalion and arrived on October 6. He had been allocated the service number of 889958 and was five foot seven inches tall. A month later he arrived in France, on November 12, and was assigned as a reserve to the 69th Battalion. On November 13 he was transferred to the 22nd Royal Regiment (5th Canadian Infantry Brigade) of the 2nd Canadian Division, the only French Canadian Regiment to serve on the Western Front and who had suffered heavy casualties in the Battle of the Somme. After the battle it was being reorganized to the northwest of Lens at Bully–Grenay and was to remain there for much of the winter before taking part in the capture of Vimy Ridge in the battle of Arras in April 1917. During the fighting on the 24th,when the troops were still under fire, Kaeble suffered gunshot wounds to the right shoulder and was out of action for twenty-five days during which time he was in hospital in Boulogne. However, he was soon back with his battalion, on May 25, and was once more made a machine gunner. On September 5, Kaeble was sentenced to twenty-eight days of Field Punishment Number One for being outside the billeting area without a pass on August 29. During the rest of 1917 the battalion took part in the fighting for Hill 70 in August and then in the autumn the struggle for possession of Passchendaele Ridge in Belgium. At the end of March 1918 the battalion moved to the Neuville-Vitasse sector and on March 23 Kaeble was promoted to corporal.

Six months after he won a VC the posthumous award was presented to his mother by the Duke of Devonshire, Governor General of Canada, in Rimouski, Quebec, on December 16. As well as his VC his decorations included the MM, BWM, and VM and together with a plaque are in the care of the Royal 22e Regimental Museum, the Citadel, Quebec. He was the first French/Canadian to be awarded the Military Medal (*LG* October 7, 1918) as well as the VC.

Kaeble's name is remembered in Sayabec Parish Church in Quebec and in recent times he has been commemorated in a number of ways including being honoured at the Canadian Forces Base Valcartier with a Mount Kaeble east of Vimy Camp; also on the camp is a street named after him and an NCO's club as well. The base, sixteen miles north of Quebec City, has been used for military purposes since 1914 when the 22nd Canadian Bn. trained there.

On November 5, 2006, the Governor General unveiled the Valiants Memorial in Ottawa, which included a series of five busts and nine statues commemorating some of Canada's heroes. A bust of Joseph Kaeble can be found on the northeast side of the National War Museum.

In February 2011 the Department of Fisheries and Oceans announced that nine new mid-shore coast guard patrol boats (Hero Class) would be built and the first one would be named after a Passchendaele VC, Private James Robertson, which has already been launched. Kaeble's boat was launched on September 22, 2014.

H.J. GOOD

Hangard Wood, France, August 8

The great Franco-British Offensive began on August 8, 1918, and within one hundred days the Allies had defeated the German Army, resulting in the signing of the Armistice on November 11. The Allied plan for the Battle of Amiens included a major role for the Australian, British, and Canadian Forces who, with fifteen divisions, were to be very heavily engaged. It was the Canadian and Australian Corps who were to spearhead the advance.

The major offensive was to take place to the east of the city of Amiens and plans were laid to use various ruses and deceptions in order to confuse the enemy about Allied intentions. Units of the Canadian Expeditionary Force were sent northwards to the Ypres Salient and put into the line on the Kemmel Front, where they were duly identified by the enemy. Corps headquarters was prepared and casualty clearing stations were set up in places where they could be seen. Wireless activity was also stepped up on the First Army Front and the impression was given to the enemy of a great concentration of tanks gathering in the area of Saint-Pol. Training operations, too, were carried out, which in turn were noted by enemy reconnaissance. The rumour that the British were about to begin a large offensive on the Northern Front quickly spread.

While the decoy units were busy near Ypres, the whole of the Corps — nearly 100,000 men — were being moved secretly from the Arras sector to Amiens, some fifty miles to the southwest. Preparations for the advance were carried out as much as possible during the hours of darkness and sounds of tanks or troop movements were muffled by either aerial or artillery activity. The assault began in the early hours of August 8 with a well-timed artillery barrage, combined with the use of several hundred tanks accompanied by Canadian, Australian, and French troops moving forward. It was the beginning of the end of the war and the day was later described by the German commander Field Marshal von Ludendorff as the German Army's "Black Day."

The 3rd Brigade (Canadian 1st Division) had to cover a front which was originally nearly two miles in width, and which was later reduced by a quarter of a mile. The brigade was the spearhead of the 1st Division together with the 4th Tank Battalion, which had forty-two Mark V tanks at its disposal. The first Canadian troops swept forward, regardless of hostile posts, which they left for the following infantry to deal with.

Cpl. Herman Good was a member of the 13th Battalion Quebec Regiment (Royal Highlanders) of this Brigade and was a member of D Company. Although in the early morning of August 8 the barrage began very accurately, it later caused casualties to the battalion when shells began falling short. However, despite this, the Canadian advance was very swift and the village of Aubercourt to the east of Hangard was soon reached. Twenty out of an original twenty-eight tanks in this area reached the high ground and moved off ahead of the 13th and 14th battalions of the 3rd Brigade. The tanks demoralized the enemy, but the Germans still put up a stout resistance. Their supports were duly dealt with and, according to the British Official History, "the fighting went on simultaneously all over the field."

Machine-gun nests in Hangard Wood put up considerable resistance and it was in dealing with these nests that Pte. Croak and Cpl. Good won their VCs. Good's VC was gazetted on September 27, 1918, as follows:

For most conspicuous bravery and leading when in attack his company was held up by heavy fire from three machine guns, which were seriously delaying the advance. Realizing the gravity of the situation, this N.C.O. dashed forward alone, killing several of the garrison and capturing the remainder. Later on Corpl. Good, while alone, killing several of the garrison and capturing the remainder. Later on Corpl. Good, while alone, encountered a battery of 5.9 inch guns, which were in action at the time. Collecting three men of his section, he charged the battery under point-blank fire and captured the entire crews of three guns.

Having overcome the machine-gun nests in Hangard Wood, the 13th Battalion moved swiftly, killing numbers of the enemy and capturing several German batteries. However, at a position called Croates Trench, the Royal Highlanders were held up for forty-five minutes by some enemy machine guns that proved to be very stubborn. A shortage of bombs was giving the battalion great concern and according to the Regimental History:

Rifle fire was ineffective and two tanks, which went forward in response to the infantry's request for aid, were put out of commission as soon as they got astride the trench and before they could deal with the occupants. Eventually, two Stokes guns were brought up and opened fire. After a few rounds from these had burst in the enemy position, a shirt, once white, appeared on the end of a rifle and the German garrison surrendered. By 8 a.m. the 3rd Bde. had reached nearly three miles into enemy territory and the objective, the Green line had been reached. Here the battalion halted and consolidated and the 2nd Bde. passed through their lines in order to continue the attack. It was at this point that the British Cavalry made an appearance. The day had been a great success.

Good was presented with his VC by the king on March 29, 1919, in the ballroom of Buckingham Palace.

Herman James Good was one of six brothers and eight sisters, children of Walter and Rebecca (*née* Sealy) Good. He was born in South Bathurst, New Brunswick, on November 29, 1887, where he attended Big River School. After leaving school he was involved in lumbering operations in the Bathurst area. By this time he had developed into a heavily built man, just under six feet in height, with sandy hair and blue eyes.

On June 29, 1915, Good enlisted in the Canadian Army in Sussex, New Brunswick, and was given the service number 445120. He left for Europe on the SS *Corsican* on October 30 and arrived in England on November 9. He joined the 5th (2nd Pioneer) Battalion and later transferred to the 13th Battalion on April 15, 1916. Over a period of three years he served in the 55th, 2nd Pioneer, and 13th battalions. He was wounded three times, the first time when he was shot in the buttocks on June 5, 1916, and was subsequently moved to the 2nd Canadian Field Ambulance.

Six weeks later he rejoined his unit but nearly three months after that he was suffering from shell shock and was sent to the Convalescent Depot for Shell Shock Cases at Le Tréport on October 6. He spent

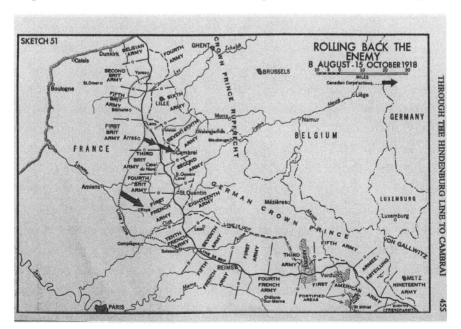

some time at base and rejoined his unit on November 11. A few weeks later he was back in hospital and rejoined his unit on January 6, 1917. Toward the end of May he caught a severe bout of mumps and was sent to a general hospital. On recovering he returned to base once more. By now he wore three wound stripes. On August 29, 1917, he was made an acting lance corporal, and this rank was confirmed four months later, on December 29. On May 18 the following year he was made a full corporal and on September 25, 1918, he was promoted to lance sergeant after winning his VC.

When Lance Sergeant Good returned on the *Olympic* he was met by his parents from Big River and the mayor of Bathurst, a town close by, on April 22, 1919, and given a hero's welcome. He was struck off strength on April 26, and on September 3 he was discharged at Saint John, New Brunswick.

Much of his later life was spent in lumber operations in the Bathurst area and he later became a warden for game and fish, as well as acting as fire warden in the same district, a position he held for nearly twenty years.

Ten years after the war he travelled to London for a dinner hosted by the Prince of Wales and Admiral of the Fleet Earl Jellicoe, president of the National Executive Council of the British legion, on November 9, 1929, in honour of all holders of the VC. The dinner took place in the Royal Gallery of the House of Lords. Dress was lounge suits with medals. As a souvenir of this famous dinner each winner of the VC was presented with a copy of the Legion Book, signed by the Prince of Wales, and copies of this book and signature have subsequently become highly collectable. They can be found in second-hand shops, but usually with the autograph removed.

Good was a modest man and made one of his rare public appearances in August 1962, when he laid the cornerstone of a new legion building on St. Peter Avenue, which was subsequently named after him. He was also made a life member of the Gloucester branch which was renamed "Herman J. Good, V.C. Branch No. 18" in September 1966. He was also a member of St. George's Anglican Church.

On April 13, 1969, Good suffered a stroke and died five days later at home in Bathurst. His body was taken from the hospital to rest at Elhatton's Funeral Home, St. George Street, Bathurst, before it was placed in the West Bathurst Protestant Receiving Vault until later in the spring. His funeral service took place in St. George's Church with full military honours, being attended by the CO of the Black Watch, Royal Highland Regiment of Canada, Lt.-Col. G.S. Morrison, together with six other officers, a firing party of one sergeant, and fourteen other ranks. A band with pipes and drums was also in attendance and took part in the service. Good was laid to rest in St. Alban's Cemetery, Sand Hill, Bathurst, where a cairn was later put up to his memory at the Salmon Beach Road entrance to the cemetery.

Good had three sons, Frank, Alfred, and Milton (who died in childhood); he bequeathed his VC to Frank. His wife, Martha, predeceased him in 1941.

A second soldier from New Brunswick to win the VC was a great friend of Good's, Dr. Milton F. Gregg; Good named one of his sons after him.

Good's decorations, including the VC, British War Medal, Victory Medal, King George VI Coronation Medal (1937), Queen Elizabeth II Coronation Medal (1953), and the Canadian Centennial Medal (1967) were acquired by the Canadian War Museum in December 2013.

J.B. CROAK

Hangard Wood, France, August 8

Private John Croak, like Cpl. H. Good VC, was a member of the 13th Battalion Quebec Regiment (Royal Highlanders of Canada) (3rd Brigade, 1st Division) and he also gained his VC at Hangard Wood. The village of Hangard is to the north of the Amiens–Roye road and, on the morning of August 8, the Canadian Corps' front line ran roughly north to south through Hangard Wood West to a line to the west of Hangard village. The 1st Divisional boundary was between the wood and the village.

The 13th Battalion led the attack in a heavy fog at dawn, with the 16th Battalion to their right and the 14th to the left. A huge barrage was set down, which was the prelude to a charge across no man's land into the German positions. During the advance, accompanying tanks found themselves blinded as a result of the barrage. During the attack Pte. Croak took on a German machine-gun nest with a supply of grenades, which resulted in seven Germans being captured. Although he was wounded in the arm during the action, Croak led the group of prisoners to company headquarters and, once there, was instructed to have his arm attended to. Ignoring this order he took on a second machine gun, which was targeting the Canadian command post. Croak rallied some of his colleagues and together they charged the enemy position, managing to overcome it with the bayonet. During this second deed Croak was mortally wounded and died within a few minutes.

Croak became the first man born in Newfoundland (not then part of Canada) to win the VC; his citation was published in the *London Gazette* on September 27, 1918:

> For most conspicuous bravery in attack when, having become separated from his section, he encountered a machine gun nest, which he bombed and silenced, taking the gun and crew prisoners. Shortly afterward he was severely wounded, but refused to desist. Having rejoined his platoon, a very strong point, containing several machine guns, was encountered. Private Croak, however, seeing an opportunity, dashed forward alone, and was almost immediately followed by the remainder of the platoon in a brilliant charge. He was the first to arrive at the trench line, into which he led his men, capturing three machine guns and bayoneting or capturing the entire garrison. The perseverance and valour of this gallant soldier who was again severely wounded and died of his wounds, were an inspiring example to all.

This official citation was added to by Capt. Harwood Steele in his book *The Canadians in France*:

> Private John Bernard Croak distinguished himself greatly. In the early stages of the attack he went hunting by himself, found a machine gun in action and bombed it with such fury that gun and crew became his captures. He then rejoined his platoon, although wounded, and went with it to the attack. Shortly afterward, a machine gun nest in a trench was encountered. Private Croak led a magnificent charge under heavy fire, was first into the trench, and was largely instrumental in killing or capturing the whole garrison.

John Croak was buried in Hangard Wood British Cemetery, Plot 1, Row A, Grave 9, very close to where he fell. The track leading to the cemetery is close to the no man's land crossed by the 1st Canadian Division on August 8 and between the two sections of

Hangard Wood. The epitaph on his headstone reads: "Do you wish to show your gratitude? Kneel down and pray for my soul."

On November 23, 1918, Lieutenant Governor John James Grant of Nova Scotia presented Croak's VC to his mother, Mrs. James Croak, at a ceremony at Government House, Halifax. Mrs. Croak, who was accompanied by her husband and daughter, was also awarded a second medal, that of the international Order of the Allied Mothers in Suffering.

At the conclusion of the proceedings, the Croak family were presented with two "handsome and valuable chairs" by their son's former employers, local No. 7. The opening address from local No. 7 to Mr. and Mrs. James Croak began with the following sentence:

We are here to-night to tender you the sincere and heartfelt congratulations of the officers and members of local No. 7 A.M.W. of Nova Scotia, New Aberdeen on the high honour and distinction just conferred upon you in memory of the noble and valiant deeds of your brave boy, who made the supreme sacrifice in the service of his King and Country.

At Mr. Croak's request a Mr. McAulay expressed the thanks of the family for the gifts and tributes on their behalf. A musical interlude then followed and the function ended with the playing of the National Anthem. In addition to receiving a letter of condolence from the 13th Battalion Chaplain, Mrs. Croak also received a letter of sympathy from Brig.-Gen. G.S. Tuxford of the 3rd Canadian Infantry Brigade.

John Croak was the son of James and Seeley Croak, born in Little Bay, Newfoundland, on May 18, 1892, and baptized into the Roman Catholic Church the same day. His name in Newfoundland was spelt Croke but he preferred Croak as the spelling of his name. In 1896 his parents moved to Nova Scotia and lived at New Aberdeen, later part of Glace Bay, when John attended St. John's High School, New Aberdeen, and later Aberdeen Public School. John left school at the age of fourteen when he became a miner, working in Dominion No. 2 colliery at Glace Bay.

In 1914 John Croak moved westwards and for a time took up trapping and enlisted in the following year as a member of the 55th Battalion in Sussex, New Brunswick, on August 7. His service number was 445312 and he was five foot five inches tall with light hair. His basic training was carried out in Camp Sussex. He volunteered for overseas service with the 55th Battalion and left for for England in November 1915, arriving there on the ninth.

After arriving at Bramshott Camp in Surrey he was in trouble with the military authorities right from the start of his service. On November 12 he was placed in detention for drunken behaviour and on December 30 he was given six days field punishment for being in possession of whiskey. He was punished for similar offences later in the war and had even been absent without leave for three days. He had been transferred to the 13th Battalion Quebec Regiment (Royal Highlanders of Canada) and served in France and Flanders between April 1916 and and August 1918, and saw action on the Somme, at Vimy, Arras, Hill 70, and Passchendaele. In early October 1916 he was given a ten day sentence for drunkenness and in June 1917 he was being treated for venereal disease. Throughout his service he was very often drunk or violent, and on at least one occasion resisted arrest. He was also penalized with a loss of pay.

After his death Croak was commemorated by Branch 125 of the Royal Canadian Legion in Glace Bay being named after him, but owing to lack of funds the branch was shut down. A chapter of the Imperial Order of the Daughters of the Empire was also named after him, but it too became defunct. After that a school was named after him in St. John's. Much later Croak was commemorated with a plaque, hewn out of a block of Cape Breton rock to symbolize the "unpolished virtue" of the character of Pte. Croak of Glace Bay. This was placed in the Memorial Park in Glace Bay, which is also named after him. The site was formerly the grounds of the former Dominion No. 2 Colliery reservoir. The plaque was unveiled on Croak's centenary, on May 18, 1992, and the ceremony was preceded by a Memorial Mass at St. John the Baptist Church in New Aberdeen. Croak, together with the the seventeen-year-old Private Thomas Ricketts, were the only two men born in Newfoundland to win the VC in the War.

Croak's decorations were presented to the Army Museum at the Citadel, Halifax, by Bernard Croak, a nephew, on August 19, 1972. Apart from the VC, they included the BWM and the VM and are now on display at the Canadian War Museum in Ottawa.

H.G.B. MINER

Démuin, east of Hangard, France, August 8

Corporal Harry Miner won a posthumous VC at Démuin, to the east of Hangard on August 8, 1918, when he took on an enemy machine gun and bombing posts single-handed, despite being wounded. He was a member of the 58th Battalion (2nd Central Ontario Regiment, 9th Brigade, 3rd Canadian Division). The 9th Brigade also included the 43rd, 52nd, and 116th battalions. The 43rd was responsible for capturing Rifle Wood, to the west of the Démuin–Moreuil road, which they duly accomplished by 7:30 a.m. The 116th attacked Hamon Wood from the north and Miner's battalion, which had also been involved in the fighting at Rifle Wood, pushed on to Démuin and had cleared the hamlet of Courcelles, northeast of Démuin, by 7:05 a.m. It was during this fighting that Miner was severely wounded in the head, left arm, and face. He later died from these shell wounds at No. 5CCS and was awarded a posthumous VC, which was gazetted on October 26, 1918, and presented to his parents, who lived in Ridgetown, by His Excellency, the Duke of Devonshire, Governor General of Canada. The citation reads as follows:

> For most conspicuous bravery and devotion to duty in attack, when, despite severe wounds, he refused to withdraw. He

rushed an enemy machine gun post single-handed, killed the entire crew and turned the gun on the enemy. Later, with two others, he attacked another enemy machine gun post, and succeded in putting the gun out of action. Corpl. Miner then rushed single-handed an enemy bombing post, bayoneting two of the garrison and putting the remainder to flight. He was mortally wounded in the performance of this gallant deed.

Miner was buried at Crouy British Cemetery, ten miles northwest of Amiens, Plot V, Row B, Grave 11. The commanding officer of the 58th Battalion, Maj. R.L. Smythe, wrote a letter of sympathy to his parents, as did several of the officers in his unit.

Harry Garnet Bedford Miner, the son of John and Sarah Orphra Miner, was born on June 24, 1891, in Cedar Springs, Ontario. He attended school at Selton and continued his schooling in Highgate School in Oxford Township. After leaving school he went into farming and at some point lived in Ohio and Detroit in the U.S. In London, Ontario, he enlisted in the Canadian Army on December 1, 1915, and was posted to the 142nd Battalion, and promoted to lance corporal on October 1, 1916. On his attestation papers he was described as being five foot seven inches tall with blue eyes and brown hair. His service number was 823028 and his next of kin was his father of 130 Stanley Avenue, Chatham, Ontario. Miner left Canada on October 30 and arrived in Britain on November 11, when he asked for his rank to be altered to private, acting lance corporal, so that he could join the 58th Battalion, 2nd Central Ontario Regiment. He then trained for a few weeks before making the transfer and arrived in France on November 29. He was in hospital with tonsillitis from December 11 to 16, and was made a full corporal on January 1, 1918, after he had won the French Croix de Guerre for a deed carried out in the Saint-Émile sector between Hazebrouck and Lens at the end of December 1917.

His citation for this award (August 17, 1918) reads as follows: "During the night of 30–31 December 1917, being in charge of a wiring party, he did excellent work, by his example and energy, in keeping his men together for seven hours in spite of enemy machine guns which were firing on his position."

In January he was in hospital again, this time being treated for scabies.

On September 22, 1963, an historical plaque to his memory was unveiled in Cedar Springs, Miner's birthplace. This plaque was one of several that commemorate the Canadian holders of the VC. The idea was instigated by the Ontario Department of Travel and Publicity, who acted on the expertise and advice supplied by the Archeological and Historic Sites Board of Ontario.

This particular ceremony was organized and sponsored by the local branch of the Royal Canadian Legion. The legion invited various local dignitaries to the unveiling, which included a legion drum head service. The plaque itself was unveiled by Mr. Ross Miner, a brother of Cpl. Harry Miner. It was dedicated by the Rev. A. Meecham of Blenheim United Church, Ontario. There is also a plaque to Miner's memory in the United Church in Cedar Springs. Branch 185 of the Royal Canadian legion in Blenheim was also named after him.

Harry Miner's decorations, including the VC, BWM, VM, and Croix de Guerre, are kept in the Huron County Museum, Goderich.

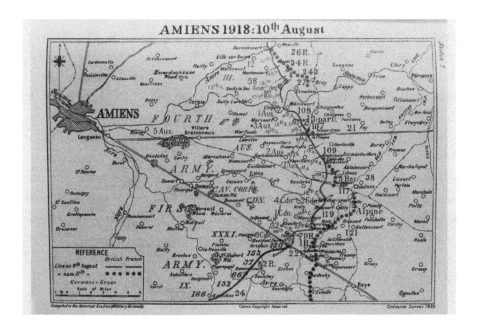

AMIENS 1918:10th August

J. BRILLANT

Near Wiencourt, France, August 9

Between August 8, 1918, the first day of the Battle of Amiens, and August 11, no fewer than eleven men gained the VC, of whom eight were serving with Canadian Forces. One of the Canadians, who in fact was a French Canadian, was Lieutenant Jean Brillant of the 22nd Canadian Infantry Battalion (5th Brigade, 2nd Canadian Division). On August 8 his battalion was operating southeast of Villers-Bretonneux, engaged in mopping-up operations to the west of the village of Wiencourt-l'Équipée, during which he rushed an enemy machine-gun post that was holding up the left flank of his company. He killed two machine gunners but in doing so was injured in his left arm.

At 10:00 a.m. the following day his battalion moved from Wiencourt and, supported by artillery, proceeded in a southeasterly direction toward the village of Caix, and took over enemy positions after very arduous fighting in the village of Vrély, to the south of Rosières-en-Santerre. The enemy had entrenched machine-gun positions close to the village of Vrély and any advance over open ground would prove to be very costly. Companies were organized into groups that used the cover of ditches and sunken roads. By 3:15 p.m. the leading groups had managed to progress through

Vrély and beyond, and proceeded to consolidate 500 yards east of Méharicourt, which they reached by 5:30 p.m. By then they were too far ahead and had to wait for their neighbours to catch up, which they did two hours later. Although the battalion had been successful it came at a very high cost in casualties of six officers and 176 other ranks either killed, wounded, or missing.

During the attack on Vrély, athough Brillant was already wounded, he led a group of two platoons using bombs and grenades in a skirmish, which led to the capture of no fewer than fifteen machine guns together with 150 prisoners. During this action he was wounded again, this time in the head, yet still managed to organize a party to capture an enemy four-inch gun that was engaging the battalion over open sights. It was for this bravery during this fighting, in addition to his work the previous day, that Lt. Jean Brillant won his VC. In two days of hard fighting he had been wounded three times but tragically succumbed to his injuries on August 10. His citation was published in the *London Gazette* of September 27, 1918.

For most conspicuous bravery and outstanding devotion to duty when in charge of a company which he led in attack during two days with absolute fearlessness and extraordinary ability and initiative, the extent of the advance being twelve miles. On the first day of operations, shortly after the attack began, his company's left flank was held up by an enemy machine gun. Lieut. Brillant rushed and captured the machine gun, personally killing two of the enemy crew. While doing this he was wounded, but refused to leave his command. Later on the same day his company was held up by heavy machine gun fire. He reconnoitred the ground personally, organized a party of two platoons, and rushed straight for the machine gun nest. Here 150 enemy and fifteen machine guns were captured, Lieut. Brillant personally killing five of the enemy, and being wounded a second time. He had this wound dressed immediately, and again refused to leave his company. Subsequently this gallant officer detected a field-gun firing on his men over open sights. He immediately organized and led a "rushing" party toward the gun. After progressing about 600 yards he was again seriously wounded. In spite of this third wound he continued to advance for some 200 yards more, when he fell unconscious from exhaustion and loss of blood. Lieut. Brillant's wonderful example throughout the day inspired his men with an enthusiasm and dash which largely contributed toward the success of the operations.

Brillant's last words were said to have been: "I am through. Take charge of the company because I know I won't be here long." He died of his wounds and loss of blood on August 10 at 48 CCS and was buried in Villers-Bretonneux Military Cemetery, Plot Via, Row B, Grave 20, to the left of the Cross of Sacrifice. His posthumous VC was presented to his father in Rimouski, Quebec, on December 16, 1918, by His Excellency the Duke of Devonshire, Governor General of Canada.

Jean-Baptiste-Arthur Brillant, a French Canadian, was born of a military as well as Roman Catholic family, in Assametquaghan, Quebec, on March 15, 1890. His father was Joseph, a railway maintenance worker, and his mother Rose-de-lima Raiche Brillant. He studied at St. Joseph University, Memramcook, New Brunswick, and later at the Seminaire de Rimouski (1904–05). He became a railway telephone operator. In 1903 he volunteered to serve in 89th (Temiscouata & Rimouski) Regiment (which in 1920 was renamed les Fusiliers du St. Laurent) and claimed later to have been a member for thirteen years, becoming a lieutenant. He quit his job on March 20, 1916, when he applied to join the CEF in Valcartier. After six months' training there he filled out an Officer's Declaration Form at the camp on September 20 and was made a member of the 189th Battalion. He was five foot ten inches tall and his father was his next of kin. The family address was Le Bic, Co. Rimousky, Quebec. Brillant sailed for Liverpool a week later on board SS *Lapland*. When he attested, his address was Bic. Co., Rimouski, Quebec.

Arriving in England on October 6 he was assigned to the 69th Battalion and left for France on October 29. He then became an officer with the only French-Canadian battalion serving in the field at that time, the 22nd Battalion, Quebec Regiment (Canadian Français), CEF who were part of the 2nd Division. He proceeded to his new battalion, joining it at Bully-Grenay.

In 1917, between April 9 and 14, Brillant took part in the fight for Vimy Ridge and subseqently spent a few days in hospital with trench fever. Three months later he was wounded briefly and became a patient in the Duchess of Westminster Hospital in Le Touquet on July 21. He was suffering from Orchitis VDG. Soon afterward he was transferred to 51st General Hospital in Etaples. After two months he was discharged to base on September 18.

Brillant won the MC (*LG* 16 September) for his work during the night of May 27–28 in the vicinity of Boiry-Besqerelle, 110 miles north of Paris, when he was called to assist in the silencing of an enemy outpost defended by two machine guns and fifty men. During the attack he spied a small of group of five Germans making their escape. He managed to dispatch four of them, and captured a fifth and took him back to battalion headquarters for interrogation. During the fighting Brillant was slightly wounded. On July 6 he was able to go to Paris for a week for what was to be his last leave. Four weeks later he was mortally wounded, on August 9, and died the following day.

His posthumous MC was gazetted on September 16, eleven days prior to his VC. Apart from these two decorations, his medals included the BWM, VM, and King George V Coronation Medal of 1911. They became the property of his regiment and are displayed at the Royal 22 Regiment Museum at the Citadel, Quebec, together with a Dead Man's Penny and other related items to his life. In addition, his name was the first to be listed on the Rimouski War Memorial, and his name is also included as the name of a park in Montreal that also includes a memorial to him. Streets are also named after him in Rimouski, where his father lived, and in Montreal. His name was also used by the Royal Canadian Legion Branch in Quebec City and in the Canadian Forces base in Valcartier. Unusally, his name has also been used for a retirement home group in Montreal.

J.E. TAIT

Beaucourt Wood, France, August 8–11

Lieutenant James Tait of the 78th Battalion (Winnipeg Grenadiers, 12th Brigade 4th Canadian Division) won his VC for action over a period of three days between August 8 and 11. By late afternoon of August 8, 1918, the Canadian advance to the southeast of Amiens had reached Beaucourt, near Le Quesnel and north of the road to Roye. To the south of Beaucourt Wood the landscape was very open and devoid of cover. Because of this the Canadians lost heavily from machine-gun fire coming from the direction of Fresnoy-en-Chaussée as well as the northern edge of Le Quesnel. As a result any idea of a frontal attack was ruled out. The right flank of the 12th Brigade in particular was strongly attacked by fire coming from Beaucourt Wood and it left a company from each of the 38th and 78th battalions in order to deal with it. The 78th Battalion took on the enemy machine guns at the north end of the wood and with artillery and tank support overcame them when they then formed a defensive flank. It was during this action that Lt. Tait, in command of C Company, won his VC when he knocked out an enemy machine-gun post single-handed. In addition, his men captured a dozen machine guns and twenty prisoners. The 72nd Battalion, despite heavy rifle and machine-gun fire, succeeded in passing through the lines of the 78th Battalion to reach its final objective at about 6:15 p.m., a dozen miles from its starting point.

The rest of the 12th Brigade dealt successfully with enemy resistance and reached the southern edge of the wood to the south of Caix at about 4:45 p.m. In this section of the battlefield the day had been a most successful one, with considerable territorial gains and the capture of 13,000 prisoners.

Lt. Tait's citation was gazetted on September 27, 1918, as follows:

For most conspicuous bravery and initiative in attack. The advance having been checked by intense machine gun fire, Lieut. Tait rallied his company and led it forward with consummate skill and dash under a hail of bullets. A concealed machine gun however, continued to cause many casualties. Taking a rifle and bayonet, Lieut. Tait dashed forward alone, and killed the enemy gunner. Inspired by his example, his men rushed the position, capturing twelve machine guns and twenty prisoners. His valorous action cleared the way for his battalion to advance. Later, when the enemy counterattacked our positions under intense artillery bombardment, this gallant officer displayed outstanding courage and leadership, and, though mortally wounded by a shell, continued to direct and aid his men until his death.

Tait died in action at Hallu on August 11, 1918, and was probably first buried in the village prior to being moved to Fouquescourt British Cemetery, where he is now believed to be buried. He has a headstone which is number eight of a section of similar casualties but gives his age as thirty-one and not thirty-two. The village of Fouquescourt is sixteen miles south of Albert, to the southwest of Hallu, and the cemetery is just outside the village, which was captured by the Canadian Corps in August 1918. Tait's VC was presented to his widow, Jessie, by His Excellency the lieutenant-governor of Manitoba. She was living in Winnipeg at the time.

James Edward Tait was the son of James Bryden and Mary (*née* Johnstone) and born in Greenbrae, Dumfries, Scotland, on May 27, 1886, although some accounts say his birthplace was

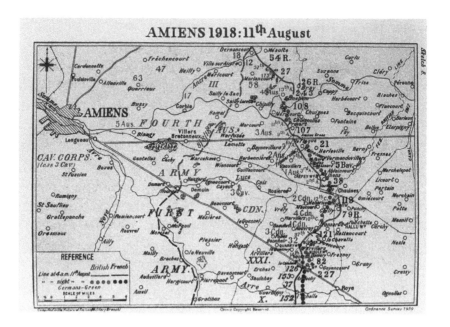

Kirkcudbrightshire. On his Officer's Declaration Form he gave his date of birth as May 27, 1888. He attended Laurieknowe School, Maxwelltown, and later Dumfries Academy. In 1911 he emigrated to Winnipeg where he worked as a surveyor and later civil engineer. Prior to the war he was a member of the the the 100th Winnipeg Grenadiers and had served for five years in the Imperial Yeomanry, one year in Squadron and four years in the Regimental Scouts. He signed up for overseas service on February 4, 1916. On joining the CEF he gave his religion as Presbyterian and his address as 19 Thelmo Park, Bunell Street, Winnipeg, and his next of kin as his brother Robert of 799 Camerons, Winnipeg. As an officer he left Halifax for England on September 11, 1916, and arrived in Liverpool on September 20. He was sent to Shorncliffe for further training and left for France on February 18, 1917, when he became a member of the 78th Battalion. Before gaining what was to be a posthumous VC in the Battle of Amiens in August 1918. Previously he had won the MC when taking part in the capture of Vimy Ridge in April 1917 (*LG* August 16, 1917), and he published an article about the Canadian victory entitled "The Vimy Ridge" on July 28, 1917, in the periodical *Canada*. He was also involved in the capture of a German post and during the action was severely wounded. It was probably when he was convalescing in England that he married Jessie Spiers Aitken from El Camino Real, West Arcadia, California. His parents still lived in Maxwelltown in Scotland.

By November 1917 he was promoted to acting captain. During 1917 until his death in August the following year Tait was wounded several times; firstly in early April when, with gunshot wounds to his knee, he was treated at No. 14 General Hospital, Boulogne, prior to being transferred to London, and later to Matlock where he was a patient in the Canadian Convalescent Home for Officers. He was also wounded in the hand in mid September. At the time of his death his widow, Mrs. Jessie Tait, was living at 71 Thelmo Mansions, Winnipeg. Tait's decorations consisting of the VC, MC, BWM, and VM, are in the collection of the Glenbow Museum, Calgary, Alberta.

Tait is commemorated in a number of ways: on the Laurieknowe School War Memorial, which took the form of a brass plaque erected after the war to honour the dead from the school. His name is also commemorated in the vestibule of Troqueer Parish Church, Dumfries. He is remembered in two other places in Maxwelltown: firstly, on the town's war memorial, and secondly, with a plaque in Troqueer Road with "bevilled sides mounted on a white headed stone background" on a blackboard. This latter memorial was funded by the residents of Maxwelltown.

A.P. BRERETON

Hatchet Wood, France, August 9

On August 9, north of the Amiens–Roye road, the 2nd Canadian Brigade (1st Division) advanced against the villages of Warvillers and Vrély across a flat and open landscape covered with growing corn. After the euphoria of the great Allied advance the day before, the 8th Canadian Battalion (Winnipeg Rifles), Manitoba Regiment (2nd Brigade, 1st Division), unsupported by either artillery or tanks, neverthless played a full role in coping with enemy machine-gun nests at Hatchet Wood and adjacent copses to the northwest of the village of Warvillers to which it provided the key. To their right was the 5th Battalion which had flat ground covered with crops to pass through. A task they accomplished in short rushes.

Although the enemy was waiting for them and hidden in woods and copses, the Canadians, after hard fighting, still managed to occupy Hatchet Wood before dusk and then the battalion struck forward to the north of Warvillers. During this fighting Cpl. Alex Brereton of the 8th Battalion gained a VC as a result of dealing with one of the machine-gun positions single-handed. The citation for his VC was gazetted on September 27, 1918, and told the story as follows:

For most conspicuous bravery during an attack, when a line
of hostile machine guns opened fire suddenly on his platoon,
which was in an exposed position and no cover available.
This gallant NCO at once appreciated the critical situation,
and realized unless something was done at once his platoon
would be annihilated. On his own initiative, without a
moment's delay and alone, he sprang forward and reached
one of the hostile machine gun posts, where he shot the man
operating the machine gun and bayoneted the next one who
attempted to operate it, whereupon nine others surrendered
to him. Corpl. Brereton's action was a splendid example of
resource and bravery, and not only undoubtably saved many
of his comrades' lives, but also inspired his platoon to charge
and capture the five remaining posts.

Brereton was decorated by the king at Buckingham Palace on
October 24, 1918, together with Sergeant Coppins of the same
battalion who won his VC in the same action. A third Canadian,
Sgt. R.L. Zengel of the neighbouring 5th Battalion, also won the VC.

Alexander Picton Brereton was born in Oak River, Alexander,
Manitoba, on November 13, 1892, the son of a farmer, Claude Picton
Brereton, and his wife, Annie Frazer (*née* Black). Alexander was one
of six children, four sons and two daughters, and went to school in
Oak River. After leaving school he worked on a farm.

Brereton gave his home address as being 378 Rose Avenue,
Winnipeg, when he enlisted in the Canadian Army in Winnipeg on
January 31, 1916. He was five foot seven inches tall and gave his
occupation as barber. He made his father his next of kin and was
allocated the service number 830651. He left Halifax for England
on September 11 and reached Liverpool two weeks later. After being
taken on strength at Shorncliffe he arrived in France on February 7,
where he joined the 8th Battalion Manitoba Regiment (2nd Brigade,
1st Canadian Division), with whom he remained for twenty-two
months. He was promoted to corporal and later to company quarter

master sergeant. Six weeks after he won his VC on August 9 he was in hospital at Etaples with appendicitis and later transferred to England.

At the end of the war he returned to Canada and was welcomed home by his parents and other members of his family, as well as Lt.-Col. A.W. Morley and other officers from the 144th Battalion. During his stay he spent a few days with friends before returning home to a hero's welcome in the town of Violadale, Manitoba. He was discharged from the Canadian Army in 1919 and returned to farming, eventually acquiring 640 acres of farmland in the Elnora district of Alberta, where he made his home. On June 17, 1925, he married Mary Isabel McPhee. The couple had three children, one son and two daughters. Brereton attended the November 1929 VC Dinner in the House of Lords.

During the visit of the recently crowned King George VI and the Duchess of York to Canada in 1939, Brereton was presented to them in Edmonton on June 2. Three months later, when the Second World War broke out, he rejoined the army, serving as a company quartermaster sergeant at an army training camp in Red Deer, Alberta. After he was discharged in 1944 he ran a butcher shop at Bashan for a short period and later a general store at Newbanan, until he returned to his farm at Elnora in early 1946. He was then responsible for only a small section of the family farm and his son, Mac, was responsible for the rest. The farm boasted a fine herd of Aberdeen Angus cattle.

In June 1956 Brereton attended the Hyde Park VC/GC Review, in London. He later moved to Fort St. John in British Columbia.

Brereton's wife predeceased him by four years, dying in 1972, and Alex himself died in the Colonel Belcher Hospital Calgary, on June 11, 1976. His funeral took place at Knox United Church, Three Hills, four days later. He was buried in Elnora Cemetery, Elnora, Alberta.

Alex Brereton was survived by his son, Mac, of Three Hills and his two daughters, Mrs. Betty McPhee of Edmonton and Mrs. Gwen Wik of Fort St. John, British Columbia. After his death the only Alberta man left who had won the VC in the First World War was Brig. F.M.W. Harvey. Alberta had produced no fewer than eighteen VC winners during the war.

Having been acquired by Lord Ashcroft in 2006, Brereton's decorations are on display in the Lord Ashcroft Gallery in the IWM, London. Apart from the VC, they include the BWM, VM, Canadian Volunteer service Medal (1939–45), War Medal 1939–45, and Coronation Medals for 1937 and 1953. He is also commemorated at Elnora with a Royal Canadian Legion Post named after him.

In recent years Brereton, together with Robert Cruickshank VC, Coulson Mitchell VC, and Harcus Strachan VC, all of whom had links with the province of Manitoba, have had lakes named after them to the east of Thompson.

F.G. COPPINS

Hatchet Wood, France, August 9

On August 9, 1918, Cpl. Frederick Coppins gained the VC on the same day as his colleague Cpl. Alex Brereton. Both men were members of the 8th Canadian Battalion (Winnipeg Rifles), Manitoba Regiment (2nd Brigade, 1st Division). As the battalion moved forward over the flat agricultural plain in the direction of Warvillers, the enemy was waiting for them and held its fire to the last moment. The battalion faced serious resistance from the enemy when they began to fire out of Hatchet Wood and adjoining copses to the north. The Manitoba Battalion found itself in a precarious position against an overwhelming German force, but far from shirking danger, Corporals Coppins and Brereton courted it and became the means of saving many lives and of materially helping achieve military objectives. Coppins' citation was published on September 27, 1918, as follows:

> For most conspicuous bravery and devotion to duty when during an attack his platoon came unexpectedly under fire of numerous machine guns. It was not possible to advance or retire, and no cover was available. It became apparent that the platoon would be annihilated unless the enemy

machine guns were silenced immediately. Corpl. Coppins, without hesitation and on his own initiative, called on four men to follow him, and leaped forward in the face of intense machine gun fire. With his comrades he rushed straight for the machine guns. The four men with him were killed and Corpl. Coppins wounded. Despite his wounds, he reached the hostile machine guns alone, killed the operator of the first gun and three of the crew, and made prisoners of four others, who surrendered. Corpl. Coppins by this act of outstanding valour, was the means of saving many lives of the men of this platoon, and enabled the advance to be continued. Despite his wound, this gallant N.C.O. continued with his platoon to the final objective, and only left the line when it had been made secure and when ordered to do so.

The 117 graves provide the mournful evidence of the losses from the 8th Manitoba Battalion in the nearby Manitoba Cemetery, revealing the high human cost paid for by the Canadians in order to reach their objectives on August 9, 1918.

Together with Cpl. Brereton, Cpl. Coppins was decorated in the ballroom of Buckingham Palace on October 24, 1918, when both men were then wearing their sergeant's stripes. Sgt. R.L. Zengel was also invested with his VC at the same time.

Frederick George Coppins was born in London on October 25, 1889, and spent four years with the Royal West Kents before emigrating to Canada where he joined the 19th Alberta Dragoons. He had enlisted as a Trooper in Valcartier Camp, Quebec, on September 23, 1914, his height was five foot six inches, and he had brown hair. He gave his profession as cattle buyer and was allocated the service number of 1987. After being transferred he served in France with the 8th Manitoba Regiment and was promoted to corporal and then sergeant. His brother Joseph, who also fought in the war, was his next of kin. In January 1919 he was transferred to the 18th Reserve Bn.

Coppins' medical records indicate that he spent a great deal of time in hospital, and the range of his ailments fell between veneral disease and scarlet fever. He was also wounded, and in April 1918 gassed. In November 1916 he had also spent time in a military prison. He was demobilized on April 30, 1919, when his home address was 562 Rosseau Avenue, Winnipeg.

Between the wars Coppins was involved in a collision between police and strikers in the Winnipeg General Strike, when serving as a special constable. He was dragged off his horse and severely injured.

He later lived in California and worked for the Pacific Gas and Electric Company in Oakland as a construction foreman. At the end of 1942, during the Second World War, he enlisted in Angel's Camp in Averas County, California, but we have no details of what role he played.

At the age of seventy-three Frederick Coppins died on March 30, 1963, in the U.S. Administration Hospital in Livermore, California. Three days later his funeral took place in Oakland and his ashes are kept in the Chapel of the Chimes Crematorium, where his name is listed on a vault. His VC was originally presented to the Valour Road Branch of the Royal Canadian Legion, Winnipeg, on September 26, 1965. It had, though, been bequeathed to the 8th Battalion Association, and is now in the collection of the Royal Winnipeg Rifles (Little Black Devils) Museum. His other decorations were the BWM, VM, and Coronation Medals for 1937 and 1953.

R.L. ZENGEL

Near Warvillers, France, August 9

On August 9, 1918, the 2nd Canadian Brigade of the 1st Canadian Division attacked over open farmland in its advance against the villages of Vrély and Warvillers. Serious opposition came from hidden German machine-gun nests and Sgt. Raphael Zengel gained a VC to the east of Warvillers, when serving with the 5th Battalion (Saskatchewan Regiment). According to the Official History

The 5th Battalion reached the enemy's front line, capturing twenty machine guns, and then halted for half an hour for the 8th Battalion to come up. An attempt by a squadron of the 16th Lancers (3rd Cavalry Brigade) to charge and round up a party of German machine gunners holding out in a copse after the Canadian infantry has passed by, completely failed. When the advance was continued Warvillers village and wood were captured about 4.30 p.m. though at the cost of heavy casualties.

Zengel was the third member of the CEF to win the coveted medal on the same day in the area of Warvillers and Beaufort. He won the decorations to the east of Warvillers, in what was known as the Triangle, which consisted of an area of land flanked by three roads to the southwest of the village. At first the advance had been pretty rapid, but later Zengel's platoon was pinned down by a machine-gun nest in a wheatfield. Zengel then decided to go it alone and crawled along a gully, which led him indirectly to a position from which he was able to observe a party of the enemy retreating toward a white château. At the same time he found himself close to the enemy machine-gun nest that had been causing all the trouble. After firing from the hip and killing the officer, Zengel managed to shoot two members of the gun crew; the remaining man rushed at him, but Zengel disposed of him with his bayonet. After this success Zengel waved his platoon on and they continued the advance. By late afternoon the assaulting 2nd Brigade had reached ground near the Méharicourt–Rouvroy road.

At the end of the action only sixteen men were left out of the original thirty-one.

The citation of Zengel's VC was gazetted on September 27, 1918, as follows:

> For most conspicuous bravery and devotion to duty when protecting the battalion right flank. He was leading his platoon gallantly forward to the attack, but had not gone far when he realized that a gap had occurred on his flank, and that an enemy machine gun was firing at close range into the advancing line. Grasping the situation, he rushed forward some 200 yards ahead of the platoon, tackled the machine gun emplacement, killed the officer and operator of the gun, and dispersed the crew. By his boldness and prompt action he undoubtably saved the lives of many of his comrades. Later, when the battalion was held up by very heavy machine gun fire, he displayed much tactical skill and directed his fire with destructive results. Shortly afterward he was rendered unconscious for a few minutes by an enemy shell, but on recovering consciousness he at once continued to direct harassing fire on the enemy. Sgt. Zengel's work throughout the attack was excellent, and his utter disregard for personal

safety, and the confidence he inspired in all ranks, greatly assisted in bringing the attack to a successful end.

Zengel was decorated at Buckingham Palace on December 13, 1918.

Raphael (Ray) Louis Zengel was born in Faribault, Minnesota, on November 11, 1894. In 1906 he and his mother, Mary Jane Zengel, moved to a homestead near Burr south of Humbolt in Saskatchewan. By 1914, when war broke out, he was working on a farm as a labourer near Virden in Manitoba. In December, as an American citizen, he enlisted in the 45th Battalion and was provided with the service number of 424252. He attested for overseas service on July 16, 1915, in Shorncliffe and was five foot nine inches tall with brown hair. His mother was his next of kin. On June 10, 1915, he was transferred from the 45th Bn at Shorncliffe and in the field to the 5th Bn in July. When he reached France on July 18 and after further training he took part in several trench raids and fought in the Battle of the Somme when he was badly wounded in the face and jaw on September 23. A few days later he was sent to a hospital in London and on October 17 he was a patient at West Cliff Hospital and was medically discharged from there on March 3, 1917. At a medical board in April it was noted that he was still having problems with his eating. On May 18 he was taken on the strength of the 15th Canadian Reserve Bn, and returned to France and was was transferred to the 5th Battalion on June 20. He later took part in the battle of Passchendaele during which time he won the Military Medal, which was gazetted on March 13, 1918. When as acting sergeant he had taken over command from his wounded officer.

After the announcment of his VC on September 27 he was granted two weeks in England. He then "disappeared," seemingly "having had enough." Once discovered by police in London he was confined to barracks as he had already missed the date of his presentation. In the end it didn't take place until December 13, 1918, when he returned to France in time to catch influenza.

After he was demobilized in Calgary in April 1919 he worked

for a short time as a fireman in Calgary, before eventually moving to Rocky Mountain House, where he took up farming again. In November 1929 he travelled to London for the VC dinner at the House of Lords, but this visit appears to be the only time that he visited London after the war.

During the Second World War Zengel held the rank of sergeant-major at Suffield Experimental Grounds, Alberta. He remained there throughout the war in charge of military components that were attached to civilian scientific groups involved in wartime experiments. In 1966 he married a second time, a lady named Myrtle.

The Royal Canadian legion allocated numbers to the various areas covered by their branches and in 1968 Zengel's local Branch No. 8 was renamed as a tribute to him, becoming the R.L. Zengel VC Wing of the Alberta command. After he moved and arrived in the legion's District 69 he became a member of Parksville Branch No. 49 and in 1975 was made an honorary president.

Two years later Raphael Zengel died in Nanaimo Regional Hospital, Victoria Island, British Columbia, on February 27, 1977, and was buried at Pine Cemetery, Rocky Mountain House, Alberta. Later a commemorative plaque to his memory was set up outside the Pine Cemetery. There is also a mountains named after him in Jasper National Park, Alberta. In 1936 a lake in northeastern Saskatchewan was named after him, but his name was wrongly spelt as Zengle. In recent years an historical plaque has been erected at reference point SE114, Section 2, Township 355, Range 24, west of the 2nd Meridian.

Zengel's decorations, apart from the VC and MM, include the BWM (1914–20), VM (1914–19), Canadian Volunteer Service Medal (1939–45), War Medal (1939–45), King George VI Coronation Medal (1937), Queen Elizabeth II Coronation Medal (1953), and Canadian Centennial Medal (1967). They are held in the Royal Canadian Legion Post, Rocky Mountain House.

In the display room of the Arlington Amphitheatre, in November 2014, Princess Anne unveiled a memorial in Raphael Zengel's honour as well as those three other Americans who served in the CEF, Bellenden Hutcheson, William Metcalf, and George Mullin, and won the nation's highest military honour during the First World War.

T.F. DINESEN

Parvillers, France, August 12

Private Thomas Dinesen was a member of the 42nd Battalion (Royal Highlanders of Canada), 7th Brigade, 3rd Division, and won the VC at Parvillers, northwest of Roye, on August 12, 1918. On August 8 the Canadian Corps had some of its greatest successes and the advance continued until August 14, when Sir Douglas Haig decided to break off the battle. Before this, though, on August 12, the 7th Canadian Brigade was sent to the vicinity of the village of Parvillers, where the 42nd Battalion was involved in a fierce battle.

The battalions went into the line with orders to keep up pressure on the enemy, which was fighting a rearguard action. The Canadian battalions were to be involved in clearing miles of enemy trenches which linked up the villages of Fouquescourt, Parvillers, and Damery. About one and a half miles behind this defensive system was another that connected the villages of Hattencourt, Fresnoy, and Goyencourt. The fortified village of La Chavatte was at a point midway between the two systems of defence.

Spread across the landscape were the remains of many derelict tanks, which were often adapted by the enemy as suitable cover for machine guns. Communication trenches on the battalion front connected the German frontal positions with those of the La Chavatte defences. The task of capturing these heavily defended villages presented a very strong task for the 42nd Battalion. On the left of the battalion the 44th Battalion (10th Brigade, 4th Canadian Division) penetrated the German line and managed to capture Fouquescourt. It was then decided to attempt to take the trench system at Parvillers to the south by using a bombing attack from the northern flank. The method used was to send men over in pairs, as it was hoped they would not attract enemy observation. The trenches to be attacked were defended by heavy wire and by deep-timbered dugouts.

In the middle of the afternoon of August 12, the enemy, although taken by surprise at the Canadians' attack, fought on stubbornly. During the fighting the 16th Platoon under Lt. Adam Sheriff Scott reached so far forward into enemy lines, at least 1,500 yards, that they became cut off. They had reached the railway crossing on the outskirts of Fransart. Owing to strong opposition, the small group had to retire, and at first they had to cross a section of trench that was in a very exposed position. They were then in danger of becoming trapped between the railway embankment and the road, nearly a mile from their objective. Their successful withdrawal was greatly assisted by the action of three privates, including Thomas Dinesen, who not only sniped the enemy, but managed to keep the German heads down by showering bombs over the railway embankment. Dinesen's two colleagues were both killed in this covering defence. Later in the day Scott's platoon was again in trouble, and at some point Scott was wounded. Again, he took a hand to protect the platoon while the officer was removed to safety. A report written by Maj. D.B. Martyn MC (and included in the unit history) notes the as follows:

> There never was greater dash nor perseverance shown by men than that by the Company of the 42nd who cleared about four miles of a network of trenches and fought steadily and at deadly close range for ten hours. The spirit was such that throughout the men continually cheered. Every man played his part ...

Throughout the action Dinesen was an outstanding figure and according to the unit history he was the "spearhead" of C Company's thrust into the German lines. According to Martyn again:

> ... he led the way into the midst of groups of the enemy, wielding bayonet and clubbed rifle with irresistible effect. Repeatedly, also, he rushed forward alone in the face of machine gun fire from which it seemed impossible to escape unhurt and personally put the machine guns out of action ...

On October 10 the 42nd Battalion moved to the Quéant area and stayed there for ten days. On October 17 they were visited by the Prince of Wales. By the time the war ended, on November 11, the battalion found themselves in the city of Mons and set up outposts on the outskirts of the eastern side of the city. Battalion headquarters was in the Hôtel de Ville in the Grand Place.

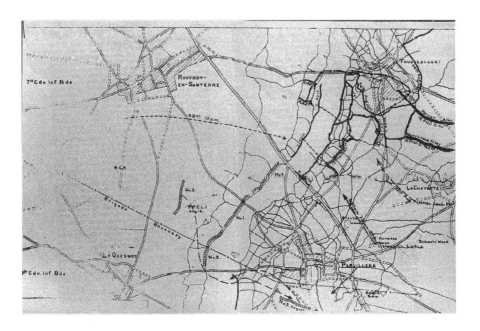

The citation for Dinesen's VC was gazetted on October 26:

For most conspicuous and continuous bravery displayed during ten hours of hand-to-hand fighting, which resulted in the capture of over a mile of strongly garrisoned and stubbornly defended enemy trenches. Five times in succession he rushed forward alone, and single-handed put hostile guns out of action, accounting for twelve of the enemy with bomb and bayonet. His sustained valour and resourcefulness inspired his comrades at a very critical stage of the action, and were an example to all.

Dinesen was almost immediately promoted to lieutenant in the field and was decorated by the king at Buckingham Palace on December 13.

Thomas Fasti Dinesen was born in Rungsted, Denmark, on August 9, 1892, into a well-off Danish family of army officers and landed gentry. He was educated at the local state school, followed by the Polytechnical School, Copenhagen, where he graduated in civil engineering in 1916. He was keen on sports, including hunting and sailing.

On the outbreak of the war there was a very real invasion threat from Germany, which encouraged him to try and join up on the Allied side and he approached the British and French legations in Copenhagen with a view to joining one of their armies, but they told him that only their own nationals could join up — a ruling which was not to last for the duration of the war. After a great deal of difficulty, he finally achieved his wish and joined up in the Canadian Recruiting Office in Montreal on June 26, 1917. He gave his address at the Hotel Biltmore in New York. He was six feet seven inches tall with fair hair. His mother, Mrs. Ingleborg of Rungsted, was his next of kin. His profession was civil engineer. He became a member of the 5th Regiment, Royal Highlanders of Canada (2nd Reinforcing Company) and was allocated the service number of 2075467.

On entering the Canadian Army in June 1917, Dinesen was first sent to Guy Street Barracks in Montreal as a member of the Black

Watch reinforcement unit. Three months later, in early October, he left Halifax for England, where he trained at Bramshott and later at Aldershot. It was not until March 1918 that he was sent to France. (During the spring and early summer and now serving in 42nd Battalion (not involved in any major battle, while they were in a very active part of the Canadian Corps front), Dinesen volunteered to take part in as many trench raids as he could and rose through the ranks.) On August 20, 1918, he was sent to England to take part in an officer cadet course. He was commissioned on November 5, 1918, and afer the war resigned his commission in January 1919.

After Dinesen was discharged he returned to Denmark and moved to Kenya in the early 1920s, where he took up farming, civil engineering, and writing. He remained there for five years before returning to Denmark for good in 1925. He continued with his writing, combining this activity with extensive farming and forestry interests. These were based on his home at Leerbeck, his estate in Jutland.

He wrote ten books, including *Merry Hell! A Dane with the Canadians,* first published in 1930, and translated from the Danish as *No Man's Land*, dealing with his war experiences. It was reprinted in 2005. In it he wrote the following fatalistic comments: "When I was sent to the front from England last year I did not expect to come back any more.... Once and for all, I shook off the fear of Death by looking death straight in the face."

Describing the day he received his VC from the king at Buckingham Palace he has this to say in his book:

At Buckingham Palace the King gave me the Victoria Cross. There were three others who received the cross at the same time. One was to be given to a sergeant who had been killed, so his parents had come to get it in his place — two old, frail people. The King said a few gracious words to each of us. We saluted and stepped back. That afternoon I went for a long tramp through the rain across Hampstead Heath and came home in the evening deadly tired, sick of the whole world.

On his time spent in training in England, he made some scathing comments about his military training:

> We might have learned how to find our way about after dark, to judge distances and recognize objects and people in the dark or in moonlight. It seems almost too stupid a thing to be recorded, but never once in Bramshott did we try to load or fire rifles unless it was in broad daylight, nor did we practice in the dark any of the jobs a soldier has to do at night such as putting up wire entanglements, putting on gas masks or thrusting with the bayonet.

Although Dinesen had lived in Canada for only three months, during his army training he always retained a soft spot for the country and in particular the comrades who he had met while serving with the 42nd Battalion. He kept in touch with them and visited Canada several times, for reunions and other meetings. Apart from the VC, his decorations included the Croix de Guerre (France) and he was awarded with a Knight of the Order of Dannebrog by the king of Denmark.

Dinesen was a fine-looking man and also a very brave one: after all, having been born in a country that was not even directly involved in the war he didn't have to get involved at all.

He had a sister, Karen, Baroness Blixen, who wrote under the name of Isak Dinesen. One of her most famous books was *Out of Africa*, which was based on her life in Kenya and which was turned into a film starring Robert Redford and Meryl Streep. Thomas and his sister would have been in active partnership in the early 1920s in Kenya, and one of her business interests was called Karen Coffee Company. She had also met the German general Paul von Lettow-Vorbeck, when he was on the same boat to East Africa at the end of 1913, and they struck up a friendship. In 1958 she visited the former enemy general in Hamburg in 1958; he died six years later, when he was in his early nineties.

Thomas Dinesen attended the House of Lords VC Dinner in November 1929 and the VC centenary review in London in June 1956, and was a guest at the Canadian Victoria Cross and George Cross holders' reunion in Ottawa in 1967. He died at the age of eighty-six at his home in Leebaek, Denmark, on March 10, 1979, and was buried in the family plot at Horsholm Churchyard, Rungsted, Fredereriksbard, Denmark. His decorations were in private hands until December 2013, when they were acquired for the Lord Ashcroft collection held at the Imperial War Museum. Apart from the VC they include the BWM, VM, King George VI Coronation Meal (1937), Queen Elizabeth II Coronation Medal (1953), Queen Elizabeth II Silver Jubilee Medal (1937), Knight Order of Dannebrog (Denmark), Croix de Guerre (France), and Pro Benignitate Humana Medal (Finland).

R. SPALL

Near Parvillers, France, August 12–13

During the period August 12–14, 1918, the 3rd Canadian Division, which had taken over the right of the Canadian Corps front, was involved in clearing the strongly held German trenches between the villages of Fouquescourt and Parvillers, to the northwest of Roye. Except for the 32nd Division's advance southwest of Damery on August 11 the enemy was still holding their trench network system between the Roye road and Fouquescourt.

The 7th and 9th Canadian Brigades, working in tandem, pushed close up to Parvillers and it was during this period that Pte. Thomas Dinesen and Sgt. Robert Spall, both of the 7th Brigade, won their VCs. Spall was a member of the No. 3 Company of Princess Patricia's Canadian Light Infantry in former trenches immediately behind Nos. 2, 1, and 4 companies. They were to the northwest of Parvillers.

At 3:30 in the afternoon of August 12 the neighbouring 42nd (East Lancashire) Division attacked Parvillers from the north. The CO of the PPCLI organized a supporting bombing attack to the south of the village in which Spall's No. 3 Company, under the leadership of Capt. C.M. MacBrayne, were to be used. At 8:00 p.m. they attacked across the Parvillers–Damery road and it was during the fierce fighting that Robert Spall gained a posthumous VC while involved in clearing the enemy trenches. His citation was gazetted on October 26, 1918, and tells the story briefly as follows:

> For most conspicuous bravery and self-sacrifice [August 13] when during an enemy counterattack, his platoon was isolated. Thereupon Sergt. Spall took a Lewis gun and, standing on the parapet, fired upon the advancing enemy, inflicting severe casualties. He then came down from the trench, directing the men into a sap seventy-five yards from the enemy. Picking up another Lewis gun, this gallant N.C.O. again climbed the parapet, and by his fire held up the enemy. It was while holding up the enemy at this point he was killed. Sergt. Spall deliberately gave his life in order to extricate his platoon from a most difficult situation, and it was owing to his bravery that the platoon was saved.

On the next day the Princess Patricia's Canadian Light Infantry managed to gain an entry into Parvillers but were quickly forced out; however, the village was finally taken the following day.

The former chief justice and twelfth lieutenant governor of Quebec, the Hon. Sir Charles Fitzpatrick, presented Spall's posthumous VC to his father Charles Spall, at Château Frontenac, in Quebec City on December 11, 1918. Robert has no known grave and his name is listed on the Vimy Ridge Memorial, one of 11,000 Canadian servicemen who died during the war who also have no known grave.

Robert Spall was the son of Charles and Annie Maria (*née* Morgan) and born in the district of Brentford at the Royal India Asylum, Ealing, on March 5, 1890. Charles worked as a gardener in the grounds of the asylum, which had been set up for the benefit of infirm pensioners who had worked for the East India Company. Two years later, when the asylum closed, the Spall family emigrated to Montreal with Robert and three other sons and two daughters. Charles took up gardening work once more.

Robert was a pupil at Aberdeen school and later, prior to the war, he worked in an office in Winnipeg as a customs broker. In around 1910 he moved to Winnipeg, and on July 28, 1915, he enlisted in Montreal, joining a draft of the 90th Winnipeg Rifles with the service number of 475212. He was five foot five inches tall with blue eyes and brown hair. His home address was 2642 St. Urbain Street, Montreal. His first next of kin was his father, who on his death was replaced by his mother. Spall arrived in England on September 6 and was taken on the strength at Shorncliffe and posted to the 11th Battalion. On November 29 he transferred to the Canadian Army Service Corps (CASC) at their training depot. In mid December/early January he spent some time in a convalescent hospital at Monks Horton Eight, where he was treated for gonorrhea. Ten weeks later he proceeded to France, arriving on February 12, 1916. Once in France, he joined the CASC unit at the headquarters of the Canadian Cavalry Brigade.

He was promoted to sergeant, but at his own request and wishing to be part of a fighting unit he chose to remain as a private, and on July 14, 1916, joined the Princess Pat's. The regiment attracted volunteers from all over Canada and gave preference to those men who had already served in the army. After initial training, he joined his new regiment in the field at Courcelette on September 18, 1916. They later fought in the battle for the Ancre Heights, and in April 1917 took an active part in the Battle of Vimy Ridge. On April 7 he was made lance corporal (unpaid) and from June 11 he was paid an NCO's salary. Seven months later this was followed by service at Passchendaele. In early March he had a few days leave in Paris, and on March 26, 1918, he was made a lance sergeant, and on May 21 his sergeant's rank was confirmed. On June 8 he was again in hospital at Etaples with veneral disease, and was discharged at the end of July. A few days later he took part in the Battle of Amiens in early August 1918, before his death on the 13th.

An article by Dr. N.J. Skinner was published in the *Suffolk Roots* (Journal of the Suffolk Family History Society), page 156, volume 23, in November 1997, in which the writer tries to find out more about Robert Spall, who had a familiar surname in the county of Suffolk. Skinner writes that Spall was born in Ealing on March 5, 1890, and that his parents were Charles and Annie Maria Spall (*née*

Morgan), who had married in South Kensington on July 11, 1882. Charles was a gardener and at the time of Robert's birth he was working for the East India Company at their Royal India Asylum for Infirm Pensioners in Ealing. Three years later a Neville Skinner wrote an extended article in *Stand To!* No. 59.

The Royal British Legion, Brentford branch, organized a special service on November 1, 1998, when Spall's name together with two others were added to those names already included on the cenotaph. In what is a memorial garden Spall's name is commemorated at the foot of the front of the Brentford War Memorial, close to the local public library in Boston Manor Road, Brentford. The Canadian maple leaf and badge of the Princess Pat's are featured as well.

Spall's decorations were donated to his regiment in Calgary by his sister Mrs. Isobel Stoneman in 1969, and apart from the VC included the BWM and VM, and are held in the Museum of the Regiments in Calgary, Alberta.

In 2013 his family was sent a Memorial Cross (Princess Pat's) and it was offered for sale on eBay and purchased for $8,000. Many of the contributions came from Veterans and the cross is now with his other decorations.

In August 2018 his commemorative paving stone will be laid in Ealing.

C.S. RUTHERFORD

Monchy, France, August 26

On August 26, 1918, the 2nd and 3rd divisions of the Canadian Corps began an attack which straddled the Arras–Cambrai road. The latter town was twenty miles away and the essential village for the Canadians to capture was Monchy-le-Preux two and a half miles away. It was during the fighting for possession of this village that Lt. C.S. Rutherford of the 5th Canadian Mounted Rifles Battalion, Quebec Regiment (8th Brigade, 3rd Canadian Division), won his VC in what became known as the Battle of the Scarpe. The Canadian Mounted Rifles (CMR) had been converted to infantry and provided four infantry battalions for the Canadian Corps. All four of them — 1st, 2nd, 4th, and 5th — formed the 8th infantry Brigade of the 3rd Canadian Division. Rutherford's VC was gazetted on November 15, 1918, when he was on leave in Scotland, as follows:

For most conspicuous bravery, initiative and devotion to duty. When in command of an assaulting party, Lieut. Rutherford found himself a considerable distance ahead of his men, and at the same moment observed a fully-armed strong enemy party outside a pillbox ahead of him. He beckoned to them with his revolver to come to him; in return, they waved to him to come to them. This he boldly did, and informed them that they were prisoners. This fact, an enemy officer disputed, and invited Lieut. Rutherford to enter the pillbox, an invitation he discreetly declined. By masterful bluff, however, he persuaded the enemy that they were surrounded, and the whole party of forty-five, including two officers and three machine guns surrendered to him. Subsequently he induced the enemy officer to stop the fire of an enemy machine gun close by, and Lieut. Rutherford took advantage of the opportunity to hasten the advance of his men to his support. Lieut. Rutherford then observed that the right assaulting party was held up by heavy machine gun fire from another pillbox. Indicating an objective to the remainder of his party, he attacked the pillbox with a Lewis gun section, and captured a further thirty-five prisoners with machine guns, thus enabling the party to continue their advance. The bold and gallant action of this officer contributed very materially to the capture of the main objective, and was a wonderful inspiration to all ranks in pressing home the attack on a very strong position.

At the time of the Armistice on November 11, 1918, Rutherford was on leave in Scotland, and it appears that he was only informed of his VC when he bumped into his commanding officer in London, Col. George Pearkes, who told him the good news. He remained in London until the investiture at Buckingham Palace on November 23, 1918, when he received his VC from the king. He left for France and remained there until March 1919.

Charles Smith Rutherford was born on January 9, 1892, at a farm in Haldimand Township near Colborne, Ontario. He was the son of John T. and Isabella Rutherford. Charles attended Dudley Public School before taking up work on the family farm.

On March 2, 1916, he enlisted in a reserved battalion to the 3rd Battalion (Queen's Own Rifles) of Canada as a private in Riverside Barracks, Toronto. He was five foot nine inches tall with black hair. He trained at Valcartier Camp. He left Halifax for England on April 28, 1916 and reached France on June 7. After a short spell with the 2nd

Quebec Regiment he was transferred to the 5th Canadian Mounted Rifles with whom he took part in the Ypres and Somme battles. He subsequently suffered gunshot wounds to his arm in Regina Trench near Courcelette, during the Somme battle of 1916, and convalesced in Leicester, but returned to France in time to take part in the assault on Vimy Ridge in April 1917. Two months later he was wounded again, this time in the face, at Arvillers, near Amiens, when helping to hold the line prior to it being handed over to the French Army.

Rutherford was a sergeant at the time of the Passchendaele campaign in 1917, when he won the MM and was one of thirteen members of the 5th CMR who captured two farms, Vapour and Source, on the left of the Canadian advance. The small group then proceeded to hold on to these two farms despite repeated counterattacks. It was for his gallantry on that occasion that Capt. George Pearkes, his company commander, won his VC on October 30–31.

After an officer's course in Bexhill-on-Sea, Rutherford was commissioned in April 1918, and when back in France was put in charge of No. 9 Platoon and won the MC on August 8, 1918, the German Army's Black Day. On this pivotal day Rutherford led his platoon in an advance to Arvillers in front of Amiens, from which the enemy had very recently withdrawn. The village was then handed over to French troops whose objective it was, but who had been delayed in their advance. Nearly three weeks later Rutherford won his VC at a time when the Allies were beginning to have the mighty German Army on the run.

After the war Rutherford returned to a hero's welcome at Ottawa Central Station. He resumed farming and worked in Colborne as such for the next eighteen years. In 1921 he married Helen Haig from Baltimore, who was a graduate of the University of Toronto and a trained dietician. The couple were to have four children, one son and three daughters. In the early 1930s Rutherford was a charter member of Lt. Charles Rutherford VC Branch in Colborne, and was later made the branch president. He had also served as the clerk-treasurer of Halimand.

On Christmas Eve 1935 Rutherford accepted the post of sergeant-at-arms of the Ontario Legislature, when he took over from another holder of the VC, Capt. Walter Rayfield, who won his VC east of

Arras between September 2 and 4, 1918. Rayfield had recently been appointed the deputy governor of Don Jail, Toronto. For his new position Rutherford wore a uniform consisting of flowing robes, a tricorn hat, and a sword.

In 1939 Rutherford became postmaster of Colborne and was one of the VC holders introduced to King George VI and the Duchess of York during their tour of Canada. When the Second World War broke out he enlisted in Ottawa, becoming a member of the Veterans' Guard of Canada. His duties included supervising German prisoners in prisoner-of-war camps. For a year he later served in the Bahamas as part of the guard to the Duke of Windsor when the latter was governor of Bahamas. Rutherford was promoted to captain in 1943 and in 1944 he was transferred to the Royal Military College in Kingston.

When the war ended in April 1945 Rutherford finished his service in July with the rank of captain and returned to his job at Colborne Post Office until 1955. Later, he and his wife opened a dry goods store in Keswick, north of Toronto, until their retirement in 1960, during which time they moved to Coburg in 1973. Six years later the couple returned to Haldimand Township and to Colborne in August 1979, when they were given a public welcome home complete with motor motorcade. At this point the couple lived with Dora Grant, one of their daughters. Helen died the following year.

During the last years of his life Rutherford became quite a celebrity as one of a dwindling group of VC survivors from the First World War, and on occasions he discussed how his three main gallantry medals were won. In an interview with a Toronto newspaper when he was quite elderly he talked of the time that he won his MM at Passchendaele at the end of October 1917:

> George (Pearkes) — he was a captain then — was leading us. I was a sergeant. We were digging in when I looked up. I saw 100 Germans coming toward us. We were only a handful but we started shooting and they disappeared.
>
> George got the VC that day for getting us to the top of that ridge. I guess we'd never have got there if he hadn't been along ... I got the MM that day too.

After the war the two Canadian winners of the VC from the same regiment met up in London, and Rutherford recalled that Pearkes congratulated him for winning the VC. However, Rutherford spoke of other things he had experienced in the war, and of the first time in the trenches on the Somme he said: "... all the men around me were killed." His second experience was as bad, when: "I carried a dead comrade through a four-foot tunnel that had a foot of water in it. The hardest thing I had to do."

Of becoming an officer, which he did in April 1918, Rutherford said:

> The government gave us money to buy our uniforms. But we had to have a revolver, a compass and field glasses. I managed to get a revolver from someone who had no more use for it. And I used it until the end of the war. We captured two towns, first Arvillers, the German division headquarters where I managed to get a paymaster and a lot of German money. The only other things they left behind were a box of pigeons and 300 new machine guns. Then we captured Bouchoir and that was as far as we could go.

However, it seems unlikely that the Germans left as many as 300 machine guns behind, and perhaps Rutherford's memory was at fault on this occasion.

That day (August 8, 1918) Lt. Rutherford won the MC and during the next few days the Canadian Corps moved to the Arras sector in preparation for an attack against the village of Monchy-le-Preux. On August 26 he and his men began to move forward for an attack in the pouring rain in the middle of the night: "Three miles up we ran into four field guns. We captured about twenty men who came out of their dugout and surrendered. Then we went on to Monchy." At one point Rutherford became separated from his men: "I was gone about ten minutes. When I came back I couldn't see my men. I thought they'd gone into the town as the barrage lifted. So I ran as hard as I could to catch up with them." But his men had gone into some woods:

When I was within a 100 yards of the town all I could see were Germans. So I decided to go and do the best that I could with them. All I had was my loaded revolver. I walked up to the Germans and demanded they surrender. They were my prisoners. One German who spoke English said "no prisoners ... No you prisoner." They asked me to go to their dugout but I wouldn't.

He [the German] went in and when he came out, he gave an order for the others to drop their rifles. They did. Boy, was I in a fix! I didn't know what to do next.

Then one of their machine guns opened fire on A company. I said "your machine gun is firing at my men." I was afraid that my men might start firing back. So I said "you go and stop your machine gun and I'll stop my mine ..."

I ran back. When I was out of sight of the Germans I took my hat off and waved my men to come on. They were soon there and I sent two men back with 40 prisoners. Then we went over to the other machine gun and got 30 prisoners here.

The records show that the 3rd Canadian Divison took Monchy-le-Preux that day. I was in the 3rd Canadian Division.

At the time of this interview, which was about 1983, Pearkes would have been ninety-five and Rutherford would have been about four years younger, and readers should take Rutherford's age into account. The two men were the oldest winners of the VC from the First World War to be still living in Canada, Rutherford living at this time on his daughter's farm to the north of Colborne, Ontario, and Pearkes in Victoria, British Columbia.

During his final two years Rutherford lived at the Rideau Veteran's Home in Ottawa, where at the age of ninety-seven he died on June 11, 1989, the very last of the men to win the VC in the First World War. Three days later he was given a full military funeral at Colbourne United Church, which was attended by a sixty-member guard of honour from 1st Canadian Signal Regiment of Kingston. Also in attendance at the Union Cemetery in Colborne was Christine Stewart

MP and Fred Tilston, a VC holder from the Second World War.

Rutherford was survived by his son and three daughters, and thirteen grandchildren. He earned thirteen medals and, according to his granddaughter Mary Ellen Cain, kept his VC in a sock drawer. Apart from the VC, MC, and MM, they included from the First World War the BWM and VM. From the Second World War he was awarded the 1939–45 Star, Defence Medal (1939–45), Canadian Volunteer Service Medal (1939–45), and War Medal (1939–45). His other decorations included Coronation Medals for 1937 and 1953, the Queen Elizabeth II Silver Jubilee Medal (1977), and the Canadian Centennial Medal (1967).

After his death his obituaries were fulsome and *The Times* wrote the following of his career:

> Few exploits in the annals of the Victoria Cross equal the extraordinary courage which gained Rutherford his award. Indeed his three major medals, achieved in a single year of fighting, attest to phenomenal bravery over months of unremitting combat, which saw the Allies pass from deep despondency, through acute crisis, to the verge of complete victory.

Rutherford's decorations are privately owned and he is commemorated by having a mountain named after him in Jasper National Park, Alberta. He is also remembered in the Royal Canadian Military institute in Toronto, where his service revolver, which he used during the war, is kept. As we have seen the Legion Branch 187 in King Street, Colborne is named after him.

W.H. CLARK-KENNEDY

The Fresnes–Rouvroy Line, France, August 27–28

Lieutenant-Colonel William Clark-Kennedy gained the VC between August 27 and 28, 1918, on the second day of the Battle of the Scarpe in the renewed Arras offensive, and it was gazetted on December 14, 1918. The citation explains how Clark-Kennedy won his VC:

For most conspicuous bravery, initiative and skilful leading on the 27 and 28 August 1918, when in command of his battalion. On the 27th he led his battalion with great bravery and skill from Crow and Aigrette trenches in front of Wancourt to the attack on the Fresnes–Rouvroy line. From the outset the brigade, of which the 24th Battn. was a central unit, came under very heavy shell and machine gun fire, suffering many casualties, especially amongst leaders. Units became partially disorganized, and the advance was checked. Appreciating the vital importance to the brigade front of a lead by the centre, and undismayed by annihilating fire, Lieut.-Colonel Clark-Kennedy, by sheer personality and initiative, inspired his men and led them forward. On several occasions he set an outstanding example by leading parties straight at the machine gun nests which were holding up the advance and overcame these obstacles. By controlling the direction of neighbouring units and collecting men who had lost their leaders, he rendered valuable services in strengthening the line, and enabled the whole brigade to move forward. By the afternoon, very largely due to the determined leadership of this officer and disregard for his own life, his battalion, despite heavy losses, had made good the maze of trenches west of Cherisy and Cherisy Village, had crossed the Sensée River bed, and had occupied Occident Trench in front of the heavy wire of the Fresnes-Rouvroy line; under continuous fire he then went up and down his line until far into the night, improving the position, giving wonderful encouragement to his men, and sent back very clear reports. On the next day he again showed valorous leadership in the attack on the Fresnes-Rouvroy line and Upton Wood. Though severely wounded soon after the start, he refused aid, and dragged himself to a shell hole, from which he could observe. Realizing his exhausted troops could advance no further, he established a strong line of defence, and thereby prevented the loss of most important ground. Despite intense pain and serious loss of blood, he refused to be evacuated for over five hours, by which time he had established the line in a position from which it was possible for the relieving troops to continue the advance. It is impossible to overestimate the results achieved by the valour and leadership of this officer.

Clark-Kennedy was presented with his VC, CMG, and bar to his DSO in the ballroom of Buckingham Palace on March 1, 1919, by the king.

William Hew Clark-Kennedy was the son of Capt. A.V.M. Clark-Kennedy and the Hon. Mrs. Clark-Kennedy, and was born in Dunskey, Wigtownshire, Scotland, on March 3, 1879. His parents rented a house there, although the family home was actually at Knockgray, Carsphairn, Galloway, and included a house and farms together with shooting and fishing. William's father, who died in 1894, served in the Coldstream Guards and his mother died on the eve of the Second World War in 1939. William was educated at St. Andrew's College, Southborough, Kent, and Westminster School, and in 1897 joined the Standard life Assurance Company in London.

On the outbreak of the South African war he became a trooper as a member of the yeomanry regiment "Paget's Horse," and served with distinction in the yeomanry in the Boer War 1900–01. During this time he was mentioned in despatches and also received the Queen's Medal with four clasps. In 1903 he emigrated to Canada when still on the staff of the Scottish Life Assurance Company and later became assistant manager for Canada. He joined the Canadian Militia and subsequently joined the 5th Royal Highlanders of Canada as a Reserve Officer. He married Kate (*née* Redford) of Montreal on September 5, 1914, a month after the war broke out, when he was still in a training camp in Quebec City. She later became his next of kin. Her address was 260 Drummond Street, Montreal. Clark-Kennedy signed up for overseas service on September 23 at Valcartier. He was five foot nine inches tall.

Clark-Kennedy left Canada for England with the First Canadian contingent as a company commander of the 13th Battalion Royal Highlanders of Canada. Once in Belgium, at the time of the Second Battle of Ypres in April 1915 he was reported killed, and very nearly was. He was knocked over three times by shells, the third time being completely buried and left unconscious, the men on either side of him being killed. However, eventually he managed to dig himself out, although the enemy was close by. For his role in the Ypres battle he was awarded the French Croix de Guerre with Palm. On June 2 he was a patient at No. 4 CCS with a back injury.

On January 14, 1916, his first DSO was gazetted for service in the Battle of Festubert in May 1915 and he was promoted to major at the same time. He held the rank of brigade major in 1916 and in the following year was promoted to lieutenant-colonel. He left the Royal Highlanders in order to command the 24th Battalion Victoria Rifles, with whom he gained his VC. Just over three years later Clark-Kennedy was created a Companion of the Order of St. Michael and

St. George, and later awarded a bar to his DSO, which was gazetted on January 11, 1919, for activities on August 8, 1918, during the advance on the Somme. The citation was as follows:

> For great gallantry in action during which the battalion under his command reached the objective allotted to it. On several occasions, at great risk, he personally directed the capture of strong points obstinately defended by the enemy. The success which his battalion obtained in these attacks was due in no small degree to the example, courage and resourcefulness of its commander.

On August 28 he was in hospital in Le Treport with gunshot wounds to his leg. He was transfered to the Prince of Wales Hospital in London and then to hospital in Hyde Park Place. He was discharged from hospital on November 23.

Clark-Kennedy returned to Canada on March 28, 1919, and was demobilized on April 7. During his war service Clark-Kennedy was wounded on several occasions, especially with gunshot wounds, and was mentioned in despatches four times. After the war he was appointed brevet lieutenant-colonel, Corps Reserve, Canadian Militia. He was proficient at sports and especially keen on fishing, and in addition was a first-rate shot. In November 1929 he travelled to London for the House of Lords VC Dinner. He later became manager of the Scottish Life Assurance Company in Montreal, Canada. He also became a director of the Guardian Insurance Company of Canada in 1927, and in 1943 became its chairman. He was also chairman of the advisory board of the Guardian-Caledonian group of insurance companies.

In November 1945 Clark-Kennedy retired from the Scottish Life Assurance after fifty years' service. In June 1956 he attended the VC/GC Centenary Review. He later resided in Montreal, where he died on October 25, 1961, and was buried in Montreal Royal Cemetery three days later in Pine Hill Section of the Reford family plot, lot 258.

His numerous decorations, which are in private hands, include the CMG, DSO & Bar, Order of St. Michael & St. George, the

1914–15 Star, BWM, VM, two Coronation Medals for 1937 and 1953, Efficiency Decoration (ED), and Croix de Guerre (France). He was survived by two sons, both of whom became lieutenant-colonels.

On October 13, 2006, in the 150th-anniversary year of the Victoria Cross, Clark-Kennedy's name, together with the names of nine other winners of the VC, were commemorated with a sculpture in Tunbridge Wells set up in the Victoria Cross Grove in Dunorlan Park. The grove was originally planted in 1995.

C.J.P. NUNNEY

Near Vis-en-Artois, France, September 1–2

Private Claud (Red) Nunney of the 38th Battalion Eastern Ontario Regiment (Ottawa) (12th Canadian Brigade) 4th Canadian Division won what was to be a posthumous VC southeast of Arras. The objective was to attack the Drocourt-Quéant Line, an action which had been delayed. On September 1 the 38th Battalion positions were close to the village of Vis-en-Artois prior to the previously delayed but eventually successful Canadian capture of the line.

Private Nunney was one of seven men serving in the Canadian Expeditionary Force to be awarded Britain's highest military honour in connection with the capture of this very important enemy defence line, which was a very strongly held backbone of the German resistance. Together with a support line it boasted a very sopisticated system of interlocking trench systems as well as tunnels, concrete shelters, machine-gun posts, and a dense mass of barbed wire. It even boasted a light railway system. The Buissy Switch linked the line with the Hindenburg support system. The lines joined on the forward slope of a position known as Mont Dury between the village of that name and the Arras–Cambrai road and the support line was on the reverse slope. The switch line ran in front of Buissy and Villers-lès-

Cagnicourt in a southeasterly direction. The Canadian plan was to use the 4th and 1st Divisions to attack the section of the line closest to the Cambrai road and to then roll up the German defences to the north and south. Six companies of Mark V tanks were also to be used. The British 57th (West Lancashire) Division was to the right of the Canadians.

On September 1 the Canadian positions recently captured by them were then subjected to a heavy enemy artillery barrage. The Official History noted the following of the actions on September 2:

> When at 5 a.m. the 72nd, 38th and 85th battalions of the 12th Canadian Brigade advanced, each on a five-hundred yard front, the twenty-two tanks allotted to this brigade had not arrived, and some opposition was experienced from enemy outposts, some of which were so close to the jumping-off line as to be untouched by the barrage. Then, aided by the tanks, the D-Q front and support systems were taken without difficulty; in places the Germans fought stoutly and three tanks were lost, whilst in others they were eager to surrender ...

Nunney's VC was gazetted on December 14, 1918, as follows:

> For most conspicuous bravery during the operations against the Drocourt–Quéant Line on 1 and 2 Sept. 1918. On 1 Sept., when his battalion was in the vicinity of Vis-en-Artois, preparatory to the advance, the enemy laid down a heavy barrage and counterattacked. Private Nunney, who was at this time at company headquarters, immediately on his own initiative proceeded through the barrage to the company outpost lines, going from post to post and encouraged the men by his own fearless example. The enemy were repulsed and a critical situation was saved. During the attack on 2 Sept. his dash continually placed him in advance of his companions, and his fearless example undoubtedly helped greatly to carry the company forward to its objectives. He

displayed throughout the highest degree of valour until severely wounded.

Private Nunney died of his wounds sixteen days later at Vis-en-Artois CCS on September 18 and was buried twelve miles east of Saint-Pol at Aubigny Communal Cemetery Extension, Plot IV, Row B, Grave 39. His brother Alfred, who was a member of the 80th Battalion, had been killed in action a few weeks before, on August 10, 1918.

Stephen Sargent Claud Patrick Joseph Nunney was born in 24 Bexhill Road, Hastings, on December 24, 1892, although many accounts of his life, including his own, state he was born in Dublin, a fiction that came from Nunney himself. There is no question of him being Irish though, and he inherited an Irish temperament from his Irish mother, whose maiden name was Sargent. His father was William Percy Nunney. Stephen was the fourth of eight children and known as Claud. In 1895 the family moved to Kentish Town in St. Pancras, London. His mother died of food poisoning when Claud was seven years old. Details about his childhood are very sketchy and the sources are inconsistent, although it is known that when he was about thirteen years of age Claud and several of his siblings were packed off to Quebec in October 1905, when his family was very poor and it was thought the children would have a better chance in life if they emigrated to Canada. Two of the children had died in infancy and the survivors passed into the care of the Catholic Church. Three of the boys became "Home Children." George had arrived in Canada in 1904, and in October 1905 he was placed in an orphanage, at St. George's Home at Hintonberg, Ottawa. The family had been split up and the rest of the children and their father lived in North Lancaster, Ontario.

It was at St. George's Home that Claud caught the eye of a Dr. D.D. McDonald, who took took an interest in the boy. Claud was subsequently moved to live with McDonald's mother, who lived in the community of Pine Hill in nearby Glengarry County in Lancaster Township. At this point Claud attended Separate School No. 9 in the township. It was in this way that Claud became a Canadian citizen.

Mrs. D.J. McDonald, Claud's foster mother, died in 1912 and, having finished his schooling, Claud became a painter and travelled to work in Trenton and St. Catharines and returned to the Nunney family in North Lancaster in early 1915.

Claud decided to join the army and became a member of the 59th Stormont and Glengarry Regiment, which was a non-government militia unit. After the outbreak of war he attested in the 38th Eastern Ontario Regiment Battalion on February 8, 1915, in Alexandria, Glengarry County, and re-attested on March 8. He was a painter, and five foot five inches tall with red hair. He was given the service number 410935 and gave the name of his next of kin as Gordon Calder. His battalion left for Bermuda on August 8, 1915, where it relieved the Royal Canadian Regiment and, after a few months, moved to England, arriving in Plymouth in May 1916. Three months later the 38th Battalion left for France on August 11, as part of the 4th Canadian Division in August 1916, and took part in the Battle of the Somme. A few months later Nunney won the DCM during the Canadian capture of Vimy Ridge in April 1917. The citation published in the *London Gazette* of September 14 was as follows:

> For most conspicuous gallantry and devotion to duty. Although wounded in two places, and his section wiped out, he continued to advance carrying his gun and ammunition, and alone stopping an attack by over 20 enemy. He continued on duty for three days, showing exceptional fearlessness and doing magnificent work. He also won the MM at Gouy Souvins on 17 September 1917.

On April 12 he was wounded and spent two days at No. 12 Canadian FA. He was back on duty a few days later, and in May he was in hospital again with gunshot wounds to his left shoulder and right leg By the end of May 1917 he had been promoted to sergeant. He was gassed at the end of July and became a patient at No. 23 CCS. He was transferred to several hospitals and finally discharged at Rouen on September 21. On September 14 he was awarded the DCM, and on October 17 the MM. On April 25, 1918, he struck a superior officer and was sentenced to one year's hard labour. However, after the sentence was confirmed on May 6 it was suspended. Meanwhile he had been wounded yet again, on May 3. On June 3 he was a patient at No. 57 CCS, this time with burns to his hands and face. On September 2, when he won his VC, he was wounded in the early morning and hung on until wounded again in the afternoon, when he was carried away. He died of these wounds at 42 CCS on September 18.

A document from the collection of a Miss H. Menzies, daughter of Sgt. A. Menzies (who used to be Nunney's sergeant), includes some pithy comments about Nunney's Irish character, although the wording is not always consistently accurate:

He did some excellent work in France under me, but owing to his Irish temperamant, generaly caused trouble when fighting under others.

As a sergeant in D. Company, whilst on duty in the front line, he lost his temper and threw the Company Sergeant Major down the steps to a dugout, breaking his arm and causing other minor injuries.

Sentenced to five years detention, but whilst under guard in the horse lines a British plane crashed and immediately went into flames. Red broke through his guard, entered the burning plane and brought out the pilot. He was severely burnt, and evacuated to Étaples Military Hospital. Whilst there the Germans made a very heavy air-raid on the whole area, causing great damage. Red dashed out of bed and for hours kept bringing in wounded.

Sentence suspended on the recommendations of British H.Q. and Red rejoined the Battalion. Previously he had been awarded certain decorations.

At the battle of Amiens, 1917 [sic 1918], the Battalion made great progress (I was not there, being in hospital in London). When stiff resistance on the third day of the battle was encounterted. Red, as private Nunney, dashed ahead through the barrage and killed or wounded the crews of three enemy machine gun posts.

The following day Red, now once again a platoon sergeant, was in charge of a platoon in an advanced position. The enemy attacked and Red stood up in front of his men in the open shouting "Come on Boys, let them have it."

Red was shot through the throat, died shortly afterward, the platoon, now very much below strength, held off the attack ...

In 1962, forty-four years after his death, a plaque to commemorate Nunney's memory was erected at the Glengarry Municipal Building by the Glengarry Historical Society in conjunction with the Claud Nunney VC Memorial Branch. It was unveiled on August 22 by William H. Proctor, a former member of the 38th Battalion, at the municipal building, County Roads 18 and 26, North Lancaster. It was one of several plaques erected by the Department of Travel and Publicity on the advice of the Archaeological and Historic Sites Board of Ontario. The dedication part of the service, which was attended by local dignitaries, was conducted by Monsignor E.J. Macdonald, vicar-general of the Diocese of Alexandria, who had served in the First World War and had won the MC. In 2008 the branch received government funding to help toward the costs of restoring the Lancaster Cenotaph and at the same time repositioning it.

There is also a plaque on Main Street, Lancaster, to the First World War dead from Glegarry in 1921, set up in the grounds of the library by the Red Cross Society of Glengarry. The names of the fallen listed include that of Claud Nunney. Another memory of him is with the naming of an air cadet squadron, the 253 Claud Nunney VC Royal Canadian Air Cadet Squadron.

Nunney's posthumous VC, DCM, MM, and service medals the BWM and VM are in the collection of the Cornwall Armoury in Ontario.

B.S. HUTCHESON

East of Arras, France, September 2

Capt. B.S. Hutcheson was a Medical Officer in the Canadian Army Medical Corps and in September 1918 was attached to the 75th Battalion, 1st Central Ontario Regiment. The main action on September 2 was the Allied penetration of the German defensive position known as the Drocourt–Quéant line, during which the Canadian Expeditionary Force distinguished itself when attacking this line together with the assistance of British infantry Divisions on either flank. During this day Capt. Hutcheson was east of Arras and won the VC, which was gazetted on December 14, 1918, as follows:

For most conspicuous bravery and devotion to duty on 2 Sept., when under most intense shell, machine gun and rifle fire, he went through the Quéant–Drocourt Support Line with the battalion. Without hesitation and with utter disregard of personal safety, he remained on the field until every wounded man had been attended to. He dressed the wounds of a seriously wounded officer under terrific machine gun and shellfire, and, with the assistance of prisoners and of his own men, succeeded in evacuating him to safety, despite the fact that the bearer party suffered heavy casualties.

Again using an undated letter written in answer to an enquiry from a Capt. Gwynn, Hutcheson wrote of when he won the VC as follows:

My medical detail and I worked along the crest attending to the wounded when the battalion was held up short of its objective. The rifle, machine gun and artillery fire was intense. We got to the wounded by crawling or running in a stooping position and when the field of fire became too hot flattened out on the ground like limpets on a rock ...

Capt. Hutcheson was presented with his VC and the MC in the quadrangle of Buckingham Palace on May 22, 1919.

Bellenden Seymour Hutcheson was born on December 16, 1882, at Mount Carmel, Illinois, son of Mr. Hutcheson and Luella Bellenden Hutcheson. After a high school education he then graduated in medicine in Chicago, Illinois, at Northwestern University and later worked as a physician and surgeon at Mound City, Illinois.

He served in the 13th Royal Regiment and a year after the war began, in 1914 when his profession was physician and surgeon, he decided to join the Canadian Army. After renouncing his American citizenship, he made an officer's declaration form in the 97th Canadian Battalion on December 14, 1915. He was five foot eight inches tall and his father was his next of kin. He gave his address as Exhibition Camp, Toronto. After being commissioned as a lieutenant in the Canadian Army Medical Corps he was later attached to the 75th Battalion (later the Toronto Scots). He left Halifax on September 8, 1916, and arrived in France toward the end of 1916. He was promoted to captain a month later. On January 11, 1917, he was in hospital with pleurisy in Seaford and discharged a fortnight later. He was also in hospital from December 21, 1917, until discharged on Februay 19, 1918. He won his MC on August 8, 1918, on the first day of the August Allied offensive (gazetted November 3, 1918) and in a reply to an enquiry from a Capt. Gwynn he later wrote a graphic account of this action as well as his later VC on which the following is based.

On the left of the Amiens–Roye road about twenty-six kilometres southeast of Amiens the Canadian advance passed between Beaucourt and Le Quesnel. The latter had fallen to the enemy on March 27, 1918. The Canadian advance was under observation from enemy balloons that were linked to artillery batteries and accurate pinpoint shelling made the treatment of the wounded a very hazardous business. The casualties were scattered throughout the whole town of Le Quesnel and thus several searches had to be made in order to find them all. A cellar area was used by Hutcheson as a dressing station, which was staffed by Hutcheson, two NCOs, and two privates. A company belonging to the 4th Canadian Mounted Rifles suffered grievously from enemy shelling when passing close to a street corner and Hutcheson's team dealt with the many casualties. In spite of these setbacks the village was retaken on the 9th by Hutcheson's 75th Canadian infantry Battalion.

After gaining a VC in September, Hutcheson was demobilized in December 1919 and appointed captain in the Canadian Militia. Returning home he reclaimed his American citizenship. After some time he resigned from this post and became City Health Officer in Cairo, Illinois, later marrying a Frances Young from Nova Scotia. The couple had met prior to the war but had decided to postpone getting married until after the war. Frances had been a nurse during the war, and after the couple moved back to Souhern Illinois. During the summer months Frances used to take their son, who was schooled in Canada, back to Nova Scotia.

In 1939 Hutcheson travelled from Illinois in order to be presented to King George VI and Queen Elizabeth during their visit to North America, at a reception at the British Embassy in Washington on June 9, 1939. During the proceedings he was invited to accompany the king and queen to Arlington Cemetery to lay a wreath at the Tomb of the Unknown Soldier.

Bellenden Hutcheson died of cancer after a long illness at Cairo, Illinois, on April 9, 1954, and was buried at Rose Hill Cemetery in Mount Carmel, Section B, Lot 145, Grave C. In commemoration he has a memorial in Mount Carmel Court House and his decorations are in the care of the York Armoury, Toronto. Apart from the VC, they include the MC, BWM, and VM, together with Coronation Medals of 1937 and 1953. They had been donated to them by his widow. The Armoury also holds an oil painting of Hutcheson working on the battelfield.

On September 12, 2009, the successors of the 75th Battalion, namely the Toronto Scottish Regiment (Queen Elizabeth, the Queen Mother's Own), moved into a new armoury, which they shared with the Toronto Police Service. It was named after Capt. Hutcheson and can be found in 70 Birmingham Street, Toronto. His decorations are in the collection of the Hodden Grey Museum in the same complex.

In November 2014 the four Americans who won the VC when serving with the Canadian forces were commemorated by Princess Anne in Arlingtson Cemetery, Washington. The bronze plaque was unveiled by her in the display room of the Arlington Amphitheatre. The other men include Sgt. R. Zengel, Lt.-Cpl. W.H. Metcalf, and Sgt. G. Mullin.

A.G. KNIGHT

Villers-lès-Cagnicourt, France, September 2

Sgt. Arthur Knight, 10th Battalion (2nd Brigade, 1st Canadian Division), won his VC as one of six members of the CEF in the fight for the Drocourt–Quéant Line on September 2, 1918, at a point just south of the Arras–Cambrai road at a village called Villers-lès-Cagnicourt, halfway between Arras and Cambrai. On the front of the 2nd Brigade the 5th Battalion engaged in hand-to-hand fighting for the jump-off line and then, aided greatly by a shrapnel barrage, the 7th Battalion passed through their lines to begin the assault on their portion of the Drocourt–Quéant Line, experiencing little difficulty in taking part of the line and mopping up. At 8:00 a.m. the 10th Battalion took over the advance in an area that was beyond the barrage zone. Until then tanks had been in the forefront, knocking out one enemy post after another, but several of them were destroyed during the process. East of the Drocourt–Quéant Line, the German artillery slowed the 10th Battalion's advance with intense fire from machine guns and trench mortars in the Buissy Switch, east of Villers-lès-Cagnicourt. However, the 10th Battalion still managed to capture the village by late afternoon. The battalion established a line to the east of the village and, after an allied barrage targeted the enemy positions, the Canadians managed to move forward to capture the Buissy Switch just before midnight. By now the 1st Canadian Division had captured two systems of the Drocourt–Quéant Line and was approaching a further objective, the Canal du Nord.

Sergeant Arthur Knight's VC was gazetted on November 15, 1918, and tells the story as follows:

> For most conspicuous bravery, initiative and devotion to duty when, after an unsuccessful attack, Sergt Knight led a bombing section forward, under very heavy fire of all descriptions, and engaged the enemy at close quarters. Seeing that his party continued to be held up, he dashed forward alone, bayoneting several of the enemy machine gunners and trench-mortar crews, and forcing the remainder to retire in confusion. He then brought forward a Lewis gun and directed his fire on the retreating enemy, inflicting many casualties. In the subsequent advance of his platoon in pursuit, Sergt. Knight saw a party of about thirty of the enemy go into a deep tunnel which led off the trench. He again dashed forward alone, and, having killed one officer and two N.C.O.s, captured twenty other ranks. Subsequently routed, single-handed, another enemy party which was opposing the advance of his platoon. On each occasion he displayed the greatest valour under heavy fire at very close range, and by his example of courage, gallantry and initiative was a wonderful inspiration to all. This very gallant N.C.O. was subsequently fatally wounded.

Knight, who would have been unaware of winning the VC, died of wounds the following day in a field hospital near Hendecourt-lès-Cagnicourt and was buried ten miles southeast of Arras in the Dominion Cemetery, Plot I, Row F, Grave 15. The cemetery was begun by the Canadian Corps after the storming of the Drocourt–Quéant Line on September 2, 1918.

In the National Archives of Canada is a "Circumstances of Death card," which goes some way into pinning down the date of Knight's death. It states: "Killed in Action. While taking part in operations with his Company he was struck in the head by shrapnel from an enemy shell, at about 3 p.m. on 3 September 1918, when 500 or 600 yards left of Buissy. He died shortly after being wounded." This was the day after his VC action, in which he wasn't wounded, although his citation suggests that he was. His casualty form states that he actually died on September 10.

Arthur George Knight, the son of Edward Henry and Ellen Knight, was born in Haywards Heath, Sussex, on June 26, 1886 although he stated he was born in Mead Vale, Redhill. He became a pupil at St. Wilfrid's School and when he was still quite young his family moved to Redhill, Surrey, when their home was No. 1 Somerset Road, Mead Vale, in the southern part of the town.

Arthur attended the local school of St. John's School and later attended Redhill Technical and Trade School, where he studied carpentry. He was subsequently apprenticed to a local firm of builders, Bagaley & Sons. At the age of twenty-five, in 1911, he decided to move to Canada where he lived and worked as a carpenter in Regina. Three years later he enlisted in Regina, on December 19, 1914, having served for a year with the Grenadiers. He was posted to the 46th (Saskatchewan) Battalion for training. He was five foot nine inches tall with blue eyes and fair hair. His service number was 426402. Seven months later he sailed to England on July 5, 1915, when he was transferred to the 32nd Battalion at Shorncliffe on July 19, 1915. In the following month he travelled to France arriving on August 29. He became a member of the 10th (Battalion) Alberta on September 28. On November 20 he was wounded and taken to No. 3 Field Ambulance, and on December 8 he returned to England to recuperate. He was suffering from nephritis.

Afer returning to active service he was promoted to lance corporal in June 1917; full corporal on September 29, 1917, and in the following year to acting sergeant, on August 7, 1918. Despite being sick he still managed to serve in the Battles of the Somme, Vimy, Passchendaele, and Amiens.

In November 1917 he had been awarded the Belgian Croix de Guerre, which was gazetted on July 12, 1918. On December 15 he was wounded in the left hand and five days later, on December 20, 1917, he was accidentally injured while carrying some rations from a supply train when his foot caught in some loose barbed wire in the dark. This caused him to twist his ankle and he was forced to go to hospital. At an enquiry on April 20, 1918, no blame was attached to him.

Three months after his death, in September 1918, his parents were presented with their son's posthumous VC at Buckingham Palace on December 19, 1918. At some point the decoration was presented to his regiment, and is on display in the Glenbow Museum, Calgary. It is one of three VCs in the museum's collection and, apart from his VC and Croix de Guerre (Belgium), his decorations include the 1914–15 Star, BWM, and VM.

Arthur Knight has been commemorated in many ways: two roads in Coventry Park in west central Regina are named after him as Knight and Sussex. He is also remembered with a memorial plaque outside 1843 Rae Street, Regina, which was his last home. The previous house he lived in, 1646 Albert Street (North), has been demolished. A lake is also named after him in north Saskatchewan, and a mount in Jasper National Park.

Back in England, Knight as a young man was a member of the Reigate Church Lad's Brigade in Surrey. In the close by town of Redhill his name is listed at the top of the war memorial of St. John the Evangelist Church, where he used to sing in the church choir. Arthur Knight's name also appears on the church's draft Roll of Honour in the August and September 1919 editions, published prior to the production of the war memorial, which takes the form of a framed list on vellum that hangs within the church. A commemorative stone memorial was also erected outside the church, but carried no individual names on it. As he was also a young pupil in St. Wilfrid's School, Haywards Heath, his name was listed on a Roll of Honour Board of former pupils killed in the war. It now hangs in the new replacement school in Eastern Road. In 2008 the Royal British Legion asked the Haywards Heath Town Council to arrange for Knight's name to be added to the town's war memorial. This request was carried out in 2008.

W.H. METCALF
and C.W. PECK

Near Cagnicourt, France, September 2

Two of the six members of the Canadian Expeditionary Force who gained the VC on September 2, 1918, in the attack on the Drocourt–Quéant Line were members of the same battalion, the 16th Manitoba Battalion (Canadian Scottish): American-born Lt.-Cpl. W.H. Metcalf and the battalion commanding officer Lt.-Col. C.W. Peck. In the early hours of September 2, 1918, the Drocourt–Quéant Line was attacked by three battalions of the 1st Canadian Division, namely the 16th and 13th of the 3rd Brigade on the right of the attack opposite Cagnicourt, and the 7th Battalion of the 2nd Brigade to the left.

The two battalions of the 3rd Brigade had a 1,600-yard front and were assisted by eight tanks. They pushed forward, up a long slope, toward the very heavily enemy-wired positions. Initially, there was little resistance and many of the enemy were quite happy to surrender. By 7:30 a.m. the 13th Battalion had already taken two trenches of the front system of the Drocourt–Quéant Line. Moving forward the battalion then took the support system as well, but murderous machine-gun fire from the right, where the British 57th (West Lancashire) Division had not yet arrived, began to strike the 16th Battalion after about 200 yards and checked progress. It was during the following period that Metcalf and Peck were to earn their

VCs. The history of the 16th Battalion (CEF), tells the story of what happened in considerable detail.

Men from Numbers 1 and 4 companies had reached as far as a second of five belts of wire, when the artillery covering them suddenly ceased firing on the Drocourt–Quéant front line. Almost immediately, the enemy took advantage of the situation, setting up two or three of their machine guns from the parapet to begin firing at the Canadian attackers. The 16th Battalion was not stopped in its tracks, though, and despite the heavy fire managed to move forward in rushes. When they had reached another belt of wire — which was from eight to ten feet wide — they were forced to take cover in shell holes, as the Germans had started bringing up more machine guns.

The battalion history quotes from a narrative compiled by a member of No. 4 Platoon of Number 1 Company, a Sgt. F.E. Earwaker:

> We had been there [in a shell hole] but a short time when Lieut. Campbell-Johnson passed word along to try once more, we all got up together and didn't get more than five yards before we met up with the heaviest fire from the trench in front of us that I had ever faced. Down I went into a shell hole; Lieut Campbell-Johnson flopped on his stomach right in the wire about twelve feet to my right.

Shortly afterward, Campbell-Johnson was shot in the head and a Sgt. Reid came back into a shell hole, while Earwaker threw a smoke bomb. The two men felt helpless as every time they showed themselves they were shot at. They then decided to wait for a tank to assist them and soon afterward they heard the sound of one approaching:

> Suddenly a heavy fire started from the trench in front of us. We looked up to see what it was about and there we saw the tank with Lance-Corporal Metcalf walking beside it, a little to the right in front of it, pointing with his signal flags in our direction. It was still pretty early and you could hardly recognize him except by his flags. The tank was coming on

at an angle from the left flank. I saw Metcalf walking about thirty yards and then we decided it was our turn to help. We made a dash for the trench and made it before the Germans got their guns on us. When we captured the trench, we found a nest of machine guns on not more than a fifty foot frontage. Behind them was a big dugout. The tank started to amble out in front the minute we got into the trench; about fifteen minutes later I saw it in the smoke five hundred yards in front.

Another witness, Pte. J.H. Riehl, took up the story:

When the tank came to within three hundred feet of the German wire, a heavy machine gun fire was opened upon it from the front trench. Cpl. Metcalf jumped up from the shell hole where he was with his flags pointing toward the enemy's trench, led the tank toward it and then along it. The enemy kept heavy machine gun fire on the tank and as it got close to the trench commenced to throw at it clusters of bombs tied together.

When we afterward got into the trench, we found seventeen German machine guns at the same place, and all of them had been well used. How Metcalf escaped being shot to pieces has always been a wonder to me.

As a result of this defiant action the heavily wired Drocourt–Quéant Line was broken. William Metcalf's VC was gazetted on November 15, 1918, four days after the Armistice as follows:

For most conspicuous bravery, initiative and devotion to duty in attack, when, the right flank of the battalion being held up, he realized the situation, and rushed forward under intense machine gun fire to a passing Tank on the left. With his signal flag he walked in front of the Tank, directing it along the trench in a perfect hail of bullets and bombs. The machine gun strong points were overcome, very heavy casualties were inflicted on the enemy, and a very critical situation was relieved. Later, although wounded, he continued to advance until ordered to get into a shell hole and have his wounds dressed. His valour throughout was of the highest standard.

Metcalf was presented with his VC at York Cottage, Sandringham, on January 26, 1919, when he was accompanied by Cyrus Peck, his commanding officer who was also presented with his VC.

Although the 16th Manitoba Regiment (Canadian Scottish) Battalion had broken into the front of the main Drocourt–Quéant Line, we have seen it was subsequently held up in front of the support line. It was at this point that the battalion commander, Lt.-Col. Cyrus W. Peck, took what was to be a very active role in the battle. Despite the bursting of shells, together withering machine-gun fire, he went forward to make a personal reconnaissance. As a result, he set about organizing several tanks to protect his open flank before leading his battalion forward to their objective. The 16th Battalion history notes of this action that a Capt. Johnston, who was second-in-command of No. 1 Company, found that a flanking battalion had no knowledge of any planned attack and furthermore had no intention of taking part in it. After Johnson had delivered this message to his CO there was a total silence until one of the NCOs present spoke up, saying:

"There's the Colonel!" All turned, and were able to distinguish the form of Colonel Peck, followed by his piper a few yards away, coming toward them. The officer commanding Number 1 told the Commanding Officer what Johnston had just reported and the Colonel replied: "Well, it doesn't make any difference, we've got to go forward whether they do or not, that settled matters."

A reserve battalion, the 15th, later pushed through the 16th's lines and, moving forward slowly, suffered huge casualties before reaching the Bois de Bouche, which was about 3,000 yards from the Buissy Switch and linked the line with the Hindenburg support system. The lines joined on the forward slope of a position known as Mont Dury between the village of that name and the Arras–Cambrai road. The support line was on the reverse slope. The switch line ran in front of Buissy and Villers-lès-Cagnicourt in a southeasterly direction.

Lt.-Col. Cyrus Peck's VC was gazetted on November 15, 1918, and takes up the narrative as follows:

> For most conspicuous bravery and skilful leading when in attack under intense fire. His command quickly captured the first objective, but progress to the further objective was held up by enemy machine gun fire on his right flank. The situation being critical in the extreme, Colonel Peck pushed forward, and made a personal reconnaissance under heavy machine gun fire and sniping fire across a stretch of ground which was heavily swept by fire. Having reconnoitred the position, he returned, reorganized his battalion, and, acting upon the knowledge personally gained, pushed them forward and arranged to protect his flanks. He then went out under the most intense artillery and machine gun fire, intercepted the Tanks, gave them the necessary directions, pointing out where they were to make for, and thus pave the way for a Canadian infantry battalion to push forward. To this battalion he subsequently gave requisite support. His magnificent display of courage and fine qualities of leadership enabled the advance to be continued, although always under heavy artillery and machine gun fire, and contributed largely to the success of the brigade attack.

Later, the general officer in command of the Canadian First Division, Sir Archibald Macdonell, described Peck's actions in the following way:

> When the advance was held up in front of the Bois de Bouche, MacPeck walked along the front of his line and the Fifteenth Battalion, cheering up the men, and constantly repeating: "She's a bear, boys, she's a bear!"

William Henry Metcalf was an American, born at Waite Township, Walsh County, Maine, on January 29, 1894. After leaving grammar school in his hometown he became a barber. During a fishing trip to New Brunswick on the Miramachi River with a few friends in the summer of 1914 he learnt that war had been declared a few days earlier.

In August, having decided he wanted to enlist, he crossed the border to Canada and joined the Canadian Forces on August 29. He was five foot six inches tall and had brown hair. He was given the service number of 22614.

In the main sources for Metcalf's life the year of his birth is often given as 1885 and this confusion was caused by Metcalf himself who wanted to be seen as nine years older than he actually was when he joined the Canadian Forces in September. He did not inform his mother of this deception. His first regiment in 1914 was a militia unit, the 71st Regiment at Fredericton in New Brunswick. A few weeks later, on September 22, he joined the 12th Battalion, a regular battalion at Valcartier, Quebec. After initial training the 12th Battalion left for England on October 14 and, on reaching England, Metcalf was questioned on behalf of his mother by the American ambassador, who asked whether he was the man that all the letters had been written about. Metcalf lied his way out of this one, convincing the ambassador that he had got the wrong man. Subsequently Metcalf joined the 16th Battalion (Canadian Scottish) and served in France and Flanders, from mid May 1915 this time, with the 3rd Canadian Infantry Brigade of the 1st Canadian Division. The Canadian Scottish wore kilts and when taking part in marches were accompanied musically by the sound of bagpipes.

The battalion took part in the 1915 Battle of Ypres, then fought on the Somme in October 1916, during which time Metcalf won the first of two Military Medals. He was promoted to lance corporal, but after gaining his VC in September 1918 during the Second Battle of Arras he was wounded on September 6 and had to remain in hospital for nine months. Later his bullet-ridden kit was put on display in London. Altogether he was wounded six times during the war and won a bar to his MM on January 6, 1917. At the end of hostilities he married a hospital nurse, Dorothy Winifred Holland, who had been born in 1898.

On June 3, 1919, Metcalf was demobilized in Quebec and discharged two days later. He was then appointed as an officer with the Canadian Militia, later returning to the U.S. with his new wife to live in New York, before moving to Eastport, Maine, where he worked as a mechanic. The couple later moved again, to South Portland.

For the remainder of his life Metcalf attended as many VC functions as possible, including the House of Lords Dinner in November 1929, his rank by that time being a captain.

In June 1953 he visited London for the Coronation of Queen Elizabeth II, and in June 1956 he again travelled to London, this time to attend the ceremonies in Hyde Park for the centenary of the VC, where he was the only American-born man among the 300 VCs on parade. Three years later Metcalf attended a reception and dinner at the Royal Canadian Military institute on November 17, 1959.

Again putting the record straight, William Metcalf died in his home in South Portland, Maine, on August 8, 1968, and not in a nursing home in Lewiston. His funeral, three days later, was attended by more than forty members of the Royal Canadian Legion, including a contingent of bagpipers. He had requested to be buried at Bayside Cemetery, Eastpoint, Maine, which overlooked a part of Canada across the St. Croix River, the international boundary. He left behind him Dorothy, his wife, together with three sons and Sheila, a daughter. His sons had served with the American Forces during the Second World War. Dorothy was presented with the Union Jack, which was used to cover her husband's coffin during the ceremonies as she had no wish for her husband's coffin to be draped with the new Canadian maple-leaf flag or the Stars and Stripes. She outlived her husband by twenty-four years, dying in November 1992. Metcalf was one of six American-born men who were awarded the VC. For many years he was a member of the St. Croix New Brunswick Branch of the Royal Canadian Legion.

At the beginning of 1998 the Canadian Scottish Regimental Museum in Victoria asked one of William's sons, Stanley, if they could borrow his father's VC for use in an eightieth-anniversary display. Stanley asked the museum director whether he would take the whole collection. William Metcalf's VC, which was kept in a manila envelope in his son's home in Bucksport, was presented to the Canadian Scottish Regimental Museum in Victoria, British Columbia, by Stanley, together with his father's other war memorabilia of newspaper clippings and old photographs. On October 1, 1998, an armoured car arrived at Stanley Metcalf's house on Route 1 in Bucksport to collect his father's medals and the other mementoes. Apart from the VC, the medals consist of the MM and Bar, 1914–15 Star, BWM, VM, and Coronation Medals for 1937 and 1953.

The original headstone above Metcalf's grave never showed the design of the Victoria Cross, and as it was getting into a poor state the Royal Canadian legion decided to replace it with a new headstone that would also incorporate the VC design. This new stone was dedicated at a ceremony on October 4, 2012. Metcalf's grave also includes the remains of his wife, Dorothy, who died in 1992, and their daughter Sheila.

In 2014, in the display room of the Arlington Amphitheatre, Princess Anne unveiled a memorial in Metcalf's honour as well as those three other Americans, Raphael Zengel, Bellenden Hutcheson, and George Mullin, who served in the CEF and won the nation's highest military honour during the First World War.

The Peck family migrated from New England to New Brunswick in 1763, and Cyrus Wesley Peck was born in Hopewell Hill, New Brunswick, on April 26, 1871, and was educated in the local public schools. On June 27, 1887, when he was sixteen years old, his family moved to New Westminster, British Columbia, so that his father could work in the lumber business in the Fraser River port city on the lower British Columbian mainland. At the same time Cyrus took up military training and sailed to Britain, with the idea of enlisting in the British Army. However, he later changed his mind and volunteered for service in South Africa, but his application was rejected. Returning to Canada, he went to the Klondike and eventually worked in business in Prince Rupert, British Columbia, as a salmon canner. Later, he was elected Unionist MP for Skeena.

Cyrus Peck and Katie Chapman got married in March 1914, and in time the couple had three sons: Horace Wesley, Edward Richard, and Douglas Cyrus. Peck had been a member of the militia and joined the Canadian Expeditionary Force in 1914 in Victoria, when he was already forty-three years old, and was made a captain in the 30th Battalion on November 1. He gave his occupation as broker on his attestation papers. He was not a tall man, but even so he was a very impressive one, being five feet eight inches tall and weighing 225 pounds. Peck left for France on February 23, 1915, and was promoted to temporary major two months later, on April 25 when he arrived in France. He was then transferred to the 16th Battalion and promoted to major. A few days later, on the 21st, he was wounded in the legs by gunshot in Festubert and on May 23 was invalided to England on the hospital ship *St. Patrick*. On July 5 he returned to the 16th Battalion and became its commander a year later in November during the Battle of the Somme.

On January 6, 1917, he was promoted to lieutenant-colonel. In mid-April 1917 Peck was invalided to England again, this time suffering from gastritis. In the same year, during his absence, he was re-elected to the Canadian House of Commons in what was called the Khaki Election. (He was the member for Skeena and a supporter of Sir Robert Borden's Union Government.) He returned to France on June 7 to rejoin his battalion, and his DSO was published in the Birthday Honours Award of June 4.

The *London Gazette* citation reads:

During an attack he showed fine courage and leadship. He led his battalion, under great difficulties caused by heavy mist, to its final objective, nearly three miles. After severe fighting he personally led his men in an attack on nests of machine guns and protecting the enemy guns, which he captured. Some of the guns were of 8 in calibre.

On January 10, 1918, Peck assumed temporary command of the Canadian 3rd Infantry Brigade until January 15, but on January 23 he was a patient in 4 Canadian FA for a few days, and then again between February 15 and March 15, 1918. He then spent eight days in a Canadian CCS.

A month after winning his VC, on September 2, Peck was gassed on October 4 and was in hospital for ten days. He was Mentioned in Despatches on October 12, and was back in England on January 5, 1919. A bar to his DSO was gazetted a few days later, and he received his VC at York Cottage, Sandringham, on January 26, 1919. He was with his colleague, William Metcalf, who was also presented with his VC on the same occasion. In February he returned to Canada, where he attended to business in the House of Commons. He was demobilized in Ottawa in early June.

Peck, whose nickname in the war was MacPeck, introduced to his Canadian Scottish Regiment a Highland tradition of being piped into battle. During the war his name was mentioned in despatches five times. After ending his four-year war service on June 11, 1919, he remained in contact with his military connections and in November 1921 was transferred to the Reserve of Officers with the rank of colonel. In the same year he commanded the Canadian rifle team at Bisley. In 1920 he was made commanding officer of the newly formed Canadian Scottish Regiment after the amalgamation of the 88th and 50th battalions.

After being defeated in the federal elections in 1921, Peck went to the British Columbia legislature in 1924 as member for the islands, when he lived in Vancouver Island for a time. His island constituency was said to be unique in Canada and no longer exists as an electoral district. The constituency was made up of a hundred islands, both large and small, which were off the inner coast of Vancouver Island. In 1928 he was re-elected as Conservative. In the following year he travelled to London for the dinner given by the Prince of Wales in the House of Lords, where he was the most senior member of the

Canadian VC contingent. In 1930 the Gulf Islands Ferry Company purchased the Canadian Pacific Car Ferry *Island Princess* and re-named it *Cyrus Peck*. It was in service until 1966.

Peck was appointed aide-de-camp to two governor generals, Lords Byng and Tweedsmuir, and in 1936 he was appointed to membership of the Canadian Pensions Commission, a position that he held for five years. In April 1956, on the occasion of his eighty-fifth birthday, a group of members of the Canadian Scottish Regiment paid their respects, wishing him luck for his forthcoming June trip to England when he and his wife were to attend the VC centenary commemorations in London. After their London visit, the couple stopped off in Toronto for four days to meet up with old friends from Hamilton, Toronto, and other parts of Ontario, and some former comrades from the Canadian Scottish and 48th Highlanders called on the Pecks at the Royal York Hotel, where they were staying. Afterward they went on to British Columbia. In his last years Peck lived at Hopewell, Sidney, and Vancouver, where he died in hospital on September 27, 1956, having suffered a heart attack nine days earlier. He was cremated, half of his ashes being interred in the family plot in Fraser Cemetery, while the other half were taken by a former colleague to be scattered at sea off the Pacific coast of Prince Rupert Sound. Peck's wife, Kate, survived him and was still alive in 1987 at the age of 101. Peck had also left three sons, although by 1987 only two of these (Joe and Ed) were still living.

During that same year the two sons presented their father's VC to the Canadian Scottish Regiment (Princess Mary's). The ceremony took place during a parade at the Bay Street Armoury, involving 150 members of the Canadian Scottish Regiment from all parts of British Columbia. Ed described his father as being "an extremely loyal and enthusiastic Canadian." In 1993 Peck's decorations were presented by his family to the Canadian War Museum in Ottawa, and the presentation took place seventy-five years to the day from when he won the VC on September 2, 1918. His name is also commemorated with a plaque which is on display in the Canadian Houses of Parliament. His decorations, in the Canadian War Museum in Ottawa, apart from the VC, include the DSO & Bar,

1914–15 Star, BWM, VM, and MiD with Oakleaf, the King George V Silver Jubilee, and Coronation Medals for 1937 and 1953. His Christian name of Cyrus would have been taken from Cyrus the Great Master of Asia Minor, who died 529 B.C. He was said to have been a "Mighty Warrior."

J.F. YOUNG

Arras, France, September 2

During the hectic fighting of September 2, 1918, no fewer than eleven Victoria Crosses were awarded for gallantry beyond the call of duty. In the Dury–Arras sector Pte. John Young was a stretcher-bearer attached to D Company of the 87th Canadian Grenadier Guards Battalion (11th Brigade, 4th Division). The battalion had penetrated the Drocourt–Quéant Line and then had to attack the German-held ridge at Dury.

There was no cover and the battalion was an open target for enemy gunners, and as a consequence the Canadians suffered very heavy casualties. Young went forward to dress the wounds of some of the injured in this open ground which was still being swept continuously by murderous machine-gun and rifle fire. Despite this, he calmly continued his life-saving work for more than an hour before returning for more dressings. He went out again and again to bring in the wounded over the following days.

Private Young was awarded a VC for his magnificent work, which was gazetted on December 14, 1918, as follows:

For most conspicuous bravery and devotion to duty in attack at Dury Arras sector on 2 Sept. 1918, when acting as a stretcher-bearer attached to D Company of the 87th Battn. Quebec Regt. This company in the advance over the ridge suffered heavy casualties from shell and machine gun fire. Private Young, in spite of the complete absence of cover, without the least hesitation went out and in the open, fire-swept ground dressed the wounded. Having exhausted his stock of dressings, on more than one occasion he returned, under intense fire, to his company headquarters for a further supply. This work he continued for over an hour, displaying throughout the most absolute fearlessness. To his courageous conduct must be ascribed the saving of the lives of many of his comrades. Later, when the fire had somewhat slackened, he organized and led stretcher parties to bring in the wounded whom he had dressed. All through the operations of 2, 3 and 4 Sept. Private Young continued to show the greatest valour and devotion to duty.

He was presented with the VC by the king in the ballroom of Buckingham Palace on April 30, 1919.

John Francis Young was son of Robert Charles Young and Mary Ann Young, and was born in Kidderminster, Worcestershire, on January 14, 1893, and later emigrated to Canada where he became a tobacco packer in Montreal. Prior to the war he had served for four months with the McGill Bn. He enlisted in the Canadian Army on October 20, 1915, being given the service number of 177239. He was five foot six inches tall and his father was his next of kin. He gave his address as 376 St. Philip Street, Montreal. After a few months he became a member of the 87th Quebec Regiment (Grenadier Guards) and arrived in France on May 4, 1916. During the war he was wounded on several occasions, mainly by gunshots to his face, head, and neck. On October 20 he was awarded the Good Conduct Badge. He left England for Canada on August 15, 1919. After demobilization Young resumed his work as a tobacco packer in Montreal, and married Ida Thatcher. The couple were to have one son. He had joined the Militia and was made a sergeant.

John Young was never a well man, and died from TB at the early age of thirty-six on November 7, 1929, in the Sainte-Agathe Sanatorium, Quebec. He was buried in Mount Royal Cemetery, Montreal, Section l/2, Plot 2019. He is commemorated in the Canadian Grenadier Guards' Junior Ranks Mess, which is called the John Francis Young Club, and he also has a plaque to his memory in the sergeants' mess.

Young left his VC to his son, John F. Young, of 10479 Laurentide Avenue, Montreal North 459, Quebec, and his two service medals, the BWM and VM, remain in private hands. His VC was acquired in March 2012 for display at the Canadian War Museum in Ottawa.

In recent years a plaque has been placed infront of his headstone in Mount Royal Cemetery. In September 2018 a commemorative paving stone will be laid in Kidderminster, the town of his birth.

W.L. RAYFIELD

East of Arras, France, September 2–4

Private Walter Rayfield, 7th Battalion (British Columbia Regiment) (2nd Brigade, 1st Division), won his VC on September 2–4, 1918, for several acts of bravery during the fighting for the Drocourt–Quéant Line. After the 14th Battalion (3rd Brigade, 1st Division) captured the village of Cagnicourt with very few casualties, the Bois de Loison was overrun and the Buissy Switch reached. However, at that point the opposition stiffened. On the left of the 3rd Canadian Brigade, the 2nd Brigade attacked with its 7th Battalion, using four tanks on a front of 1,000 yards with the 10th Battalion and three more tanks in support. Despite an accurate Allied barrage, the 7th came under heavy fire from advanced machine-gun posts. These were gradually captured and, with the tanks doing good work, the battalion assaulted and took the forward system of the Drocourt–Quéant position with the assistance of seven tanks. The support system and northern end of the Buissy Switch were then taken without much difficulty, with a large number of the enemy surrendering.

Walter Rayfield's VC was gazetted on December 14, 1918. When he received the news of his decoration he was stationed in Germany with his battalion a few weeks after the war had finished, and he was pulled out of bed to be told that his VC was listed in army orders. Later in the day he was escorted out on to the parade ground for the public announcement of his VC. It was the third VC won by the 7th Canadian Battalion, and the citation was as follows:

> For most conspicuous bravery, devotion to duty and initiative during operations east of Arras from 2 to 4 Sept. 1918. Ahead of his company he rushed a trench occupied by a large party of the enemy, personally bayoneting two and taking 10 prisoners. Later, he located and engaged with great skill, under constant rifle fire, an enemy sniper who was causing many casualties. He then rushed the section trench from which the sniper had been operating, and so demoralized the enemy by his coolness and daring that thirty others surrendered to him. Again, regardless of his personal safety, he left cover under heavy machine gun fire and carried in a badly wounded comrade. His indomitable courage, cool foresight and daring reconnaissance were invaluable to his company commander and an inspiration to all ranks.

A few weeks later, on September 27, 1918, Rayfield was promoted to corporal, then on January 7, 1919, to acting sergeant. On March 8, 1919, he was presented with his VC by the king in the ballroom of Buckingham Palace and in the following month he returned to Canada and was demobilized on April 25.

Walter Leigh Rayfield was born in Richmond, Surrey, on October 7, 1881. He was educated at a private school in London and in Richmond Grammar School. His family emigrated to Canada a few years later, and from the age of ten Walter's education was completed in Canada and America, although he lived mainly in Ontario. In America he graduated from Oakland Agricultural College and began a career in California, but he returned to Canada shortly before the outbreak of war.

When the war began in August 1914 Rayfield was a lumberjack in Vancouver, and when trying to enlist in the Canadian Army he was twice rejected on medical grounds. Eventually, though, he was successful and enlisted in Victoria, British Columbia, on July 10, 1917, when he was allocated the service number of 2204279 and became a member of the 7th Battalion (British Columbia) CEF. He was five feet six inches tall. He gave his address as Gray Hotel, Los Angeles. His next of kin was his mother, Mrs. John Stretting of Washington. He left Canada in early January for Liverpool, when he was sent to Seaford on January 27 and was taken on the strength of the 1st Canadian Reserve Bn. on February 15. He was in hospital from mid September to mid October 1918, and granted leave from January 1, 1919, which was extended.

After the war Rayfield returned to England on March 3, 1919, and left for Canada on April 10. He was discharged in Vancouver, but he had to he remain in a Vancouver hospital for some time, presumably as a result of the war. He then took up farming with the hope of improving his health, and was later put in charge of the transfer of shell-shocked and other seriously disabled soldiers at a military hospital under the DSCR.

In November 1929 he travelled to London for the House of Lords VC Dinner, and on the same trip visited Belfast where he laid a wreath in the Garden of Remembrance on behalf of the Canadian winners of the VC. On his return to Canada he moved to Toronto, and was later an official of the Toronto Harbour Commission. He was interested in politics and on one occasion stood for membership of the federal parliament, but was narrowly defeated. In 1934 he was appointed sergeant-at-arms of the Ontario legislature, when he "fulfilled his duties efficiently and to the credit of all concerned." While acting as a sergeant-at-arms he used to wear a sword, cocked hat, and satin waistcoat, but during his term of office the ceremonial uniform was replaced by a more moden garment. In 1935 Rayfield was made deputy governor of Toronto Jail, later becoming its governor. He was considered to be a very suitable candidate as during his life he had a wide experience in the handling of men. He was also an officer in the Queen's Own Rangers.

In 1939, during the king and queen's visit to North America, Rayfield was one of the winners of the VC to be presented to the royal couple on May 22, 1939, in the Commons Chamber, Toronto; others were Benjamin Geary, Henry Robson, Colin Barron, Thomas Holmes, and Charles Rutherford.

Walter died very suddenly, at home in Toronto on February 19, 1949, and at his own request was buried in the Soldiers' Plot, Prospect Cemetery, in Toronto, Section & Grave 4196. Apart from his VC, BWM, VM, and King George VI Coronation Medal, he was also awarded the Silver Medal of the Crown (Belgium) in recognition of his services. His son, Victor, presented his father's decorations to the Canadian War Museum, Ottawa, in February 1970.

M.F. GREGG

Near Cambrai, France, September 27–October 1

In the Marcoing section of the Hindenburg Line — Germany's famous "impregnable" defensive system — Lt. Milton Gregg of the Royal Canadian Regiment (RCR) won the VC for gallantry during the period between September 27 and October 1, 1918. The aim of the Canadian 3rd Division was to take the village of Fontaine-Notre-Dame, to the east of Bourlon Wood, and then force the Marcoing Line, which would then open the way to the very important town of Cambrai.

Led by the Royal Canadian Regiment, the 7th Brigade began well and, by 8:50 a.m., had captured the Marcoing Line on September 28. But then strong enemy resistance from the Marcoing support line slowed the advance down. The Germans were out to delay the fall of Cambrai and the crossings of the Canal de l'Escaut for as long as they possibly could. By mid-morning the RCR were pinned down under heavy fire from the front, and from Sailly on the left flank. The Princess Patricia's Canadian Light Infantry (PPCLI) then joined the action and, by early afternoon, the two battalions had secured the Marcoing position between the Arras and Bapaume roads. Many of Gregg's achievements were carried out during this period of the advance, and the VC citation, published on January 6, 1919, takes up the story:

For most conspicuous bravery and initiative during operations near Cambrai, 27 Sept. to 1 Oct. 1918. On 28 Sept., when the advance of the brigade was held up by fire from both flanks and by thick uncut wire, he crawled forward alone and explored the wire until he found a small gap, through which he subsequently led his men, and forced an entry into the enemy trench. The enemy counterattacked in force, and through lack of bombs the situation became critical. Although wounded, Lieut. Gregg returned alone under terrific fire and collected a further supply. Then, rejoining his party, which by this time was much reduced in numbers, and, in spite of a second wound, he reorganized his men and led them with the greatest determination against the enemy trenches, which he finally cleared. He personally killed or wounded 11 of the enemy, and took 25 prisoners, in addition to 12 machine guns captured in this trench. Remaining with his company in spite of wounds, he again on 30th Sept. led his men in attack until severely wounded. The outstanding valour of this officer saved many casualties and enabled the advance to continue.

Gregg was decorated with his VC by the king at an investiture in the ballroom of Buckingham Palace on February 26, 1919.

Milton Fowler Gregg was born in Mountain Dale, King's County, New Brunswick, on April 10, 1892. He grew up on a farm owned by his father, George Lord Gregg, who had previously been a successful farmer in Devon; his mother, Elizabeth Celia Myles, came from Ireland. Gregg was educated at the local public school, and at the Provincial Normal School in Fredericton. He then went on to Acadia University, and then to Dalhousie University, graduating in 1916. After leaving university, he became a schoolteacher in Carleton County, New Brunswick.

The first step in his military career was as a trooper in the 8th Princess Louise's New Brunswick Hussars in 1910. Soon after the war began Gregg enlisted in Halifax as a private in the CEF in November 1914, and served with the 13th Canadian Infantry

Battalion (Royal Highlanders), who wore the Black Watch tartan. Gregg was five foot nine inches tall with dark brown hair. He gave his religion as Baptist and his service number wass 50051. On February 8, 1915, he sailed from Canada to Liverpool and arrived on May 20, when he was sent for further training and found himself alongside many of his countrymen, training on Salisbury Plain. He later went to Shorncliffe, and sailed to France on April 16 while he remained with the 13th Battalion and took part in the Second Battle of Ypres, and was wounded in the fighting at Festubert on May 31. He was promoted to corporal on September 1 and to sergeant on November 25. In 1916, while recovering from his wounds in England, he attended an Imperial Officers' Training Course between May and August in Cambridge. He was commissioned as temporary lieutenant on November 1, 1916. His service papers at this time suffered from a mix-up, which resulted in him becoming briefly an officer serving in the British Army and a member of the King's Own Royal Lancaster Regiment. However, this was not for long as he soon transferred to the 40th Canadian Battalion. He was transferred to the 26th Reserve Battalion in January and on April 25 to the Royal Canadian Regiment.

Gregg was wounded at Lens, near Vimy, on June 9, 1917, and was also awarded the MC when leading a trench raid. The citation of August 25 read as follows:

> For conspicuous gallantry and devotion to duty in leading a bombing attack against a hostile machine-gun which he outflanked and annihilated the crew, thus permitting the advance of his party to continue unchecked. His prompt action greatly assisted the success of a much larger operation. Later, although himself wounded, he carried a seriously wounded officer out of action to a place of safety.

Four days later he was invalided and detached to the Nova Scotia Regimental Depot. He was in hospital for four weeks and was then granted three weeks sick leave. He returned to France on November 22, and rejoined the RCR on the 27th. In August

1918, during fighting in the Arras battles, he won a bar to his MC (*London Gazette*, October 8) when serving with the RCR, to which he had transferred:

> During an attack on the Bois de Sart on 26th August 1918 he became detached from his company with his platoon, and being subjected to withering machine-gun fire, he led a bombing party forward and rushed two machine-gun crews, killing them. Pushing on with his platoon he found his position isolated and dug in, and by a personal reconnaissance connected up with the left flank, and by skillfully dispersing his men enabled an enemy counterattack to be repulsed....

He returned to England for a fortnight's leave at the end of August. After winning his VC, Gregg was wounded again on October 1, having been made adjutant to the RCR the day before. He rejoined on October 11 and, at the end of the year, was granted another two weeks' leave. He returned to England on February 6, 1919, and left with his unit for Canada on March 1. He was demobilized on April 8, and on his return to Canada in 1919 he married Dorothy Alward of Havelock, New Brunswick. The couple were later to have a daughter. Gregg was then transferred to the Canadian Militia. After the war he went into private business, trying his hand at advertising, then became a company secretary to a mining company, and later worked as a motorcar dealer. On November 9, 1929, he attended the House of Lords Dinner. In 1934 he was invited to become the sergeant-at-arms at the House of Commons in Ottawa, a post which he held from 1934 to 1939, when he was given a leave of absence. His job was no sinecure and his duties on Parliament Hill included the traditional one of mace-bearer; he was also responsible to the Speaker of the House for the smooth running of the administration of the buildings and for supervision of the large staff. Gregg was Dominion Treasurer of the Canadian Legion (1934–39), and took part in the ceremonies connected with the unveiling of the Vimy Ridge Memorial in France in July 1936.

On the outbreak of the Second World War Gregg rejoined the Canadian Army. Posted as second-in-command RCR, he proceeded to England with the unit in 1939. In the following year he was made lieutenant-colonel commander of West Nova Scotia Regiment, and in April 1940 his unit was inspected by the king. In 1941 he became commandant of the Canadian OTCU in England, until it was abolished. He returned to Canada in 1942, where he took charge of the Officers' Training Centre in Brockville, Ontario. In the following year he was made brigadier and commandant of the Canadian School of Infantry in Vernon, British Columbia, a position that he held until the middle of 1945. He then retired from the army.

Although Gregg had not had much academic experience, he had been invited to become chancellor of the University of Brunswick in 1944. He was later elected to Parliament (1947–57), serving in Prime Minister Mackenzie King's Liberal Cabinet, in which he was minister of fisheries (1947–48), minister of veterans' affairs (1948–50), and minister of labour (1950–57). In 1957 he was defeated by a Conservative in the general election held in June. Between 1952 and 1958 he was the Royal Canadian Regiment's honorary colonel, and he was a member of the Canadian contingent at the 1956 Hyde Park VC review in London. In the late 1950s he served with the UN's Children's Fund in Iraq for a year before occupying a similar post in Indonesia from 1960 until 1963. In 1964 he became the Canadian high commissioner to Guyana, holding this position for three years. Gregg retained a home in Ottawa, in addition to his home at Fredericton. In 1977, when in his eighties, he attended the sixtieth-anniversary commemorations of the Canadian capture of Vimy Ridge.

Gregg listed his recreations in *Who's Who* as rugby, football, hunting, motoring, and fishing. It is surprising that a man with such an active life had any time for recreations. He died in New Brunswick on March 13, 1978, at the age of eighty-five, and was buried near his home in Snider Mountain (formerly Mountain Dale) Baptist Church Cemetery, Fredericton. He was survived by his second wife, Erica Deichmann. Later, the names of both of his wives were inscribed on his headstone.

His medals were stolen on Christmas Eve in 1978 from the Royal Canadian Regimental Museum in London, Ontario, and have never been found. However, a replacement set has been cobbled together for display purposes. The length of the list of his awards underpins his very considerable service to Canadian life: he had been a soldier, politician, administrator, and diplomat.

The award list for the First World War, apart from the VC, MC and bar, included the 1914–15 Star, BWM, and VM. His other awards included Officer of the Order of Canada (OC), Defence Medal 1939–45, Canadian Volunteer Service Medal (1939–45) with "Maple Leaf" clasp, War Medal 1939–45, King George V Silver Jubilee Medal (1935), King George VI Coronation Medal (1937), CBE, Queen Elizabeth II Coronation Medal (1953), Canadian Centennial Medal (1967), Queen Elizabeth II Silver Jubilee Medal (1977), Colonial Auxiliary Forces Long Service Medal, Efficiency Decoration (ED) with "Canada" clasp, Canadian Forces DFC (1949), and Commissionaires Long Service Medal. Also on display in the museum are his officers' service dress and a bust. The University of New Brunswick also has a Gregg Centre in Fredericton, which was set up for the study of war and society. An Annual Student Bursary is also in operation in Gregg's name, as is a trophy called the "Mons Box," an award for officer trainees who have displayed a high quality of leadership skills.

The Hon. Milton Gregg is also remembered in a number of other ways, including having a mountain named after him in Jasper Natural Park. He also had a barracks named after him, which carries the following inscription:

So named in this centennial year of the Royal Canadian Regiment to honour the memory of a gallant soldier, statesman and scholar. A native of New Brunswick, Brigadier the Honourable Milton F. Gregg, VC, OC, CBE, MC, ED won the Victoria Cross in 1917 [sic] while serving as a Lieutenant with the Regiment. He died in Fredericton, New Brunswick on 13 March 1978 at the age of 85.

S.L. HONEY

Bourlon Wood, France, September 27

Three members of the Canadian Army won VCs during the capture of Bourlon Wood on September 27, 1918. The wood was a vital part of the strongly defended German Hindenburg Line and, in the past, had provided a major stumbling block for the Allies. General Currie, the Canadian Army Corps Commander, planned to carry out the tasks allotted to him in two parts. First would come the crossing of the Canal du Nord and the capture of Bourlon Wood, together with the high ground close to the Arras–Cambrai road; then, in the second part of the action, the Canadian Corps would capture the bridges over the Canal de l'Escaut, to the northeast of the German-held town of Cambrai. This would lead to a firm line being established as far as the Canal de la Sensée.

Zero hour on September 27 was 5:20 a.m., and the Allied armies opened a heavy barrage against the enemy positions. To the right of the line, the 10th Canadian Brigade quickly crossed the canal, meeting little opposition; but the 11th and 12th brigades, who were leading the 4th Division on the right and left respectively, soon met trouble from the south of their attack. In tough fighting the 87th Canadian Battalion reached the southern part of Bourlon village by 9:45 a.m., and the 54th Battalion, passing through, then went around the north of the wood in order to reach the far side. The relative slowness of the British attack to the south led to the plan for encircling the wood to be abandoned. The 54th Battalion then found itself in a salient, but did manage to reach the village of Fontaine-Notre-Dame to the east of Bourlon Wood. The 75th and 87th battalions came up on their left. To the north, the 12th Brigade fought all day, and their 85th and 38th battalions were severely hit in their attempts to capture part of the Marquion trench system. However, their work allowed the 78th and 72nd battalions to reach most of their objectives, with the final resistance in the wood overcome by 8:00 p.m. The day had turned out to be a complete triumph for the Canadian Corps and a disaster for the German 188th Infantry Regiment, who lost very heavily. Lt. Samuel Honey, of the 78th Battalion, performed outstandingly. He was heavily involved in clearing German strongpoints, leading to the eventual capture of Bourlon Wood, and was awarded the VC, gazetted in the *London Gazette* on January 6, 1919, as follows:

> On 27 Sept., when his company commander and all other officers of his company became casualties, Lieut. Honey took command and skillfully reorganized under most severe enemy shelling and machine-gun fire. He continued the advance with great dash and gained the objective, but finding his company was suffering casualties from enfilade machine-gun fire, he made a personal reconnaissance and, locating the machine-gun nest, he rushed it single-handed, capturing the guns and ten prisoners. Having organized his position, he repelled four enemy counterattacks, and when darkness fell he again went out himself alone, and having located an enemy post, he led out a party and captured the post of three guns by stealth. He immediately advanced his line, and his new position proved of great value in the jump off the following morning. On 29 Sept., he led his company against a strong enemy position with great initiative and daring, and continued on the succeeding days of the battle to display the same wonderful example of leadership and bravery.

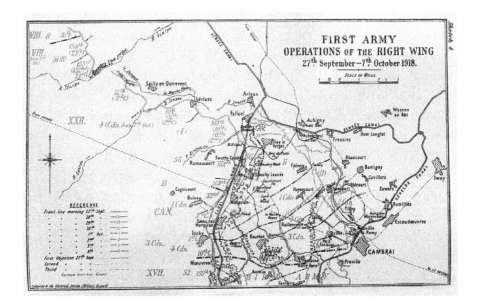

Sadly, Honey died on September 30 at 12 Canadian Field Ambulance of gunshot wounds to his legs, received during the last stages of the attack by his battalion, and was buried at Quéant Communal Cemetery, British Extension, Row C, Grave 36. The cemetery is quite some distance from where he fell and is twelve miles southeast of Arras, roughly midway between the Arras–Cambrai and Bapaume–Cambrai main roads. His posthumous VC was sent by the War Office to Canada, then by post from the Governor General of Canada on March 27, 1919, to his father. No presentation ceremony took place.

Samuel Lewis Honey was the son of the Reverend George E. and Metta Honey (*née* Blaisdell), who came from Boston, Massachusetts. Samuel was born on February 9, 1894, at Conn, near Mount Forest, Wellington County, Ontario. His father was a Methodist minister of the Hamilton Conference, a calling that required continuous moves, which is reflected in the number of schools and colleges the boy attended. Always known by Lewis, his middle name, he attended school at Drayton and when his father was sent to Princeton in 1908. He graduated from the Princeton Continuation School with a junior matric in July 1910, and took charge of a school on the Six Nations Reserve close to Brantford. In the following spring he taught for a brief time at a school near Drumbo, before he joined a teachers' college at Normal School in London, Ontario, that autumn. He graduated in June 1912 with a public-school teaching certificate and then spent a year in western Huron County at Londesborough school. He then continued his education, studying for the senior matriculation at Walkerton High School, where he won a scholarship and passed the Honour Matriculation examinations with first-class honours in English and French, and second-class honours in Latin and German. After his graduation in June 1914 he resumed teaching in York County and also completed a cadet instructor's course. In the autumn he took up teaching again, this time in Whitchurch, York County

Honey had planned to enroll at Victoria College, but the outbreak of war intervened and, a few months later, he joined the army in Walkerton, Ontario, on January 22, 1915, as a private in the 34th Battalion (Ontario) Regiment instead. He was five foot five and a half inches tall with grey eyes and dark-brown hair, and his service number was 602174. His father was his next of kin. Eight months later he left Canada for Britain on October 23, arriving in Devenport a week later. Sensibly teaching experience had clearly been recognized by the army and he was sent on a course in physical training and bayonet fighting in Aldershot. Following this course from January to August he was made an instructor in these disciplines in Bramshott camp, during which time he was promoted to sergeant.

On August 12, 1916, he left for France with the 78th Battalion (Winnipeg Grenadiers) of the 4th Division, and six months later won a Military Medal (MM) in a trench raid on February 22, 1917 (*London Gazette*, April 26, 1917). "He did most excellent work in clearing an enemy's communication trench and establishing a block in spite of heavy opposition. He personally covered the withdrawal of his own and another squad under very heavy grenade fire...."

He later earned a Distinguished Conduct Medal (DCM) for his deeds in the 1917 Arras battles at Vimy Ridge (*London Gazette*, August 16, 1917):

... when his platoon commander was wounded he assumed command, leading his men forward in the face of terrific fire, until compelled by casualties to dig in. He held the position for three days, encouraging his men by splendid example.

In May 1917 Honey returned to England for officer training, and was appointed a temporary lieutenant on September 2 with the 11th Reserve Bn. On June 23, while still in England, Honey was one of an eight-man bearer party that took part in the presentation of the Colours of the 78th Battalion for safe keeping in Canterbury Cathedral. Fifteen months after he had returned to France, Honey died of wounds at 12 Canadian Field Ambulance, having received gunshot wounds to the leg at Bourlon Wood on September 30.

Nearly fifty years after the war began, on July 26, 1964, a plaque commemorating Honey's life was unveiled by his sister beside the Westcott United Church, in 10 Central Street, Conn. The plaque was one of several to be erected in the province by the Department of Tourism and Information. The ceremony, attended by several local dignitaries, was sponsored by the Mount Forest Branch (134) of the Royal Canadian Legion, and the township of West Luther. The inscription on the plaque is virtually a retelling of the original VC citation. This plaque has been relocated to a position ouside the Legion building in 14 King Street West, Mount Forest. A similar plaque is to be found in Valour Place, Cambridge, Ontario, and in the Galt Armoury in Ainslie Street. Honey's name is also included on a Roll of Honour to Canadian school teachers who served in the war from Ontario. Honey was survived by two brothers, George B. Honey and C.S. Honey, who lived in Fort Erie.

His decorations which, apart from the VC and DCM, included the MM, BWM, and VM and are in the collection of the Canadian War Museum having been presented by his family in 1975.

If one visits Bourlon Wood in France today, it becomes very clear how important it would have been to hold on to, as it is on high ground and offers a spectacular view over a wide area. A section of the wood, which still contains many trench lines, was later presented to the Canadian people as a memorial to their fighting troops for their efforts in September 1918. A Canadian memorial, similar to the one at Maple Copse on the Somme, is in the centre and the local villagers use the wood as a recreational park. A more recent war memento is close by in the form of a memorial to local members of the Free French who were killed by the Gestapo in June 1944.

G.F. KERR

Bourlon Wood, France, September 27

To the left of the Canadian 4th Division's attack on September 27, 1918, against the Canal du Nord and Bourlon Wood, the 1st Division was also successful. Guns of the 1st Canadian Field Artillery allowed the 1st Brigade to move quickly into the village of Inchy-en-Artois on the west side of the Canal du Nord. The dry bed of the canal was quickly negotiated and the 4th Battalion, moving northeasterly, managed to capture its allotted section of the Marquion Line. The 1st Battalion then moved on, but the 2nd and 3rd battalions were delayed by heavy fire coming from a railway embankment to the north of Bourlon Wood. With the timely assistance of the 72nd Battalion, the enemy resistance was overcome and the advance continued. The role played by George Fraser Kerr, commander of the 3rd Battalion's left support company, in dealing with a German strongpoint close to the Arras–Cambrai road at Raillencourt was crucial. As a result, four machine guns and thirty-one prisoners were captured. His almost inevitable VC was gazetted on January 6, 1919, as follows:

For most conspicuous bravery and leadership during the Bourlon Wood operations on 27 Sept. 1918, when in command of the left support company in attack. He handled his company with great skill, and gave timely support by outflanking a machine-gun which was impeding the advance. Later, near the Arras–Cambrai road, the advance was again held up by a strongpoint. Lieut. Kerr, far in advance of his company, rushed this strongpoint single-handed and captured four machine guns and thirty-one prisoners. His valour throughout this engagement was an inspiring example to all.

Lt. Kerr was decorated at an investiture with the VC, together with an MC and bar, on May 20, 1919, in the Quadrangle of Buckingham Palace.

George Fraser Kerr was born in Deseronto, Ontario, on June 8, 1895. He was the son of John James Kerr, who ran a dry goods store in the town, and Isabell Fraser. He was educated in local schools and, later, in Toronto after the family moved there in about 1903. When the war began in 1914, Kerr, who was working in a bank, decided to join up as a private in the 3rd Battalion (Toronto Regiment) at Valcartier, Quebec, on September 22. He was five foot seven inches tall with light hair. He sailed for Britain in early October. After further training he arrived in France on February 11. Two days earlier he had been promoted to corporal and his leadership qualities had been noted. Despite that, his record as not perfect as at a Field General Court-Martial held on April 7, 1916, he was found guilty of drunkeness and was punished by being reduced to the ranks.

Two months later, on June 13, 1916, he won the MM at Mount Sorrel in the Ypres Salient. This was an important position, which allowed the Canadian troops good observation over enemy positions. It had been captured by the Germans on June 2, but following a huge artillery bombardment on June 13 it was recaptured by the Canadians. The Canadians remained in the Salient for three more months. During this time the enemy made several attempts to recapture Mount Sorrel, but these attacks were repulsed. Toward the end of July, Kerr was seriously wounded and, on July 31, he was sent back to England for medical treatment and was hospitalized in Cambridge with wounds in his left leg. He was discharged from Epsom Hospital on December 12.

Approximately six months later Kerr was judged fit enough to return to active service. By this time he had been commissioned in the 12th Reserve Battalion, although once in France he rejoined his former unit, the 3rd Battalion. On February 24, 1918, he was in hospital in Boulogne suffering from scabies and was discharged on March 13.

During the war he had served from private to captain, and by 1918 his military record had become outstanding, demonstrating his courage and initiative. As an example he won the MC during the Allied offensive at Amiens on August 8, 1918, when during the fighting he discovered a gap opening up in the Allied lines and, together with his platoon, he quickly filled this gap and subsequently put an enemy machine gun out of action. Thirty of the enemy were killed and a battery of 77-milimetre guns were captured in the process. Later he filled a further gap in the line and went forward with advancing troops. This time he was wounded, but still continued to the final objective. On the way, a machine-gun nest of two guns was accounted for. Despite his wounds, Kerr still continued to serve for another couple of days.

While he was recovering from his latest wounds, he learnt about an impending attack against the Canal du Nord and Bourlon Wood. His unit was to take part in this assault and he was determined not to miss out. Despite still being ruled unfit by his doctors, he discharged himself from hospital and promptly rejoined his unit at the front. It was during the subsequent fighting that he won a bar to his MC at Quéant on September 2/3. The *London Gazette* date of his MC was December 2, 1918, and the bar was added on February 1, 1919. The citation was as follows:

For conspicuous gallantry, initiative and skill during the Drocourt–Quéant attack on the 2nd and 3rd September 1918, when he led his company forward with great dash. Later he led two platoons to the assistance of one of the attacking companies, which was held up by heavy machine-gun fire, surprising the hostile machine-gun crews, and personally accounting for several of the enemy. His splendid courage afforded a most inspiring example at a critical time.

On January 3, 1919, while out riding in France with a colleague, Kerr had an accident when his horse bolted and broke away from him when passing through a wood. The horse smashed its rider against a tree. Kerr ended up in hospital at Wimereaux. He later returned for treatment to England and was discharged from hospital in Buxton on May 21. A few weeks later, on July 4, 1919, he was declared free of venereal disease. His military career ended on July 16, 1919, when he was discharged as medically unfit. He arrived back in Canada as one of the country's most decorated soldiers.

Returning to peacetime, Kerr became a manager of a firm of metal suppliers called Lewis, Lazarus and Sons in Toronto. He was still active in the militia and, on March 1, 1921, was promoted to captain in the Toronto Regiment. He travelled to England for the House of Lords Dinner on November 9, 1929, but during the voyage broke his arm. Because of this he suffered a great deal of pain and had to consult a specialist once his ship had docked in port. He requested that his injury should not be reported, in order to prevent his wife becoming alarmed about his health. However, much worse was to follow, for within a month he died after a tragic accident. His body was found sitting in his car. Apparently, while waiting for the car engine to warm up, he had been poisoned by carbon monoxide fumes and asphyxiated. The accident, which was described in a local newspaper as a "Peacetime Tragedy," happened on December 8, 1929, at his home at 38 Cheltenham Avenue, Lawrence Park, Toronto.

Kerr was buried in Mount Pleasant Cemetery in Toronto, Plot 14, Section 36, Lot E- ½, with full military honours. Representatives from the government and numerous organizations attended. Kerr's coffin, draped with a Union Jack, was followed by a soldier carrying his decorations on a cushion. Other holders of the VC also attended; men who only a few weeks ago had attended the House of Lords Dinner in London with Kerr. At the gates of the cemetery on Yonge Street, a guard of honour was drawn up, comprising members of the

3rd Canadian Infantry Battalion. The coffin was then transferred to a gun carriage and the procession moved slowly toward the Kerr family plot. At the graveside, a short burial service was conducted, while a biting cold wind blew snow across the ground. Rifle volleys rang out over the grave and the "Last Post" and "Reveille" were then played. The Canadian Governor General sent a cable to Kerr's family in which he commiserated with their loss.

Kerr's wife, Mary Beeman (1886–1952), shares the family plot, together with their daughter, Mary Louise Kerr (1925–77).

On November 11, 1973, an Ontario Heritage Foundation plaque to his memory was erected in Valour Place, Cambridge, Ontario, formerly named Galt. On Remembrance Day 2001 it was replaced by a bilingual one. Frederick Hobson and Samuel Honey are also commemorated there.

Forty-four years later, on November 2, 1973, a plaque commemorating the life and career of Capt. George Kerr was unveiled in Centennial Park, between Main Street and the waterfront in Deseronto, his birthplace, one of a series erected throughout the province. It was arranged and sponsored by the Earle J. Brant Memorial Branch, Royal Canadian Legion. The unveiling ceremony was performed by Capt. Kerr's grandchildren, David, Carol, and Allison Ross. His decorations apart from his VC and MC and Bar included the MM, 1914–15 Star, BWM, and VM, are in the collection of the Canadian War Museum in Ottawa.

G. T. LYALL

North of Cambrai, France, September 27

Lt. Graham Lyall was an officer in the 102nd (Central Ontario) Battalion, and won his VC during the operations of the 4th Division at Bourlon Wood on September 27, together with another VC winner, Lt. S.L. Honey. They both had to deal with German strongpoints during the capture of the Wood. Lyall's VC was gazetted on December 14, 1918, as follows:

For most conspicuous bravery and skillful leading during the operation north of Cambrai. On 27 Sept. 1918, whilst leading his platoon against Bourlon Wood, he rendered invaluable support to the leading company, which was held up by a strongpoint, which he captured by a flank movement, together with thirteen prisoners, one field-gun and four machine guns. Later, his platoon, now much weakened by casualties, was held up by machine guns at the southern end of Bourlon Wood. Collecting any men available, he led them toward a strongpoint, and, springing forward alone, rushed the position single-handed and killed the officer in charge, subsequently capturing at this point forty-five prisoners and five machine guns. Having made good his final objective, with a further capture of forty-seven prisoners, he consolidated his position and thus protected the remainder of the company. On 1 Oct., in the neighbourhood of Blecourt, when in command of a weak company, by skillful dispositions he captured a strongly defended position, which yielded sixty prisoners and seventeen machine guns. During two days of operations Lieut. Lyall captured in all three officers, 182 other ranks, twenty-six machine guns, and one field-gun, exclusive of heavy casualties inflicted. He showed throughout the utmost valour and high powers of command.

A Canadian newspaper described Lyall's actions in the following way:

This most remarkable record is probably unexcelled in all the annals of war. His feat required not only courage and resource, but also the very highest type of military intelligence; a thorough understanding of military technique, and a personality of the most inspiring character.

Lyall received his VC from the king on March 15, 1919.

Graham Thomson Lyall was the only son of the Rev. R.H. Lyall, and was born in Chorlton, north of Manchester, on March 8, 1892. His father was vicar of St. John's, Farnworth, from 1894 to 1900, and the family then moved to Nelson, Lancashire, where Lyall's father became vicar of St. John's, Darwen. The family home was in Turncroft Lane, Darwen. Lyall was educated at Nelson Municipal Secondary School, and later he atttended a naval engineering college. He was a keen sportsman throughout his life: an expert swimmer and he also excelled at tennis, cricket, and hockey, as well as going in for shooting, canoeing, and rowing.

After he left college in 1912 he emigrated to Welland, Ontario, where he completed his education at the University of Toronto, qualifying as a mechanical engineer. He subsequently acquired a job with the Canadian Steel Foundries at Welland, and later worked for the Canadian Niagara Power Company at Niagara Falls, Ontario. He was to become a member of the British Institute of Engineers. Prior to the war he served with the XIX Regiment for a year. He enlisted on September 24, 1915, in St. Catharines, Ontario. He was five foot ten iches tall and had auburn hair. His service number was 158524. He was placed on active duty and served with the Welland Canal Force as Canal Guard in Niagara and, after serving for several months on Lock Seven, he left Halifax on April 28 and arrived in England on May 6. On June 6 he was made a member of the 81st Canadian Infantry Battalion, becoming an acting corporal. He left for France on June 7, and a week later joined the 4th Canadian Mounted Rifles. He took part in the Battle of the Somme, and on September 7 he was in hospital with a sprained ankle. He was back on duty four days later. In April 1917 he took part in the Battle of Vimy Ridge. During this period he had been promoted through the ranks for conspicuous bravery and was made a temporary lieutenant on April 28, 1917, after a short course at the Canadian Officers' Training School in Bexhill, Sussex. He then joined the 102nd Battalion, 2nd Central Ontario Regiment. Lyall was in and out of hospital throughout his service. He was wounded on November 18, 1917, and suffered bouts of bronchitis, tonsilities, gastric problems, adenoids, hearing problems, effects of gas poisoning, and trench mouth.

After the war, Lyall returned to his former home at Darwen, where the local inhabitants presented him with a French bronze clock, together with other ornaments. He was married on April 24, 1919, in the High United Free Church, Airdrie, Lanarkshire, to Elizabeth Moffat, eldest daughter of Alexander Frew, the provost of Airdrie, and Elizabeth Moffat Frew. Lyall's father took part in the marriage ceremony. Later, Lyall became a manager of Drumbathie Brickworks (Alexander Frew & Co.), and the couple lived at Forrest Park, Drumgelloch, Airdrie. He later became managing director of Aerocrete (Scotland) Ltd., Victoria Works, Airdrie. On June 26, 1920, he attended the Garden Party for VC winners and their families in the grounds of Buckingham Palace, and was also a guest at the House of Lords Dinner on November 9, 1929.

Lyall joined up again in the Second World War, having been called up in the Territorial Army (TA) Reserve of Officers, and was promoted to major (Ordnance Mechanical Engineer, 2nd Class), temporary lieutenant-colonel (Ordnance Mechanical Engineer, 1st Class), and acting colonel, Royal Army Ordnance Corps (RAMC). Sadly he died of heart failure in his sleep on November 28, 1941, at Mersa Matruh in Egypt, and is buried in Halfaya Sollum War Cemetery in Egypt, Plot XIX, Row B, Grave 2. His service number was 48647.

On June 5, 2005, the Countess of Wessex, colonel-in-chief of the Lincoln and Welland Regiment, which emerged from the 19th Regiment, unveiled a plaque to his memory in St. Catharines. It was set up on the northwest corner of Lake Street and Welland Avenue. In Remembrance Week of 2006, Lyall's decorations, together with those of Cpl. Fred Fisher, were placed on display in St. Catharines Historical Museum. They had been on loan from 2002 to the REME Museum in Aborfield, England.

His decorations still belong to his family and apart from the VC, they include the BWM, VM, 1939–45 Star, Africa Star, WM (1939–45), King George V Silver Jubilee (1935), and a Coronation Medal for King George VI of 1937.

Nearly ninety years after he won his VC in September 1918, a commemorateive plaque in Lyall's memory was unveiled close to Bourlon Church in the cenre of the village on September 6, 2008. It was set up by the British Columbia Regiment (Duke of Connaught's Own) and tells his VC story in both English and French.

J. MACGREGOR

Near Cambrai, France,
September 29–October 3

The operations to capture the Hindenburg Line were well advanced by September 29, 1918, with the attempt to cross the dry Canal du Nord having begun successfully on September 27. The Canadian Corps' involvement was very successful in the initial assault and, in addition to crossing the canal, the Canadians captured two heavily defended wired trench systems: the Marquion Line and the Marcoing Line. At the end of operations on September 29, the Canadians were close to the walls of the enemy held city of Cambrai.

During the actions of September 30, the 3rd and 4th Canadian divisions managed to advance two miles to Ramillies, Eswars, and Cuvillers, while the 8th Brigade, which was part of the 3rd Division, covered Cambrai. A company commander, Capt. John MacGregor, was a member of the 2nd Canadian Mounted Rifles (CMR) and they, together with their sister unit the 1st Canadian Mounted Rifles, were ordered to capture bridgeheads in the Canal de l'Escaut area of the northern part of the city. However, they were delayed by fierce fire from the direction of Sainte-Olle, a village that had not yet been taken, and the regimental historian of the 2nd CMR describes the fighting on that day "as the most desperately fought engagement of the war for our battalion." However, once Sainte-Olle had fallen, the two Canadian battalions were able to move forward into the outskirts of the suburbs of Cambrai in the area of Neuvilly-St-Rémy. On their left flank, two battalions of the 7th Brigade were held up opposite Tilloy.

On October 1 the four Canadian divisions took part in an early attack, which began at 5:00 a.m., and they advanced for about a mile, capturing the high ground to the east of Tilloy. During the advance they coped with intense fire and several counterattacks. On the following day, the Canadians, expecting a German attack, brought their artillery heavily down on the German front line. Obviously, this barrage was designed to catch any planned enemy counterattack, but the foe had already withdrawn. Capt. John MacGregor had been deeply involved in the fighting and was awarded a VC, which was gazetted on January 6, 1919, as follows:

> For most conspicuous bravery, leadership and self-sacrificing devotion to duty near Cambrai from 29 Sept. to 3 Oct. 1918. He led his company under intense fire, and when the advance was checked by machine guns, although wounded, pushed on and located the enemy's guns. He then ran forward in broad daylight, in face of heavy fire from all directions, and, with rifle and bayonet, single-handed put the enemy's crew out of action, killing four and taking eight prisoners. His prompt action saved many casualties and enabled the advance to continue. After reorganizing his command under heavy fire he rendered most useful support to neighbouring troops. When the enemy were showing stubborn resistance he went along the line, regardless of danger, organized platoons, took command of the leading waves and continued the advance. Later, after a personal daylight reconnaissance under heavy fire, he established his company in Neuvilly St. Rémy, thereby greatly assisting the advance into Tilloy. Throughout the operations Capt. MacGregor displayed bravery and heroic leadership.

He was presented with his VC in the ballroom of Buckingham Palace on February 26, 1919. James MacGregor, one of John's two brothers, was killed in 1918 while serving as a corporal in the Cameron Highlanders.

John "Jock" MacGregor was born in Cawdor, Nairn, Scotland, on February 11, 1889, one of five children born to William, a farmer, and his wife, Jessie (or Hannah) Mackay. On his attestation papers he gave his date of birth as 1888. He was educated first at Clunas School, then at either Cawdor Public School or Nairn Academy. In 1908, at the age of nineteen, he emigrated to Canada, where he trained as a mason and carpenter. Prior to the war he served three years in Garrison duties in Nairn.

When the Great War broke out he was working in British Columbia, but on March 26, 1915, he enlisted in Vancouver as a trooper in the Canadian Army, after travelling 120 miles on snowshoes in order to reach the recruiting office at Prince Rupert. His service number was 116031. He was five foot nine inches tall and gave his mother as his next of kin. He became a private in the 11th Canadian Mounted Rifles and, after training, served in France from September 22, 1915, with the 2nd CMR. In June 1916 the battalion was part of 8th Brigade, 3rd Canadian Division, and lost much of its strength during the fighting around Sanctuary Wood, near Zillebeke. McGregor had influenza in early June. In September 1916, he was promoted to sergeant and, in April 1917, he won a DCM at Vimy Ridge. On May 12 he was commissioned in the field as a lieutenant and, two months later, the citation for his DCM was published in the *London Gazette* of July 26, 1917, as follows:

> For conspicuous gallantry and devotion to duty. He single-handed captured an enemy machine-gun and shot the crew, thereby undoubtedly saving his company from many casualties.

He was also awarded the MC, which was gazetted on August 16, 1918, for attacks on German trenches and three pillboxes on January 12, as follows:

For most conspicuous gallantry and devotion to duty. Whilst he was assembling his men prior to a raid the enemy bombed the trench. He, however, changing his point of attack, led his men over the wire into the enemy's trench, and successfully dealt with the garrison of the trench and three concrete dugouts, himself capturing one prisoner. He then withdrew his party and his prisoner successfully to our trenches. Before the raid he, together with a sergeant, had made several skillful and daring reconnaissances along the enemy wire, which materially assisted in the success of the enterprise.

On February 5, 1918, he was promoted to temporary captain and subsequently won a bar to his MC. The citation was published in the *London Gazette* on December 10, 1919:

For conspicuous gallantry and leadership from 5th to 8th November, 1918, at Quievrain and Qulevrechain. Through his initiative the bridges over the Hounelle River were secured. His personal reconnaissances and the information he derived from them were of great use to his commanding officer. His prompt action in seizing the crossings over the river did much toward the final rout of the enemy.

In April 1918 he was treated for pleurisy for two months. He was confirmed in his rank of captain and sailed to Canada on March 15, 1919, where he was demobilized. He was gazetted as a major in the Canadian Militia. He returned to his home in British Columbia, moving to Powell River in 1925 and worked with construction crews. On the occasion of an announcement of a forthcoming House of Lords Dinner in 1929 for holders of the VC, MacGregor was tracked down by a friend, who wished to inform him of the forthcoming event. At the time MacGregor was working in the mountains of British Columbia on a hydroelectric plant, and he told the story of what then happened:

I was in my cabin one night, when suddenly a friend burst open the door. He told me that several wireless stations were asking if anybody knew where I lived, for the authorities wished me to attend the Prince's banquet.

My friend had motored 100 miles to tell me, and he simply rushed me into his car and off to the nearest railway station at Salmon Arm. There we caught the Toronto Express with only ten minutes to spare. I was not even able to let my wife and family know that I had caught the train.

There was a two hours' stop at Toronto where I bought some spare gear, and we got to New York only two hours before the *Olympic* sailed. The presence of the Canadian contingent at the House of Lords Dinner was partly subsidized by the Canadian National and Canadian Pacific Railways, Cunard and White Star Steamship Lines, in addition to several Canadian provinces.

MacGregor was quoted to have said at the time:

I have not been home since 1919, when I was demobilized. My old mother, who is nearly eighty, does not know I am here. I did not have the chance to send her a cable before leaving, and my visit will be a big surprise to her.

During the visit to his mother in Nairn, the local citizens presented him with a clock and a silver tea service.

In 1933 MacGregor was persuaded by friends to stand in the Canadian provincial elections as an independent candidate, but he was unsuccessful. Six years later, in 1939, when the king and queen visited Vancouver, MacGregor was presented to them. At the outset of the Second World War, MacGregor again joined the army, this time as a private in the Canadian Scottish Regiment, where he was soon promoted to captain. In 1941 he was made second-in-command of the 2nd Battalion Canadian Scottish and promoted to major. In early 1942 he became commander of the 2nd Battalion. In 1943 he proceeded overseas, returning a year later to command the Kent (Canadian) Regiment. He then served as acting brigadier while commanding the 2nd Battalion during its training at Wainwright, Alberta. After the Second World War, MacGregor was awarded the

Efficiency Decoration (ED) which he received for his services in both world wars.

At some point he married Ethel, who had nursed him when he had a hand injury. They returned to British Columbia, where he established a concrete plant at Cranberry Lake, which was later sold to his son, Don. Powell River is a "company town" about seventy-three miles to the north of Vancouver, and on a day when Viscount Alexander, then Governor General of Canada, visited the town, Jock MacGregor was appointed to be his aide for the day.

After a long illness MacGregor died at Powell River Hospital, British Columbia, on June 9, 1952, having suffered from cancer for six years. Three holders of the VC attended his funeral, C.W. Peck, Charles Train, and G.R. Pearkes. Jock was survived by his wife, two sons, James and Donald, two sisters, and a brother. His ashes were buried in Cranberry Lake Cemetery, Powell River. Fifty-four years later, the Commonwealth War Grave Commission (CWGC) considered the grave was in need of a better stone and a standard commission headstone replaced the original plaque. His two eldest sons attended the ceremony; both were in wheelchairs and both died shortly afterward. Seven years before, James had published a biography of his father, *MacGregor VC*.

MacGregor had always been a very shy man and one who was impatient of inactivity; he was at his best as a front-line soldier. His career as one of Canada's most-decorated soldiers was summed up by Sir Arthur Currie, onetime commander-in-chief of the Canadian Army:

> MacGregor ... combines good judgement with sound military knowledge and wide experience. Good power of command and leadership; he inspires men. Excellent character, good appearance, strong personality; tactful, resourceful, and co-operative.

MacGregor was to become one of Canada's most highly decorated soldiers of the First World War. Apart from his VC, MC and bar, and DCM, he was also eligible for the following medals and decorations: 1914–15 Star, BWM and VM. For the Second World War he received a 1939–45 Star, Voluntary Service Medal (Canada) and clasp, 1939–45 War Medal, Coronation Medal 1937, and the Efficiency Decoration. His VC and Efficiency Decoration were the two decorations that most pleased him.

In mid-November 1996 MacGregor's decorations were put up for sale at Messrs Spinks in London by a member of his family. His younger son, Donald, was very keen to get them back to Canada where they belonged. They had probably left the MacGregor family in the early 1980s. However, on the eve of the sale the medals were suddenly withdrawn. Owing to the lack of an export licence they should never have been allowed out of Canada in the first place. By that time Donald had endeavoured to raise at least $100,000 in assurances, as he wished to present the medals to Powell River or a suitable museum where they could be seen by the public. The story ended happily, with the medals being duly presented to the Canadian War Museum on August 11, 1997, by Don MacGregor: $40,000 was raised by private sources; $35,000 came from the Canadian government; and $100,000 from Canadian Heritage.

Apart from his decorations, he is also commemorated at Cranberry Lake Cemetery, Cranberry Lake, Powell River. During his life Jock MacGregor was described as a man of action, who became extremely impatient with the paperwork that was part and parcel of his military seniority. He was described by one journalist as being big, blunt, and burr voiced. He was obviously a great character.

W. MERRIFIELD

Abancourt, France, October 1

Sergeant William Merrifield was a member of the 4th Battalion, 1st Central Ontario Regiment, CEF, and won his VC on October 1, 1918, during the fighting at Abancourt. The village was to the north of the German-held town of Cambrai. All four Canadian divisions were to take part in the advance toward the town on October 1. The 2nd Division was to be prepared to move through the lines of the 3rd Division and then to cross the Saint-Quentin Canal, exploiting the ground captured to the northeast of Cambrai. It was a very wet night, which made conditions treacherous, and the advance commenced with an artillery barrage which extended from Neuvilly-St. Rémy northwestwards to Epinoy.

The artillery played a significant role, firing more than 7,000 tons of ordnance, which contributed to the early success of the advance. However, later in the day, the 1st Canadian Division suffered a severe setback. The enemy resistance was mostly on the left, or northern, flank and was partly a result of the British 11th (Northern) Division's failure to make progress on the same day. The history of the CEF tells the story of what happened to two of the Canadian battalions:

> Attacking north of Bantigny Ravine, the 1st and 4th battalions had been thwarted in attempts to free Abancourt by the

heavy fire coming from in front of the British division. That formation, assigned the task of protecting the 1st Division's left, had been halted by heavy uncut wire almost before it began to advance. The two Canadian battalions were pinned down all day at the line of the railway. The 1st Brigade's 388 casualties brought to more than a thousand the losses sustained by the 1st Division on 1 October.

It was during this fighting that Sgt. William Merrifield won his VC, gazetted on January 6, 1919, as follows:

For most conspicuous bravery and devotion to duty during the attack near Abancourt on the 1st Oct. 1918. When his men were held up by an intense fire from two machine-gun emplacements, he attacked them both single-handed. Dashing from shell hole to shell hole he killed the occupants of the first post, and, although wounded, continued to attack the second post, and with a bomb killed the occupants. He refused to be evacuated, and led his platoon until again severely wounded. Sergt. Merrifield has served with exceptional distinction on many former occasions, and throughout the action of the 1st Oct. showed the highest qualities of valour and leadership.

He received his VC from the king at York Cottage, Sandringham, on January 26, 1919.

William Merrifield was born in Brentwood, Essex, on October 9, 1890. As a young man he emigrated to Canada and lived in Ottawa. At one point the family moved to Sudbury, where William became a fireman and worked for the Canadian Pacific Railways for eighteen months. He joined the 97th Regiment Algonquin Rifles, who were based in the same town, for a year.

After the war broke out he enlisted at Valcartier on September 23, 1914, from his hometown at Sault Ste. Marie, Ontario, with the 4th Battalion, 1st Central Ontario Regiment, CEF. He had served prior to the war in the 97th Regiment for a year, and gave his occupation as fireman. His service number was 8000. He had taken part in the

Second Battle of Ypres in 1915, and was awarded the MM in early November 1917 at Passchendaele for "serving with exceptional distinction." Although wounded, he carried on with his work as a stretcher bearer and continued to bandage the wounded. He also organized their return to safety while still continuing with his work. During his service he was regularly in hospital, and at different points suffered from shell shock, influenza, gunshot wounds, and appendicitis. He was promoted through the ranks, and by the end of August 1918 was a sergeant.

After the war he was declared free of venereal disease and left England, returning to Canada in April 1919, and was discharged from the CEF in Toronto on the 24th of the same month. He married Maude Bovington two years later. During a visit to the Dominion by the Prince of Wales in September 1919, the royal train was halted to allow Sgt. Merrifield to climb on board. He had been demobilized by then, with the rank of lieutenant in the Canadian Militia.

Just over ten years later he met up with the Prince of Wales again, in November 1929, when he came to London as a member of the group of six Canadian Army VC winners who attended the House of Lords VC Dinner. His next meeting with royalty was in May 1939, during the king and queen's visit to Canada, when he was a guest of honour at a celebration of their visit, in Toronto, held by the 4th Battalion, CEF.

In 1939 William Merrifield suffered a severe stroke, from which he never really recovered, and at the early age of fifty-two he died in Christie Street Military Hospital, Toronto, on August 8, 1943. He was buried in West Korah Cemetery, Sault Ste. Marie. He left a wife and four children. His decorations were in the hands of his family until November 2005, when they were donated to the Canadian War Museum in Ottawa. Apart from the VC and MM, he was also awarded the 1914–15 Star, BWM, VM, and Coronation Medal for King George VI (1937).

Merrifield is also remembered with a statue in front of the courthouse of Sault Ste. Marie, and the name of a public school in Sault Ste. Marie. There is also a small display at the Sgt. William Merrifield VC Armoury in Brantford, Ontario, which includes a replica VC. It was founded in the 1890s.

C.N. MITCHELL

Canal de l'Escaut, North-East of Cambrai, France, October 8/9

By the beginning of the second week of October 1918, the British First Army, which included the Canadian Corps, had reached a line about one mile west of Cambrai. The line ran in a northwesterly to southeasterly direction. As the Allies wished to limit the damage done to the city of Cambrai, their plan was to encircle it. The divisions to the right and in the centre had no specific obstacles to overcome, but to the left the Canadian Corps had the task of crossing the wide Canal de l'Escaut. Most of the canal bridges had already been destroyed and those which survived would have been prepared by the enemy for demolition at a moment's notice.

The plan for the Canadian Corps on the night of October 8/9, 1918, was for the 2nd Division to make the initial canal crossing, followed by the 3rd Division, which would cross on its own front, in order to establish bridgeheads in Cambrai. The position selected for the Canadian attack was the bridge named Pont d'Aire (close to the D61 road), across the Canal de l'Escaut. This would allow the Canadians to reach the village of Escaudoeuvres to the east. The situation was complicated by the fact that, in addition to the main bridge, there were also two further obstacles in the form of millstreams about twenty feet wide to the west of the canal.

Most of the following details were based on accounts written by Capt. Coulson Mitchell, which differ at certain points from accounts of the action in the *Official Histories*. Mitchell was a member of the 4th Battalion, Canadian Engineers, 2nd Canadian Division, who through his extreme gallantry won his VC at the Pont d'Aire in preparation for the Canadians to make the canal crossing. The 4th Battalion, Canadian Engineers, led by Capt. Mitchell, were instructed to prevent the enemy blowing up the main bridge before the Allies reached it.

Mitchell's small group left the jumping-off trench in Tilloy Wood, to the north of Cambrai, at midnight, accompanied by A Company from the 26th Battalion. The engineers moved quickly for about one and a half miles before reaching a road where they parted company with the infantry, who were to remain there for a couple of hours. The road led to the first millstream, which they reached at about 2:00 a.m., only to find the crossing destroyed, leaving a twenty-foot gap. Mitchell sent a couple of runners back with this information. The sappers located a footbridge across a stream about one hundred feet to their left, but this ended at a door in a brick wall that opened into a warehouse. The group then sought out the second millstream, where they discovered a stone arch that appeared to be unmined. Two more runners were sent back with this information, and also to act as guides to lead the infantry to the second bridge. Assistance then came from the artillery, who provided a box barrage around the bridges to protect it from the enemy.

Depleted by the number of runners who had to be used for communication, Mitchell's party was down to four. Years later, Mitchell said the men became quite excited when they ran across the 500-foot area toward the main canal bridge. The bridge was found to be a double-span steel girder, with a concrete base which rested on two abutments, together with a pier and canal locks in the middle of the stream. The bridge was about fifteen feet above the water and there was a towpath on each side of the canal. The sappers felt their way very gingerly across the bridge, after a while locating the various wires that were connected to the German explosives, and finally reached the far side of the bridge, which was about 200 feet long. Mitchell sent one man back as lookout to guard the western end of the bridge and left another sentry at the German end. After the fuses had been cut, there was a shout from one of the sentries who had shot two of the enemy when they had suddenly appeared from the back of a building to the left of the bridge. It was now about 4:00 a.m. and dawn light was beginning to show. The three remaining men were wondering what was going to happen next when a third German appeared on the scene, but Mitchell disposed of him. Mitchell and his colleague, Sgt. Jackson, then quietly slipped into the cold water of the river to search for the explosives. Finding a large box of explosives close to one of the seventy-five-foot steel girders, they cut the electric circuit and began a search for similar charges.

Suddenly the Germans realized what was happening and began to tackle the small group. Down to just three men, they were "yelling like madmen" in an effort to convey to the enemy that they were up against a whole battalion. Surprisingly, the group of Germans scuttled off, which allowed Mitchell's men to finish the job of cutting any remaining fuses; as it became lighter, they dismantled the four main charges, which they threw down on the towpath. They then came across a small party of twelve Germans who were only too anxious to give themselves up, together with a group of eight more. The small group had managed to save the bridge, which allowed the advance of the Canadian infantry to continue, followed by the field artillery. For their role in capturing this bridge intact, Jackson and the sapper who had held the German end of the bridge were both awarded the DCM. Capt. Mitchell won a VC, which was gazetted on January 31, 1919, as follows:

> For most conspicuous bravery and devotion to duty on the night of 8–9 October 1918, at the Canal de l'Escaut, northeast of Cambrai. He led a small party ahead of the first wave of infantry in order to examine the various bridges on the line of approach and, if possible, to prevent their demolition. On reaching the canal he found the bridge already blown up. Under a heavy barrage he crossed to the next bridge, where he cut a number of 'lead' wires. Then, in

total darkness, and unaware of the position or strength of the enemy at the bridgehead, he dashed across the main bridge over the canal. The bridge was found to be heavily charged for demolition, and while Capt. Mitchell, assisted by his N.C.O. [Sergeant Jackson], was cutting the wires, the enemy attempted to rush the bridge, in order to blow the charges, whereupon he at once dashed to the assistance of his sentry, who had been wounded, killed three of the enemy, captured 12, and maintained the bridgehead until reinforced. Then, under heavy fire, he continued his task of cutting wires and removing charges, which he well knew might at any moment have been fired by the enemy. It was entirely due to his valour and decisive action that this important bridge across the canal was saved from destruction.

Mitchell remained with the 4th Battalion in its advance toward Mons and, at the time of the Armistice, was in the area of Elouges. A week later the unit marched toward the Rhine, which it crossed at Bonn on December 13. He remained with the army of Occupation and returned to England on April 1, 1919. Two days later he was decorated by the king in the ballroom of Buckingham Palace.

Coulson Norman Mitchell, later known as Mike, was born at Ross Street, Winnipeg, on December 11, 1889. He was the third son of Mr. Coulson Nicholas Mitchell and his wife, Mary Jane. Mitchell's father also came from a military background, which included serving in the 90th Winnipeg Rifles. After Coulson's birth the family moved to a terraced house in Edmonton Street, Winnipeg. Coulson was educated at Mulvey Public School and Winnipeg Collegiate Institute, and while at school he became a keen sportsman. In 1912 he graduated in engineering at the University of Manitoba, and before the war was working as an electrical engineer with the Foundation Company of Canada on projects both in Manitoba and British Columbia. When the war broke out he was working on the construction of the Transcona elevator and was keen to see the job completed before enlisting. Prior to the war he was a member of the 2nd Field Troop Canadian Regiment.

On November 10, 1914, Mitchell attested in Winnipeg and gave his father as his next of kin. He was five foot nine inches tall and had brown hair. He was a Presbyterian. He joined the Canadian Engineers as a sapper, being posted to 4 Field Company, in Ottawa. In December a signal company was set up and Mitchell, together with other university graduates, joined the 2nd Divisional Signal Company. Mitchell remained with this unit until May 1915, having a pretty easy time in the hilly country around Ottawa with "flag and heliograph." Later he was transferred to the Canadian Overseas Railway Construction Corps and, leaving New Brunswick on June 14, 1915, sailed for England. He arrived in Plymouth on June 25, and then moved to Longmoor Camp. He remained in England for two months before he and his unit moved to France on August 26. From Calais they proceeded to Alveringen in Belgium, where the unit was attached to the Belgian Army and their role was to build a narrow gauge track as far as the support line. When this job was completed, the unit returned to Longmoor Camp in England on October 5.

In November 1915 Mitchell was promoted to sergeant and recommended for a commission in the Canadian Engineers; he was made a lieutenant on April 28, 1916. In the following month he was transferred to the 1st Canadian Tunnelling Company, which he joined in Belgium in July; he was posted to the left half-company operating between Verbrandenmolen and the Ypres–Comines Canal, and was sent up to the Bluff. Mitchell's work was ninety feet below ground level, and he was later involved in the capture or destruction of German tunnels at the bluff. He was in that area until the end of the year, and it was during this time that he won the MC on December 11, gazetted on February 13, 1917. The citation includes that "he was cut off from our lines for twelve hours." On May 24 he was promoted to captain.

At the beginning of January 1918 the 1st Canadian Tunnelling Company was moved to Vimy Ridge in readiness for the much-heralded German Spring Offensive, which began at the end of March. The 1st and 2nd Tunnelling companies were broken up in the summer of 1918 and the personnel distributed among the newly formed engineer battalions. Mitchell was posted to D Company of the 4th Battalion, Canadian Engineers, taking part in the Battle of Amiens in August. During the period from September 2 to the Armistice he was in the areas of Drocourt–Quéant, the Canal du Nord, Cambrai, and Valenciennes. In 1919 he sailed to Canada on April 14 and, after being demobilized as captain at the end of the month, Mitchell returned to Winnipeg to rejoin the Foundation Company of Canada as manager of a high-power electrical station in British Columbia. Later, in 1926, he joined the Power Corporation and became the general superintendent of construction and development of steam and hydroelectric power plants for their subsidiary and other companies.

Mitchell attended the House of Lords VC Dinner in November 1929, returning home on the *Duchess of Atholl* on November 22, 1929. In 1930 he joined 16 Field Company, 4th Reserve Engineers (M), as a captain, remaining with them for three years. In July 1936 Mitchell attended the unveiling of the Vimy Ridge Canadian Memorial and took his eighty-two-year-old father with him. While in France, Mitchell revisited the Pont d'Aire bridges where he had won his VC. In 1940 Mitchell was asked to raise a company of pioneers and, with the rank of major, take it overseas. The unit sailed for England in August and he remained with it for eleven months, before being appointed OC 11 Field Company, Royal Canadian Engineers. In February 1942, as a lieutenant-colonel, he was transferred to the 1st Royal Canadian Engineer Reinforcement Unit and remained in that position as OC of the Training Wing. In September 1943 he returned to Canada, working at National Defence HQ special duties. In April 1944 he was appointed to command the Royal Canadian Engineer Training Centre at Petawawa. There he was responsible for the training of officers and other ranks in units serving overseas. The training program was "hard and intensive."

In 1944 Mitchell was involved in the building of a Legion Hall at Chilliwack, which was opened in May that year. Also in 1944 he was active in raising money for the erection of a memorial in Vedder Crossing to the memory of members of the Canadian Corps who had been killed in battle. At the end of the war, Mitchell was a key figure in a campaign to build the first permanent married quarters in the camp. In September 1946, after a very distinguished war service, Mitchell left the army and returned to his home in the town of Mount Royal, Quebec. He continued working as an executive with the Power Corporation, finally retiring in 1957.

Mitchell had always taken a keen interest in the Canadian Legion and, in 1942, the "Norman Mitchell VC Branch" was named in his honour. He was also instrumental in suggesting a housing project, which was built on a street named after him. In 1956 he attended the VC Centenary commemorations in London. In 1973 the married quarters he had campaigned for were renamed the "Mitchell Gardens," and a memorial cairn to his own achievements was unveiled by him on October 12, 1973. Mitchell had never let his association with the Royal Canadian Engineers lapse and he later became a member of the VC/GC Association, attending several of their meetings over the years.

At the age of eighty-eight Coulson Mitchell died on November 17, 1978, at his home at Mount Royal, Montreal, while watching television. Even among the hallowed ranks of winners of the Victoria Cross, Mitchell stands out as a very courageous and public-spirited man. His funeral took place at the Mount Royal United Church on November 21 and he was buried at Pointe-Claire Field of Honour Cemetery, Quebec, Section M, Grave 3051. He left behind a widow, Gertrude Hazel Bishop, who died in her mid-nineties in 1985; she was buried next to her husband. There were two daughters from the marriage.

Mitchell was commemorated in several ways. A mountain in Jasper National Park was named after him to mark his work in bridge-building on the Alaska Highway, and a street in Mount Royal was named after him. He is also commemorated with the Royal Canadian Legion Post in Montreal. In CGB Gagetown the main building of the Canadian Forces School of Military Engineers is named after him. A panel at the All Sappers' Memorial Park and Cenotaph also recognizes his personal vision and leadership.

Mitchell is also remembered with the name of a lake to the east of Thompson, Manitoba. His family requested it to be known as the Norman Mitchell Lake. In addition in 1980 the Royal Canadian Engineers Museum at Chilliwack was able to acquire not only Mitchell's decorations, but also a large collection of documents, maps and photographs. The decorations in addition to the VC and MC, include the 1914–15 Star, BWM, DM, Canadian Volunteer Service Medal and clasp (1939–45), King George VI Coronation

Medal (1937), Queen Elizabeth II Coronation Medal (1953), the Canadian Centennial Medal (1967), and the Queen Elizabeth II Silver Jubilee Medal (1977). The museum already owned Mitchell's uniform and the weapon that he was using at the time of winning his VC, and provides a permanent exhibit to honour the only Canadian military engineer to have won a VC. If readers wish to visit the site of Mitchell's VC action, which hasn't changed a great deal since 1918, then they would be advised to go around Cambrai in a northeasterly direction and take the D61 road to Morenchies.

W.L. ALGIE

North-East of Cambrai, France, October 11

On October 11, 1918, five miles to the northeast of Cambrai, the 4th and 6th Canadian Brigades of the Canadian Corps of the First Army attacked at 9:00 a.m., and the enemy replied strongly with artillery and machine-gun fire. In particular, the 6th Brigade met heavy resistance from their objective, the village of Iwuy. The Germans defended Iwuy by piling up stacks of lumber and this, together with masses of wire, allowed them to maintain a steady fire against the Canadian attackers. In addition, the enemy could be seen bringing up more guns in small handcarts, to enfilade the Canadian positions.

Lt. Wallace Lloyd Algie won his VC during the fighting as a member of the 20th Battalion, Central Ontario Regiment, 4th Brigade, 2nd Canadian Division. Assessing the situation, Algie called for volunteers in order to thwart the enemy intentions. His thinking was that if his group moved to the left, beyond the battalion boundary, then they could perhaps clear out the east end of the village. Taking a leading role he rushed forward, used his revolver to shoot the crew of a machine gun and, after turning it on the enemy, his group was able to cross a railway embankment. He then rushed a second machine gun and killed its crew; in the process he cut off the escape of an officer and ten enemy troops, forcing them to surrender. With the use of the captured machine guns he then cleared the east end of the village of the enemy:

Having placed his men in a good position and showed them how to use the German machine guns, he went back for reinforcements, but was killed in bringing them forward. The posts he had established were able to hold their positions until the situation was relieved by the troops on the left occupying the village.

By early afternoon Algie's group, together with troops of the 28th and 31st Canadian battalions, were able to completely clear the village. After the capture of Iwuy, the town of Le Cateau fell the next day and the Allies reached the Solesmes–Le Cateau road to the east of Cambrai. Algie's VC was gazetted on January 31, 1919, as follows:

For most conspicuous bravery and self-sacrifice on the 11th Oct. 1918, northeast of Cambrai, when with attacking troops which came under heavy enfilade machine-gun fire from a neighbouring village. Rushing forward with nine volunteers, he shot the crew of an enemy machine-gun, and, turning it on the enemy, enabled his party to reach the village. He

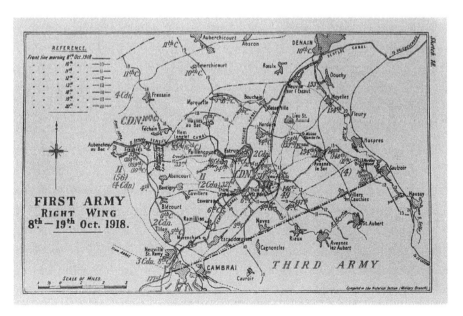

then rushed another machine-gun, killed the crew, captured an officer and ten enemy, and thereby cleared the end of the village. Lieut. Algie, having established his party, went back for reinforcements, but was killed when leading them forward across the railway. His valour and personal initiative in the face of intense fire saved many lives and enabled the position to be held.

Algie was buried at Niagara Cemetery, Iwuy, Row C, Grave 7, which is five miles northeast of Cambrai, and his posthumous VC was presented to his father by the lieutenant governor of Toronto on March 28, 1919.

Wallace Lloyd Algie was born in Alton, Ontario, on June 10, 1891. The family home was 1155 King Street and Wallace's parents were Rachel and James Algie, who had practised medicine for twenty-five years in Peel County. In about 1908 the family moved to Toronto and settled down at 75 Dawson Street, Toronto. Algie was educated at Alton Public School and, after he left, he took up banking, working in various branches in Toronto and Vancouver. In 1916 he was manager of the Elm Street Bank of Toronto.

He graduated from the Royal Military Academy of Canada and, prior to his enlistment, served for four months with the Queen's Own Rifles of Canada as a lieutenant, and also for two months with the 40th Regiment. He was also a member of the band of the 18th Highlanders for eight years

One of Algie's brothers had already enlisted and Wallace joined up in Toronto on April 19, 1916, in Camp Borden. He signed an Officer's Declaration Form for overseas service. He was five foot ten inches tall with light brown hair. The family was still living in Toronto when war broke out. He was allocated the service number if 916711 and left Halifax for Liverpool on September 27, 1916. After basic training he was drafted from the Reserve of Officers to the 95th Battalion, and by October he was serving with the 20th Battalion, arriving in France in 1917 when he was transferred to the 198th Battalion. On April 26 he was in hospital in Rouen.

At the time of his death on October 11, 1918, when serving with the 20th Battalion, he left two sisters, Bessie and Ethel.

On March 23, 1995, Algie's VC, in its original Hancocks-fitted case with tissue, was sold at Glendinings to Lord Ashcroft for £17,800. At the present time it is in his collection at the Imperial War Museum. Algie's other decorations were the BWM and VM.

T. RICKETTS

Near Ledegem, Belgium, October 14

In October 1918, during the advance to victory, the 1st Battalion Royal Newfoundland Regiment (28th Brigade, 9th [Scottish] Division), was involved in an attack from Ledegem, nine miles to the east of Ypres, on the morning of October 14. The morning was very misty and, at 5:35 a.m., the Royal Newfoundlanders moved over a ridge, through some barbed-wire entanglements, to descend the other side of the ridge, before crossing a beet field to reach a shallow ditch 300 yards beyond. By then the mist had begun to lift and one of the companies was held up by a German field battery, which was firing at point-blank range from the shelter of two farmhouses. The shallow ditch gave very little protection and the company began to take heavy casualties. The men were trapped, and it was at this point that Pte. Thomas Ricketts seized a Lewis gun and worked forward, together with L.-Cpl. Matthew Brazil MM of B Company, his section commander, to try to outflank the enemy battery and prevent any more casualties. Moving from the far right of the ditch, the two men advanced in short rushes over the open ground, but when 300 yards from the farmhouses they ran out of ammunition. Immediately, Ricketts returned for more ammunition and, picking up two carriers, returned to his colleague. However, L.-Cpl. Brazil was nowhere to be seen. By now the enemy gunners were taking shelter in the partially destroyed farm buildings, so, grabbing his chance, Ricketts rushed forward. Firing from the hip, he planted the gun in the doorway of one of the buildings and the whole crew quickly surrendered. By his presence of mind in anticipating the enemy's intentions and his utter disregard of personal safety, Pte. Ricketts secured the further supply of ammunition which directly resulted in these important captures and undoubtedly saved many lives. It's possible that Ricketts had been spurred on by the recent news of his elder brother, George, being recently killed in the Battle of Cambrai.

Brazil was awarded the DCM and, two months later, on December 14, the announcement of Ricketts' VC was made at a parade by Maj. Bernard, who read out the official citation and then congratulated the private. Nearly a month later, on January 13, Ricketts left the regiment, returning to England for his investiture. His VC was gazetted on January 6, 1919, as follows:

Thomas Ricketts, No. 3102, Private, 1st Battn. Royal Newfoundland Regt. (Canadians). Near Ledegem on 14 Oct. he volunteered to go with his section commander and a Lewis-gun to attempt to outflank a battery causing casualties at point-blank range. Their ammunition was exhausted when still 300 yards from the battery. The enemy began to bring up their gun teams, Private Ricketts doubled back 100 yards under the heaviest machine-gun fire, procured ammunition, dashed back again to a Lewis-gun, and by very accurate fire drove the enemy and the gun teams into a farm. His platoon then advanced and captured the four field-guns, four machine guns and eight prisoners. A fifth field-gun was subsequently intercepted by fire and captured.

Thomas Ricketts was anxious to return home to Newfoundland in order to resume his studies, and on January 18 he received a message informing him the king agreed to invest him with his VC at York Cottage, Sandringham, the following day, which was a Sunday.

The young Canadian travelled by train to Wolferton, the nearest station to Sandringham, the then royal residence. Here he was met by an equerry with a car, who explained the formal procedure before he met the king. Once at York Cottage, Ricketts was given a splendid lunch, which he ate in a room by himself. In the afternoon he was taken to meet the king, who was not in uniform but in civilian clothes, and who, as well as presenting him with the VC, talked to him for at least ten minutes. While at Sandringham, Ricketts was also introduced to other members of the royal family. At that point he was the youngest holder of the VC in the army. On January 29 Ricketts was promoted to sergeant and he left Liverpool for home the following day. Together with Private John Croak he was the only man born in Newfoundland to win the VC in the war. In addition he was the only member of the Royal Newfoundland Regiment to win the nation's highest military honour as well.

Thomas Ricketts was the son of John Ricketts, a fisherman, and Amelia, whose maiden name was Castle, and was born at a small fishing settlement in White Bay called Middle Arm, on the Baie Verte Peninsula, Newfoundland, on April 15, 1901. His mother died when he was still very young and he was probably brought up by an aunt. Overstating his age as eighteen when it was fifteen and a quarter, he joined the Newfoundland Regiment in St. John's on September 2, 1916, with the service number 3102, and sailed to England on January 31, 1917. He then carried out further training and left Southampton for France on June 10, 1917, and joined the Newfoundlander Battalion on July 2 at Rouen. He first saw action at Steenbeek at the Battle of Langemark in August. His regiment was part of 28th Infantry Brigade of the 9th Division. Three months later, during the Battle of Cambrai, he was wounded in the right leg at Marcoing on November 20. After a five-month break, during which time he spent eighteen days in hospital in Wandsworth, he returned to the Western Front on April 4, 1918. By now his regiment had been honoured by the king with the "Royal" as a prefix. He joined them on the field on April 30.

In mid December the Royal Newfoundlanders crossed the Rhine and occupied billets at Hilden in the center of the steel industry.

News of Ricketts's VC was announced to the regiment just before Christmas, and he was the recipent of a great many congratulary handshakes and slaps on the back. In adition his health was drunk in German beer over Christmas lunch.

In addition to becoming one of the youngest men to win the VC in the First World War, Ricketts was also awarded the French Croix de Guerre. It was awarded at Holickshen on September 27 by the commander of II Corps, Lt.-Gen. Sir Claud Jacob.

He was promoted to sergeant on January 29, 1919, and left the army after he returned to Canada in early 1919, but his demobilization wasn't formally completed until July 1. Returning to St. John's on February 10, he was given a huge welcome and acclaimed by the whole town. He was drawn in a sleigh by young men through the streets of the capital. A fund was set up to cover his college education, which reached more than $10,000. At one point he was considering a career in medicine, but decided on pharmacy instead. He attended a course at Bishop Field College and, in 1925, entered an apprenticeship. In 1937 he opened his own drug store in Water Street, St. John's.

In November 1929 he attended the House of Lords Dinner. On July 17, 1962, he attended a Garden Party at Buckingham Palace given by the queen for members of the VC/GC Association, and on the same day he also attended a banquet given by the Lord Mayor of London for the Association at the Mansion House. On the next evening he attended a dinner for the association, which took place at the Café Royal in Regent Street, London. It appears that Thomas Ricketts was a very shy and modest man, and disliked having his photograph taken.

Sadly, Ricketts suffered from poor health for many years and, at the early age of sixty-five he died of a heart attack on February 10, 1967, while working in his drug store. Three days later he was given a full military funeral and his remains lay in state for three hours before the funeral at St. Thomas' Anglican Church. Large crowds turned out on an extremely cold day to line the route of the procession. His decorations were placed on the flag-draped coffin. The cortège included a guard of honour drawn from the Royal Newfoundland

Regiment and the Royal Canadian Legion. Also represented were men from the Royal Canadian Mounted Police, Newfoundland Constabulary, and the Royal Canadian Legion. Local dignitaries, including Prime Minister J.R. Smallwood, walked behind the coffin.

Ricketts was buried in the Anglican Cemetery, St. John's, and many of the nearby graves belong to former members of the Royal Newfoundland Regiment. A three-volley salute was fired by the Royal Newfoundland Regiment and veterans dropped poppies into the open grave. The "Last Post" and "Reveille" were then sounded.

Ricketts left a widow, Edna (*née* Edwards), a daughter, and a son. A painting of him is displayed at the Royal Canadian Legion in Corner Brook, Newfoundland. For many years his VC was on display at the Confederation Building, but in the early 1980s it was returned to his family. On June 10, 1972, a monument to the memory of Thomas Ricketts was unveiled in Water Street, St. John's, close to the site of his pharmacy store, which described him as a "Soldier-Pharmacist-Citizen." A play based on his life, *The Known Soldier,* was first performed in Newfoundland in 1982. In October 2002 a display about his service life was opened in the Royal Newfoundland Regiment Room in the Canadian Forces Station. On October 22, 2003, his widow donated his decorations to the Canadian War Museum, Ottawa. Apart from the VC and French Croix de Guerre, his medals included the BWM, VM, and Coronation Medals for King George VI (1937) and Queen Elizabeth II (1953).

At the time of writing a Belgian farmer whose land is in Ledegem east of Ypres is building a memorial to Thomas Ricketts who won his VC on his family's land in October 1918.

W.G. BARKER

Forêt de Mormal, France, October 27

In October 1918 the Allied forces were advancing rapidly into France and Belgium, areas where the original BEF had seen action in August 1914 and, as then, it was a war of movement. In order to keep pace with the ever-changing situation the Allied airfields were also moved nearer to the retreating enemy.

No. 201 Squadron RAF was based at Beugnâtre airfield, two miles from Bapaume and, the squadron's aircraft were Sopwith Camels. On October 17 Major William Barker joined the squadron on a ten-day roving commission. He had requested this particular posting as the commanding officer, Major Cyril Leaman, was a friend. Barker was flying the RAF's newest scout aircraft, a Sopwith Snipe E8102, powered by a Bentley engine and equipped with refinements such as oxygen for the pilot. Although evaluation of this machine in action was part of Barker's mission, his role did not always endear himself to the squadron's other pilots when the Snipe outperformed the Camel, and he was able to fly much higher, "waiting for targets."

Cloudy and wet weather hindered operations against the retreating enemy and Barker was unable to fly patrols for four days, but in the next three he took part in squadron sorties with other pilots but with no enemy contact. This frustrated Barker and when, on October 26, he received orders to return the Snipe to the Aircraft Supply Depot and then go to London, he was annoyed he had not been able to attack any enemy aircraft.

The following morning there were few clouds when Barker took off in the Sopwith Snipe before 8:00 a.m. He quickly reached over 15,000 feet and was still climbing. He was over the Forêt de Mormal, south of Mons, less than thirty minutes later when he spotted a white Rumpler two-seater aircraft above him at a height of over 21,000 feet. Barker engaged the enemy machine and the two aircraft exchanged a few short bursts of fire while each manoeuvred for a favourable attacking position. At a range of over one hundred yards Barker again fired and either wounded or killed the German observer. He then closed in on the Rumpler and fired several short bursts into the aircraft and the Rumpler began to break up. One of the German airmen fell free of the aircraft and Barker became distracted as he watched the unusual sight of the man's white parachute open. He did not notice the approach of a Fokker D.VII whose pilot had witnessed the fight and flown up toward the British aircraft. The first indication Barker had of this opponent was the sound of machine-gun fire and he was hit in his right thigh, which caused him to release the controls and the Snipe descended several hundred feet in a spin.

When he regained control of his aircraft, Barker found himself amongst a formation of fifteen Fokker D. VIIIs. He fired bursts at two and then from very short range fired at a third, which then burst into flames. The other Fokkers attacked him from all sides and he was hit again, this time in the other leg. He passed out and his plane went into another downward spiral and when he came to he had dropped to about 15,000 feet and was in the midst of yet more enemy aircraft. Barker then attacked one Fokker from behind and set this aircraft on fire at the same time as another aircraft fired at him from behind. One bullet hit his left elbow and others damaged his aircraft. By now the fuel tank was holed, the ignition ruined, and smoke was streaming from his engine. British aircraft crew did not carry parachutes at the time, so escape by this method was not possible. Barker then flew straight toward the nearest enemy aircraft with his guns firing and was fortunate to set this Fokker on fire and it dived out of his path. With both legs and his left arm now useless and faint from his injuries, he was unable to operate the throttle on his left, and as this was still in the full-on position he had very little control of his Snipe as it spiralled downwards.

Barker then saw a British balloon and flew in its direction. He managed to crash-land close to it when the Snipe turned over after it was quickly stopped by barbed wire. Men of No. 29 Kite Balloon Section rushed to Barker's aid and extricated the semiconscious pilot from the wreckage. It was obvious he was badly wounded and Lt. Frank Woolley Smith, serving with the balloon unit as an observer, had him driven to the nearest field dressing station while he applied pressure on an artery near Barker's groin to stem bleeding. After Barker's wounds were dressed he was taken by ambulance tender to No. 8 General Hospital, Rouen, where he was soon operated upon. Although his left arm had been virtually severed at the elbow the surgeons managed to save it. Barker remained in a critical condition for the next week but by November 7 he was able to write a letter to his friend at No. 201 Squadron, Major Leman, in which he admitted "By Jove I was a foolish boy but anyhow I taught them a lesson. The only thing that bucks me up is to look back & see them going down in flames...."

When this letter was written it was known throughout the hospital that Barker had been recommended for the award of a VC and a supplement to the *London Gazette* No. 31042, dated November 30, 1918, carried the citation for his award.

Barker's family was notified by telegram shortly after he was badly wounded but it was not until December that the Canadian Department of Militia informed the family of his condition or whereabouts.

Barker was transferred from No. 8 General Hospital, Rouen on January 16 and sailed to England on HMHS *Grantully Castle*. Ten days earlier, Barker had been visited at the hospital by a Capt. B. Johnston from Canadian GHQ, who had been ordered to report on the pilot's condition. This report contained a description of the award-winning action in which Barker admitted that "he did not act with his usual care...." Johnston also advised on the current state of Barker's recovery, "The arm wound is healing very satisfactorily and Major Barker will have a certain amount of use of the arm ... The wound in the left hip ... will be rather a long time in healing...."

Later, on February 4, he sent a letter home from the Anglo-Chilean Hospital, Grosvenor Square, London, and wrote that soon he would be able to sit up but his "left hip is still troublesome [and] my left elbow... will take a long time yet."

By late February Barker was able to walk short distances with the aid of a cane, and on the morning of March 1, at a Buckingham Palace investiture, he received his VC from the king. After receiving his award he was taken on a short tour of the palace by the Prince of Wales. According to his diary entry King George V presented 344 medals that day, including six VCs.

William George Barker was born on November 3, 1894, the first of nine children of George Barker and his wife, Jane Victoria (née Alguire), at their homestead at Dauphin, Manitoba. George was a farmer and blacksmith and in addition he ran a sawmill. In 1902 the family moved fifty miles west to a farm near Russell.

William was educated first at Londonderry School and then Russell High School, and attained good marks despite frequent absences to help his father. He became an excellent shot as well as an experienced horseman, and as his father was the first in the local area to use steam engines it followed that William became well-acquainted with the workings of the combustion engine. During his teenage years he also attended farm exhibitions in Manitoba, where pioneer aviators would appear, and the young man was enthralled by these early flyers.

William enlisted as a trooper in the militia, the 32nd light Horse, in 1912 and the following year the Barker family moved back to Dauphin, a rapidly growing town where he attended classes at the Dauphin Collegiate institute. On December 1, 1914, Barker enlisted in 1st Regiment, Canadian Mounted Rifles (CMR), and his attestation papers record that No. 106074 Private Barker, W. G. was five foot ten inches tall.

Barker's regiment trained in Manitoba, and by March 1915 he had been assigned to operate one of the regiment's four Colt-Browning machine guns. The 1st CMR Brigade, of which his regiment was part, entrained for Montreal, and on June 12 it sailed for England on board the SS *Megantic*. Barker disembarked at Devonport and entrained for Shorncliffe, Kent, on June 19, where the regiment trained for three months. On September 16 Barker received his first-class machine gunner's certificate and four days later he embarked at Southampton for France. By the end of the month the 1/CMR was in trenches near Ploegsteert, Belgium, and it was in this area and in the vicinity of the River Douve that the regiment, serving as dismounted troops, was to stay for the next few months. It was a relatively quiet section of the front and consequently the regiment suffered few casualties, but trench conditions were pretty miserable.

Unhappy with life in the trenches, Barker had made an application to be transferred to the RFC, which was rejected, but on December 1 a second application was approved and he was posted to No. 9 Squadron at Saint-Omer as a trainee observer with the rank of corporal. Later in the month the squadron flew its BE2c aircraft to Bertangles, six miles north of Amiens, from where Barker took part in many reconnaissance patrols as an observer. His aircraft claimed one Fokker shot down in March 1916.

Barker was commissioned into the RFC as a second lieutenant on April 2, and then posted to No. 4 Squadron at Baizieux, west of Albert. The Battle of the Somme started on July 1, and six days later he was posted to No. 15 Squadron then based at Marieux, northwest of Albert. On July 21 Barker's aircraft was credited with a Roland machine which was driven down out of control near Miraumont, and on August 15 with another, similar enemy aircraft shot down, which crashed in flames near Achiet-le-Grand. It was during this period that he was mentioned in despatches. Less than two weeks later, on August 27, he qualified as an observer and was recommended for pilot training.

The British attempted one final attack before the winter, and on November 13 the Battle of the Ancre began in thick mist, which hampered the artillery spotting of No. 15 Squadron. In the following days Barker, whose pilot was Capt. W.G. Pender, helped in the attempted contact of Scottish troops isolated in Frankfurt Trench near Redan Ridge, following the British attack of November 13. Unfortunately, despite brave rescue attempts and stubborn resistance by these men of 16/Highland Light Infantry, they were eventually attacked and overwhelmed. In addition, again piloted by Capt. Pender, over Y Ravine, Beaumont Hamel, Barker "engaged large numbers of infantry in trenches with Lewis gun fire, and reported their position to the artillery."

Barker returned to England from France on November 16, and began his pilot training at Narborough, Norfolk. After spending his Christmas leave in London he completed his training at Netheravon, Wiltshire. He was promoted to Capt. and Flight Commander on January 15 and returned to France as a fully qualified pilot on February 24, 1917. He rejoined C Flight, No. 15 Squadron, stationed at Clairfaye Farm, Lealvillers, four miles south of Marieux.

The supplement to the *London Gazette* No. 29898 of January 10 carried the citation for the award of the Military Cross: "For conspicuous gallantry in action. He flew at a height of 500 feet over the enemy's lines, and brought back most valuable information. On another occasion, after driving off two hostile machines, he carried out an excellent photographic reconnaissance."

The aircraft of No. 15 Squadron were mostly employed in close co-operation with ground troops and flew numerous low-level sorties that invited attack from enemy fighter aircraft in addition to fire from ground troops. Barker flew on an almost daily basis, and on March 23 he shot down a Fokker Scout which crashed near Cambrai. His name was frequently to appear in RFC communiques for reconnaissance work in co-operation with the 7th Infantry Division.

On April 9 Lt. Goodfellow and Barker, flying very low and under ground attack, directed accurate artillery fire on enemy troops in support trenches preparing to counterattack Australian positions. During the following weeks, while the Battle of Arras was in progress, they also reported the positions of hostile artillery, machine-gun positions, and concentrations of infantry in addition to attacking parties of enemy troops.

The supplement to the *London Gazette* No. 30188 of July 18 published the citation for the award of a bar to Barker's Military Cross, "For ... continuous good work in co-operation with the artillery ..." and he was again mentioned in despatches.

During May the squadron's BE2 aircraft were replaced by RE8s. Barker was injured by shrapnel, which narrowly missed his right eye, while on a contact patrol on August 7, and after almost continuous flying for six months he was posted back to England as an instructor. This was RFC policy meant to give pilots a rest from operational duties. This appointment held no attraction for Barker and after being refused another posting in France he made "a thorough nuisance of himself" by performing stunts in flying-school aircraft, and on one occasion a very low flight over London, very near the Air Ministry. Eventually he was offered the choice between a posting to 56 Squadron in France, flying SE5as, or 28 Squadron being formed at Yatesbury, Wiltshire, who were equipped with Sopwith Camels. He chose No. 28 Squadron and on October 2 was posted to this squadron in command of A Flight. Within a week this squadron flew to their new base at Droglandt near Poperinge, Belgium.

On the evening of his arrival in Belgium, October 8, Barker led the three inexperienced flight commanders on a "familiarization" patrol along the trench lines and, against squadron orders, crossed into enemy-held territory. A formation of enemy aircraft was seen beneath them, later described by one of the pilots as "a circus of 22 gaudily-painted machines." Barker dived down toward these aircraft and fired a burst into the rear machine which caused it, an Albatros DV, to break up in mid-air and crash between Ypres and Dixmude. The British aircraft returned to base but Barker did not claim a victory or submit a combat report for this event, only recording that Camel B6313 was taken out for a test flight.

The squadron recorded its first official victories on October 20, when British bombers attacked Rumbeke aerodrome near Roulers with No. 28 Squadron Camels as part of the escort. A total of nine enemy aircraft were shot down, which included two by Barker. He was in action the following day over Houthulst Forest and fired at another Albatros which glided down. During the following week he badly damaged a Gotha, and shot down two Albatros DV machines two days later between Roulers and Thielt. After this last encounter Barker admitted in his combat report that he had lost his bearings and had run out of petrol before he landed near Arras. Two days later, 28 Squadron was warned of a move to Italy as part of the Anglo-French support following the Italian defeat at Caporetto, and this transfer began on the following day.

The squadron arrived in Milan on November 12, and after their aircraft had been reassembled, moved to Verona ten days later and after six days to their base at Grossa airfield near Padua. On the 29th, patrols began and Barker led three other Camels in B6313 over Senegalia and at about 10,000 feet they were attacked by five Albatros DV aircraft of Jasta 1. One enemy aircraft was driven down and another destroyed in the ensuing fight, and Barker was credited with one of these victories. Less than a week later, on December 3, after completing escort duty for RE8s, Barker with two other pilots attacked an observation balloon northeast of Conegliano.

When a brightly painted Albatros of Jasta 39 attempted to attack one of the Camels, Barker left the balloon and drove this enemy aircraft down to about 300 feet when he was able "to get a burst of fire into him." The Albatros dived and crashed in flames, Barker returned to the balloon and, at very close range, fired again and it also caught fire and crashed. He then fired at the balloon ground crew and later attacked a staff car that overturned in a ditch. In addition he strafed and dispersed small parties of enemy troops. Barker's aggressive attitude was typified when he and another Camel pilot strafed an Austrian airfield at Motta on Christmas Day 1917.

Further successes for Barker followed with a balloon destroyed in flames on December 29, and three days later an Albatros of Jasta 1 shot down over Vittorio followed, on January 24, by another kite balloon at Conegliano. On February 2 four enemy aircraft were shot down in one encounter by the squadron, two each by Capt. W.G. Barker and Lt. C. McEwen, and three days later three more enemy machines were brought down, two by Barker and one by 2/Lt. H.B. Hudson, all in the vicinity of Oderzo. A week passed before Barker and Hudson found and destroyed a group of five observation balloons near Fossamerlo, on February 12. Barker had noticed that the thick ground mist made conditions ideal for attacking the balloons, which were at a height of 1,000 feet.

Barker went on leave from February 13 to March 7, and although he logged almost twelve hours flying time from then until March 16 he did not achieve another victory until two days later. On the 18th Barker, flying B6313 with three other Camels, spotted seven Albatros at 17,000 feet and climbed to attack. The enemy aircraft dived; Barker followed one down and at 3,000 feet and about forty yards range he fired a long burst with both guns. This aircraft crashed in a field near Villanova, while the remainder avoided combat. The next day Barker, again with lieutenants Cooper and Forder, spotted a group of enemy aircraft at 17,000 feet and attacked them. Barker forced two Albatros to spin down and fired at another which went down to 800 feet when he closed in and fired 200 rounds at close range, causing this D.III to crash north of Cismon. Capt. Barker had further operational flights with 28 Squadron and his last patrol with this squadron was on April 8 when the squadron was then part of the RAF, formed when the RFC had amalgamated with the RNAS on April 1.

Due to his tendency to fly unofficial patrols and not always to follow orders properly, Barker was not given the command of No. 28 Squadron when it became vacant. Consequently he requested a transfer, and on April 10 he joined No. 66 Squadron at Liettres. He still retained his "personal" Camel B6313, which was continually customised. In addition to paintwork and engine modifications he had fitted sights of his own design to the twin machine guns, which improved his aim. Other squadron pilots commented that Barker's enemy target would often be seen breaking up before they considered it even to be within range. Barker also kept a running tally of his victories with small flashes of white painted on the struts.

Barker claimed a further sixteen victories while with 66 Squadron. The first was Oberleutnant Gassner-Norden of Flik 42J in an Albatros D.III on April 17 and, less than three months later, on July 13, he shot down a Berg Scout and another D.III near Godega. While with this squadron, on May 19, he was presented with the Croix de Guerre (gazetted on September 20) and again mentioned in despatches.

On July 14 Barker, with promotion to major, took command of No. 139 Squadron at Villaverla. This squadron's aircraft was the Bristol Fighter, but Barker was permitted to take his Sopwith Camel B6313 with him and he continued flying patrols. He claimed his first victim four days later on July 18 when his patrol attacked five enemy aircraft over Asiago. Barker was credited with one LVG shot down and another victory shared with Lieutenant G. May.

Two more Albatros scouts were destroyed by Barker on July 20, and he shared victory over a third with two other pilots three days later. On July 21 the supplement to the *London Gazette* No. 30801 had announced the award of the DSO for Barker, the citation confirming that he had "... on five different occasions brought down and destroyed five enemy aeroplanes and two balloons...."

No victories were recorded for Barker during August, as he was much involved in preparations to put an Italian agent into enemy-held territory. It was Barker's task to fly a modified Savoia-Pomilio SP.4 bomber at night using radio and searchlight signals, drop off the agent, and, return to base. He was assisted in this mission by Lieutenant William Wedgwood Benn RAF, who as well as navigation was responsible for the safe exit of the agent, Lt. Allesandro Tandura. Sixty officers and men were involved in the experiments and planning of this operation, and as the use of parachutes was in its infancy the method developed was for the agent to be positioned over a trap door in the aircraft, where he was attached by a long rope to a parachute slung beneath the undercarriage. At the appropriate moment Barker shut down the engines and Wedgwood Benn, from the observer's seat, pulled a rope connected to the release bolts on the trap door. Amazingly this plan worked, and on the night of August 8 Tandura was dropped near his hometown of Vittorio Veneto and was able to provide much valuable information. Barker's service records showed that forty hours' flying time were logged as "Spy Dropping. Italy." The *London Gazette* No. 30895 of September 12 announced the award of the Italian Silver Medal of Military valour for this episode.

The award of a second bar to his Military Cross was published in the supplement to the *London Gazette* of September 16 and the citation included "... on one occasion [Barker] attacked eight hostile machines, himself shooting down two ... in two months he himself destroyed four enemy machines and drove down one and burned two balloons." On this date when the Prince of Wales visited the squadron at Villaverla, Barker took him on a forty-five-minute flight in Bristol Fighter 7972 and probably flew over enemy territory. The prince was taken up on other flights as one of a fifteen-minute duration was recorded with another pilot later in the month.

Barker claimed three more Albatros scouts shot down on September 18, while on patrol near Feltre. These were his last victories in Italy and he flew his last patrol with 139 Squadron on September 29 in Camel 6313. Orders were issued that this aircraft was to be sent to 7th Aircraft Park and dismantled but that "Major Barker will be allowed to take off any souvenirs." Despite this official authorization, Barker was asked to return the timepiece from this Camel.

Having flown more than 1,400 operational hours since early 1916, Barker was posted to England at the end of September 1918 to command the fighter training school at Hounslow Heath Aerodrome. He took a short leave in London and persuaded his superiors at RAF HQ that he would best achieve results at the training school if he was allowed to visit the Western Front and update himself on combat techniques. Consequently the new Sopwith Snipe E8102 was allocated for his roving commission in early October 1918.

Whilst in hospital recovering from his injuries incurred in the Sopwith Snipe, the supplement to the *London Gazette* No. 30989 of November 2 had published the citation for the award of a bar to his DSO:

CAPT. (T/MAJOR) WILLIAM GEORGE BARKER, D.S.O., M.C.

A highly distinguished patrol leader whose courage, resource and determination has set a fine example to those around him. Up to 20 July, 1918, he had destroyed thirty-three enemy aircraft — twenty-one of these since the date of the last award (second Bar to the Military Cross) was conferred on him.

Major Barker has frequently led formations against greatly superior numbers of the enemy with conspicuous success.

Consequently at his VC investiture at Buckingham Palace, on March 1, 1919, Barker had received a total of six awards!

The following month Barker flew a Handley Page 0/400 over parts of London with a number of passengers, including the Prince of Wales, and in May he again took the prince on a flight, this time at Hounslow where the aircraft was the prototype Sopwith Dove. The subsequent aerobatics were witnessed by Thomas Sopwith. This flight gave rise to such newspaper headlines as, "Prince of Wales Stunts with One-Armed VC."

On April 29 he was promoted to lieutenant-colonel in the RAF, but resigned this post and in May 1919 sailed for Canada on the *Mauretania*. With William Bishop (see page 105), a fellow Canadian VC recipient who had visited him in hospital, Barker formed Bishop-Barker Aeroplanes limited (BBAL). Barker was still receiving treatment for his injuries sustained in 1918, and was admitted into an Ottawa convalescent hospital on June 18, 1919, and not discharged until a month later. He suffered from the gradual onset of arthritis in his limbs, and as with so many other returning troops from neurasthenia and a difficulty in integrating again into civilian life. These factors led Barker to start drinking heavily and together with Bishop he gained a degree of notoriety for "anti-social episodes."

Not long after his return to Canada, Barker met and fell in love with Jean Kilbourne Smith, who had been born at Owen Sound, Ontario, where she had grown up with her cousin, Billy Bishop. She was the daughter of Horace Smith, a self-made millionaire lawyer and ship-owner who had nothing in common with his daughter's future husband and was not impressed by his war record.

There was a vast difference between the two families. On one hand the Smiths lived an affluent lifestyle, and on the other the Barkers were farmers who often struggled to make ends meet. Basically Smith considered Barker was not good enough for his daughter and thought he was a penniless opportunist. However, the marriage took place on June 1, 1921, at Grace Church-on-the-Hill, Toronto, and the best man was Billy Bishop. The couple lived at 355 St. Clair Avenue West, Toronto, and had one daughter, Jean Antoinette, born in 1923. Due in part to the vast social chasm between the families, Barker rarely visited his family in Manitoba.

By early 1922 BBAL had failed and the two men were forced to sell off their aircraft to pay the creditors. Barker joined the Canadian Air Force in the rank of wing commander in June, and was the commanding officer of the air station at Camp Borden until January 15, 1924. In 1923 Barker had been appointed aide-de-camp to King George V.

On April 1, 1924, he was made acting director of the newly formed Royal Canadian Air Force (RCAF). One of his important achievements with the RCAF was the introduction of parachutes. In June he was posted as RCAF liaison officer at the British Air Ministry in London. During May of the following year he began advanced studies at the Royal Air Force College, Andover, and graduated from there in March 1926.

When Barker and his family returned to Canada in June 1926 the director of the RCAF was Group Capt. James Scott, an officer for whom Barker had little respect. Consequently, on August 24, Barker resigned from the RCAF. He attempted tobacco farming for a while in Norfolk County, Ontario, but a severe bout of pneumonia in early 1929 forced him to sell his share of the farms.

Later in that year, when he had recovered from pneumonia, he received a number of offers from aviation companies, and in January 1930 became president of Fairchild Aviation Corporation based in Montreal. In that same month he was passed fit and received his commercial flying certificate. Fairfield was trying to sell aircraft to the Canadian government, and on March 12 a new two-seater bi-plane, the KR-21, was to be demonstrated to the RCAF at Rockliffe Ottawa Air Station.

Barker arrived at the airfield as the KR-21 took off on a flight by Fairfield's demonstration pilot, who put the plane through its paces for about ten minutes before landing. It was not necessary for any further demonstration flights as the airfield staff had witnessed a number of flights that day, but Barker insisted on taking up the aircraft. He had promised a flight to friends, but was persuaded to fly solo for the first flight. The plane took off at about 1:00 p.m. and after some steep turns, still at the relatively low height of 250–300 feet, Barker climbed steeply for another manoeuvre and he stalled the aeroplane. The aircraft started to drop backwards then rolled over and dived headlong into the frozen Ottawa River. Barker was killed instantly.

The RCAF Court of Enquiry enquiry held two days later found that the aircraft was airworthy prior to flight and that the primary causes of the crash were "an error of judgement on the part of the pilot" and "loss of control due to too steep a climb without sufficient height to recover."

Barker's wife's family did not want a church service and mourners were invited to Horace Smith's home in order to pay their respects to the dead flyer, whose coffin was guarded by an RCAF RSM. At 3:30 p.m. on March 15 a short service of fifteen minutes took place prior to the cortége starting its mile and a quarter journey to Mount Pleasant Cemetery. Led by the band of the Toronto Scottish Regiment and an honour guard of thirty-five RCAF airmen from Camp Borden, a gun carriage carried the flag-draped coffin followed by the RCAF Regimental sergeant major, who held Barker's decorations on a purple cushion. Only the men of the Smith and Barker families walked in the procession to the cemetery. The coffin was escorted by senior military officers and the honorary pallbearers included another winner of the VC. Five Canadian recipients of the VC carried a poppy wreath in the shape of the Victoria Cross. The procession also included over 3,000 military personnel, many in civilian dress, as well as senior national and local politicians. An estimated 50,000 people lined the streets and the area around Mount Pleasant Cemetery. Two three-plane V formations circled and flew down over the long procession, a number of times dropping rose petals. The cortège stopped at the Smith family mausoleum in the cemetery, two buglers sounded the Last Post and the rifle party fired three volleys. Eight airmen pallbearers lifted the coffin, and as they moved up the steps into the mausoleum the six light aircraft each flew very low and dropped the last of the rose petals. The coffin was taken inside and the bishop of Toronto delivered a final eulogy before it was placed in Crypt Room B.

The large marble facing over the crypt was engraved with his rank as a lieutenant-colonel, and the pilot's wings engraved inside the crypt are those of the RFC, not the RCAF. This was the choice of his widow, Jean, who also commissioned a stained-glass window in the back wall of the crypt to her husband's memory.

Jean later remarried Gerald Greene who, amongst other interests, had a farm near Toronto. She always kept a portrait of William Barker in her living room, together with a frame containing his medals that she refused to give to the nation during her lifetime.

On June 6, 1931, an airfield at Downsview, Toronto, was named Barker Field, but after thousands of people had learned to fly there the airfield was closed in 1953 and was later sold for commercial development. The crash site beside the Ottawa River was, for a time, marked by a plaque, but this is not now to be found.

Ernest Hemingway wrote a short story, "The Snows of Kilimanjaro," published in 1936, which fictionalized Barker's Christmas Day attack on an Austrian airfield in 1917. The story was later turned into a film in 1952 and again in 2011.

In 1940 the RCAF authorized a booklet, *Canada's Air Heritage*, which was distributed throughout the service. The book profiled only four men, Bishop, Barker, Collishaw, and McLeod (see page 228) and in addition the RCAF commissioned oil paintings of these men, copies of which were sent to schools and air bases across Canada.

During the Second World War, Jean Antoinette Barker was commissioned into the Royal Canadian Navy and was a plotter on North Atlantic convoys. Her mother, Jean, died in December 1983 and was the last to be entombed in the Smith family crypt.

In Dauphin, Manitoba, the Lt. Col. W.G. (Billy) Barker VC Airport bears his name, and a plaque to commemorate him was placed here on June 1, 2000. Six years later a statue of Barker was unveiled, on July 26, 2006, in the airport terminal. An elementary school was also named after him, as was the Dauphin Squadron of the Canadian Air Cadets. Manitoba Parkland Tourism has nominated June 1 as Billy Barker Day.

Barker's only daughter, Jean Antoinette Mackenzie (*née* Barker), died in July 2007. On September 22, 2011, a memorial at Mount Pleasant Cemetery in Toronto was unveiled to mark William Barker as the "most decorated war hero in the history of Canada, the British Empire, and the Commonwealth of Nations." This memorial was paid for by his three grandsons who were present at the unveiling. Also present were two granddaughters, Elizabeth Ede and Janice Gruneberg, daughters of William Barker Ede, who was born in Islington in the summer of 1919.

Barker had met his mother while on leave in London during the war. The following year Southport Aerospace Centre named their new flight student accommodation building after Barker.

His name, along with the other air recipients of the VC, appears on the wall left of the altar in St. Clement Danes church, the Strand, London. Barker's medal entitlement was: VC, DSO & Bar, MC & 2 Bars, 1914–15 Star, BWM, Victory Medal + MiD oakleaf, Medal of Military valour (Silver) + Bar (Italy), Croix de Guerre (France). His medals are held by the Canadian War Museum in Ottawa as is the fuselage of Sopwith Snipe E8102.

H. CAIRNS

Valenciennes, France, November 1

Sergeant Hugh Cairns of the 46th South Saskatchewan Battalion, CEF, won his VC on November 1, 1918, when the Canadian Corps reached the outskirts of the city of Valenciennes. It was the first day of what became a three-day battle to take this important city. The Canadian attack began in cold drizzling rain and was headed by their 10th and 12th Infantry Brigades. On the left, the attack initially went well and Mont Houy, identified as the key to the city, was captured and many prisoners taken. However, on the right, the 46th Battalion was held up by heavy machine-gun fire coming from the steelworks at Marly, which was known to be full of enemy troops. The Canadians were also under fire from other enemy positions in other suburbs to the southeast of the city. In addition the Canadian advance was also severely hampered by enemy artillery based to the north of the city. The 46th Battalion managed to leapfrog the 44th Battalion (Manitoba) as planned, and the infantry entered the outskirts of the city, only to be held up on the right flank. It was then that Hugh Cairns seized his opportunity. Grabbing his Lewis gun and firing from the hip, he caused havoc among the enemy positions. His VC was gazetted on January 31, 1919, as follows:

For most conspicuous bravery before Valenciennes on 1 Nov. 1918, when a machine-gun opened on his platoon. Without a moment's hesitation Sergt. Cairns seized a Lewis-gun and single-handed, in face of direct fire, rushed the post, killed the crew of five, and captured the gun. Later, when the line was held up by machine-gun fire, he again rushed forward, killing 12 enemy and capturing 18 and two guns. Subsequently, when the advance was held up by machine guns and field-guns, although wounded he led a small party to outflank them, killing many and capturing all the guns. After consolidation he went with a battle patrol to exploit Marly, and forced 60 enemy to surrender. Whilst disarming this party he was severely wounded. Nevertheless, he opened fire and inflicted heavy losses. Finally he was rushed by about 20 enemy, and collapsed from weakness and loss of blood. Throughout the operation he showed the highest degree of valour, and his leadership greatly contributed to the success of the attack. He died on the 2nd Nov. from wounds.

Lieutenant-General Sir Arthur Currie, the Canadian Corps commander, wrote a more detailed account of Cairns' actions:

Then, after consolidation, he ascertained that a battle patrol was pushing out to exploit Marly. Sergeant Cairns with his Lewis-gun broke open the door of a yard and came upon 60 Germans. They threw their hands up, but as their officer filed past he shot Cairns through the body. Cairns sank to his knees but continued firing. A moment later the butt of his gun was smashed and he collapsed from loss of blood.

Another eyewitness takes up the story:

The sergeant fell to his knees but was able to swing his beloved Lewis-gun up and fire a burst. The German officer fell dead in front of [him], but by then the Germans had regained their weapons and a wild mêlée broke out in the courtyard. Cairns was hit once again and another round shattered the butt of his Lewis-gun. Still he fired, cutting down swathes of the enemy until he himself collapsed from loss of blood.

Lt. Johnny MacLeod and two men provided a heavy covering fire as two others dragged Cairns out of the courtyard; incredibly [he] was still alive.

By now more men had arrived to assist the beleaguered patrol outside the courtyard. Cairns was placed on a door which was to act as a makeshift stretcher. As two men began to carry the unconscious Cairns away the infuriated Germans opened fire on the stretcher-bearer who was killed. Moments later, what remained of the German garrison surrendered.

Sergeant Cairns was carried to a forward dressing station, but there was nothing that could be done. On November 2, when low, grey clouds scudded overhead, the gallant sergeant succumbed to his wounds.

The operation on the November 1 was a very successful one for the Canadian Corps and in the end had gone very much to plan. A total of 1,800 enemy prisoners were taken and 800 killed in the fighting. Sergeant Cairns was to be last Canadian to be awarded a VC in the First World War. He was buried ten miles north of Cambrai at Auberchicourt British Cemetery in Plot I, Row A, Grave 8. Auberchicourt was formerly a mining village in the Department of the Nord, and is east of Douai on the road to Valenciennes. At the time it had also been the advance headquarters of Gen. Sir Henry Horne, who was in command of the British First Army. The cemetery can be found on the north side of the road to Erchin and was begun at the end of October 1918, and used until February 1919. Three Canadian casualty clearing stations used to be near by; the 1st, 6th, and 23rd.

Hugh Cairns, the son of George H. and Elizabeth Dotes Cairns (*née* Donkin), was the third of a family of eleven children and born in Ashington, Northumberland, on December 4, 1896. The family emigrated to Canada in 1911 and lived in the Caswell Hill area of Saskatoon, at 713 29th St. West, but a couple of years later they needed more space and moved the short distance to 832 Avenue G. North.,

Hugh was a member of Christ Church choir and a keen footballer. He had already completed his schooling in Ashington and became an apprentice with the Northern Plumbing Company. Later he set up his own plumbing business. On August 2, 1915, Hugh enlisted together with his brother Abbie (Albert) as members of the 65th Infantry Battalion, which was being raised in Saskatoon. His service number was 472168 and he was described as being five foot six inches tall with a chunky build and ruddy complexion. In addition he had brown eyes and black hair. His brother Albert, to whom he was very close, was to be killed on September 10, 1918.

He left Canada for England on June 20, 1916, and disembarked at Liverpool on the 28th. On reaching Bramshott, Surrey, the following day his battalion was broken up, with most of the men, including the two brothers, being transferred the following day to the 46th Saskatchewan Battalion, which was to be part of the 4th Canadian Division. He left for France on August 9.

Cairns won the DCM in June 1917, when he came to the notice of his colonel for the first time. The 46th Battalion had been ordered to provide a platoon to destroy a German machine-gun post, while at the same time two battalions of the 10th Brigade were to attack the enemy positions between the River Souchez and La Coulotte. The attack on June 3 began very well, but the success was short-lived and, by the end of the afternoon, men from the No. 13 Platoon of the 46th Battalion became isolated. In addition, they were running short of ammunition. It was at this point that Cairns, then still a private, took a hand. According to his DCM citation:

> ... he led a party forward at a critical moment and supplied covering fire to the flank of an attacking battalion. With great initiative he recovered two guns which had been left behind, and posted them, repelling three enemy attacks, and successfully covering our subsequent withdrawal. Though wounded, he held on until his ammunition was expended, when he made his way back to our line ...

At one point Cairns lost his temper with one of the Canadian battalion's inadequate advance and, in the hearing of their adjutant, roared out: "The sons of bitches may be good in training, but they're not worth a damn in the line!"

Not surprisingly, the adjutant complained to the 46th Battalion's Col. Dawson, and demanded that Cairns be court-martialled for insubordination. However, nothing more was said about the matter and Cairns was duly awarded his DCM. (*LG*, August 25, 1917). During the fighting he had been wounded in the back and had thirteen shrapnel wounds.

Cairns took part in most of the fighting that the CEF were involved in, including that at Hill 70 in August and, a few months later, at Passchendaele in November. In August 1918 he fought in the Amiens battle. He was promoted to lance corporal on November 11; corporal on July 1, 1918; and sergeant on August 15. Sadly, in early September he received the tragic news that his elder brother, Abbie, with whom he had enlisted and carried out his initial training, had died of wounds in the fighting in the Drocourt–Quéant Line. According to colleagues, this grim news inspired Cairns to greater efforts, saying he wouldn't rest until he had accounted for at least fifty Germans. Hugh, by now a sergeant, died of wounds at 1 Canadian CCS in Valenciennes on November 2, 1918. He had suffered gunshot wounds to his abdomen, and one of his hands was fractured.

After the war Hugh Cairns's VC, the last to be awarded to a Canadian, was posted on February 20, 1919, to the Colonial Office for presentation to Cairns' father, George. Later the family presented his medals to the armoury in November 1977, but at the present time they are in the care of the Canadian War Museum, Ottawa. Apart from the VC and DCM, they include the BWM, VM, and French Knight of the Légion d'Honneur. The address of the armoury, which was renamed after Cairns in 1960, is 930 Idylwyld Drive, Saskatoon.

On June 8, 1921, a twelve foot marble statue of the NCO, with a polished base, was dedicated as a central part of the local Saskatoon Football Club's war memorial in Kiwanis Park on 25th Street Bridge. The memorial had been paid for by the club. On November 13,

1933, a plaque to commemorate the 46th Battalion was unveiled in the University of Saskatchewan.

Three years later, on July 25, 1936, in the presence of his parents, Cairns was commmemorated again when he had an avenue renamed after him in Valenciennes, the city that he had helped to capture: the Avenue Serjeant Hugh Cairns. At the town's Hôtel de Ville there is also a commemorative plaque on display. These ceremonies took place in front of the Hôtel de Ville, the day before the unveiling of the Vimy Memorial by King Edward VIII. His parents' travelling expenses were paid for by an anonymous group of Canadian businessmen.

Other commemorations in his Canadian hometown include a primary school and a street name. In 1995 a plaque to his memory was erected on a house that was presumed to have been his home, but it was later relocated to 832 Avenue G North on July 7, 2005. The location reference is 418 10th Street East. He is also remembered with a lake in north Saskatchewan named after him.

RECIPIENTS WITH
CANADIAN CONNECTIONS

M.J. O'LEARY

Cuinchy, France, February 1, 1915

The year 1915 opened in northern France with the opposing forces facing each other in waterlogged trenches and fortifications, separated by a narrow strip of no man's land. On January 25, 1915, a large-scale German offensive took place along both sides of the La Basseé Canal. On the southern side, at Cuinchy, immediately south of the La Bassée Canal, the British line formed a salient from the canal on the left, running east toward the Railway Triangle (formed by the Béthune–La Bassée railway and the junction of another line toward Vermelles), then south to the La Bassée–Béthune Road, where it joined French positions.

There had been a number of German attacks in the Cuinchy sector during January, culminating in a large-scale offensive on the 25th when the enemy penetrated into the above salient, forcing men of the 1st Scots Guards and 1st Coldstream Guards (CG) (1st Bde) back to partially prepared positions 500 yards west of the Railway Triangle. The Germans renewed their attacks on January 29, but were repulsed with heavy losses.

During the evening of January 30 the 4th (Guards) Bde. moved forward to take over the front line, and 2nd CG, 2nd Bde., took over the thousand yards of front line in front of the ruins of Cuinchy with 1st Irish Guards (IG) in support. 1st IG were allocated positions east of the La Bassée–Béthune Road and in the centre of its line was a collection of huge brick stacks, originally thirty feet high. There were nearly thirty of these stacks, five held by the British and the remainder in German hands; converted for defence, they were connected by a complex system of trenches and saps. Apart from these stacks the area was flat and difficult to defend; the only raised areas were the canal and the railway, because it ran on a sixteen-foot-high embankment, separated from the canal by a towpath.

The right of the German line rested on the Railway Triangle. A little over 200 yards to the west was the area known as the Hollow: a narrow twenty-yard-wide strip lying to the south of the railway embankment. At the western end of the Hollow was a canal lock, which was crossed by the railway via a girder bridge, and about sixty yards east was a brick culvert through which the towpath was reached. The left of the line was held by 2/CG with its flank on this culvert with No. 4 Company IG in support. The enemy renewed its attacks in the early hours of February 1, and forced back men of 2/CG at a post near the canal. A counter-attack by British troops was ordered and at about 4:00 a.m. No. 4 Coy IG were ordered to retake the post. Part of the attacking force managed to get within fifteen yards of the post before being forced to take cover in shell holes, owing to enemy rifle fire and bombs. Both officers having been killed, the command of this attacking party now devolved to CQMS Carton. At the same time, a platoon of No. 4 Coy. advanced along the towpath left of the railway embankment as far as a barricade near the culvert. The two officers leading this section were wounded, so now the company had lost all its officers. At 6:30 a.m. Lt. A.C.W. Innes of No 1. Coy. was ordered to take command of the survivors of No. 4 Coy., with orders to withdraw these men to the railway bridge, leaving a party to hold the rearmost barricade. This he achieved successfully and remained with the party of men at the barricade.

Orders were issued by 1st Bde. to retake the lost position and a further attack was planned. Following an intense ten-minute artillery bombardment just after 10:00 a.m. about fifty men of 2/CG advanced on both sides of the railway, followed by thirty men of 1/IG under Lt. Graham; the Irish Guardsmen carried *filled* sandbags, spades, and two boxes of bombs as their task was to consolidate the position once it was captured. No. 2 Company IG maintained covering fire and 2nd-Lt. Innes, with his small party, was ordered to maintain his position. When the leading Coldstream guardsmen faltered at an enemy barricade, 2nd-Lt. Innes was ordered to lead his men forward, which he did "in a very bold manner."

L.-Cpl. Michael O'Leary, 2nd Lt. Innes's orderly, was with his officer in the Hollow. On the command to advance, O'Leary ran quickly on, outdistancing the men with him, mounted the railway embankment, fired five times at the German machine-gun crew at the next barricade, and killed them. At a second enemy barricade, sixty yards further on, another enemy machine gun was preparing for action. The ground between the two positions was too marshy for a direct approach, so O'Leary again climbed the railway embankment and ran toward the Germans. He was seen by them and as they attempted to turn the machine gun toward him he shot three of its crew. The remaining two Germans immediately surrendered, not realizing that O'Leary had now fired all the cartridges in his magazine. He then returned to the original line with his prisoners (in the words of CQMS Lowry) "as cool as if he had been for a walk in the park."

O'Leary's actions resulted not only in the retaking of the ground previously lost, but also a gain of over fifty yards. This new position enfiladed two enemy trenches, which were then evacuated for about 150 yards. Within days he was promoted sergeant for "Distinguished Conduct in the Field."

The IG Battalion *War Diary* records, "This was a fine piece of work and he [O'Leary] has been recommended for reward." O'Leary's reward was the Victoria Cross, which was gazetted on February 18 and he was presented with it by the king at Buckingham Palace on June 22, 1915. The citation read:

> For conspicuous bravery at Cuinchy on the 1st February, 1915. When forming one of the storming party which advanced against the enemy's barricades he rushed to the fron and himself killed five Germans who were holding the first barricade, after which he attacked a second barricade,

about 60 yards further on, which he captured, after killing three of the enemy and making prisoners of two more.

Lance-Corporal O'Leary thus practically captured the enemy's position by himself, and prevented the rest of the attacking party from being fired upon.

His VC, the first won by a member of the Irish Guards, was the first to be won on the Western Front in 1915.

The third of four children, Michael John O'Leary was probably born on September 29, 1888 (his age varies on various military documents), at Kilbarry Lodge, Inchigeela, ten miles from Macroom in County Cork, Ireland. His parents, Daniel and Margaret, ran a small farm where Michael worked after attending Kilbarry National School. In 1909 he left his father's farm and joined the Royal Navy, and was attached to HMS *Vivid* training establishment at Devonport, but was discharge unfit with rheumatism in April 1910. He returned to work on his father's farm for a few months before enlisting in the Irish Guards (Regimental No. 3556) on July 2, 1910.

On the expiration of his three years' Home Service with the 1st Battalion he was transferred to the Reserve on July 2, 1913. O'Leary applied to join the Royal North-West Mounted Police (RNWMP), in Canada. On August 2, 1913, he was engaged, as constable no. 5685, for a three-year term in the RNWMP at Regina, Saskatchewan. He was posted to Battleford, Saskatchewan, where he soon displayed his courage, taking part in a two-hour running battle with two gunmen; after their capture he was presented with a gold ring, which he wore for the rest of his life. He was posted to Regina in May 1914, and following the declaration of war with Germany O'Leary was granted a free discharge from the RNWMP on September 22, 1914, in order to rejoin the British Army. Returning to England, he was mobilized on October 22, going to France on November 23 to join his battalion, 1st Irish Guards. With a draft of nearly 300 men he rejoined the 1/IG, who were then at Meteren, near Bailleul, on the last day of the month. Like many of the original BEF regiments the Irish Guards had suffered severely since the previous August — over 600 killed, wounded, and missing, including sixteen officers — and earlier in November the battalion had been reduced to some 160 rifles.

O'Leary's previous experience no doubt helped his career, and he was appointed lance-corporal early in January 1915. (Some accounts state that he was Mentioned in Despatches not long after his arrival in France but the author has been unable to confirm this.)

After the award of his VC his deed was much publicized, and he became a celebrity in the accepted sense of the word. Newsreel footage of July 11, 1915, shows him arriving for a recruiting rally at Hyde Park, London, where over 60,000 people turned out to see him; songs, poems, and a play were written in his honour, posters and cigarette cards portrayed the young Irishman, and a fund to support Irish widows and orphans was set up in his name.

The war was not going well for the Allies at this time and "good news stories" were hard to come by, so O'Leary was much employed by the army in recruiting, and contemporary photographs show his transformation from "country boy" to a smart NCO and later a junior officer.

On his return to Ireland, O'Leary was greeted by crowds at Macroom, but when his father, a strong nationalist and a prize-winning weightlifter and footballer in his youth, was asked by a reporter to comment on his son's courage, he replied, "I am surprised he didn't do more. I often laid out twenty men myself with a stick coming from the Macroom Fair, and it is a bad trial of Mick that he could kill only eight, and he having a rifle and bayonet."

After receiving the award of the Cross of St. George, 3rd Class (Russia), in August, O'Leary was commissioned into the Connaught Rangers as a second lieutenant on October 23, and embarked on a recruitment campaign along the west coast of Ireland. On a recruiting drive in Ballaghaderrin, Ireland, he was jeered by Ulster Volunteers, an incident that led to questions being asked in the House of Commons on December 6. O'Leary's parents were also persuaded to help in recruiting, but after his father, in his maiden speech, advised the Irish audience that they should enlist and fight as the Germans would treat the Irish people in the same way the British had done for many years, but worse, the British Army did not use his services again. In early 1916 O'Leary was attached to the Northumberland Fusiliers for further recruiting duties, and in January 1917 he was posted to Salonika with 5/Connaught Rangers. It is probable that his usefulness in recruiting had waned so perhaps a forgotten hero was posted to a forgotten campaign.

He was put in charge of scouts and snipers, although one of his fellow officers was later critical of his abilities as an officer. (This criticism might easily be put down to the complete difference in backgrounds as the officer in question — Lt. Jourdain had a privileged upbringing.) O'Leary was promoted lieutenant on July 1, 1917, and was mentioned in Lt.-Gen. Milne's despatch of October 25, 1917.

Unfortunately O'Leary contracted malaria and was hospitalized when his regiment moved to Egypt in September 1917. After an attempt to join the RAF in Egypt was unsuccessful a medical board recommended that he should be sent back to England. O'Leary sailed from Egypt in August 1918, and served with the 2/Connaught Rangers at Dover until June 1920, when he was discharged to the Reserve of Officers.

Leaving his wife, Greta, and two children in Ireland, he returned to Canada in March 1921, reputedly to rejoin the Royal Canadian Mounted Police (the name of the RNWMP since February 1920), but for reasons unknown he did not do so. Instead, he first gave lectures on the war and then spent a brief period in a publishing house before joining the Ontario Provincial Police during 1921 as a licence inspector for the enforcement of prohibition, a post he held for two years. His wife and twin boys having joined him, O'Leary was then appointed sergeant of police on the Michigan Central Railway, stationed at Bridgeburg, Ontario, at a salary of £33 per month.

As he later informed a *Daily Mail* reporter:

I was with Michigan Central for two years. Unfortunately on the railway I came into contact with bootlegging and smuggling interests.... A detective has to take bribes to keep his mouth shut or else people are out to get him.

O'Leary was arrested in 1925, charged with smuggling an alien into Buffalo from Bridgeburg; after a delay of some months the court acquitted him of the charge. In the autumn of the same year he was again arrested, charged with "irregularity in a search for liquor." He spent a week in an American jail, but was again acquitted at a later trial. He was not reinstated in his job by the Michigan Central Railway.

After he had been unemployed for several months, the authorities at Hamilton, Ontario, advanced the money (£70) for passage to Ireland for O'Leary and his family, and in October 1926 his wife and four children sailed from Montreal, on the *Letitia*, for Ireland, where an uncle had promised to look after them. O'Leary stayed in Canada having been promised a "suitable position" by the Ontario attorney general and worked in Hamilton for a time, during which period he suffered several bouts of malaria, contracted in Salonika. Finally, he left Canada. The British Legion heard of his parlous state and employed him for some time as a packer in its poppy factory in England.

In 1932, while he was working as a commissionaire at the Mayfair Hotel, Park Lane, London, he took part in the "Cavalcade Ball" held there in aid of the Journey's End home for disabled officers; together with A.O. Pollard VC, he served tin mugs of rum to the distinguished audience.

He continued working at the hotel until called up from the Reserve of Officers in June 1939, and went to France with the BEF as a captain in the Middlesex Regiment. He was invalided back to England before the evacuation at Dunkirk, transferred to the Pioneer Corps, and put in charge of a prisoner-of-war camp in the south of England. Discharged from the army on medical grounds in 1945, he returned to civilian life as a building contractor, in which trade he worked until his retirement in 1954.

He attended the Victory Parade in June 1946, but at the 1956 Centenary VC Review held in Hyde Park, London, he was impersonated by a man in a bathchair.

O'Leary lived in the same district of London for more than thirty years, originally at Southborne Avenue, Colindale, but in later years at Oakleigh Avenue and Limesdale Gardens, Edgeware. He died at

Whittington Hospital, Islington, on August 1, 1961, after a long illness and was buried at Mill Hill Cemetery, Paddington. After the funeral service at the Roman Catholic Annunciation Church at Burnt Oak, the coffin was saluted by Guards officers as it left the church and it was accompanied by a "lone piper" through the cemetery. Six of O'Leary's seven children were at the funeral, including twins Daniel and Jeremiah, both winners of the DFC in the Second World War.

In July 1962 O'Leary's medals — VC, 1914 Star and Bar, BVM, with MiD, BWM, Cross of the Order of St. George, 3rd Class (Russia), Coronation Medals for 1937 and 1953, and Defence Medal 1939–45 — were presented to the Irish Guards by his family. Although O'Leary also wore his 1914 Star with a Bar, and always claimed that he was entitled to do so, his military records show he arrived in France one day too late for such entitlement.

On February 1, 2015, a commemorative paving stone was unveiled at Glasnevin Cemetery, Dublin, Ireland, to mark the centenary of L/Cpl. Michael O'Leary's VC-winning action. This is the second such stone to commemorate Irish recipients of the VC in the First World War, and by the end of 2018 all such stones will be then incorporated into a monument at Glasnevin.

Today the area previously known as the Brickstacks at Cuinchy is in some areas overgrown, with the topography changed in places, but it is still possible to walk along the embankment following in the footsteps of O'Leary's daring exploit. A visitor to the nearby Cuinchy Communal Cemetery will find in Plot I, Rows A and B, twenty-five men of both the Coldstream and Irish Guards who lost their lives one hundred years ago, on February 1, 1915. One might ponder how many more headstones would be here were it not for the bravery of Michael O'Leary.

J.A. SINTON

Orah Ruins, Mesopotamia, January 21, 1916

On January 21, 1916, during the Battle of El Hanna, Capt. John Sinton was medical officer to the 37th Dogras of the Indian Division when they were in action at Shaikh Saad in the area of the Orah ruins during one of the several attempts to relieve Kut-al-Amara, twenty-three miles away, where Gen. Townsend was besieged with troops of his 6th Indian Division.

During the fighting Sinton went forward to attend the wounded, and in so doing was shot several times, both through his arms as well as side. Despite his wounds he would not be moved, and remained at the front attending the wounded under heavy fire from the Turkish positions.

The corps war diary gave full details of how the casualties sustained on January 21, 1916, in the Battle of El Hanna were dealt with after only a few men from the attacking force had reached the Turkish trenches. After it began to rain at 11:00 a.m. a steady downpour continued into the night and turned the already marshy ground into a landscape of knee-deep mud.

The war diary of the 3 (Indian) Corps deputy director of medical services 1915 December–1917 March entry on the following day noted:

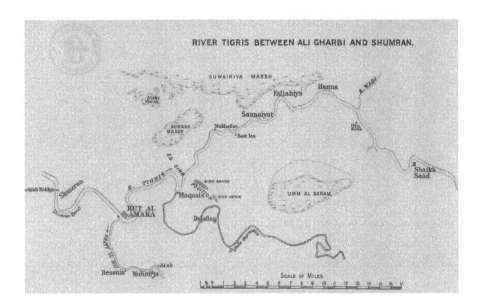

RIVER TIGRIS BETWEEN ALI GHARBI AND SHUMRAN.

22 Jan 1916 — Al Orah — Rain continued through the night. Country is a quagmire and nearly impassable for wheeled transport. Got over 1500 casualties yesterday evening and during the night. The 'Salimi' left here 6. p.m. yesterday and evacuated 6 British Officers and 450 British and Indian rank and file from a Dressing Station on the bank of the river. Another group of 120 who were 100 yards nearer the front were brought in this morning by small river craft as the "Salimi" would have been under the fire of the enemy's guns if she had gone to them. Had interview with Corps Commander 1 p.m. I told him I estimated our casualties at 3000, also that he must expect a great deal of sickness.

"Salimi" left for base at 11a.m. with 6 B.O's and about 450 British and Indian ranks referred to above. P.1 left 2p.m. for base with following wounded: BOs 6; British R & F 186, IO's 12; Indian R & F 726. Total 920.

Number evacuated on "Salimi" and P 1 approximate as owing to deficiency of Staff and urgency of getting them away they could not be properly checked.

Camp of 20 CFA [?] pitched close here is a morass and am putting as many wounded as possible on ships as they come in.

Gen. Douglas DA & QMG went out about noon with flag of truce and arranged for 6 hours armistice to allow us to collect our wounded and bury the dead. Enemy would not allow us to collect our wounded close to his trenches but took them to his ambulances.

We sent out all available A F carts — about 200 — accompanied by 3 Combatant Officers and one parson who volunteered to assist, also one troop British and one troop Indian cavalry to search the battlefield. They found all had already been collected and were in the advanced dressing station. All wounded were in by 6 p.m. with exception of 2 British Soldiers who arrived at 8.30 p.m.

A F carts bringing in the wounded had great difficulty in reaching the ships, as the country was knee deep in mud and many of them were stuck for hours. Some of them were lying out all night on the battlefield and were very much exhausted.

The citation for Sinton's well deserved VC was published in the *London Gazette* of June 21, 1916, as follows:

John Alexander Sinton, M.B., Capt., Indian Medical Service. For most conspicuous bravery and devotion to duty. Although shot through both arms and through the side, he refused to go to hospital, and remained as long as daylight lasted, attending to his duties under very heavy fire. In three previous actions Capt. Sinton displayed the utmost bravery.

Sinton was presented with his decoration on January 31, 1918, by the Viceroy of India, Lord Chelmsford, at a special ceremony in Delhi.

John Alexander Sinton was born in Victoria, British Columbia, on December 2, 1884, the third of seven children of Ulster parents, Walter Sinton and Isabella Mary (*née* Pringle). The family returned from Canada to Ulster in 1890, and from 1893 to 1899 John was a pupil at Nicholson Memorial School, Lisburn, before moving to the Royal Belfast Academic Institution, 1899–1902. He then matriculated at the Royal College of Ireland and entered the Arts School of Queen's College, Belfast. A year later he passed the First Arts Examination of the Royal University of Ireland and entered the Medical School at Queen's College. He appears to have had no difficulty in winning prizes and honours in most of the subjects he undertook.

In 1908 Sinton graduated with first-class honours in medicine, surgery and obstetrics and became the Riddell demonstrator in the pathology department. He also held an appointment in pathology at the Liverpool School of Tropical Medicine. On graduation he was appointed house surgeon and house physician at the Royal Victoria Hospital, Belfast. He was later a pathologist at the Ulster Eye, Throat and Ear Hospital, and clinical pathologist at the Mater Infirmorum Hospital, Belfast. Other qualifications included MB, DPH (Cantab and Belfast); DTM (Liverpool), and B.Ch., BAO, RUI (Indian Medical Service).

In August 1911 this very highly qualified doctor entered the Indian Medical Service, having gained first place in the entrance examination. Prior to this he had been medical officer to the 31st Bengal Lancers (31st Duke of Connaught's Own Lancers), stationed at Kohat in the North-West Frontier Province.

On the outbreak of war Sinton was on active service in India as regimental medical officer with the Movable Column, Kurram Valley, North-West Frontier, and later joined the Mesopotamia Expeditionary Force. He was made a captain on June 21, 1915, and posted to the Indian Expeditionary Force D (Mesopotamia) as regimental medical officer to the 37th Dogras together with several other units. In January 1916 he was serving with the Dogras against the Turkish forces in Mesopotamia. It was when taking part in an action brought about by the attempt to relieve Kut-al-Amara that he won his VC on the same day as the sepoy, Lance-Naik Lala.

The following is from *Biographical Memoirs of Fellows of the Royal Society*:

On return to duty (from India) after being wounded he remained on active service in various theatres of war until 1920, and for a time he was Sanitary Officer with the rank of A/Major in the Mahsud Operations on the NW Frontier, later in East African F Force (Tanganika) and then with the East Persian Cordon Field Force commanding a Cavalry Field Ambulance and Agency Surgeon, Khorassan. From August 1918 to April 1919 he was in the Turkestan Military Mission as S.M.O. and commanding a Cavalry Field Ambulance with the rank of Lt.-Col. In 1919 for a year he was D.A.D.M.S (San.) successively in the Afghanistan Campaign 1919, the Mahsud Campaign 1919–20 and the Waziristan Campaign 1920. Many times Sinton was mentioned in despatches and received many awards and medals.

In 1919 Sinton was promoted brevet major and the Queen's University conferred the honorary degree of doctor of medicine on him, in recognition of his treatment of the wounded in the field during the war.

He continued to serve on the North-West Frontier in Afghanistan and Waziristan, and was mentioned in despatches on two occasions.

Sinton was made temporary major on October 26, 1920, and received the OBE (Mil.) in 1921. After a period at home he returned to India, having retired from the army and taken up a career in research; he joined the Medical Research Department of the Indian Medical Service, taking charge of an enquiry into how malaria was treated, and he was one of the men involved in the setting up of a malaria treatment centre at Kasauli in the Punjab. As part of a team of experts he became known as a foremost authority on malarial and parasitical diseases, and in 1923 was made a full major.

On September 19, 1923, Sinton married Edith Steuart Martin, only daughter of Edward Steuart Martin, a former indigo planter; the couple had a daughter, Eleanor, born on December 9, 1924, at Kasauli, where Sinton was serving with the Indian Medical Services in a civilian appointment.

On March 24, 1927, Sinton was awarded the degree of doctor

of science and in the same year was made the first director of the Malarial Survey of India. He founded a scientific journal in order to be able to publish new information on the control of the breeding of the mosquito. He wrote over 200 papers on entomology. In 1928 he was presented with the Chalmers Memorial Medal of the Royal Society of Tropical Medicine and Hygiene and continued with his researches for a further ten years before finally retiring from the Indian Medical Services in August 1938. (He had been promoted to lieutenant-colonel on January 29, 1931.) He was then made Manson Fellow of the London School of Hygiene and Tropical Medicine, and adviser to the Ministry of Health. When war broke out again in 1939 he was recalled to India and posted as quartermaster to a military hospital, where he proved a great success. In the following April, having reached the retirement age of fifty-five, he was placed on the retired list and sent home, where he joined the Home Guard. However, between June and November 1940 he was recalled to be consultant malariologist to the East African forces, a position that was later expanded to cover the whole Middle East force. He travelled throughout the Middle East in this role, and in 1942 took part in an extensive tour in order to be able to report on health conditions on projected air routes for troops across Africa. Between March and July 1945 he took part on an inspecting and advisory tour for the army to inspect malaria conditions further afield in Assam, Burma, and Ceylon and on to Australia, New Zealand, and other countries. He was responsible for directing the advanced planning to ensure that specialized medical supplies were available to combat the dangers of malaria to the masses of troops newly arriving from the United Kingdom. Largely through his efforts incidences of malaria in the Middle East force were minimal.

In 1944 Sinton was retired a second time, but once more recalled as consultant to the War Office as there had been many outbreaks of the disease among the troops moving into Sicily and Italy. He retired for a third time at the end of the war and was awarded the Blisset-Hawkins Medal at the Royal College of Physicians in London, and in 1946 became the Robert Campbell Memorial Orator and Medallist of the Ulster Medical Society. In the same year he was made a fellow of the Royal Society for his research into the problems of malaria. On his very last retirement he returned to his home at Slaghtfreedan

Lodge, Cookstown, Co. Tyrone, where he planned "to play the role of a country gentleman" and study ornithology, fish, and gardening. In 1949 he was awarded the Mary Kingsley Medal by the Liverpool School of Tropical Medicine. Having planned a quiet retirement it did not stop him from taking part in local affairs and he became a JP, a deputy lieutenant, and in 1953 high sheriff for Tyrone.

According to the *Biographical Memoirs of Fellows of the Royal Society*:

> He was Pro-Chancellor in 1952 at Queen's and President of Queen's University Association 1953–4. Governor of the Royal Academical Institute, Belfast, 1946–50, President of the Co. Tyrone Branch of the Forces Help Society 1946–52 and Vice-President of the North Ireland Branch of this Society from 1952. He was President of the Cookstown Branch of the British Legion 1946–53, member of the Council of the North Ireland Branch 1949–52, and represented North Ireland at the 11th Conference of the British Empire Service League at London in 1951. In 1946 he was made Hon. Member of the Royal Society of St. George. He was President of the Queen's University Service Club from 1946; Vice-President 1946–52 and President 1952–3 of the Old Instonians Association. He was Magistrate (JP) for Co. Tyrone from 1947; High Sheriff for that county in 1953; and Deputy Lieutenant in 1954.

Sinton was also a member of the National Arbitration Tribunal of Northern Ireland. John Sinton died on March 25, 1956, at his home at Slaghtfreedan Lodge near Lough Fea, Cookstown, Co. Tyrone, having been ill for eight years. Described as a tall, spare man and full of energy, he was surely one of the most talented men to win a Victoria Cross, and during his career achieved a very great deal in the service of others.

Sinton's funeral took place on March 28 at his home and his coffin, on which rested his dress sword, cap, and medals and which was draped with the Union Jack, was carried into the Creggan Presbyterian churchyard by the vice-presidents of the Cookstown British Legion together with the Branch's Standard. The procession was led by two pipers from the Royal Inniskilling Fusiliers Depot at Omagh, who played the Lament. At the graveside the Final Salute was fired by two NCOs and twelve Fusiliers, and the Last Post and Reveille were sounded by a bugler from the same depot. As a final tribute members of the British Legion filed past the grave and each one dropped a poppy into it. The ceremony was also attended by the medical profession, representatives from Queen's University, and many other figures representing Sinton's considerable interests in the community at large.

Each year a ceremony takes place at Sinton's grave where a poppy wreath is laid by the local Legion branch, on the Saturday afternoon before Remembrance Sunday.

Sinton's widow, Edith, died on October 1, 1978, and is buried in the same grave as her husband. In 1987 their daughter, now Eleanor Watson, opened a small housing complex organized for the use of Legion members, named Sinton Court in honour of her father's memory. The Musgrave Park Military Hospital, Belfast, also had a ward named after him. In addition he is also remembered by the naming of Sinton Hall, a hall of residence for students at Queen's University, Belfast. In 2009 a new medical centre named after him was opened by his grandson in 2009.

Edith donated her late husband's decorations to the RAMC Museum (later Army Medical Services), in Aldershot. They were considerable in number and apart from his VC and OBE include the 1914–15 Star; BWM, VM & MiD Oakleaf, India General Service Medal 1908–36) 3 clasps, "Afghanistan NWF 1919," "Mahsud 1919–20," "Waziristand" 1919–1921, 1939–45 Star, Africa Star, Burma Star, Defence Medal (1939–45), War Medal (1939–45) and MiD Oakleaf, King George V Silver Jubilee Medal (1935), King George VI Coronation Medal (1937), Queen Elizabeth II Coronation Medal (1953), Order of St. George (4th Class), Russia and Egypt Gambia Medal.

P.E. BENT

Near Polygon Wood, October 1, 1917

As Plumer's piecemeal offensive edged across the Gheluvelt plateau, the Germans signalled their determination to hold the eastern end with a series of desperate counterattacks, each one timed to take advantage of the thick ground mist shrouding the district in the early morning hours. On September 30 one such assault, led by parties of flame-throwers and bombers, was repulsed between the Reutelbeek and the Menin road, not far from where Jack Hamilton had won his VC. The next day, undeterred by their heavy losses, they attacked again, with twelve sections of specially trained assault groups leading the way.

Some of the hardest fighting took place in and around Polygon Wood, where a scattering of shell holes was manned by units of the depleted 110th (Leicestershire) Brigade. They had only just moved on to the newly won ground and conditions were appalling. David Kelly, an officer at Brigade HQ, described the grim setting as "dreary and miserable." The night was bitterly cold and the Leicesters were, in the words of one of their number, "mud-wallowing in the open air." The headquarters party of the 9th Leicestershires dug in as best they could near a German pillbox, where they contrived to make a shelter out of some abandoned planks of wood that were lying about. Patrols were sent out and dispositions made, but preparations for defence were still incomplete when the ground quaked beneath a devastating bombardment. It was the heaviest shelling Kelly had experienced in more than two years' front-line service. It smothered the British lines to a depth of 1,000 yards and was rapidly followed by a well-timed assault by storm troops charging out of a curtain of smoke from the direction of Cameron Covert and Joist Farm.

The struggle that ensued would go down in regimental history as a minor epic distinguished by the outstanding courage of one of the army's youngest battalion commanders, twenty-six-year-old Lt.-Col. Philip Bent, a Canadian-born former Merchant Navy seaman whose substantive rank was that of a mere lieutenant. Such was the confusion and the high number of casualties that details of the action are sketchy, but it is clear that the initial storm burst heaviest on the positions occupied by A Company. An outline of the fierce battle that raged from early morning into the afternoon is provided by the battalion's war diary. The blow-by-blow account begins with the lightning bombardment:

> 5:25 a.m. Enemy put down heavy barrage on front Company and Polygon Wood and at the same time put up a smoke-screen all along Battalion front.

> 5:27 a.m. Enemy attacked through smoke-screen. SOS sent up. First wave of enemy driven off by A Company by Lewis Gun and Rifle fire. Capt. A.A.D. Lee MC, killed.

> 5:30 a.m. Enemy second wave driven off on our front, but enemy attack on Battalion of [sic] right flank successful. Right flank of A Company (front line Coy.) threatened.

> 5:40 a.m. 2 Platoons of D Company (in reserve) under Lt.-Col. P.E. Bent DSO, and B Company (in support) under Lt. Burn immediately counterattacked enemy. Counterattack was entirely successful and drove enemy from our front. Lt.-Col. Bent killed whilst leading the charge.

> 5:45 a.m. Enemy continued to make headway on right flank ... and launched his third Wave against our front. Two platoons of C Company sent up to counterattack enemy on our right flank. Lt. Burn killed.

> 6:00 a.m. C Company counterattack reported to have stopped enemy advance. 2 Platoons of C Company sent up to

reinforce and to get in touch with troops on right flank who had been driven back some distance.

Enemy attacking troops driven off but owing to heavy casualties in front Coy., a defensive line was organized approximately 100 yards in rear of our front line, along E[astern] edge of Polygon Wood. Enemy shelling Polygon Wood extremely heavy, causing many casualties. 2/Lt. Barratt killed. 2/Lts Faulkner, Scott and Hallam wounded. C Company established defensive flank ... in front of Cameron House ... Full report sent to Bde. and reinforcements asked for. Enemy repeatedly attempted to advance but was driven back by our Lewis Gun and Rifle Fire, and the line was held against further attack.

Throughout, the 9th had maintained contact with the 8th Leicestershires on the left, but the right flank lay exposed. At 9:30 a.m., as shells bracketed the track running from the western edge of Polygon Wood and Glencourse Wood to Black Watch Corner, the first reinforcements began to arrive. Two platoons of the 7th Leicestershires were sent forward, but two more companies did not fare as well. Caught by the enemy barrage, they reached the position only seventy strong. While one party was sent to bolster the defensive flank, another dug a second line one hundred yards inside the wood's eastern fringes.

Low-level strafing attacks hampered the work, but a corporal exacted partial revenge by shooting down one aircraft. No further attack came and German stretcher-bearers were seen carrying away their wounded. The war diary noted: "Enemy casualties appear to be very heavy." At noon, the CO of the 7th Leicesters arrived to take charge, and the rest of the afternoon was spent preparing to meet a fresh attack, reportedly planned for dusk. But despite numerous alarms late into the evening the Leicesters were left alone. As October 1, 1917, faded into history, the night sky was aglow with "thousands of Very lights" as a bombardment pounded the enemy lines. Next morning, pockets of Germans, cut off near the Leicesters' position, were seen running back. Few made it. What was left of

Bent's command came out of the line in the early hours of October 3, the survivors forming two companies to merge with the depleted 8th Battalion.

The Leicesters' stubborn defiance had thwarted enemy designs at heavy cost. The inspiration behind their brave defence had undoubtedly been Philip Bent. If the times in the unit war diary are accurate, his involvement in the fighting amounted to a bare twenty minutes from the moment his men recoiled from the initial shock of the enemy thrust to his death at the head of a scratch counterattack force. Yet his short-lived intervention was a decisive factor in galvanizing the defence at a critical moment when any delay or hesitation could have proved disastrous not just for his battalion but for Plumer's planned attack three days later. With SOS rockets shooting into the sky all along the front, the Leicesters' plight had seemed parlous. D.A. Bacon, a private soldier serving at 9th Battalion Headquarters, described how, as the "threatening" situation developed, Bent had called Brigade Headquarters for immediate help only to discover that he could expect no support for some hours "owing to the conditions of approach and the heavy and deep enemy barrage." It was at that point, with A Company falling back and catastrophe looming, he took matters into his own hands. In a memoir published thirteen years later, fellow Leicestershire Officer David Kelly gave a description of what followed, based on personal conversations with a company commander and the adjutant of the 9th:

> Colonel Bent ... was in a pillbox on the west side of the wood when a runner came in saying "SOS gone up from (the reserve) company." "Then we'd better get on," said the Colonel, and went forward with his headquarter personnel. Collecting the reserve company and everyone available, the Colonel led a counterattack, and, struck down in the moment of victory, was last seen — for his body, doubtless blown to pieces, was not found — waving his pipe and calling, "Go on, Tigers!"

That same stirring battle cry, or a version of it, would enter the annals of Leicestershire regimental history and even found a place in the citation for the posthumous Victoria Cross published in the *London Gazette* of January 11, 1918:

> For most conspicuous bravery, when during a heavy hostile attack the right of his own command and the battalion on his right were forced back. The situation was critical owing to the confusion caused by the attack and the intense artillery fire. Lt.-Col. Bent personally collected a platoon which was in reserve, and together with men from other companies and various regimental details, he organized and led them forward to the counterattack, after issuing orders to other officers as to the further defence of the line. The counterattack was successful, and the enemy were checked.
>
> The coolness and magnificent example shown to all ranks by Lt.-Col. Bent resulted in the securing of a portion of the line which was of essential importance for subsequent operations. This very gallant officer was killed whilst leading a charge which he inspired with the call of "Come on, the Tigers."

Philip Eric Bent, the first Canadian-born VC recipient of the campaign, was born on January 3, 1891, in Halifax, Nova Scotia, the youngest of three children, to Frank and Sophia Bent. His Canadian father was a clerk and later superintendent in the railway mail service. Philip was brought to England at an early age by his mother.

Educated at Ashby-de-la-Zouch Grammar School in Leicestershire, he spent his holidays with relatives in Weymouth and, with a view to pursuing a career at sea, he joined HMS *Conway*, the Mersey-based Merchant Navy training ship, in 1909. His time there was brief but successful. He earned a silver medal for boxing and left Conway in December 1910 with an "extra certificate" as senior cadet-capt. Port Main. His first seagoing appointment was as apprentice aboard the 2,233-ton four-masted barque *Vimeria* owned by John Hardie & Co. of Glasgow. He sailed with her for three years, gaining his second mate's ticket in early 1914.

Ashore when war broke out, Philip Bent enlisted in the army at Prince's Street recruiting office, in Edinburgh, on October 3, 1914. His attestation papers show him as having a distinctive frog tattoo on his left forearm and give his mother, then living in Oxford, as his next of kin. Quite why, as a Merchant Navy officer, he joined the army rather than the Royal Navy remains unexplained. Whatever his reasons, he served as a private in A Company, 1st City of Edinburgh Battalion, Royal Scots, until November 29 when he was granted a temporary commission in the Leicestershire Regiment. Five months later he was posted to the 7th Leicesters, a New Army battalion, based at Aldershot. Promoted to lieutenant in June, he was transferred to the 9th Battalion and sailed for France with his unit in July. Soldiering was clearly to his liking and spells in the line in Flanders and the Arras sector were sufficient to convince him to rethink his career. With the support of his commanding officer, he applied for a permanent commission in the regular army, preferably with the Leicesters. Writing in support of him on March 13, 1916, Lt.-Col. C.H. Haig noted: "He is a particularly efficient officer and a very good disciplinarian. He is at present Battalion Grenade officer and has done very good work in that appointment." A medical board stated that he had impaired vision of the right eye, but thought that glasses could overcome the problem. Either way, it proved no handicap to his ambition and the following month the former Merchant Navy officer was granted a permanent commission as a second lieutenant in the Bedfordshire Regiment. He retained the temporary rank of captain, to which he had been promoted on April 21, and remained with the 9th Leicesters. Thus far, he had experienced some discomfort but relatively little action, as was illustrated by a letter he wrote home that spring:

Life in the trenches this winter has not been very pleasant, owing to the excessive bad weather, which has made our trenches canals and our dugouts to fall in. However, the last week has been glorious, sunshine and good northwesterly winds: so we are all hoping the worst of the weather is over.

Everything is very quiet with us, a few hours' bombardment and an occasional bombing escapade make up our daily routine.

All of that was to change in July when the battalion was moved to the Somme sector. A costly attack on the Bazentin ridge was followed in September by a bloody assault on Gueudecourt. Philip Bent, who had been mentioned in despatches in June and promoted to temporary major in mid-July, escaped both actions unhurt only to suffer gunshot wounds to the neck in October. Evacuated to hospital at Boulogne, he was back with the unit in less than ten days, and his meteoric rise was made complete on October 26 when he was appointed acting lieutenant-colonel in command of the battalion. The rank was made temporary on February 1, 1917, and three months later he led his unit into action for the first time at Bullecourt. Losses were again heavy and little ground gained, but the young battalion commander's leadership was recognized by a second Mention in Despatches (gazetted May 22) and the award of a Distinguished Service Order (gazetted June 4). A second assault over much the same ground on June 15 proved equally unsuccessful and the following month the 9th Leicesters were with-drawn into divisional reserve. That same month, the Leicesters' temporary lieutenant-colonel was promoted to lieutenant!

Details of his final action at Polygon Wood were slow in reaching his family. As late as January 1918 relatives were writing to the War Office asking for information about the circumstances of his death. There was also uncertainty as to whether his body had been buried and any grave marked. Two months later, his mother, who had been appointed sole executor of his will, travelled to Buckingham Palace to receive her son's Victoria Cross and Distinguished Service Order from the king. Five years later she presented them to Philip's old school, where they remained until 1972 when they were passed to the Royal Leicestershire Regimental Museum on permanent loan.

Today, Philip Bent is remembered in England and Nova Scotia. War memorials at Hindhead in Surrey, where his mother lived for a time, and his old school honour his sacrifice. His sword was also hung in the church in Ashby-de-la-Zouch, where he had his first communion. Across the Atlantic, the Army Museum in Halifax, Nova Scotia, displays a portrait together with mementoes of his days aboard HMS *Conway*.

Despite thorough searches of the battlefield, Philip's body was never found. His name is among more than 34,000 commemorated on the Tyne Cot Memorial (Panels 50-1), a few miles from where he fell, making his last gallant gesture.

His decorations apart from his VC and DSO include the 1914–15 Star, British War Medal (1914–20), and Victory Medal (1914–19) and are on display in the Royal Leicestershire Museum.

R.E. CRUICKSHANK

North of Shunet Nimrin, East of Jordan, Palestine, May 1, 1918

Three weeks after the Gurkha Rifleman Karanbahadur Rana won the VC in the fighting at El Kefr, Pte. Robert Cruickshank gained his VC to the east of the River Jordan. It was on the first of May 1918 when he was serving with D Company of the 2/14th (County of London) Battalion London Regiment (179th Infantry Brigade), 60th (London) Division, during the battle of the second crossing of the River Jordan.

The 179th Brigade had returned to Bethany in Palestine on April 9, 1918, when they were ordered northwards to relieve one of the brigades of the 10th (Irish) Division to the north of Jerusalem on the Wadi Gharib. Soon afterward the 60th Division relieved the whole of the 10th Division. Having earlier retired, the Turkish Army had by now received reinforcements who crossed the Jordan at Jisr ed Damieh. The enemy then reoccupied the Shunet Nimrin position which, according to the divisional history, was of considerable strength. But the Allies then planned a raid in which it was intended to cut off the Turkish force.

The 179th and 180th Infantry brigades, together with troops of the Desert Mounted Corps, were given this task, which began at 2:00 a.m. on April 30. The 180th Brigade was to the right and the 179th on the left, against the position of El Haud, which had been already attacked previously but without success. The foothills were reached at dawn and the divisional history noted: "it was soon evident that very serious opposition was to be encountered.... The Scottish, with the Westminsters, on their left, in spite of a very heavy machine-gun and rifle fire gained the position on Spectacle Hill, taking seventy-six prisoners; but the enemy's fire was too heavy to permit of any further advance."

Attempts at an advance were continued and "The fighting throughout had been desperate, and the troops had done all that was humanly possible in the face of the heavy casualties sustained, which taxed to the utmost the powers of the stretcher bearers, who excelled themselves in their heroic efforts to succour the wounded...." The London Scottish had lost thirty-three men killed and 140 wounded, nearly half their strength.

It was during this desperate and ultimately unsuccessful advance that Pte. Robert Cruickshank of the 2/14th (County of London) Battalion, the London Regiment (London Scottish), gained the VC. Bernard Blaser described what happened in his book *Kilts Across the Jordan*:

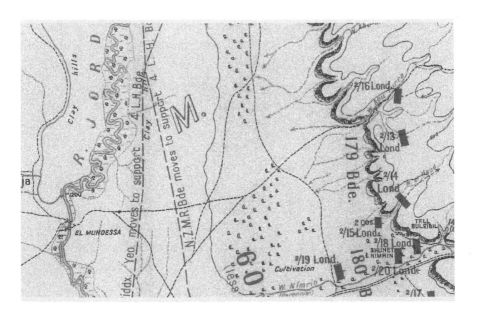

Again we tried to advance, but our endeavours were useless. In one instance the platoons had to cross a ridge, and advance up the wadi on the opposite side. They reached the ridge, but as soon as they attempted to proceed a murderous fire was opened upon them. Those who were left of the right platoon, only half of their original number succeeded in reaching the bottom, where they were comparatively safe, but the other platoon was confronted by a precipice down which it was impossible to climb.

Slowly the numbers of the platoon were reduced until there were only ten men surviving from an original thirty including a lance corporal who called for a volunteer to take a message back to Company HQ.

It was a job attended by the utmost danger, for no sooner did a man move from his little bit of cover than sure enough he attracted fire from the ever-watchful Turks. Although it meant running the gauntlet, with but a faint hope of getting through alive, one man, Private Cruickshank, offered to take that chance. Both sides of the ridge were exposed to the enemy, but Cruickshank chose that down which the remnants of the other platoon had gone earlier. As soon as he moved he was greeted with a shower of bullets, one hitting him in the arm. With as much haste as the rocky nature of the ground would permit he began the descent, but fell wounded in the thigh. Getting up again, undaunted, he hobbled on, but fell an easy target to that merciless fire, and with some half-dozen more bullet wounds in his leg he lay for a few seconds panting. It would have been fatal to have lain there long, so realizing this he began to roll. Over and over he went, bumping against stones and boulders, but never stopping till he reached the bottom. All the while the Turks, in their determination to destroy him, kept up a hot fire, but he was mercifully saved from further wounds. By a piece of amazing good fortune he alighted among several men of the other platoon, all wounded, who were sheltering behind a large rock. By dint of much squeezing into one corner they made room for him, and there they remained all the day until a party of stretcher bearers came along and carried them back to safety. For his gallantry and self-sacrifice Cruickshank won the Victoria Cross, this being the second awarded to the Battalion.

The London Scottish and the Queen's Westminsters were relieved after dark by the Civil Service Rifles and Kensingtons.

Robert Cruickshank's VC was published in the *London Gazette* of June 21, 1918:

No. 511828, Robert Edward Cruickshank, Private, 2/14th Battn. London Regt. (London Scottish) (Territorial Forces). For most conspicuous bravery and devotion to duty in attack. The platoon to which Private Cruickshank belonged came under very heavy rifle and machine-gun fire at short range, and was led down a steep bank into a wadi; most of the men being hit before they reached the bottom. Immediately after reaching the bottom of the wadi the officer in command was shot dead, and the Sergeant who then took over command sent a runner back to Company Headquarters asking for support, but was mortally wounded almost immediately after; the Sergeant having been killed in the meantime, the only remaining N.C.O. (a Lance-Corporal), believing the first messenger to have been killed, called for a volunteer to take a second message back. Private Cruickshank immediately responded and rushed up the slope, but was hit and rolled back into the wadi bottom. He again rose and rushed up the slope, but being again wounded, rolled back into the wadi. After his wounds had been dressed he rushed a third time up the slope and again fell badly wounded. Being now unable to stand, he rolled himself back amid a hail of bullets. His wounds were now of such a nature as to preclude him making any further attempt, and he lay all day in a dangerous position, being sniped at and again wounded where he lay. He displayed the utmost valour and endurance, and was cheerful and uncomplaining throughout.

Pte. Cruickshank was presented with his VC by the king in the ballroom of Buckingham Palace on October 24, 1918.

Robert Edward Cruickshank was the first of five children and born in Winnipeg, Manitoba, on June 17, 1888. His Scottish forebears came from Sutherland. Three years after his birth his family left Canada for England, where Robert was educated at Central Foundation School, Cowper Street, London, and he later attended Bancroft's School, Woodford Green, Essex. In 1908–11 he served in the City of London Yeomanry (Rough Riders) and had also been an Assistant Scoutmaster.

Robert joined the services on November 9, 1915, and began with the Royal Flying Corps before transferring at his own request to 2/14th London Scottish (County of London) Battalion, the London Regiment in France in the second half of 1916. He took part in the Battle of the Somme and was wounded at Leuze Wood on September 10. After being invalided back to England he recovered and went back to the 3rd Battalion before joining the 2nd Battalion in Salonika in February 1917. According to the *London Scottish Regimental Gazette* of October 1961 he was a member of what became known as "G.N. Smith's draft" when the battalion was based at Katerini, consisting of 200 men, many of whom were former 1st Battalion men who had served in France, including perhaps Cpl. C.W. Train, the battalion's first VC. Cruickshank then served in Egypt and Palestine in 1917–18. Robert's brother Percy died in France in early April 1917, and was buried in Duisans British Cemetery, Etrun. He was a sapper serving with the Canadian railway troops.

Soon after the war was over Lt.-Gen. Sir Robert Baden-Powell was present at a fete at Wood Green, Tottenham, at which Pte. Cruickshank was presented with a gold watch by Messrs Lipton, in whose employ he had been for a few years before the war. The fete was held in aid of a fund by which he was presented with a £200 War Bond and a cheque for £50. In addition he had also worked for Lever Brothers Ltd., for a time and was presented with a £100 War Bond by Lord Leverhulme.

Cruickshank was discharged on February 5, 1919, and a few weeks later married Miss Gwendoline May Mansell of Bush Hill

Park, London, on March 22. In the following year he attended the Buckingham Palace VC garden party on June 26, 1920, and the cenotaph and Westminster Abbey services on November 11. He also attended the November 1929 House of Lords' dinner, the June 1946 Victory Parade and dinner, the June 1956 VC centenary celebrations in Hyde Park, and the first two dinners of the VC/GC Association.

Cruickshank worked as an agent for Lever Brothers of Port Sunlight, and in the late 1920s probably lived in the southern area. During the Second World War he became a member of the 5th Leicestershire Home Guard, attaining the rank of major and company commander, until they were disbanded. He was Chairman of Essex County Committee of the British Legion. He retired from work after thirty-nine years on June 17, 1953. He was a regular attendant of 2nd Battalion regimental reunions and other functions at HQ.

Cruickshank was also actively involved in local government and local affairs, and was chairman of the parish council in Glen Parva for thirteen years, and a member of the Leicester Association of Parish Councils, of which "he was chairman for ten years and president for two years." He was also chairman of the Leicester Old People's Welfare Association, chairman of Glen Parva Parish War Memorial Committee, and a member of the Leicester Rural Community Council, the Leicester Playing Fields Association, the Leicester and Rutland Rural Industries Committee, a school manager, a member of the Local Library Committee, and chairman of the Local National Savings Committee. After his death members of Glen Parva parish council stood and paid silent tribute to their former colleague.

Cruickshank suffered a stroke on August 17, 1961, which deprived him of movement down his left side and, although he partially recovered, he died on August 30 at 13 Cork Lane, Glen Hills, Glen Parva, Leicester. His funeral took place on September 1 at Gilroes Crematorium when the London Scottish Regiment was represented. His ashes were laid to rest in the Garden of Remembrance on the north side of nearby All Saints Churchyard, Blaby. His name is also included in a Book of Remembrance. His widow, Gwen, later moved from 13 Cork Lane to No. 10. The couple had no children and she died at the age of 103.

After his death Cruickshank's miniature medals were passed to his niece. They included the VC, BWM, VM, Defence Medal (1939–45), War Medal (1939–45), King George VI Coronation Medal (1937), and Queen Elizabeth II Coronation Medal (1953). His decorations were presented by his widow to the London Scottish on October 1, 1962, and they can be seen by appointment at the Regimental Museum in Horseferry Road, London, together with those of Charles Train. After the presentaion ceremony, which took just a few minutes, the Queen Mother's personal piper played "Delaspee." In 2006 a plaque was unveiled in Bancroft's School in Woodford Green, and in 2013 the Province of Manitoba named a lake after him east of Thompson. It was one of four such lakes to be named after VC winners with links to the province.

R.R.L. BOURKE

Ostend, Belgium, May 9/10, 1918

Rowland Richard Louis Bourke was born on November 28, 1885, in Redcliffe Square, London, the son of Isidore McWilliam Bourke MD, a retired surgeon major of the 72nd (Seaforth) Highlanders, of Curraleegh, County Mayo, Ireland, and his Italian second wife, Marianna (*née* Carozzi). Isidore's first wife, by whom he had three sons, had succumbed to cholera during his service in India. He had four children by his second marriage, Rowley being the only boy among them, and two adopted nephews, and he settled in London, where he had a medical practice.

Around 1898, at the time of the gold rush in the Klondike, Isidore Bourke joined the flood of emigrants seeking their fortune out west. He went to Dawson, Yukon Territory, where he established the city's first hospital. Rowley, who was educated by a number of Roman Catholic orders in England, followed him to Canada in 1902 to try his luck in the goldfields.

The Bourkes were an unlucky family. In addition to his first wife's early death, Isidore lost a brother, who was shot and killed in Ireland, and had a son murdered in Siam. Tragedy also followed them to Canada. Not only was their house in Dawson destroyed by fire, but also one of Rowley's adopted cousins, Cecil, was accidentally killed around 1907 by the premature explosion of a dynamite charge while he was clearing tree stumps at their ranch at Crescent Bay, Nelson. Nearly blinded by the same blast, Rowley was severely injured and left with permanently damaged eyesight. Such was the shattering impact of the tragedy that the family, including Rowley, uprooted and emigrated to New Zealand. Rowley, however, returned and was farming a property at Nine Mile when war broke out.

His attempts to enlist in all three services met with rejection on account of his poor eyesight. To help the war effort he donated a waterfront lot from his land to be raffled off, with proceeds going to a local Patriotic Fund supporting the families of serving soldiers. It was not enough. Still determined to "do his bit," he left Nelson and paid his own passage back to England, where, on January 7, 1916, he finally succeeded in securing a commission as a sub-lieutenant in the Royal Naval Volunteer Reserve. After undergoing courses at Greenwich and Southampton, he was posted to Larne, on the northeast coast of Ireland, where he took command of ML341. For the next year, he toiled at the dull routine of anti-submarine patrols. "Although the work was useful as a preventative, we had only negative results ... to show for our labours [sic]," he wrote. Frustrated by the lack of action, he asked to be transferred to a more active command. Eventually, after what he described as a "considerable delay on the part of Dover," his wish was granted, and in November 1917 he exchanged command of ML341 for ML276. Rowley joined Dover Patrol, or Harry Tate's Navy as it was more popularly known, at an auspicious moment in its history.

Barely a month earlier, Roger Keyes, a man after Rowley's own heart, had taken over command with the intention of going on the offensive. By then a lieutenant, Rowley found life at Dover and its sister port Dunkirk much more to his taste. Once, during an enemy raid on the French port, a colleague recalled seeing him striding along the quay, rubbing his hands with glee as shells crashed about them, and shouting: "This is splendid, this is war!" Nevertheless when word reached him that all Canadians were entitled to a spell of home leave, he decided to apply.

The following February, having heard nothing about his application and with his launch undergoing repairs, he asked again, only to be told that "important operations" were expected soon. Later, hearing that volunteers were wanted for "special dangerous work, the nature of which was not specified," he immediately volunteered, only to be turned down. "I was very cut up when I heard this," he later wrote, "especially after postponing my Canadian leave and working hard to be ready on time." On confronting his commanding officer, he was told "it was on account of my sight."

Refusing to be put off, Bourke badgered his CO until he finally relented and agreed to appoint ML276 as a standby rescue launch. The next six weeks were the most dramatic period of his life. As well as earning a VC and a DSO, he was appointed a Knight of the Legion of Honour by the French government (*LG*, December 12, 1918), mentioned in despatches, and promoted to lieutenant-commander, with seniority back-dated to April 23, 1918.

By October, however, he was growing bored again. "I ... hope the war will end soon," he wrote to his half-brother. "I am fed up with the monotony and no signs of excitement." A month to the day after writing those words his hope was fulfilled. Back home in Canada, in 1919, he married Rosalind (Linda) Barnet, an accomplished musician originally from Sydney, Australia, to whom he had become engaged after the Ostend operations and whom he had promised to marry "as soon as the war is over."

Demobilized the following year, he returned to the Kootenays and his North Shore farm, but by 1931 his eyesight had deteriorated to the extent that he feared he might be going blind. He decided to quit farming and, with his wife, moved in 1932 to Victoria, taking a Federal Civil Service post on the staff of the Royal Canadian Naval Dockyards at Esquimalt. Shortly before the Second World War, Rowley Bourke helped organize the Fishermen's Naval Reserve, a west-coast patrol operation.

At the outbreak of war he joined the RCN Volunteer Reserve, serving variously as a recruiting officer and an extended defence officer, before being appointed as acting commander to HMCS *Givenchy*, a training ship, at Esquimalt and Burrard, Vancouver. After the war he returned to his civil service post and retired in 1950 as officer-in-charge of the civilian security guard at Esquimalt's naval dockyard.

Accompanied by his wife, he travelled to England in 1953 for the coronation of Queen Elizabeth II, and returned three years later for the VC centenary celebrations. Almost twenty years earlier Rowley Bourke had been among the distinguished Canadians who received King George VI and Queen Elizabeth during their 1938 Dominion tour, and he fulfilled a similar role shortly before his death when Princess Margaret made a visit to Canada. But such events were more the exception than the rule.

A modest man, he disliked too much attention and positively detested having his photograph taken. Judith McWilliam-Bourke, whose grandmother was his elder sister, remembered him in retirement as "a man of short stature, with twinkling eyes behind his thick spectacles, and a gentle nature, who was devoted to his wife."

Rowley Bourke VC, DSO, died at his home, 1253 Lyall Street, Esquimalt, on August 29, 1958. Following a requiem mass at Our Lady Queen of Peace Church, he was buried with full military honours at Royal Oak Burial Park, Victoria, a naval guard of honour firing a final salute of three volleys over his grave as the Last Post was sounded. In his will he left his medals to the National Archives in Ottawa, and they have since been displayed on loan in the Maritime Museum of British Columbia and the CFB Esquimalt Naval Museum, where the exhibits also included a pair of his famously thick-lensed glasses.

Apart from his VC and DSO his decorations include the 1914–15 Star, BWM (1914–20), VM (1914–19), the Canadian Volunteer Volunteer Service Medal (1939–45), King George VI Coronation Medal (1937), Queen Elizabeth II Coronation Medal (1953), and lastly the Knight, Legion of Honour (France). They are in the care of the National Archives in Ottawa.

Today a rocky outcrop northwest of Goose Island in the Golby Passage and a mountain southwest of Megin Lake bear the name of Canada's only naval Victoria Cross recipient of the First World War, grandiose memorials to a modest hero, described by one obituarist as a "steady, buoyant figure of much kindness and goodwill ... who left a fine memory of courage and integrity."

AFTERMATH

By mid December 1918 the Canadian 1st and 2nd Divs were established as part of the Occupation of the Rhine. The 3rd and 4th divisions remained in the Fourth Army area. At the end of December Lt.-Gen. Sir Arthur Currie was informed that he was to plan repatriation of the troops under his command. He was determined to treat each man's wish to return home to Canada in the fairest possible manner. He arranged for the 3rd Division to be moved to the Tournai area and then to camps southeast of Boulogne. In January 1919 the other three Canadian divisions were in the Fourth Army between Brussels and Liege.

On arrival in England the Canadian troops were sent to Bramshott, southeast of Aldershot, and later arrivals were sent to Witley, southwest of Godalming. As many men had strong links with England they were given a special eight-day leave prior to their eventual return home.

The majority of the Canadian troops serving in France and Germany in 1918/19 were able to return home by the spring of 1920. Those who did get home were keen to take up where they left off at the start of the war, and most importantly to try and get their former jobs back. However, some had been physically and mentally disabled and were unable to get employment. Civil Re-establishment centres were set up to try and assist the ex-servicemen to get employment. Others who had hardly finished their schooling when they enlisted were keen to complete their education.

After the war the role of the CEF on the Western Front was commemorated in a number of ways. One of the most memorable Canadian memorials was at St. Julien, commemorating the Canadian Army's involvement in the first enemy use of chlorine gas attack in the 2nd Battle of Ypres in April 1915. Designed by Frederick Chapman Clemesha, from Regina, this striking monument is called "The Brooding Soldier," and stands at Vancouver Corner.

The CWGC records that 64,996 Canadians lost their lives during the war (the closing date is August 31, 1921), and those who have graves all have a uniform headstone displaying the Canadian maple-leaf motif as part of its design. Those casualties in Belgium and France not fortunate enough to have a known grave are commemorated on the two Memorials to the Missing as described below. By far the largest number of "missing" casualties are commemorated in France, 39,715, with Belgium having 14,043, 61 and 21 percent respectively of fatal casualties.

Those Canadians who died in the Ypres Salient and who have no known grave are commemorated alongside soldiers from Australia, India, South Africa, and the U.K. on the Ypres (Menin Gate) Memorial to the Missing.

This imposing memorial sits beside the road to Menin, through which thousands of soldiers passed on their route to the battlefields. It was inaugurated on Sunday, July 24, 1927, by Field Marshal Hubert Plumer. Also present were King Albert I of Belgium, King George V, and General Foch, in addition to hundreds of First World War veterans and relatives of missing soldiers. The memorial was designed by Sir Reginald Blomfield, with sculptures by Sir William Reid-Dick.

At the time of writing 54,627 names are engraved on the stone panels of this memorial, 6,928 of whom served with Canadian Forces, including three VC winners: F. Fisher, F.W. Hall, and H.M. McKenzie.

In an attempt to give comfort to the relatives of the missing Field Marshal Plumer used the following words when closing his speech: "… now it can be said of each one in whose honour we are assembled here today: 'He is not missing; he is here.'"

In July 1936 the stunning Vimy Ridge Memorial, Canada's National Memorial, was unveiled to the northeast of Arras by King Edward VIII. Erected on the highest point of the ridge, which the four Canadian Divisions were all involved in trying to capture in April 1917, it was designed by Walter Allward of Toronto and overlooks the Douai Plain. It commemorates the 11,168 Canadian servicemen who have no known grave, many of whom died in the battle for the ridge. Included in their number are four men who were awarded the Victoria Cross: R.G. Combe, F. Hobson, W.J. Milne, and R. Spall.

There are six other Canadian battlefield monuments on the Western Front, apart from the Caribous for the Royal Newfoundland Regiment. They are all based on a cube design by P.E. Nobbs, an architectural advisor, and are made from a thirteen-tonne block of Stanstead granite. They have two sides of inscription, in English and French, and a wreath is carved into the other two sides. One commemorates the capture of Mount Sorrell and can be found south of Hill 62 (Sanctuary Wood). Others commemorate Courcelette on the Somme, Passchendaele at Crest Farm (Third Ypres) 1917, and Le Quesnel (Amiens) 1918. The memorial at Dury Crossroad commemorates the breaking of the Drocourt-Quéant Line, and the one at Bourlon Wood commemorates the fighting for Cambrai, Canal du Nord, Valenciennes, Mons, and, after the Armistice in November, the march to the Rhine in December 1918.

The five Caribou Memorials, designed by the British sculptor Basil Gotto for the Royal Newfoundland Regiment, are massive and set in battlefield parks. They can be found at Beaumont Hamel (Battle of the Somme); Guedecourt (Somme 1916), north of Masnières; the Saint-Quentin Canal on the Cambrai road (Battle of Cambrai, November 1917); Monchy le Preux where it is placed above a German concrete strongpoint and looks toward Infantry Hill and the Bois de Sart beyond; and in Belgium, east of Ypres, at Coutrai beside the main road close to the River Lys.

The memorials at Vimy Ridge and Newfoundland Park in Beaumont Hamel have been made major places for visitors to visit and professional guides are on hand to explain the local history of the CEF during the war.

On May 16, 2000, the remains of an unknown Canadian soldier were exhumed from Cabaret Rouge British Cemetery, Souchez, near Vimy Ridge. The grave reference was Plot 8, Row E, Grave 7. On May 25 the coffin was flown to Canada, accompanied by a guard of honour. Later, the unknown soldier was taken on an RCMP gun carriage to the National War Memorial in Ottawa and reburied in a special tomb at the foot of the memorial. A replacement headstone at Cabaret Rouge British Cemetery tells the story of what happened.

Other Canadian memorials which are not battlefield commemorations can also be found in France.

No fewer than 40 percent of VC holders didn't survive the war, and memorials to individual members of the CEF and Royal Newfoundland Regiment who earned a VC during the war can be found at the following seven places:

> Robert Hanna and Michael O'Rourke at Lens
> near Hill 70
> Filip Konowal close to the Canadian front line
> at Hill 70 near Lens
> Harcus Strachan at Masnières
> Gordon Flowerdew at Moreuil Wood/Rifle Wood
> George McKean at Cagnicourt
> Samuel Honey at Bourlon
> Hugh Cairns at Valenciennes

At the time of writing a Belgian farmer is planning to erect a memorial to Thomas Ricketts on his land at Ledegem.

Quite apart from the Canadian National War Museum in Ottawa, memorials to commemorate the Canadian VCs have also been erected in many other places than on the Western Front and can be found in Canada, U.S., England, Scotland, and elsewhere. Those commemorations in Canada have been wide ranging and have taken the form of mountains, lakes, names on war memorials, cairns, historical plaques, statues, house plaques, coastal protection boats, names of some of the branches of the Royal Canadian Legion, armouries, and other forms of remembrance.

The founding of the Princess Pat's is commemorated in Lansdowne Park, Ottawa, with a commemorative stone plaque that marks where the regiment formed up prior to marching through the main streets of Ottawa in 1914. It was first dedicated in 1974 and rededicated after it was moved to a more suitable position in September 2014.

In August 2014, with the beginning of the centenary of the four years of the First World War, there was another opportunity to remember the great deeds of these seventy-two men who were awarded the Nation's highest military honour. The first member of the CEF to win a VC in the war was L/Cpl Frederick Fisher, who won his posthumous decoration at St. Julien in Belgium on April 22, 1915. Three and a half years later Sgt. Hugh Cairns won the seventy-second and what was to be the last of the CEF VCs, at Valenciennes, ten days before the Armistice ending hostilities was signed.

Since the Victoria Cross was first awarded by Queen Victoria in 1857, ninety-nine Canadian servicemen have been awarded this highest of military honours. Five were gained prior to the South African War and sixteen in the Second World War. Canada now has its own award, but it has yet to be presented.

In 2013 the British Government decided that each of the total of 627 men who won the VC in the First World War should be commemorated with a paving stone. At first the government concentrated on those men who were born in the British Isles, but by the time of writing they had decided to commemorate all the men wherever they had been born. On March 5, 2015, 145 paving stones representing those VC winners born ouside the British Isles were unveiled at the National Arboretum in Staffordshire, England. Thirty-two of the seventy-two men written about in this book were born in Canada and the remaining forty were born in other countries including England (17); Scotland (10), Ireland (4), Northern Ireland (2), U.S. (4), Denmark (1), Ukraine (1), and India (1). The men from the United Kingdom as well as the Republic of Ireland will have paving stones dedicated to them in their own places of birth or close association, provided by the British government.

On November 10, 2014, Princess Anne, the Princess Royal, unveiled a bronze plaque at the British High Commission in Ottawa commemorating seventy of the Canadian First World War VCs. On both this plaque and at the National Memorial Arboretum in Staffordshire, the names of Michael O'Leary and Rowland Bourke, both VC recipients with Canadian connections, have been left off.

The Federal Dominion of Canada was formed on July 1, 1867, and in 2017 not only will there be commemorations of Canada's 150th anniversary but also of the capture of Vimy Ridge in April 1917 and the Third Battle of Ypres later in that year.

APPENDIX I

Country of birth of the Canadian VCs in the First World War

1915

Frederick Fisher — Canada

Frederick William Hall — Ireland

Edward Donald Bellew — India

Francis A.C. Scrimger — Canada

Frederick W. Campbell — Canada

1916

Thomas O.L. Wilkinson — England

Leo Clarke — Canada

John Chipman Kerr — Canada

James C. Richardson — Scotland

1917

Frederick M.W. Harvey — Ireland

Thain W. MacDowell — Canada

William Johnstone Milne — Scotland

Ellis Wellwood Sifton — Canada

John George Pattison — England

Robert Grierson Combe — Scotland

William Avery Bishop — Canada

Michael James O'Rourke — Ireland

Frederick Hobson — England

Harry Brown — Canada
Okill M. Learmonth — Canada
Robert Hanna — Northern Ireland
Filip Konowal — Ukraine
Christopher P.J. O'Kelly — Canada
Thomas William Holmes — Canada
Robert Shankland — Scotland
Cecil John Kinross — Scotland
Hugh Mckenzie — England
George Harry Mullin — United States
George Randolph Pearkes — England
Colin Fraser Barron — Canada
James Peter Robertson — Canada
Harcus Strachan — Scotland

1918

Edmund De Wind — Northern Ireland
Alan Arnett Mcleod — Canada
Gordon M. Flowerdew — England
George Burdon McKean — England
Joseph Kaeble — Canada
John Bernard Croak — Newfoundland, Canada
Herman James Good — Canada
Harry Garnet Bedford Miner — Canada
Jean Brillant — Canada
James Edward Tait — Scotland
Alexander Picton Brereton — Canada
Frederick George Coppins — England
Raphael Louis Zengel — United States
Thomas Fasti Dinesen — Denmark
Robert Spall — England
Charles Smith Rutherford — Canada
William Hew Clark-Kennedy — Scotland
Claud Joseph Patrick Nunney — England
Bellenden Seymour Hutcheson — United States
Arthur George Knight — England

William Henry Metcalf — United States
Cyrus Wesley Peck — Canada
John Francis Young — England
Walter Leigh Rayfield — England
Milton Fowler Gregg — Canada
Samuel Lewis Honey — Canada
George Fraser Kerr — Canada
Graham Thomson Lyall — England
John MacGregor — Scotland
William Merrifield — England
Coulson Norman Mitchell — Canada
Wallace Lloyd Algie — Canada
Thomas Ricketts — Newfoundland, Canada
William George Barker — Canada
Hugh Cairns — England

Recipients with Canadian Connections

Michael O'Leary — Ireland
John Alexander Sinton — Canada
Philip Eric Bent — Canada
Robert Edward Cruickshank — Canada
Rowland Richard Louis Bourke — England

APPENDIX II

Senior Canadian Corps and Divisional Commanders and Key Events for 1914/15

Lt.-Gen. E.H. Alderson in command of the 1st Canadian Division from September 29, 1914, until September 12, 1915.

Maj.-Gen. S.B. Steele commander of the Canadian 2nd Division from May 25, 1915, until August 16 when he was replaced by Maj.-Gen. R.E.W. Turner.

Brig.-Gen. M.S. Mercer in command of the 1st Canadian Infantry Brigade from September 29, 1914, until November 21, 1915. On December 24 he was promoted to being commander of the 3rd Canadian Division.

Brigadier A.W. Currie in command of the 2nd Canadian Infantry Brigade from September 29, 1914, until September 12, 1915, when he took over the 1st Canadian Division until June 8, 1917. He was replaced by Brig.-Gen. L.J. Lipsett from September 14, 1915, until June 15, 1916.

Brig-Gen. R.E.W. Turner in command of the 3rd Canadian Infantry Brigade from September 29, 1914, until August 11, 1915. Six days later he took over command of the 2nd Canadian Division.

When it was en route from New York to Liverpool, a German submarine sank the oceanliner RMS *Lusitania* on May 7, 1915, off the Irish coast, with the loss of nearly 1,200 passengers and crew, some of whom were U.S. citizens. The consequences of this disaster contributed partly to the U.S. later joining the war against Germany.

Sam Hughes was knighted in October 1915.

Senior Canadian Corps and Divisional Commanders and Key Events for 1916

By May 28 the public learned that Lt.- Gen. Alderson had been appointed inspector-general of Canadian Forces in England and France, and his place was taken by Lt.-Gen. Hon. Sir Julian Byng.

Major Gen. A.W. Currie was still in command of the 1st Canadian Div. In 1916 there were three other Canadian Divisions in existence.

Until December 15, 1916, Major Gen. R.E.W. Turner was in command of the 2nd Canadian Division. He was replaced by Maj.-Gen. Sir H.E. Burstall from December 15. This was a change that Lt.-Gen. Alderson had been wanting to make for some time.

From June 16 Maj.-Gen. L.J. Lipsett was in command of the 3rd Canadian Division, and from April 25 Maj.-Gen. D. Watson was in command of the 4th Canadian Division, which was formed in England in June.

The Duke of Devonshire was appointed Governor General of Canada on July 29 when he took over from the Duke of Connaught.

Up to August 31 the CEF had suffered 8,644 men killed, 27,212 wounded, and 2,005 men missing.

By early November, and by now driven to distraction by Hughes' erratic and uncontrollable behaviour, Robert Borden, the Canadian prime minister, demanded his resignation as minister of militia, which Hughes duly submitted on November 14, although this didn't stop him from still attempting to meddle in the CEF affairs.

On December 22 the Princess Patricia's Light Infantry, having served with the 80th Brigade of the 27th Division for a year, joined the new 7th Brigade as part of the 3rd Canadian Division.

Senior Canadian Corps and Divisional Commanders and Key Events for 1917

Maj.-Gen. A.W. Currie was still in command of the 1st Division until June 8, when he was replaced by Maj.-Gen. Sir A.C. Macdonell.

Maj.-Gen. N.E. Burstall had only recently taken over command of 2nd Canadian Division.

Maj.-Gen. L.J. Lipsett was still in command of the 3rd Division until September 12, 1918.

Maj.-Gen. D. Watson was still in command of the 4th Division.

In the summer the only changes to top commanders was for Maj.-Gen. A.W. Currie, when he became Canadian Corps commander in June, having succeeded the British-born Sir Julian Byng. After the victory at Vimy Ridge in April 1917 Byng was promoted to command the British Third Army.

In October the first Canadian army officer, Lt.-Col. Agar Adamson, was appointed to command the Princess Patricia's Light Infantry.

The consequences of the Ross Rifle debacle ended in July 1917 when Sir Charles Ross, its designer, was exposed as being involved in a weapons scandal and he was forced to surrender any weapons contracts outstanding with the Canadian government. He was also stripped of his knighthood.

On October 12 Prime Minister Borden was forced to form a coalition government.

On December 6 a French cargo ship full of explosives collided with a Norwegian ship in Halifax Harbour. It caught fire, which ignited the cargo and created a huge explosion that not only wrecked the city of Halifax but killed over 2,000 people and injured nearly 9,000.

By 1917 407,000 Canadians had volunteered for military service, of whom 300,000 were serving overseas. On 11 June conscription was introduced in order to increase the number of troops available.

Senior Canadian Corps and Divisional Commanders and Key Events for 1918

Sir A.W. Currie was Canadian Corps commander still and remained so until September 8, 1919, after the war had finished.

Between March and September there had been no further changes to divisional commanders, except for Maj.-Gen. Lipsett, commander of the 3rd Canadian Division, when on September 12, 1918, he was transferred to the 4th Division Headquarters. A month later, on October 14, he was killed by a sniper when was on a reconnaissance visit to the front.

Command of the 3rd Canadian Division was given to Maj.-Gen. F.O.W. Loomis on September 13.

On June 27 the RMS *Llandovery Castle*, being used as a hospital ship, was on course from Halifax to Liverpool when it was sunk by a German submarine. No fewer than 234 doctors, nurses, and patients were drowned, and there were only twenty-four survivors. It was considered a major enemy atrocity.

The 4th Company of the Princess Patricia's arrived in Mons, Belgium, early on November 11, prior to the armistice being declared.

SOURCES

The main sources used in the preparation of this book include the archives listed below, followed by additional material from other places, individuals, archives, and obituaries.

Canadian War Museum, Ottawa
Canadian Great War Project
Canadian Veteran Affairs
Commonwealth War Graves Commission, Maidenhead
Great War Forum: www.1914-1918.invisionzone.com
Iain Stewart VC Website: www.victoriacross.org.uk
The London Gazette, 1914–1920 (HMSO)
The Lummis VC files at the National Army Museum, London
The Lummis VC files at the Imperial War Museum, London
The National Archives (TNA), Kew, Surrey
The National Archives of Canada, Ottawa
Service Files of the First World War, 1914–1918 CEF (government of Canada)
Stand To! and *Bulletin* are journals published by the Western Front Association
The Victoria Cross Society also publishes a regular journal

1915

F. Fisher

Personal Record 3105-29 (National Archives of Canada)
Victor, January 14, 1967
TNA WO 95/1263 13th Canadian Infantry Battalion *War Diary*

E.D. Bellew

The Civilian, July 1919
Daily Sun (Vancouver), September 22, 1919
Globe, October 25, 1929
TNA WO 95/3768 7th Canadian Infantry Battalion *War Diary*
Winnipeg Evening Tribune, October 29, 1929
Winnipeg Free Press, October 20, 1934
Victor, May 10, 1985

F.W. Hall

Personal Record 3941-37 (National Archives of Canada)
Sentinel, May 1968
TNA WO 95/3769 8th Canadian Infantry Battalion *War Diary*

F.A.C. Scrimger

Personal Record for Nurse Carpenter 1507-52 (National Archives of Canada)
Personal Record 8/44-41 (National Archives of Canada)
Canadian Medical Association Journal, April 1916
Montreal Star
The Legionary, March 1937

F.W. Campbell

Daily Sketch, July 13, 1915
Personal Record 1432-32 (National Archives of Canada)
TNA WO 95/3760 1st Canadian Infantry Battalion War Diary

1916

T.O.L. Wilkinson

TNA WO 339/5266
Service File 10372-34
Stand To! no. 70, p. 54
The Regimental Association, *The Loyal Regiment* (North Lancashire)
The Sphere

L. Clarke

Department of Public Records and Archives, Ottawa
Service File B1755-S015

J.C. Kerr

National Archives of Canada
Service File 5118-23

James C. Richardson

Dictionary of Canadian Biography Online
Directorate of National Defence, Canada
D.A. Melville, *Canadians and the Victoria Cross* (nd)
Service File 8248-44

1917

F.M.W. Harvey

TNA WO 95/1085
Calgary Herald, December 1943, August 23, 1980, September 15, 1980

T.W. MacDowell

Bulletin, Issue 88, October/November 2010 page 21
Department of Public Records & Archives (Historical Branch), August 24, 1970

Esprit de Corps (nd)
Maclean's Magazine, February 15, 1929
Reveille, October 1, 1939
The Sunday Times, September 17, 1939
TNA WO 95/3908
Service File 6794-29

W.J. Milne

Ottawa Citizen, July 31, 1989
Service File 6229-30
TNA WO 95/3781

E.W. Sifton

Department of Travel and Publicity, May 16, 1961
Esprit de Corps, Vol. 2, No. 8
The Legionary, December 1968
Service File 8896-45

J.G. Pattison

Maclean's Magazine, February 15, 1929
Letter to Canon Lummis from Henry Pattison, September 30, 1953
Service File 7654-41

R.G. Combe

Aberdeen Grammar School Magazine
I.H. Brown
J.M. Cameron
Friends of the Canadian War Museum, Ottawa
Maclean's Magazine, February 15, 1929
Anne Park
Service File 1962-B27
TNA WO 95/3831

W.A. Bishop

D. McCaffery, *Billy Bishop: Canadian Hero* (Toronto: James Lorimer

& Company, Second Edition, 2002)
Lt. Col. W.A. Bishop, *Winged Warfare* (Bailey Bros and Swinton, 1975)
Canadian Military Journal, Autumn 2002
www.billybishop.net
Library and Archives Canada: RG 150, Accession 1992–93/166, Box 760–48

F.W. Hobson

Personal Record 57113 (National Archives of Canada)
TNA WO95/3786 2nd Canadian Division
TNA WO95/3812 4th Infantry Brigade
TNA WO95/3817 20th Canadian Battalion
TNA WO363/H1850-1 F. Hobson
Service File 4401-47

M.J. O'Rourke

Personal Record 428545 (National Archives of Canada)
Service File 7484-42
TNA WO95/3728 1st Canadian Division
TNA WO95/3765 2nd Canadian Infantry Brigade
TNA WO95/3767 7th British Columbia Regiment
TNA WO363/0250 M.J. O'Rourke

H. Brown

Personal Record 226353 (National Archives of Canada)
Service File B1147-S005
TNA WO95/3728 1st Canadian Division
TNA WO95/3765 2nd Canadian Infantry Brigade
TNA WO95/3770 10th Quebec Regiment (Appendix B)

O.M. Learmonth

Personal Record 22893 (National Archives of Canada)
Service File 5489-47
TNA WO95/3761 2nd Battalion East Ontario Regiment

R.H. Hanna

Belfast Telegraph, November 9, 1917, and June 17, 1967
Personal Record 75361 (National Archives of Canada)
Service File 4018-30
TNA WO95/3786 2nd Canadian Division
TNA WO95/3828 6th Canadian Infantry Brigade
TNA WO95/3833 29th British Columbia Regiment
TNA WO363/H250 R.H. Hanna

F. Konowal

Personal Record 1444039 (National Archives of Canada)
Lubomyr Y. Luciuk and Ron Sorobcy, *Konowal: A Canadian Hero*
(Kingston: Kashtan Press, 2000)
Service File 5247-77
TNA WO95/3881 4th Canadian Division
TNA WO95/3896 10th Canadian Infantry Brigade
TNA WO95/3899 47th British Columbia Regiment

C.P.J. O'Kelly

52nd Battalion, Canadian Expeditionary Force War Diary (National
Archives)
C.P.J. O'Kelly service papers (National Archives of Canada)
Manitoba Provincial Archives, Winnipeg, Canada

T.W. Holmes

4th Canadian Mounted Rifles War Diary (National Archives)
T.W. Holmes service papers (National Archives of Canada)
Contemporary newspaper reports
Captain S.G. Bennett, *The 4th Canadian Mounted Rifles* (Murray
Printing Company, 1926)

R. Shankland

43rd Battalion (Cameron Highlanders of Canada) War Diary
(National Archives)

Janet Shankland, family information
"War Museum pays $288,000 to Buy Victoria Cross," *National Post* and Canwest News Service, May 25, 2009
R. Shankland service papers (National Archives of Canada)
Ayr Library, contemporary newspaper reports
Manitoba Provincial Archives, Winnipeg, Canada
Vince Leah, "Valour Road," *Winnipeg Tribune, Sentinel*, May 1968
J.D. Sinclair, *The Queen's Own Cameron Highlanders of Canada* (The Regiment, 1935)

H. McKenzie

RHQ Princess Patricia's Canadian Light Infantry Archives, Calgary
Family correspondence, via Princess Patricia's Canadian LI
H. McKenzie service papers, via Princess Patricia's Canadian LI
Ralph Hodder Williams MC, *History of the Princess Patricia's Canadian Light Infantry, 1914–1919* (Hodder & Stoughton, 1923)

C.J. Kinross

49th (Edmonton) Battalion, Canadian Expeditionary Force War Diary (National Archives)
Lieutenant Colonel G.R. Stevens, OBE, *A City Goes to War: History of the Loyal Edmonton Regiment (3PPCLI)* (Charters Publishing Co., 1964)
Hillingdon Council, www.hillingdon.gov.uk
C.J. Kinross service papers (National Archives of Canada)
Cecil John Kinross VC, www.rootsweb.com/~canab/vet/kinross.htm
Papers of Canon William M. Lummis MC, IWM and National Army Museum
"Victoria Cross Symbolizes the Legend of Kinross," *Edmonton Journal*, April 1, 1989
The Fortyniner, Number 24, January 1937

G.H. Mullin

RHQ Princess Patricia's Canadian Light Infantry Archives, Calgary
Ralph Hodder Williams MC, *History of the Princess Patricia's*

Canadian Light Infantry, 1914–1919 (Hodder & Stoughton, 1923)
G.II. Mullin service papers, via Princess Patricia's Canadian LI
"Took Master Pillbox Singlehanded: Sgt. Mullin Won VC at Meetcheele," *Ottawa Citizen*, March 19, 1919
"Victoria Cross Winner Dies," *Albertan*, April 8, 1963

G.R. Pearkes

5th Canadian Mounted Rifles, Canadian Expeditionary Force War Diary (National Archives)
G.R. Pearkes service papers (National Archives of Canada)
For Most Conspicuous Bravery: A Biography of Major General George R. Pearkes VC Through Two World Wars (University of British Columbia Press, 1977)
"George Pearkes VC, Coming From Britain to Take Pacific Command," *Globe and Mail*, September 2, 1942
"VC Winner's Career in Military Ran From Bugle Boy to General," *Globe and Mail*, May 31, 1984

C.F. Barron

3rd (Toronto) Battalion, Canadian Expeditionary Force War Diary (National Archives)
C.F. Barron service papers (National Archives of Canada)
48th Highlanders Regimental Museum Archives, Toronto, Ontario
Toronto Sun Archives
Lieutenant Colonel D.J. Goodspeed, *Battle Royal: History of the Royal Regiment of Canada* (Regimental Association, 1962)
Private information from Mrs. Marjory Thompson, Barron's daughter

J.P. Robertson

27th (City of Winnipeg) Battalion, Canadian Expeditionary Force War Diary (National Archives)
J.P. Robertson service papers (National Archives of Canada)
Bruce Tascona, *From the Forks to Flanders Field* (Self-published, 1995)
"How CPR Engineer Won Victoria Cross," *Strathmore Standard*,

January 17, 1920
"Medicine Hat Honours Memory Pte. Peter Robinson VC,"
Lethbridge Herald, May 12, 1937

H. Strachan

Personal Record 15585 (National Archives of Canada)
J. Gardam, *Seventy Years After 1914–1984* (Ottawa: Canada's Wing Inc., 1983)
W. Johnston, "Who's The Sojer in the Photie Then?"
D. Law, *Harcus Strachan V.C.*
Edmonton Journal, July 15, 1989
J.E.B. Seely, *Adventure* (Heinemann, 1930)
Thirty Canadian VCs (Skeffington, 1919)
Service File 9371-01
TNA WO339/139058

1918

E. De Wind

Newtownards Chronicle
Keith Haines
Lester Morrow
Service File 2496-03
TNA WO 339/9643

A.A. McLeod

G.A. Drew, *Canada's Fighting Airmen* (Maclean, 1930)
T.B. Mason, *Scarlet & Khaki* (Cape, 1930)
W. Raleigh and H.A. Jones, *The War in the Air* (OUP, 1923–34)

G. M. Flowerdew

Eastern Daily Press
Framlingham College, *The Framlinghamian*
Dictionary of Canadian Biography Online
Service File 3158-21

G.B. McKean

Jack Cavanagh
County Chronicle
Canadian War Museum, Ottawa
TNA WO 95/3778
Dictionary of Canadian Biography Online
Service File 6941-48

J. Kaeble

Dictionary of Canadian Biography Online
Service File 4994-83
TNA WO 95/3822

H.J. Good

Canadian War Museum, Ontario
Service File 3620-25

J.B. Croak

Canadian War Museum, Ontario
Evening Telegram, Newfoundland, May 1, 1991
Legion, July–August 1991
Punching With Pemberton, vol. 3, no. 1, November 1963
The Newfoundland Quarterly (nd)
Canadian War Museum, Ottawa
Service File 2144-47

H.G.B. Miner

Canadian War Museum, Ottawa
Department of Travel & Publicity (Historical Branch), Canada
Service File 6235-48

J. Brillant

Canadian War Museum, Ontario
Dictionary of Canadian Biography Online

22nd Bn. War Diary
Service File B1069-S014

J.E. Tait

Canadian War Museum, Ottawa
Service File 9488-11

A.P. Brereton

Canadian War Museum, Ontario
Service File B1044-S033

F.G. Coppins

Canadian War Museum, Ontario
Service File B1988-S047
The World's Highest Paid Army, January 1938

R.L. Zengel

Canadian War Museum, Ontario
Service File 10677-70

T. Dinesen

Canadian War Museum, Ontario
Canada's Viking VC (nd)
The Legionary, August 1968
Service File 2524-09
Victoria Cross Society, vol. 7, p 53

R. Spall

Canadian War Museum, Ontario
Service File 9169-07
Stand To! September 2000, no. 59, pp 31–32

C.S. Rutherford

Canadian War Museum, Ontario
Article by Eileen Argyris on Capt. Chas. S. Rutherford published in
the *Colborne Chronicle*, June 27, 1984
Charles Rutherford VC, MC, MM — Out of the Shadows (2011)
Charles Smith Rutherford 1892–1989, Canadian Veterans' Hall of
Valour
Edward Storey, "Last Surviving Victoria Cross Holder from World
War 1 Has Died,"
Stand To! no. 27, winter 1989
Service File 8566-25

W.H. Clark-Kennedy

Canadian War Museum, Ottawa
Service File 1770-64

C.J.P. Nunney

Canadian War Museum, Ontario
Department of Travel and Publicity, August 1962 (Historical Branch,
Canada)
Dictionary of Canadian Biography Online
Service File 7387-20
Peter Silk

B.S. Hutcheson

Wartime letter to a Captain Gwynn as listed in the archives of the
Canadian Veterans
Service File 4654-28

A.G. Knight

Martin Barker, written communication (2000)
Peter Kefford, written communication (2000)
Service File 5223-05

W.H. Metcalf

Bangor Daily News, September 4, 1998
Stand To! no. 27, winter 1989
Service File 6140-35

C.W. Peck

Canadian War Museum, Ontario
Service File 7693-14

J.F. Young

Leslie Hunt, *Our English Heroes* (nd)
Service File 10657-15

W.L. Rayfield

Canadian War Museum, Ontario
Service File 8114-55

M.F. Gregg

Canadian War Museum, Ontario
Dictionary of Canadian Biography Online
J. Hundevad, "The Inspiring Career of Milton Gregg, V.C.," *The Legionary*, October 1968
J. Hundevad, *Veterans' Champion: The Inspiring Career of Canada's New Minister of Veterans' Affairs*
G. Melville, "Atlantic Gallantry — the Victoria Cross," *The Atlantic Soldier*, April 1996
The Regimental Rogue
"Soldier, Statesman, Politician, VC Winner Milton Gregg Dies" (Robert England papers)
Service File 3806-20

S.L. Honey

Canadian War Museum, Ontario
Department of Tourism & Information (Historical Branch, July 15, 1964)

Dictionary of Canadian Biography Online
"First World War Hero Won the Victoria Cross" (no source, nd)
Service File 4474-51

G.F. Kerr

Canadian War Museum, Ontario
Dictionary of Canadian Biography Online
Historical and Museums Branch (Ontario, November 2, 1973)
Service File 5116-08

G.T. Lyall

"English Heroes" (*This England*, nd)
"A Strange Story of the Desert" (*Eastern Daily Press*, January 1, 1973)
Service File 5803-08
Victoria Cross Society, vol. 6, March 2005, pp. 36–38
Victoria Cross Society, vol. 20, March 2012, pp. 35–40

J. MacGregor

Spinks Catalogue (November 6, 1996)
Canadian War Museum, Ontario
Dictionary of Canadian Biography Online
Service File 6893-11

W. Merrifield

Dictionary of Canadian Biography Online
Canadian War Museum, Ontario
Service File 6130-49

C.N. Mitchell

Canadian War Museum, Ontario
Dictionary of Canadian Biography Online
F.C. Swinnard, *Lieutenant Colonel Coulson Norman Mitchell, V.C., M.C., R.C.E. (1899–1978)*
Service File 6248-44

W.L. Algie

Dictionary of Canadian Biography Online
Canadian War Museum, Ontario
Glendinings Catalogue (March 22, 1995)
Service File B0085-S046

T. Ricketts

Canadian War Museum, Ontario
Canadian Dictionary of Biography (online edition)
Joy Cave
"Sergeant Thomas Ricketts, V.C.," *Evening Telegram*, St John's, February 13, 1967
"War Heroes and Their War-Torn Families," *Evening Telegram*, St John's, November 6, 1989
"V.C.s Won by Newfoundlanders: Where Are They Now?," *Sunday Telegram*, St John's, August 6, 1989
The Victoria Cross Society, no. 4, March 2004, Terry Hissey: "Sergeant Thomas Ricketts VC, 1901–67," pp. 3–4

W.G. Barker

C. Bowyer, *Sopwith Camel-King of Combat* (Glasney Press, 1978)
P.G. Cooksley, *Flight Royal* (Patrick Stephens, 1981)
W. Ralph, *Barker VC: William Barker, Canada's Most Decorated War Hero* (Toronto: Doubleday Canada Ltd, 1997)
C. Winchester, *Wonders of World Aviation* (Amalgamated Press, 1938)
Journal of the VCS, October 2013
Library and Archives Canada: RG 150, Accession 1992–93/166, Box 435–47

H. Cairns

Canadian War Museum, Ontario
Dictionary of Canadian Biography Online
Esprit de Corps (November 1991, vol. 1, issue 6)
The Legionary, June 1936

"The V.C. From Ashington," *Newcastle Evening Chronicle*, November 1967
Service File 1377-40

Recipients with Canadian Connections

M.J. O'Leary

The Sphere, July 3, 1915
Daily Telegraph, various issues
War Budget, March 6, 1915, 22, July 1915
1st Irish Guards *War Diary*
The Times, June 25, 1920, 1, November 1937
Daily Mail
Daily Express, June 17, 1940
The People, March 10, 1940
RCMP Quarterly, vol. 27, no. 2, October 1961
The Ranger, July 1962
Household Brigade Magazine
Madame Tussaud's
RCMP Historical Branch
The Scarlet Force Collectors Newsletter, vol. 18, part 1, spring 2014
TNA ADM 188/147 image 265
TNA WO95/1342
Edward Campbell

J.A. Sinton

TNA WO95/5073 3 (Indian) Corps DDMS December 1915–March 1917
Lindsay, Sidney, "Merseyside Heroes" (unpublished MS)
Biographical Memoirs of Fellows of the Royal Society, vol. 2, 1956 (The Royal Society)

P.E. Bent

9th Battalion, the Leicestershire Regiment, War Diary (National Archives of Canada)
P.E. Bent service papers (National Archives of Canada)
Biographical papers, Leicestershire Record Office
The Grammar School Archives, Ashby-de-Zouche
D.V. Kelly, *Thirty-Nine Months With the Tigers* (1930)
C.J. Willis and D.F. Rogers, *For Valour: HMS* Conway *& HMS* Worcester (Conway Club & Association of Old Worcesters, 1984)
Bob Evans ed., *The Conway Heroes* (Countyvise Ltd., 2009)
S. Lindsay, *Merseyside Heroes* (privately published, 1988)

R.E. Cruickshank

TNA WO95/4660 60th London Division
TNA WO95/4671 181st Brigade
B. Blaser, *Kilts Across the Jordan* (Witherby, 1926)
London Scottish Regimental Gazette, October 1961

R.L. Bourke

J. McWilliam-Bourke (family papers and recollections)
P.T. Maule (research notes)
Letter to John Bourke from Rowland Bourke, October 11, 1918
Family papers and correspondence, via J. McWilliam-Bourke
Nelson Daily News, July 27, 1918
"'The Kootenays' VC Winner," *Nelson Daily News*, June 17, 1932
F.D.H. Nelson, "Above and Beyond the Call of Duty," *The Lookout*, CFB Esquimalt, August 29, 1974
Claire Muir, "A Man of Courage," *Colonist*, September 3, 1958
Obituary, *Crow's Nest*, October 1958
Papers of Cdr. James Petrie, OBE, DSC, via Alastair Petrie
Recommendations for honours and awards (National Archives)
Report of ML 276 by Lieutenant Rowland Bourke, April 23, 1918 (National Archives)
Report of HMS *Brilliant*, Cdr. A.E. Godsal, April 24, 1918 (National Archives)

Report of HMS *Vindictive*, Lieutenant V. Crutchley, May 13, 1918 (National Archives)

Sir John Alleyne, "Blocking Operations at Ostende (sic) on May 10, 1918," IWM

Barrie Pitt, *Zeebrugge: St George's Day, 1918* (Cassell & Co., 1958)

C. Sanford Terry ed., *Zeebrugge and Ostend: Dispatches of Vice-Admiral Sir Roger Keyes* (Oxford University Press, 1919)

BIBLIOGRAPHY

The following list of published sources used in the preparation of this book does not include the many unit histories that were consulted.

Arthur, M. *Symbol of Courage: Men Behind the Medal*. Pan, 2005.

Ashcroft, M. *Victoria Cross Heroes*. Revised edition, Headline/ Review, 2007.

Bancroft, J.W. *Devotion to Duty: Tributes to a Region's VC*. Manchester: Aim High Publications, 1990.

———. *The Victoria Cross Roll of Honour*. Manchester: Aim High Productions, 1989.

Bishop, W.A. *Our Bravest and Our Best: The Stories of Canada's Victoria Cross Winners*. Whitby, ON: McGraw Hill Ryerson, 1995.

Brazier, K. *The Complete Victoria Cross: A Full Chronological Record of all Holders of Britain's Highest Award for Gallantry*. Barnsley: Pen & Sword, 2010.

Buffetaut, Y. *April 22nd 1915, The First Gas Attack*. Louviers: Ysec Éditions, 2008.

Canadian War Records. *Thirty Canadian VCs, 1918*. Skeffington, 1919.

Cassar, G.H. *Hell in Flanders Fields*. Toronto: Dundurn, 2010.

Christie, N. *For King & Empire, Volume 1: The Canadians at Ypres April 22–26, 1915*. Ottawa: CEF Books, 1999.

———. *For King & Empire, Volume 2: The Canadians on the Somme September–November 1916*. Ottawa: CEF Books, 1999.

Clark, B. *The Victoria Cross: A Register of Awards to Irish-born Officers and Men*. The Irish Sword, 1986.

Dancocks, D.G. *Welcome to Flanders Fields*. Toronto: McClelland and Stewart, 1988.

De la Billiere, P. *Supreme Courage: Heroic Stories from 150 Years of the VC*. Abacus, 2005.

Deeds that Thrilled the Empire: True Stories of the Most Glorious Acts of Heroism of the Empire's Soldiers and Sailors during the Great War. London: Hutchinson, no date.

Dictionary of Canadian Biography (online).

Doherty, R. and D. Truesdale. *Irish Winners of the Victoria Cross*. Dublin: Four Courts Press, 2000.

Duguid, Colonel A. Fortescue. *Official History of the Canadian Force in the Great War 1914–1919*. Volume 1. Ottawa: King's Printer, 1938.

Edmonds, Sir J.E. (ed.). *Military Operations France and Belgium*. Macmillan/HMSO, 1922–1949.

Gliddon, G. (ed.). *VCs Handbook: The Western Front, 1914–1918*. Stroud: Sutton Publishing, 2005.

Granatstein, J.L *The Greatest Victory: Canada's One Hundred Days, 1918*. Toronto: Oxford University Press, 2014.

Harvey, D. *Monuments to Courage: Victoria Cross Headstones & Memorials*. Privately Printed for the Author by Kevin and Kay Patience, 1999.

James, E.A. *British Regiments, 1914–1918*. Samson Books, 1978.

Lee, J. *The Gas Attacks: Ypres 1915*. Barnsley: Pen & Sword Books, 2009.

Location of Hospitals and Casualty Clearing Stations B.E.F.1914–19. IWM. Ministry of Pensions, 1923.

McCarthy, C. *Passchendaele: The Third Ypres. The Day-By-Day Account*. London: Arms & Armour, 1995.

McWilliams, James L. and R. James Steel. *Gas! The Battle for Ypres 1915*. St. Catharines, ON: Vanwell Publishing, 1985.

Montgomery, Sir A. *The Story of the Fourth Army in the Battles of the Hundred Days, August 8th to November 11th 1918*. Hodder & Stoughton, 1920.

Nicholson, G.W.L.N. *Canadian Expeditionary Force, 1914–1919*. Ottawa: Queen's Printer, 1962.

————. *The Fighting Newfoundlander: A History of the Royal Newfoundland Regiment.* Government of Newfoundland, 1964.

Oldfield, P. *Victoria Crosses on the Western Front, August 1914–April 1915.* Barnsley: Pen & Sword, 2014.

O'Moore, General Sir Creagh, E.M. Humphris, and E. Miss. *The VC and DSO,* Vol. 1. 1924.

Pillinger, D. and A. Staunton. *Victoria Cross Presentations and Locations.* Maidenhead, Berkshire: Woden, 2000.

Prior, R. and T. Wilson. *Passchendaele: The Untold Story.* New Haven, CT: Yale University Press, 1996.

The Register of the Victoria Cross. This England Books, 1988.

Ross, Graham. *Scotland's Forgotten Valour.* Maclean Press, 1995.

Roy, R.H. *For Most Conspicuous Bravery: A Biography of Major-General George R. Pearkes, V.C., Through Two World Wars.* Vancouver: University of British Columbia Press, 1997.

For Valour: Saskatchewan Victoria Cross Recipients. Regina: Saskatchewan Heritage Foundation, 1995.

Smith, M. *Award for Valour: A History of the Victoria Cross and the Evolution of British Heroism.* Palgrave Macmillan, 2008.

Smyth, Sir John VC. *The Story of the Victoria Cross.* Frederick Muller, 1963.

Swettenham, J.A. *Valiant Men: Canada's Victoria Cross and George Cross Winners.* Hakkert, 1973.

Torsin, R.H. *They Stayed With Us ... The Victoria Crosses in Belgium.* 1992.

INDEX

Page numbers of images are italicized
VC recipients are in bold